SOON

WTC

—

CHINESE
PAVILION

—

MALL OF
EUROPE

—

SOON

WTC (2016) video 7'34"
without sound

EN

Emma van der Put's videos originate from looking closely at (urban) public space. In her position as an observer, Van der Put tries to maintain a balance between empathy and detachment. Even though she is physically part of the crowd, the telescopic lens of her camera creates a distance, a private place within the public space.

In 2016 Van der Put made the video *WTC,* in which she focuses on the 'Quartier Nord/Noordwijk' in Brussels. In 1967, as part of the so-called 'Manhattan Plan', this area of the city's centre had to make way for the construction of eight World Trade Center towers. This urban development plan, proposed by entrepreneur and controversial politician Paul Vanden Boeynants, led to large protests and dissatisfaction among the residents of the district, but was nonetheless still implemented. After the residential area was expropriated, the area was left fallow for years to come. Due to fraud and a lack of investors, only three towers were eventually built.

For six months, Emma van der Put positioned herself high up in one of the World Trade Center towers. With a panorama view on the 'Quartier Nord/Noordwijk' district, she photographed the neighbourhood from the perspective of the building. A small park at the foot of the tower changed into an improvised tent camp where people who fled their country were waiting to register at the desk of the immigration office located at the bottom of the WTC tower. In relation to the yellowed posters of the original 'Manhattan plan' that she found in the corridors of the tower, Van der Put also integrated in her film the new simulations of building plans for a future Brussels that she noticed in the vicinity of the 'Quartier Nord/Noordwijk'. The video *WTC* shows a no man's land between ideas from the past, the current state of the area and the plans for the future. The work became a starting point for a series of videos that all originate from photographic images and that look at how the echoes of history affect the current state of different locations in the city.

WTC

FR

Les vidéos d'Emma van der Put trouvent leur origine et leur argument dans son observation minutieuse de l'espace public (urbain). Depuis sa position d'observatrice, Van der Put s'efforce de maintenir un équilibre entre l'empathie et le détachement. Bien qu'elle fasse corps avec la foule, l'objectif télescopique de son appareil photo crée une distance et ménage un espace privé dans l'espace public.

En 2016, Emma Van der Put a réalisé la vidéo *WTC,* centrée sur le quartier bruxellois appelé « Quartier Nord ». En 1967, dans le cadre du « Plan Manhattan » *(sic),* cette zone du centre de la ville devait être rasé pour faire place nette à de la construction de huit tours similaires au World Trade Center de New York. Ce plan de développement urbain proposé par Paul Vanden Boeynants, entrepreneur et politicien controversé, suscita la réprobation des habitants du quartier et d'importantes manifestations, mais fut néanmoins mis en action. Pourtant, après l'expropriation des résidents, la zone resta en friche pendant des années. À cause de fraudes et du désintérêt des investisseurs, seules trois tours furent en fin de compte érigées.

Pendant six mois, Emma van der Put s'est postée dans les étages supérieurs d'une tour World Trade Center. Profitant d'une vue panoramique sur toute la zone du « Quartier Nord », elle l'a photographiée depuis la perspective du gratte-ciel. Un petit espace vert au pied de la tour s'est transformé en camp de réfugiés improvisé où des personnes ayant fui leur pays attendaient de pouvoir s'enregistrer à l'Office des étrangers, administration en charge de l'immigration située au rez-de-chaussée d'une des tours WTC. En rappel des affiches jaunies vantant le « Plan Manhattan » qu'elle rencontrait aux murs des couloirs de la tour, Van der Put a aussi inclus dans son film les plans, modélisations 3D et autres « vues d'artiste » glanés autour du « Quartier Nord », censés préfigurer la Bruxelles du futur. La vidéo *WTC* dépeint le *no man's land* qui s'étend entre les idées du passé, la situation actuelle et les prévisions pour l'avenir. Ce travail est le point de départ d'une série de vidéos créées à partir d'images photographiques et qui examinent la façon dont l'histoire et ses effets d'écho pèsent sur l'état actuel des choses dans divers lieux de la ville.

NL

De video's van Emma van der Put komen voort uit het aandachtig bestuderen van de (stedelijke) openbare ruimte. In haar positie als toeschouwer probeert Van der Put een evenwicht te bewaren tussen empathie en distantie. Hoewel ze fysiek deel uitmaakt van de menigte, creëert de telescopische lens van haar camera een afstand, een private plek binnen de openbare ruimte.

In 2016 maakte Van der Put de video *WTC,* waarin ze zich richt op de 'Noordwijk' in Brussel. In het kader van het zogenaamde 'Manhattanplan' moest dit deel van het stadscentrum in 1967 plaats maken voor de bouw van acht World Trade Center-torens. Dit stedenbouwkundig plan, voorgesteld door ondernemer en omstreden politicus Paul Vanden Boeynants, leidde tot grote protesten en ontevredenheid bij de bewoners van de wijk, maar werd niettemin uitgevoerd. Na de onteigening van de woonwijk bleef het gebied nog jaren braak liggen. Door fraude en een gebrek aan investeerders werden uiteindelijk slechts drie van de acht torens gebouwd.

Emma van der Put stelde zich gedurende een half jaar op in één van de World Trade Center-torens. Met een panoramisch uitzicht op de Noordwijk, fotografeerde ze de buurt vanuit het perspectief van het gebouw. Het park aan de voet van de toren veranderde in een geïmproviseerd tentenkamp voor mensen die hun land waren ontvlucht en moesten wachten om zich aan de balie van de immigratiedienst onderin de WTC-toren in te kunnen schrijven. Naar aanleiding van de vergeelde affiches van het oorspronkelijke 'Manhattanplan' die ze in de gangen van het gebouw tegenkwam, integreerde Van der Put in haar film ook de nieuwe simulaties van bouwplannen voor een toekomstig Brussel die ze in de omgeving van de Noordwijk opmerkte. De video *WTC* toont een niemandsland tussen ideeën uit het verleden, de huidige staat van het gebied en de plannen voor de toekomst. Het werk betekende een beginpunt voor een reeks video's die vanuit fotografische beelden zijn ontstaan en die ieder op een eigen manier kijken naar hoe echo's van de geschiedenis doorklinken in de huidige staat van verschillende locaties in de stad.

00:00:00

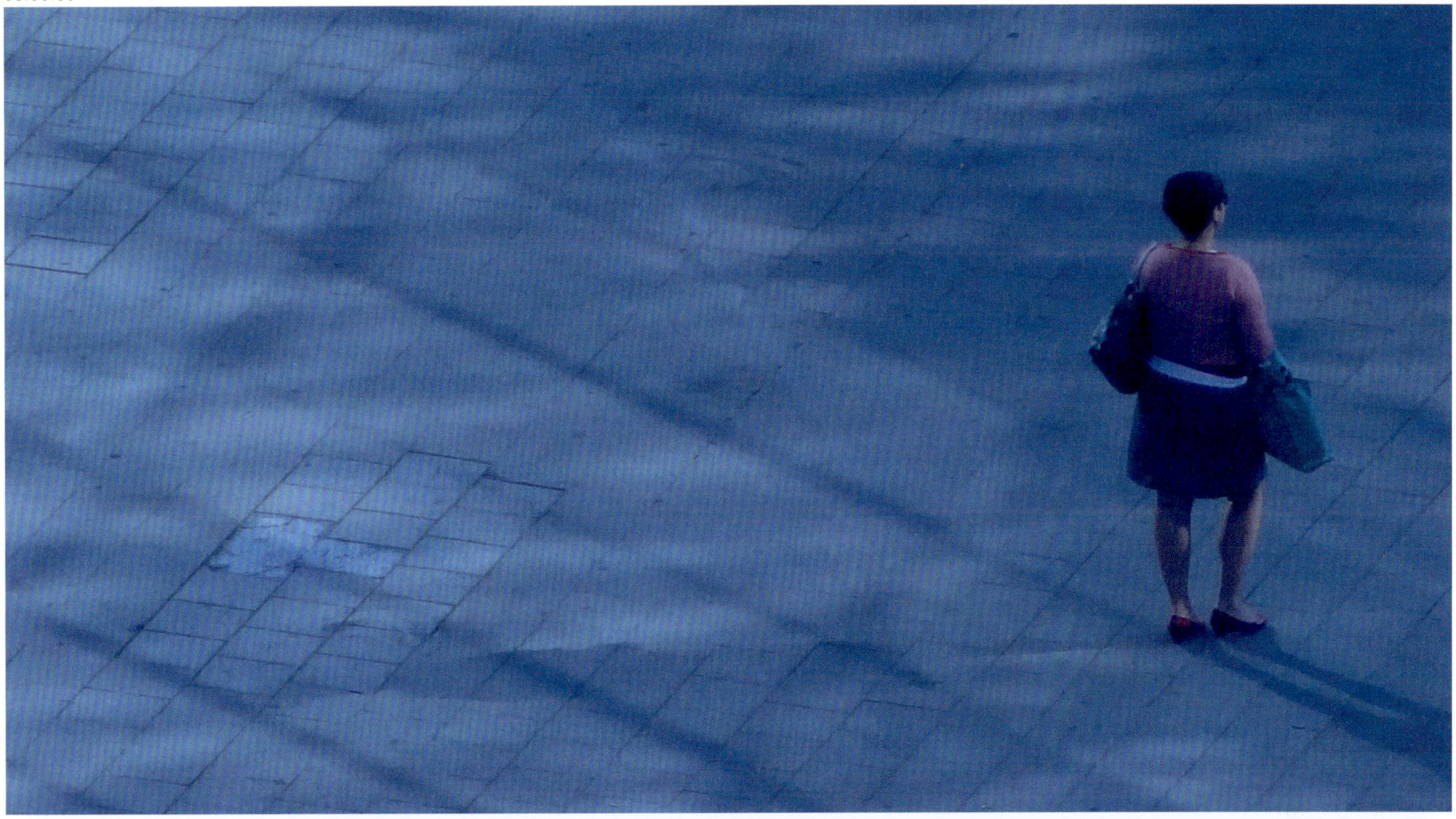

WTC

00:10:00

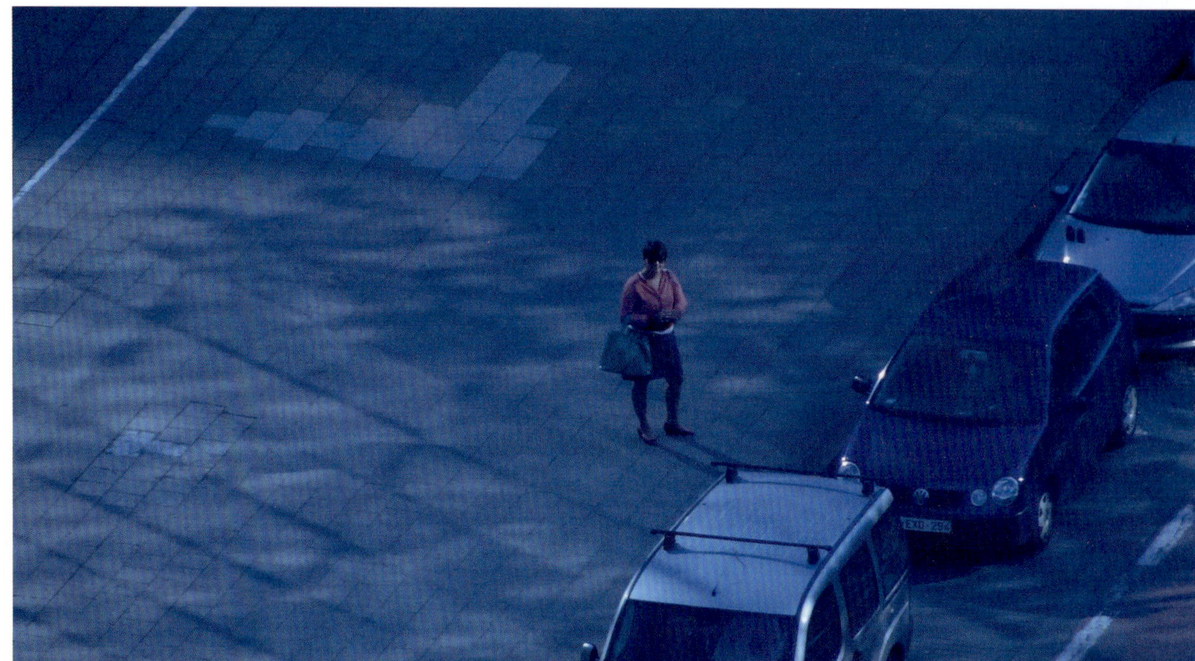

WTC

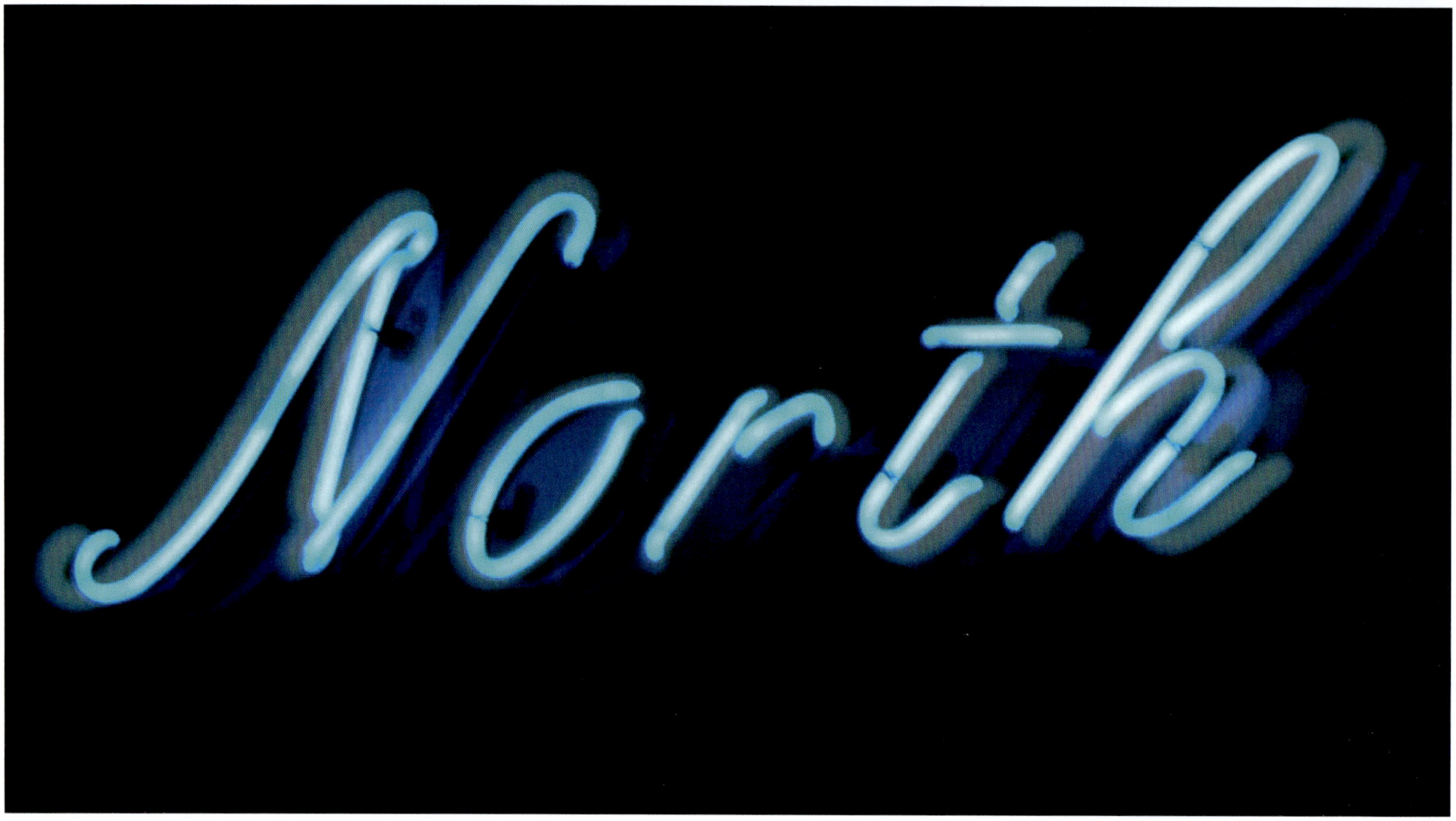

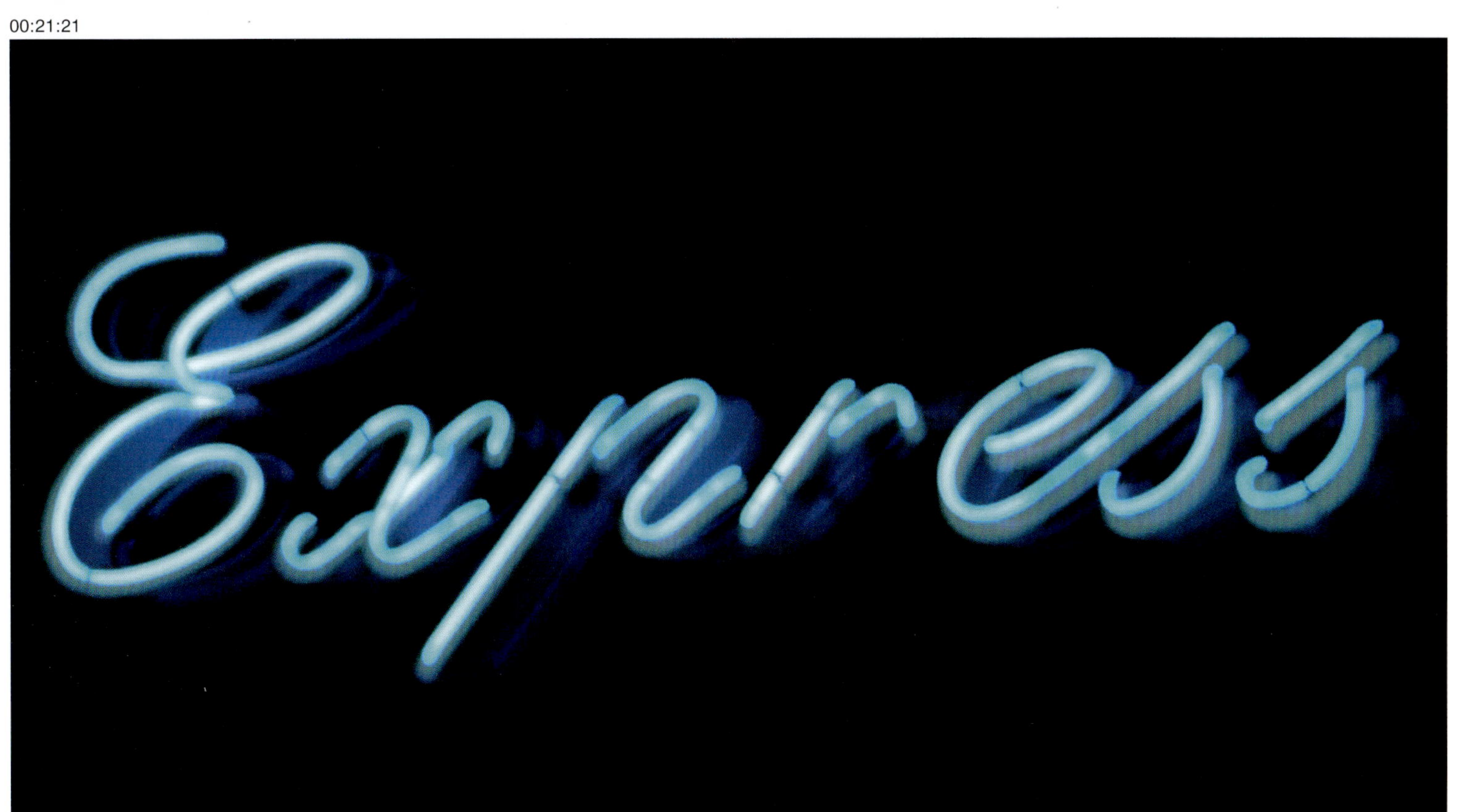

WTC

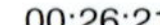
00:26:21

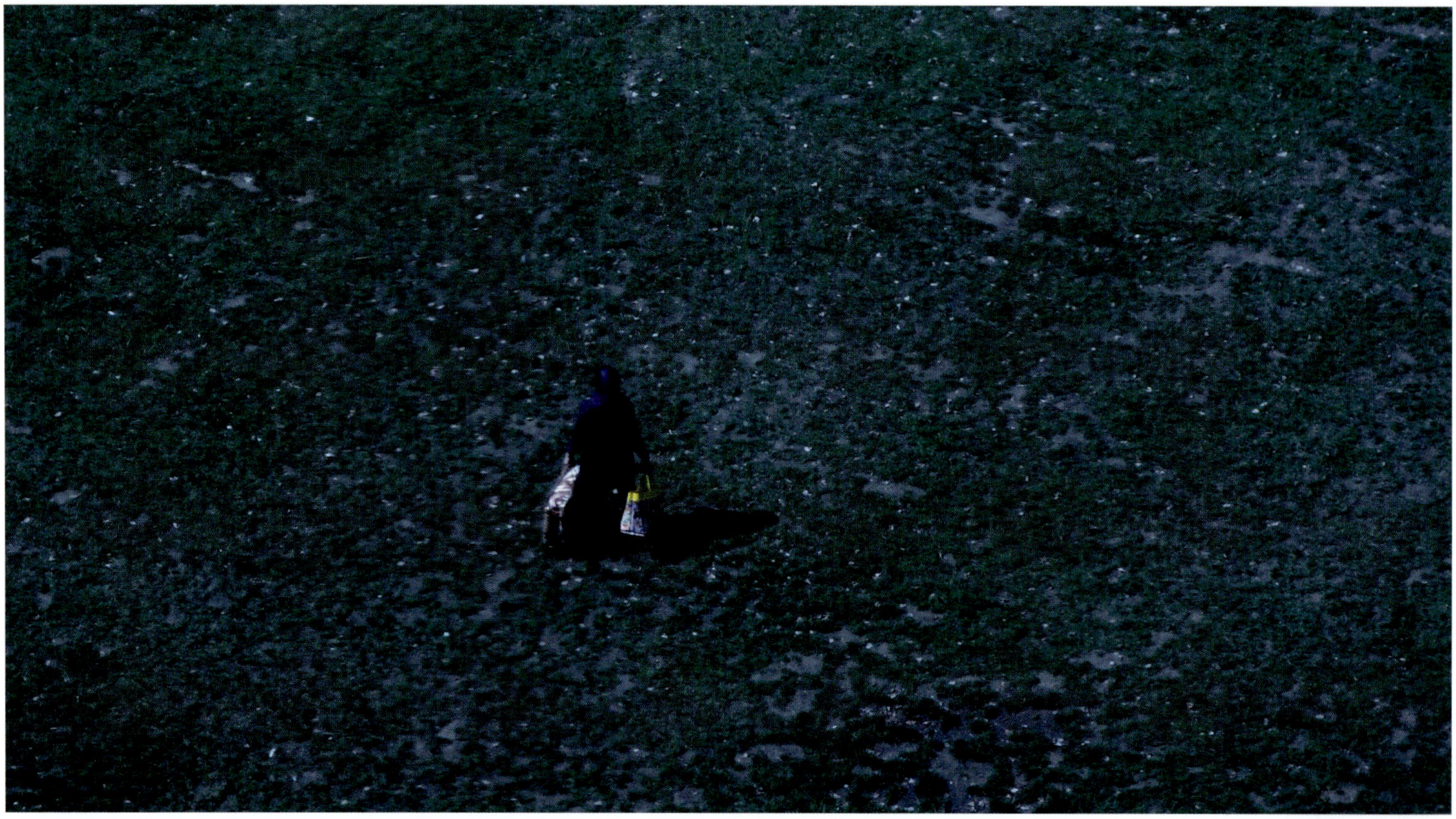

WTC

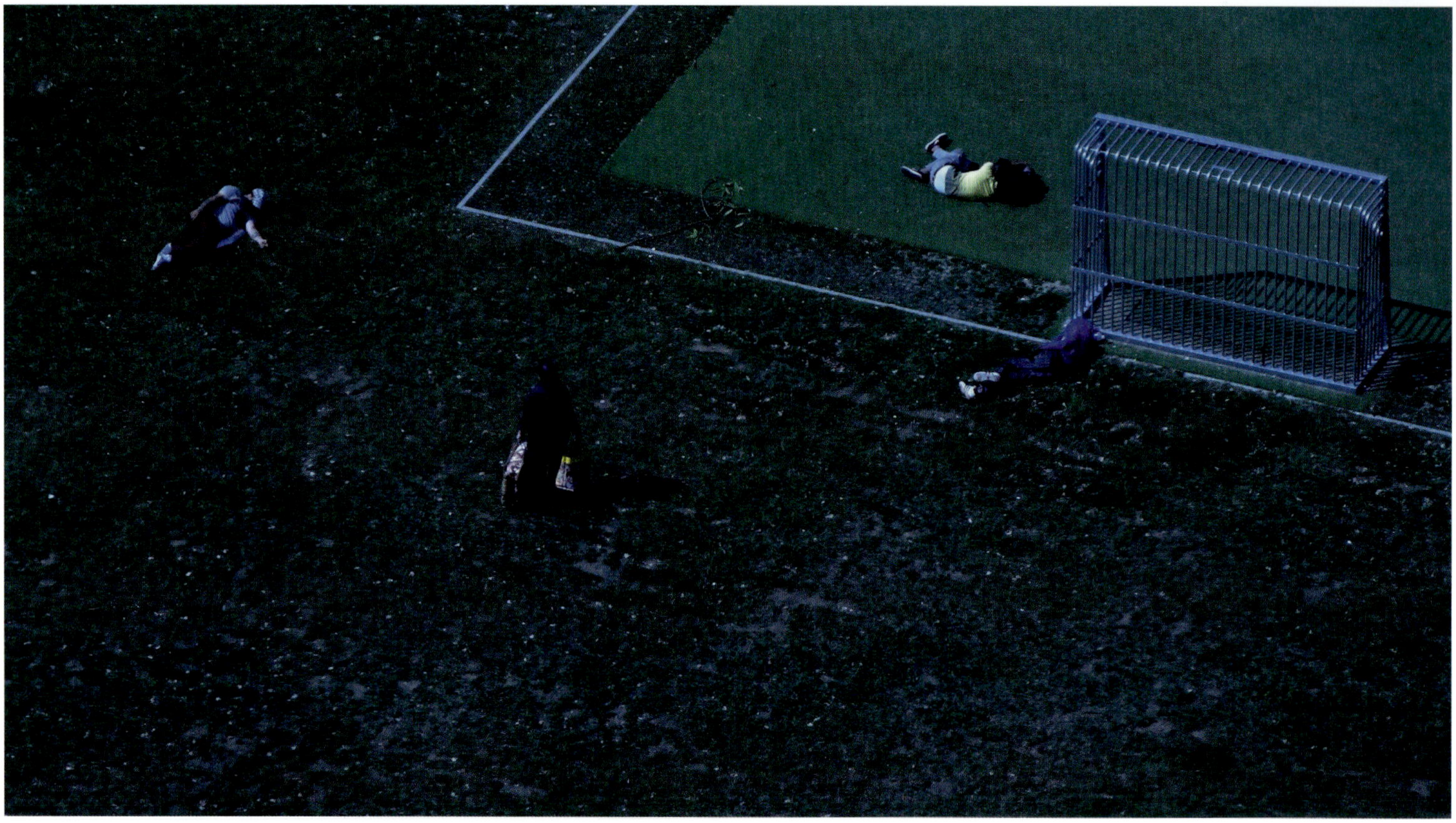

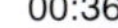

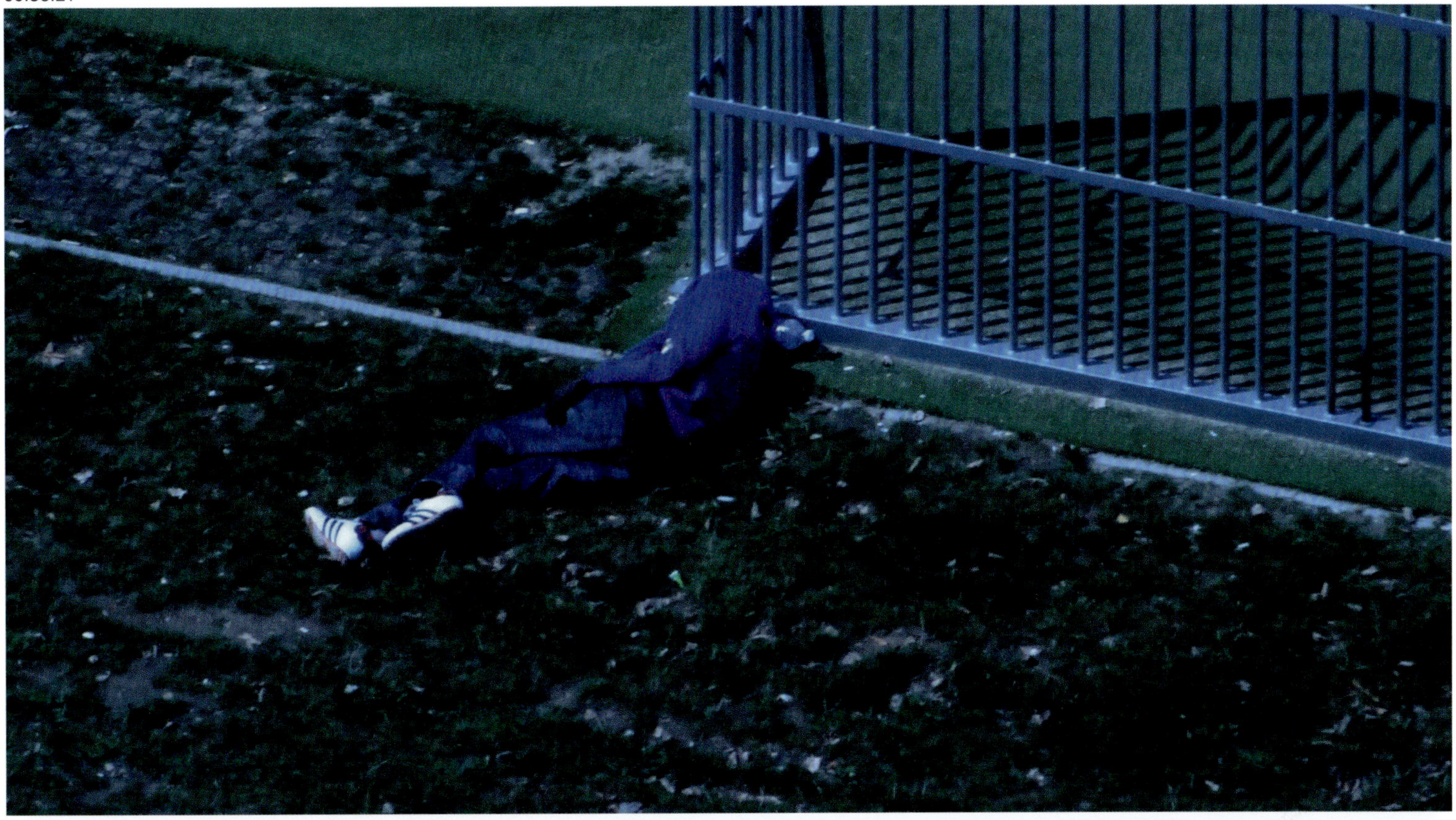

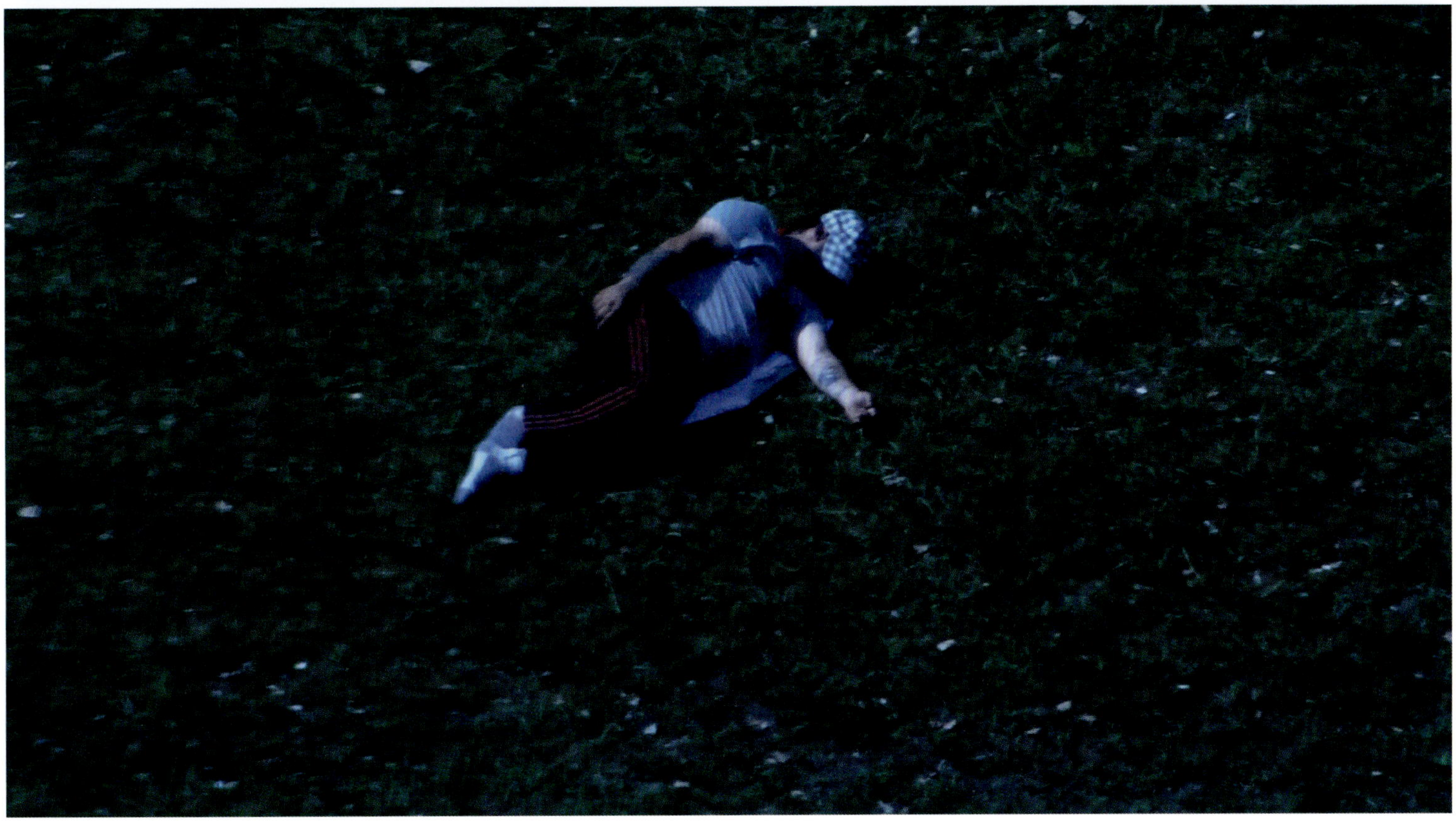

00:36:21

WTC

00:46:21

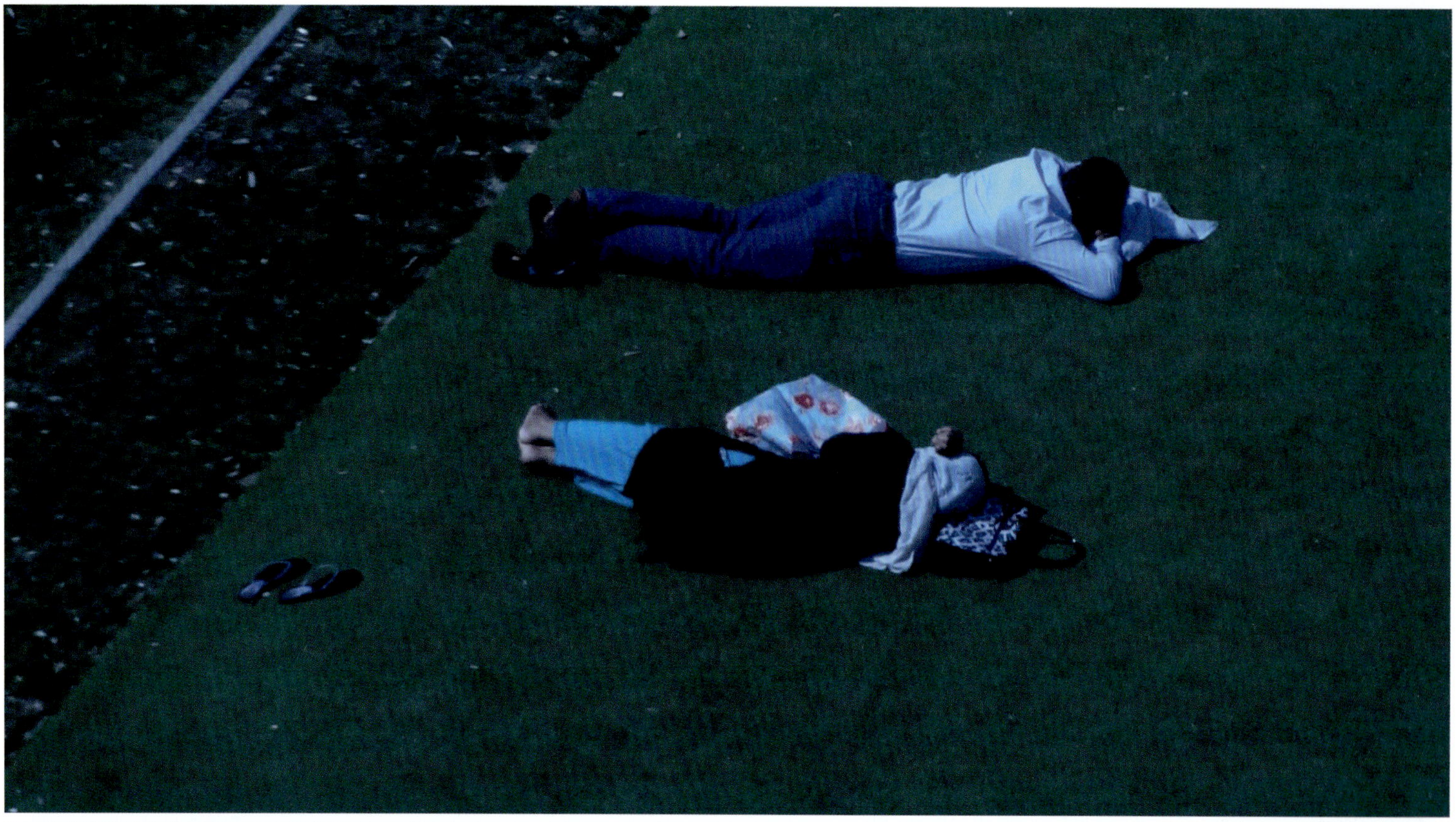

WTC

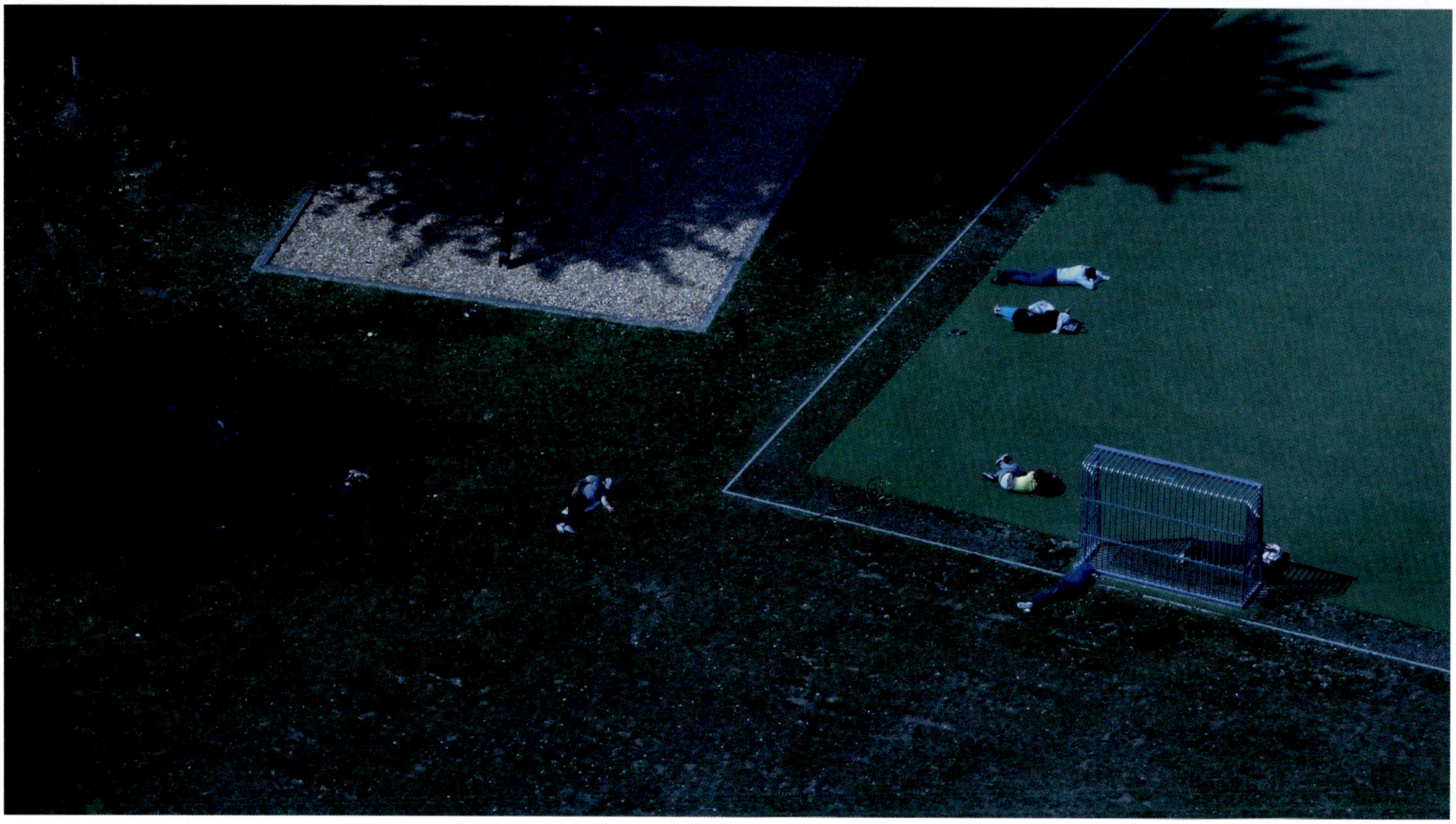

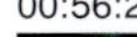

00:56:21

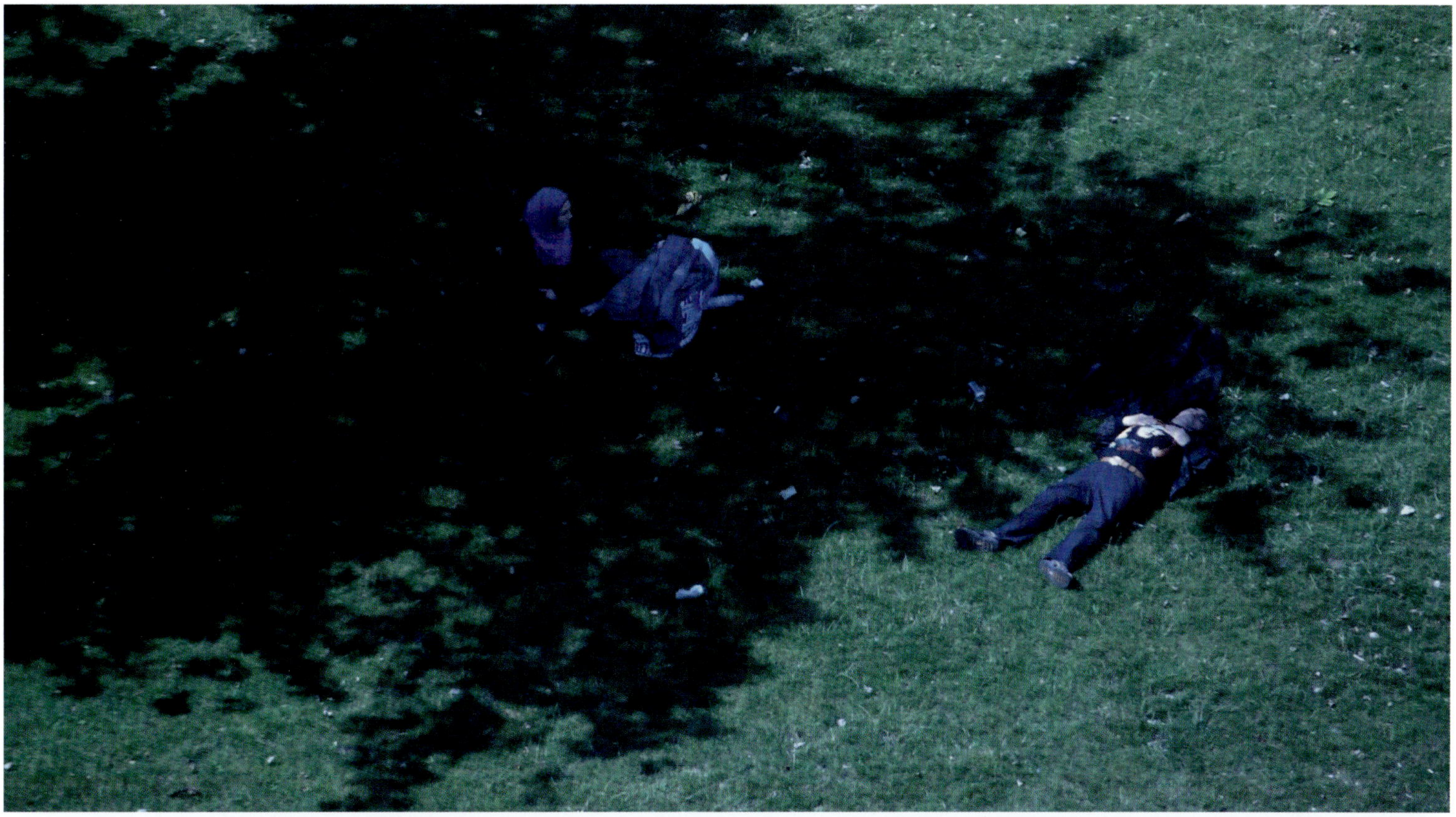

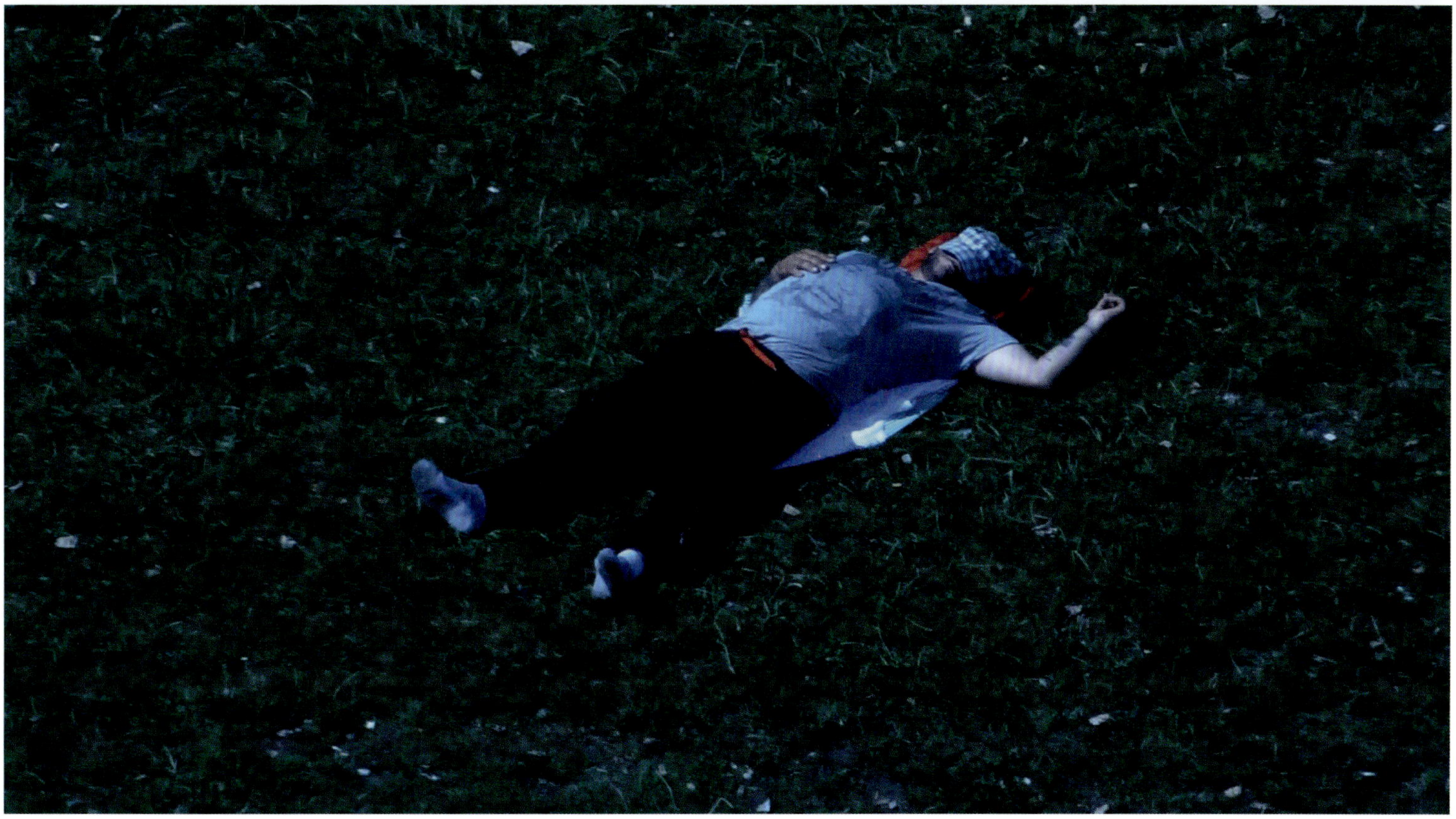

WTC

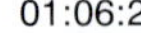
01:06:21

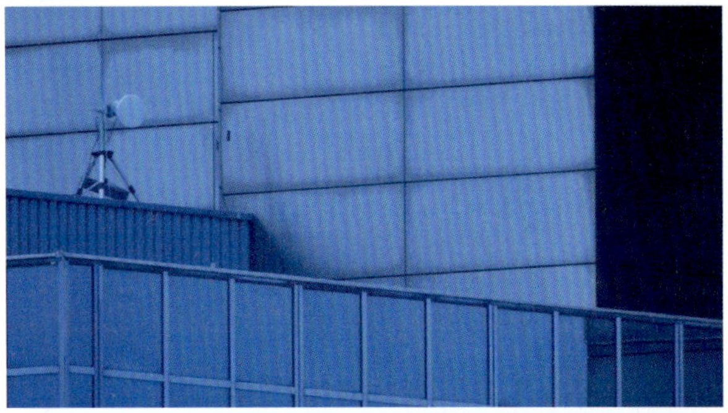

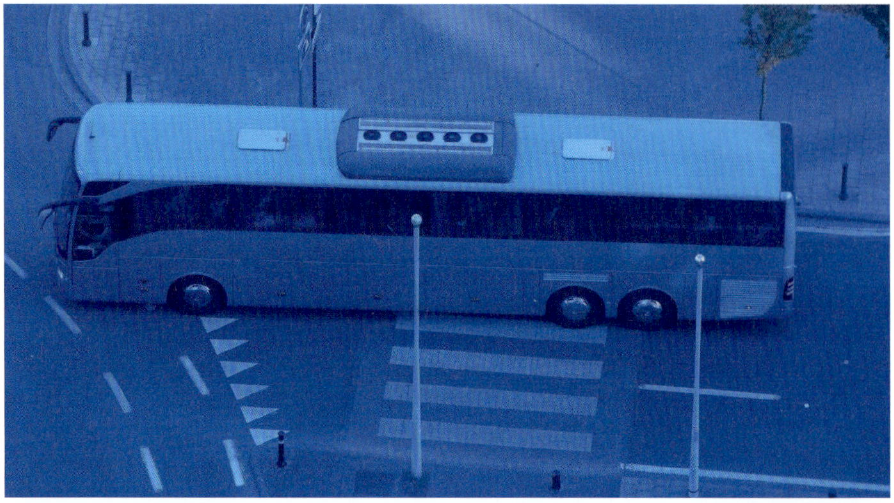

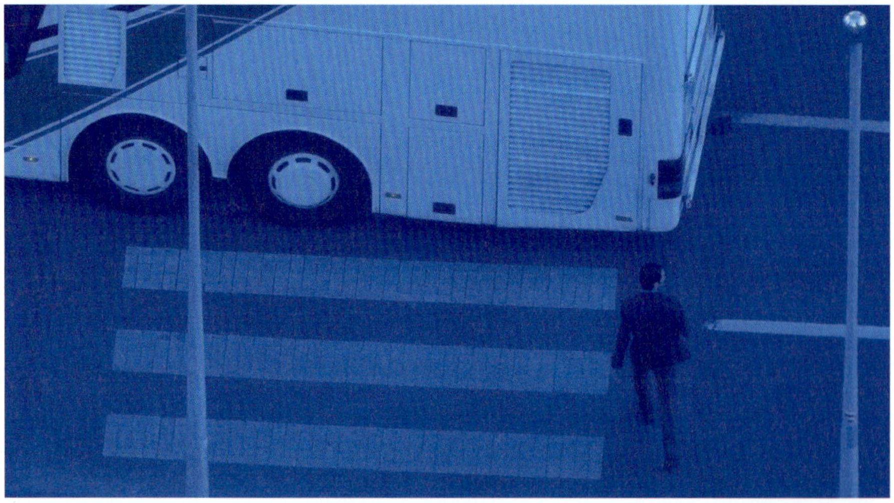

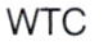
WTC

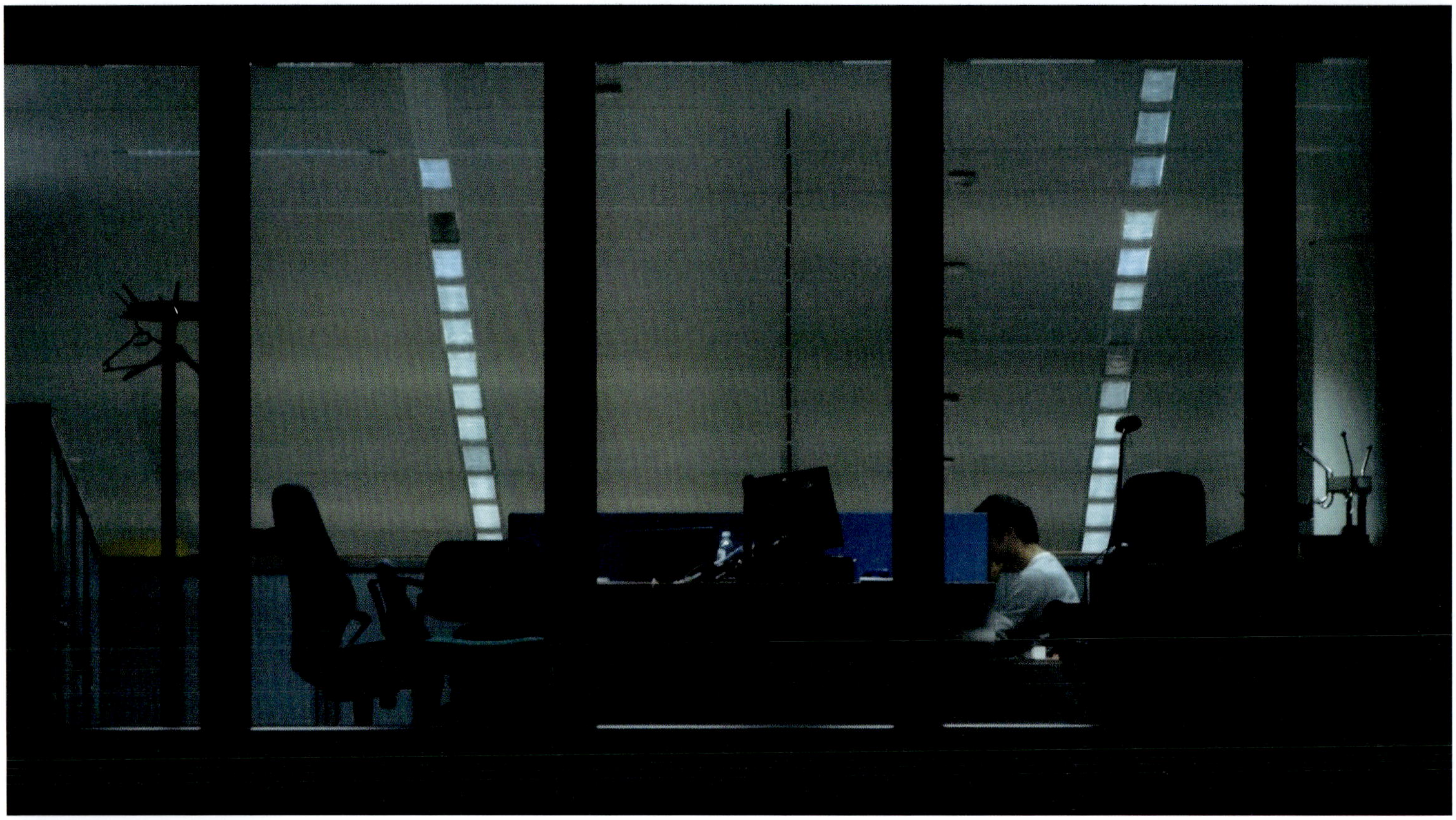

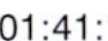

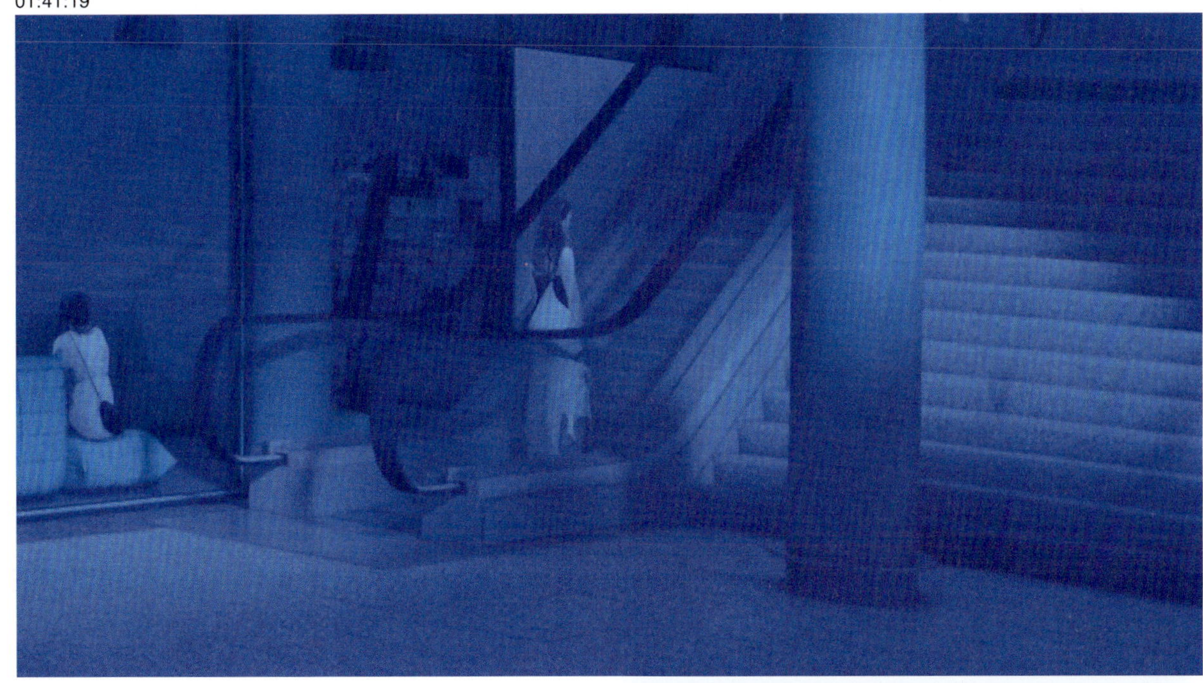

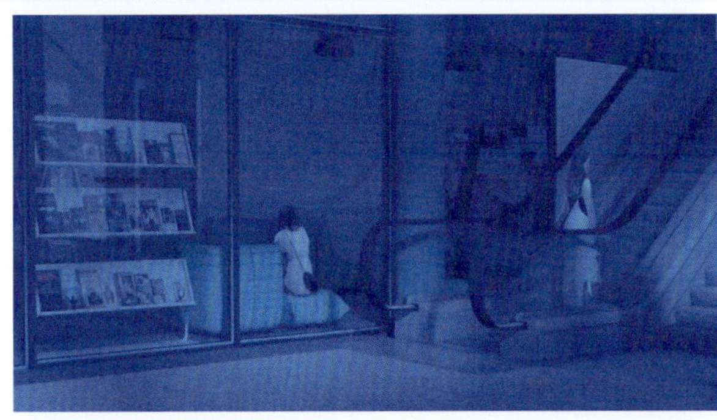

WTC

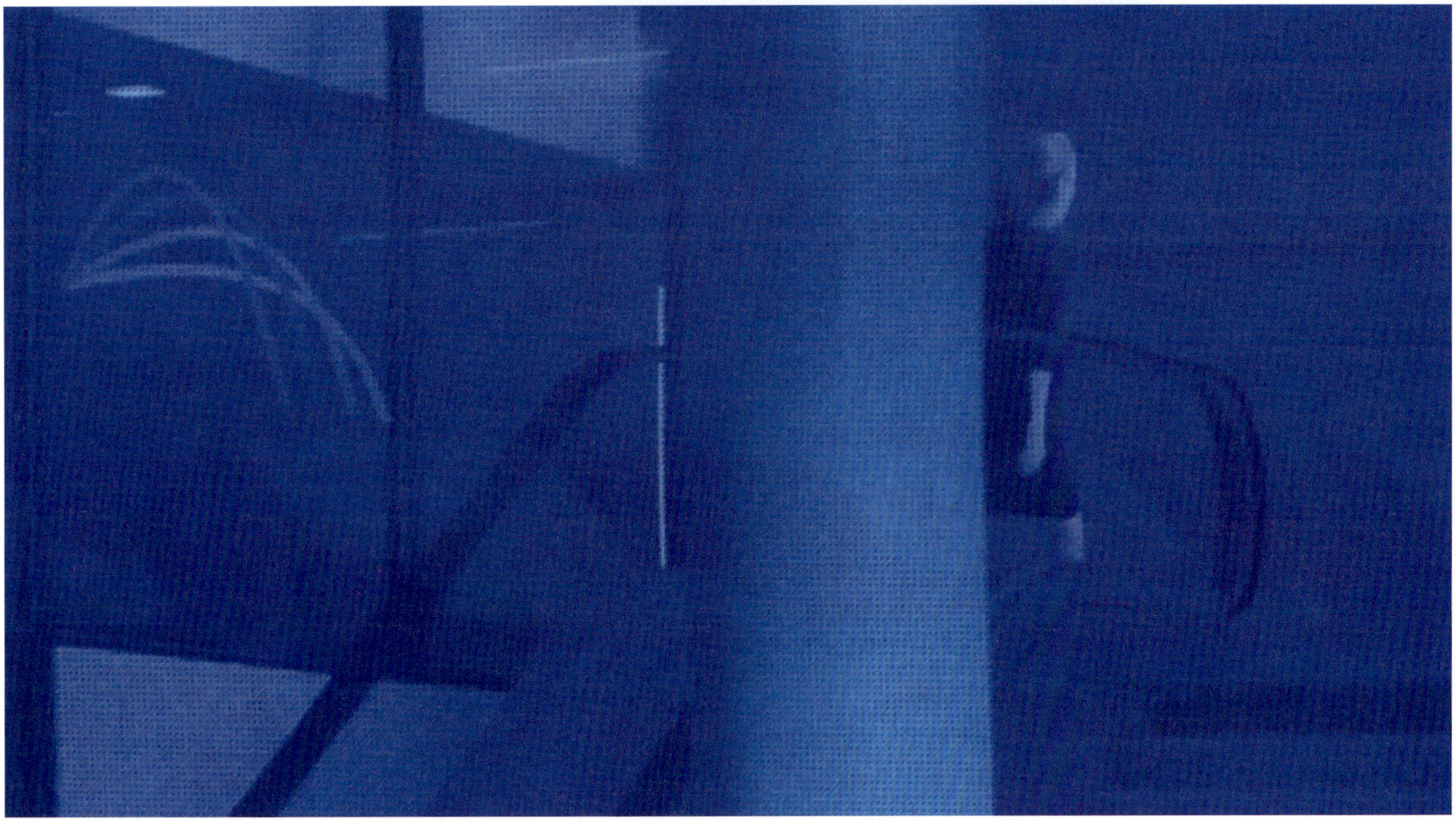

01:56:19

WTC

ElectronicImpulsSystems /// EIS
open: monday-friday
open: saturday

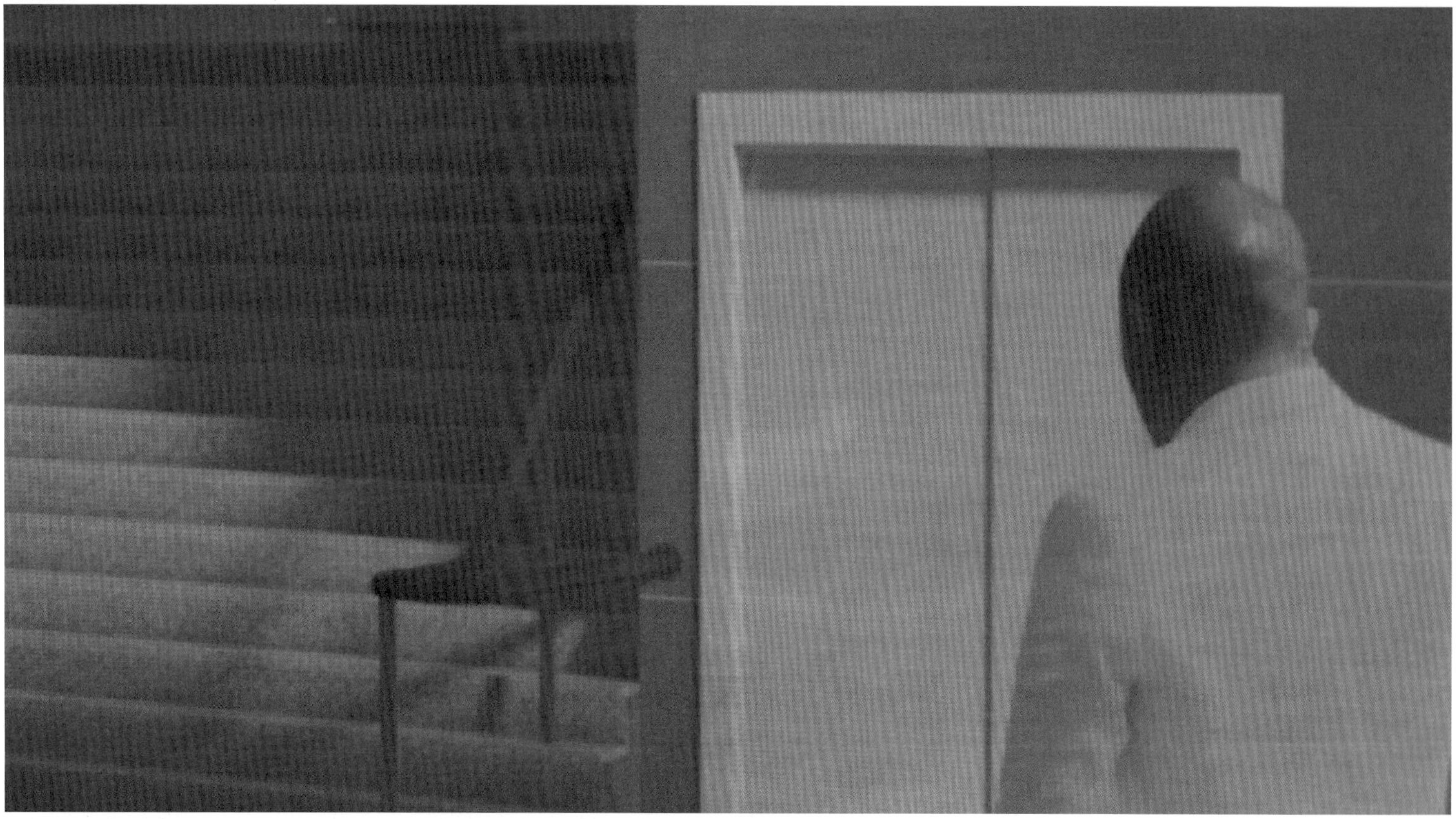

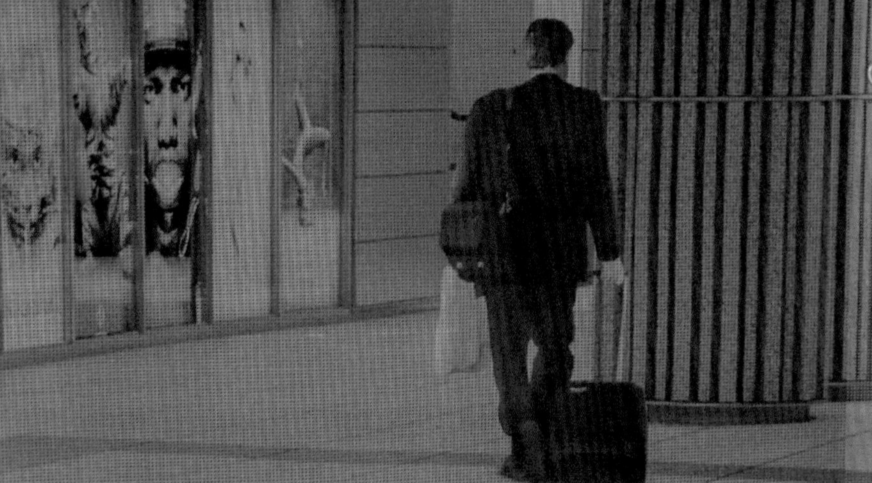

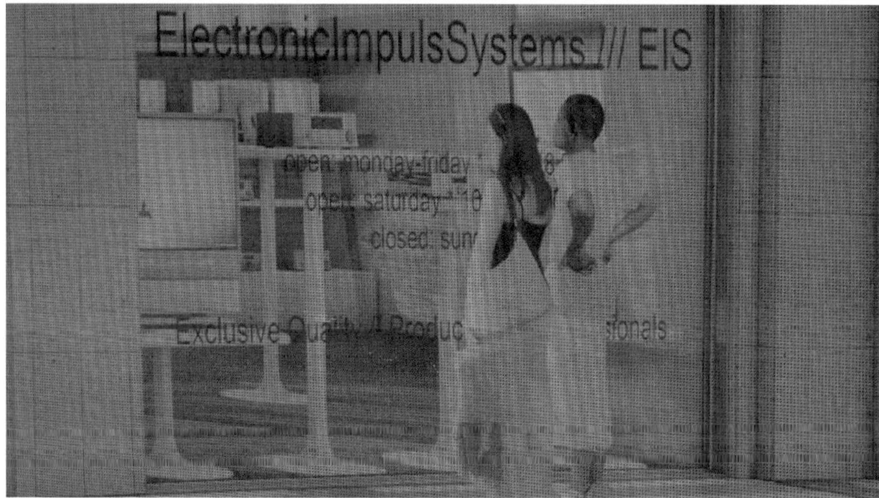

02:14:18

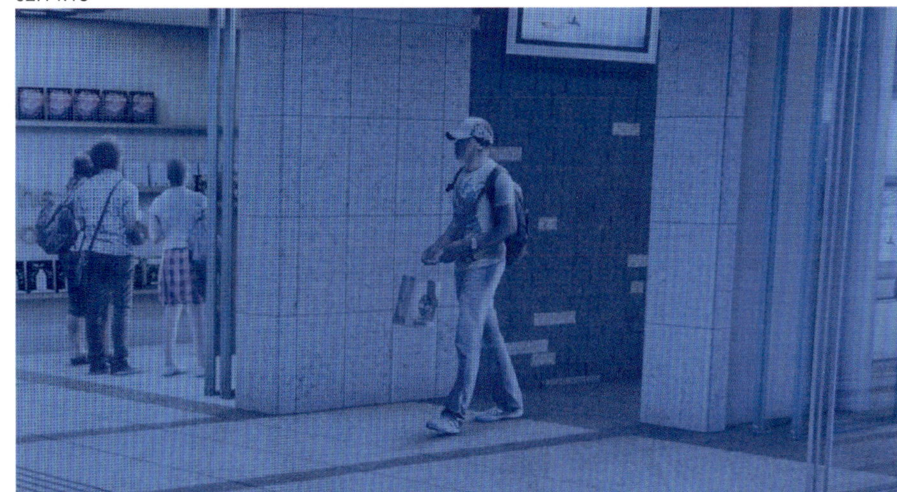

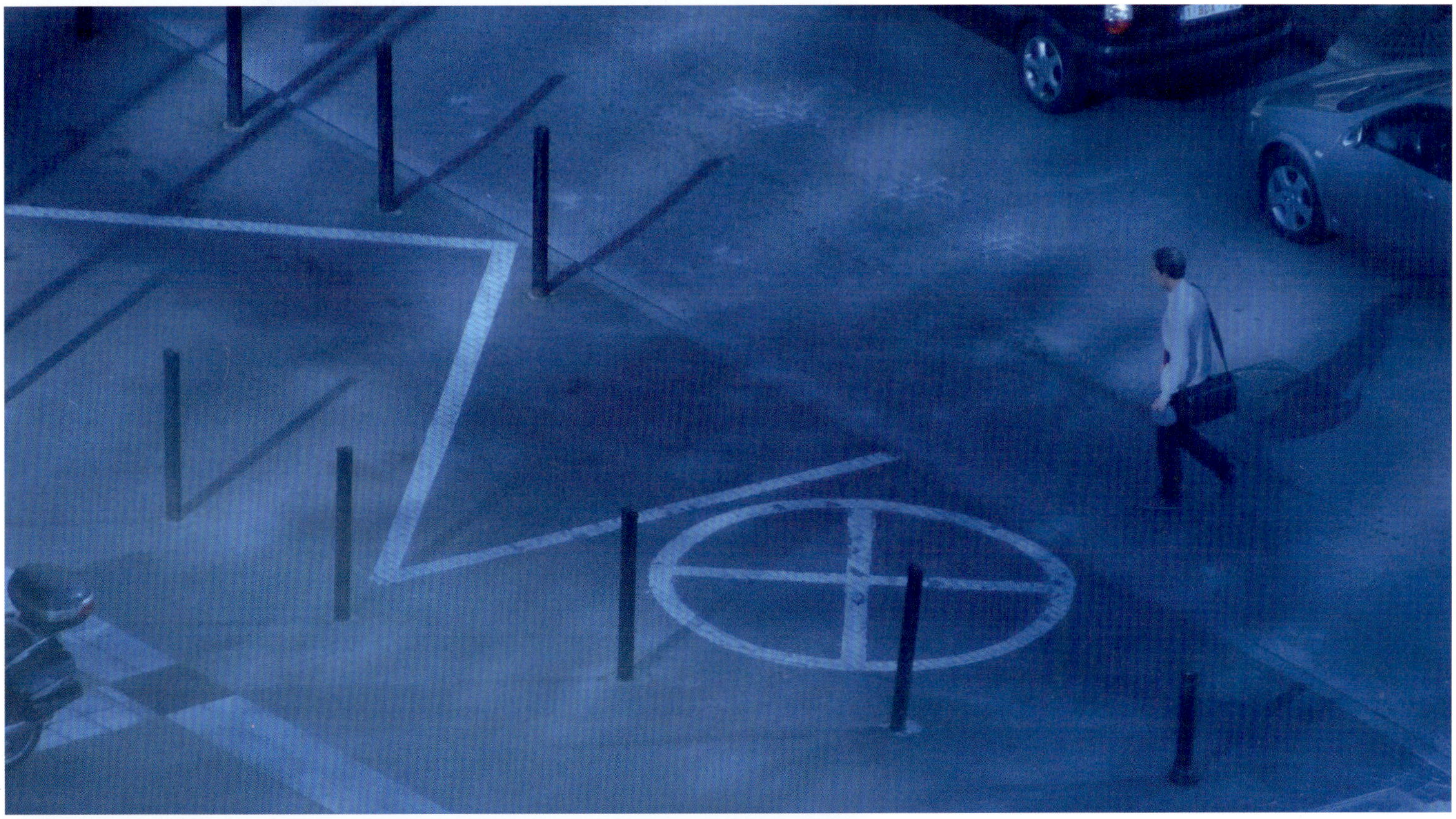

WTC

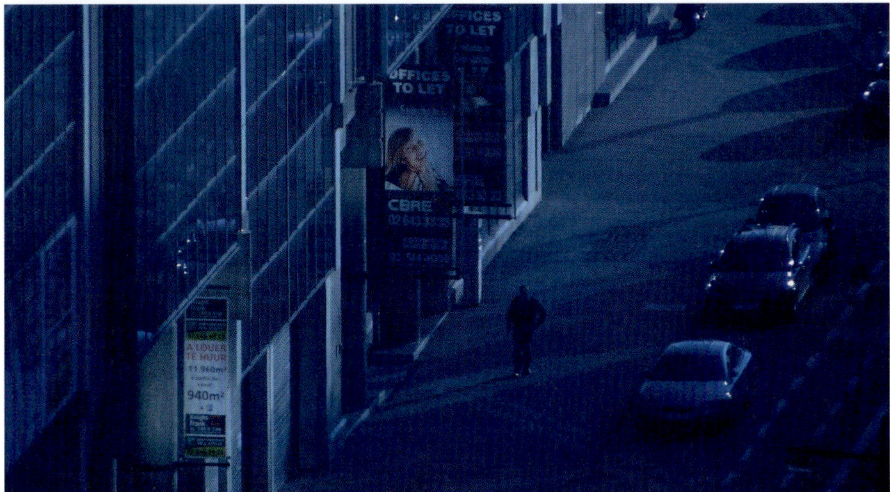

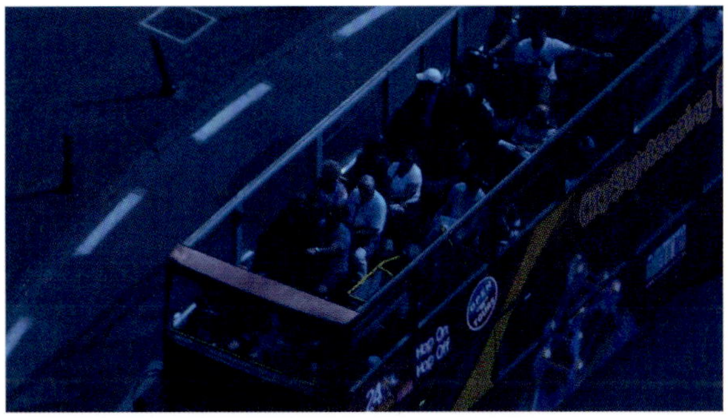

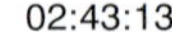
02:43:13

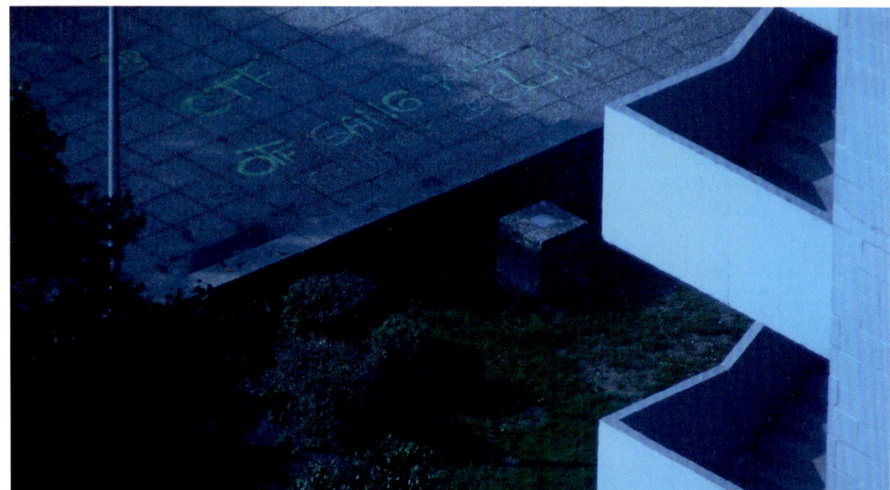

WTC

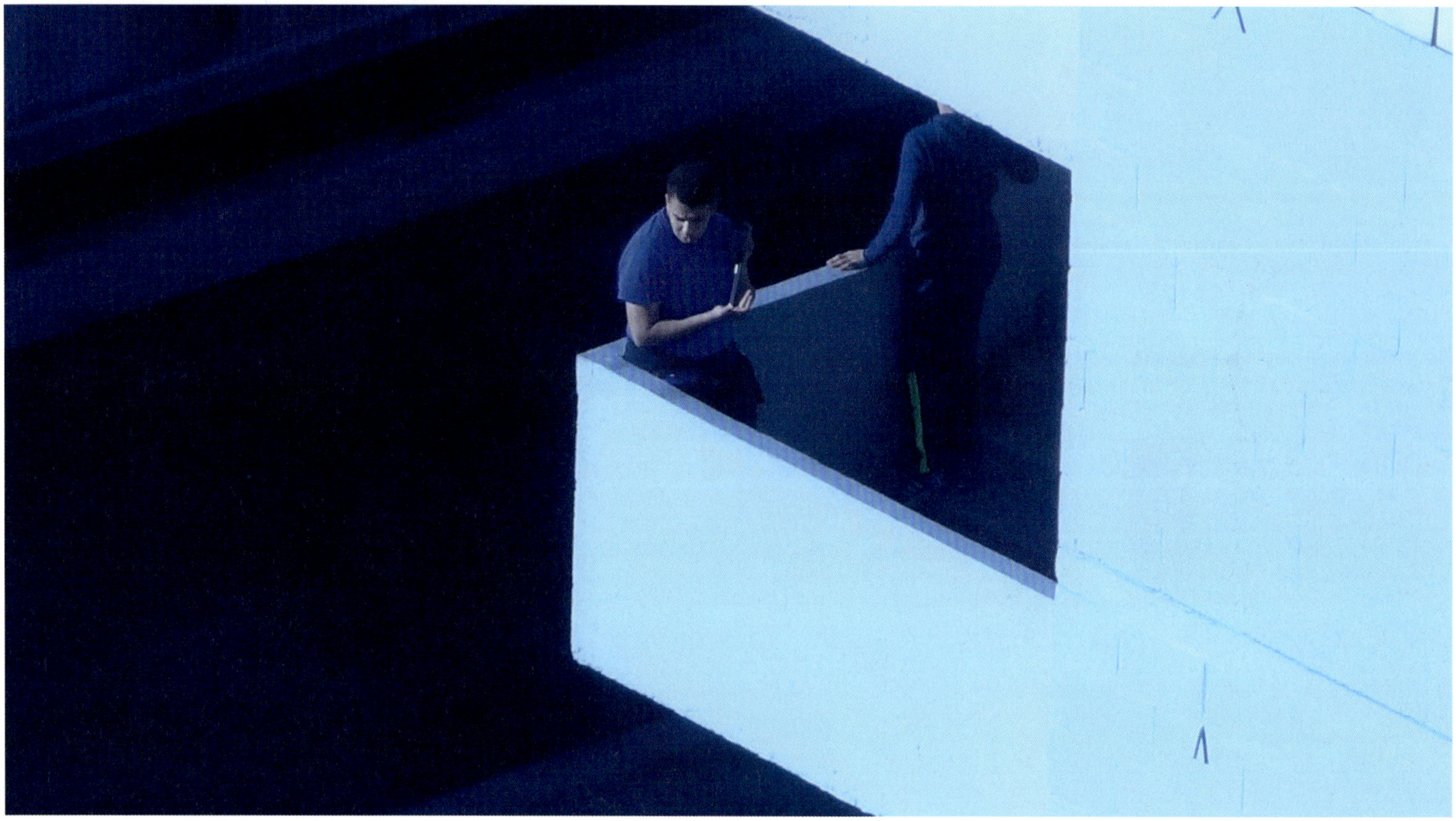

02:55:11

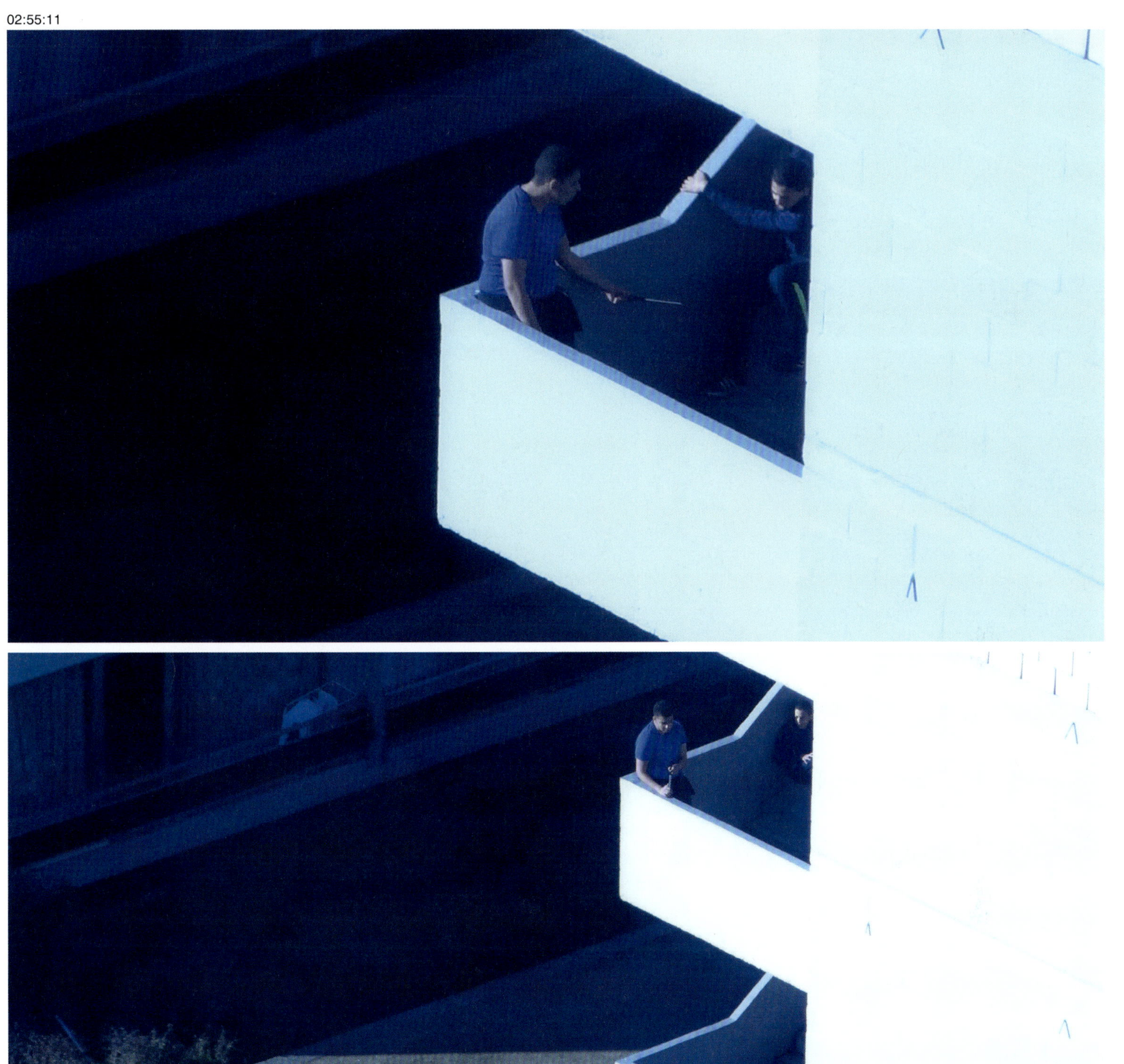

WTC

03:05:11

WTC

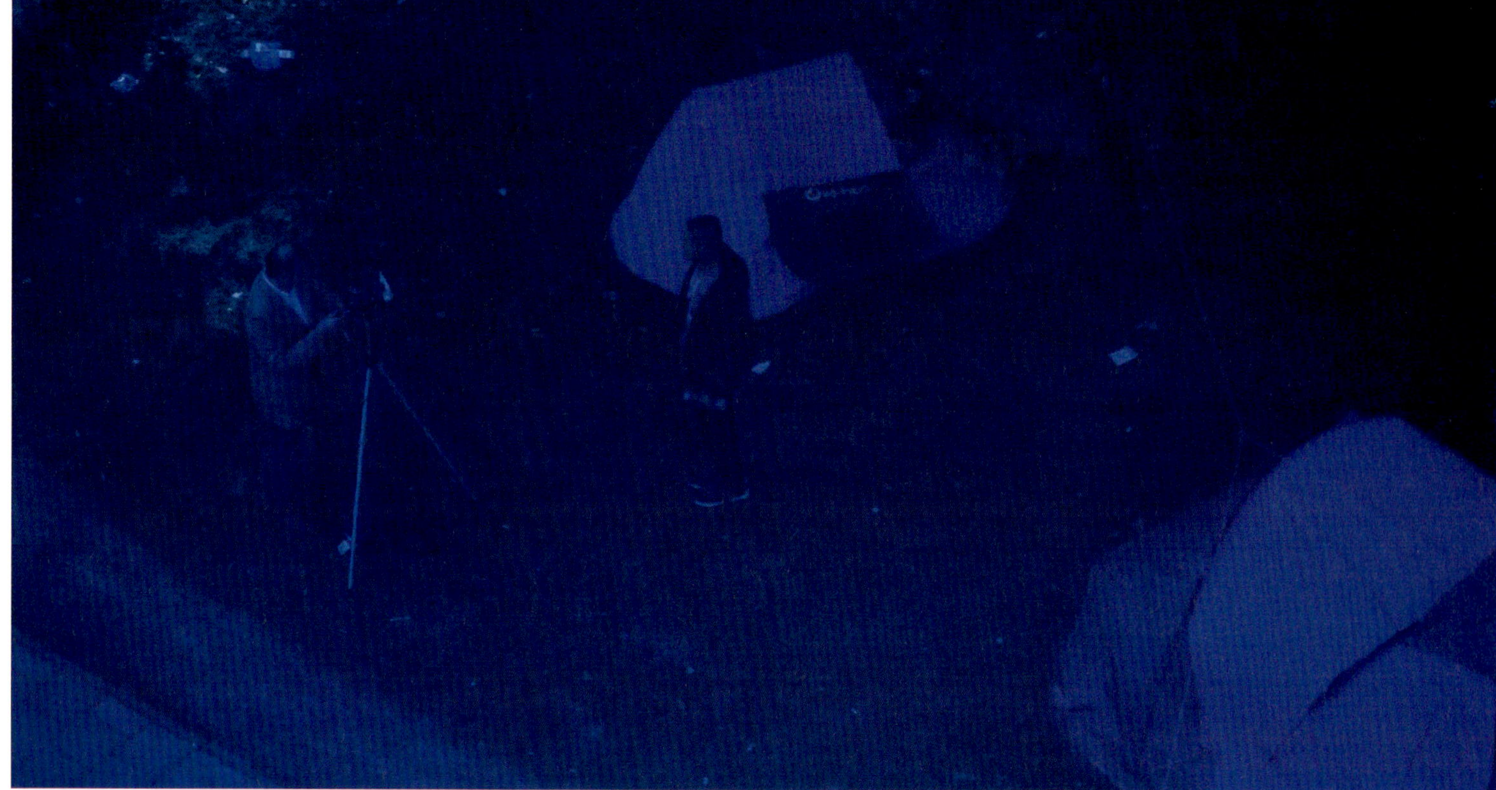

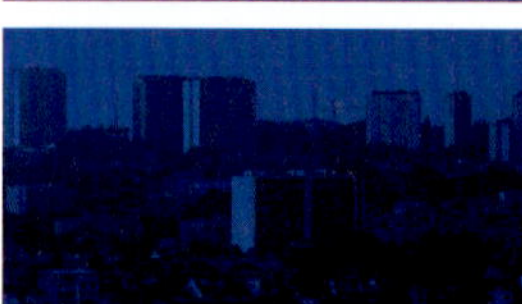

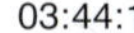
03:44:10

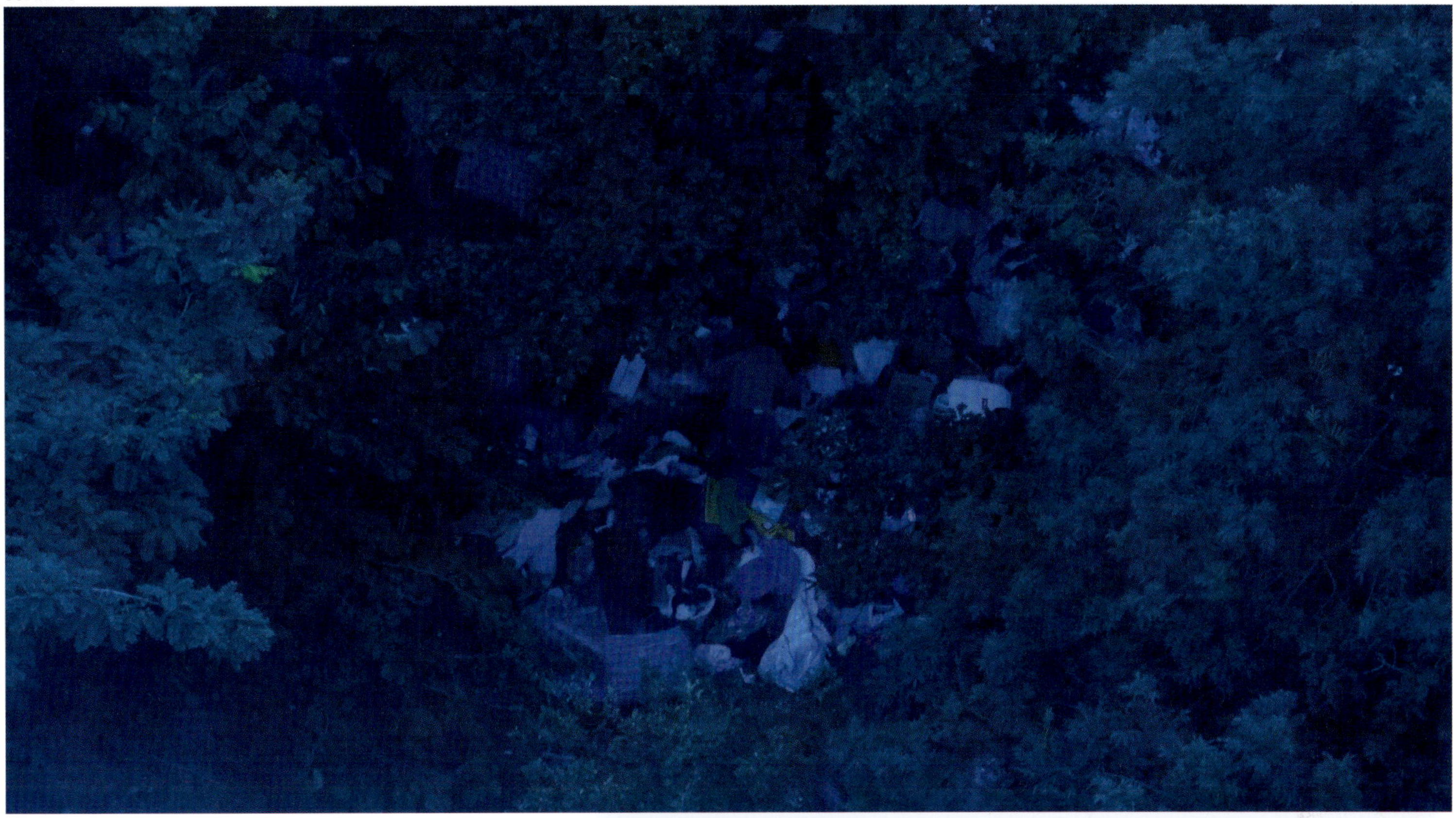

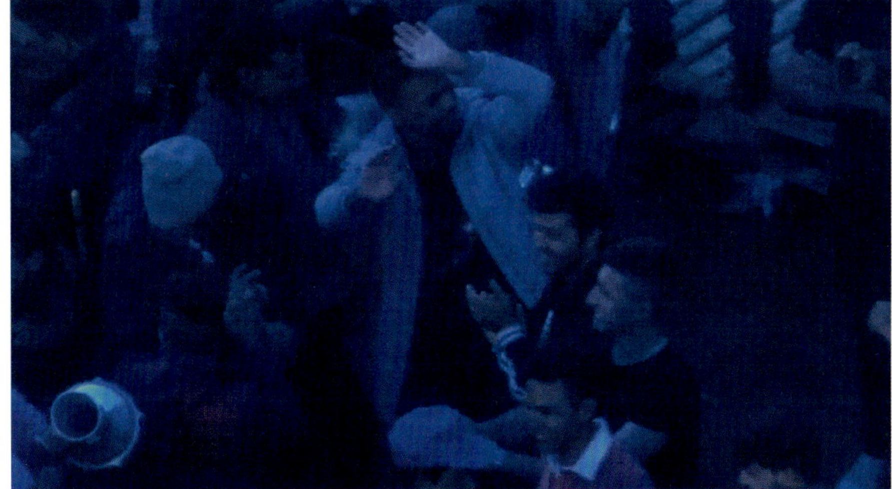

WTC

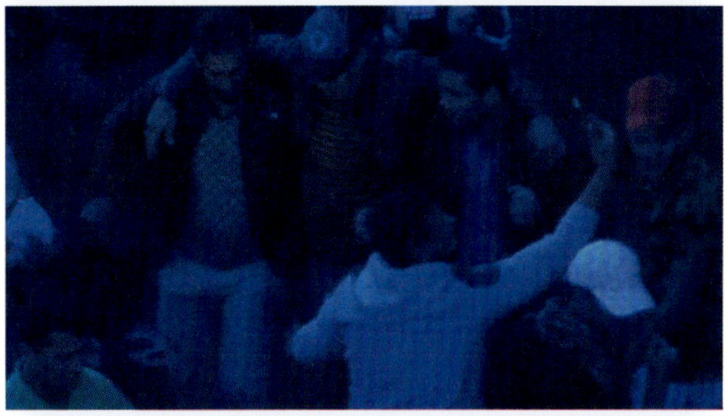

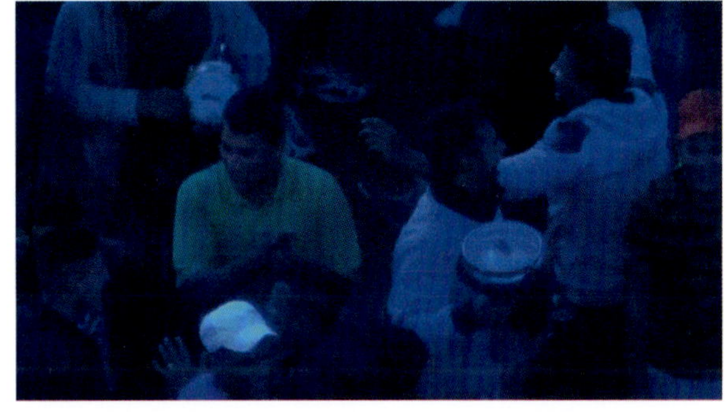

04:06:05

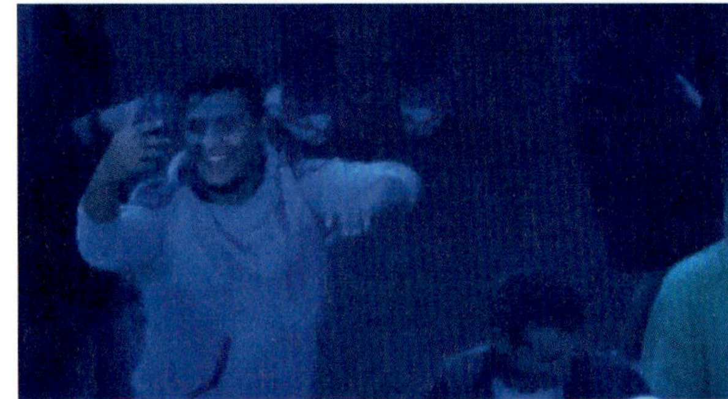

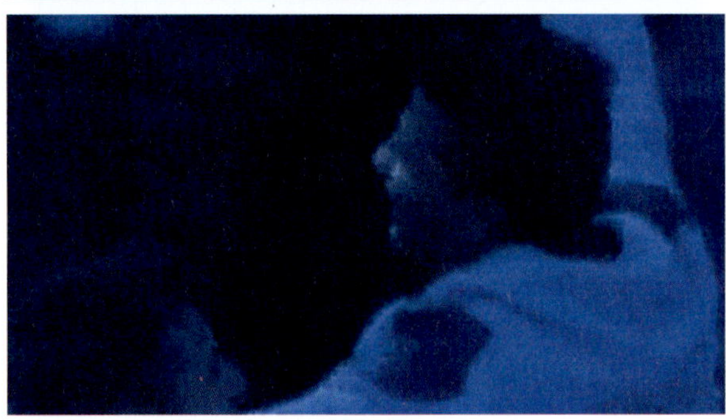

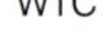

WTC

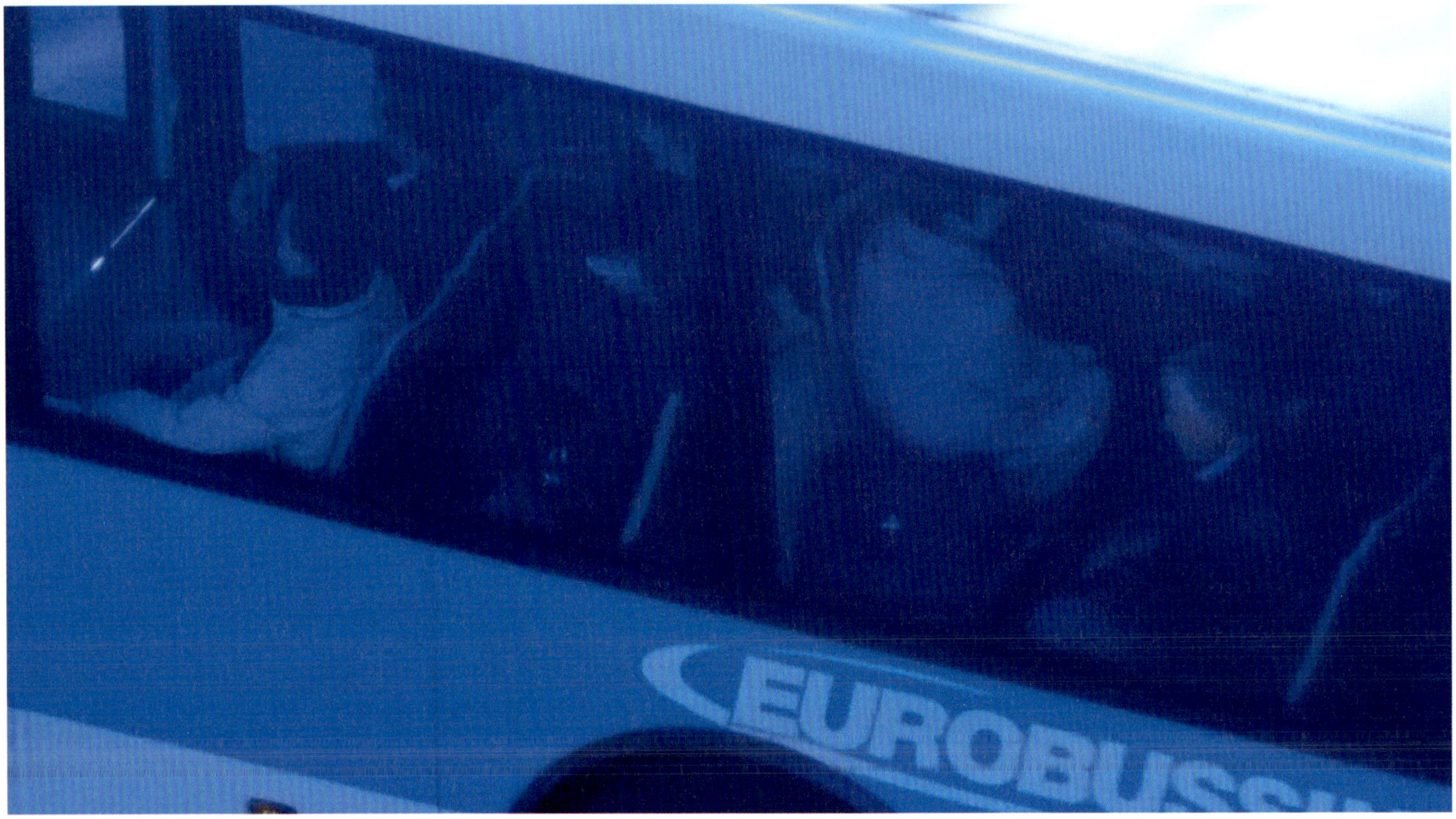

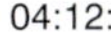

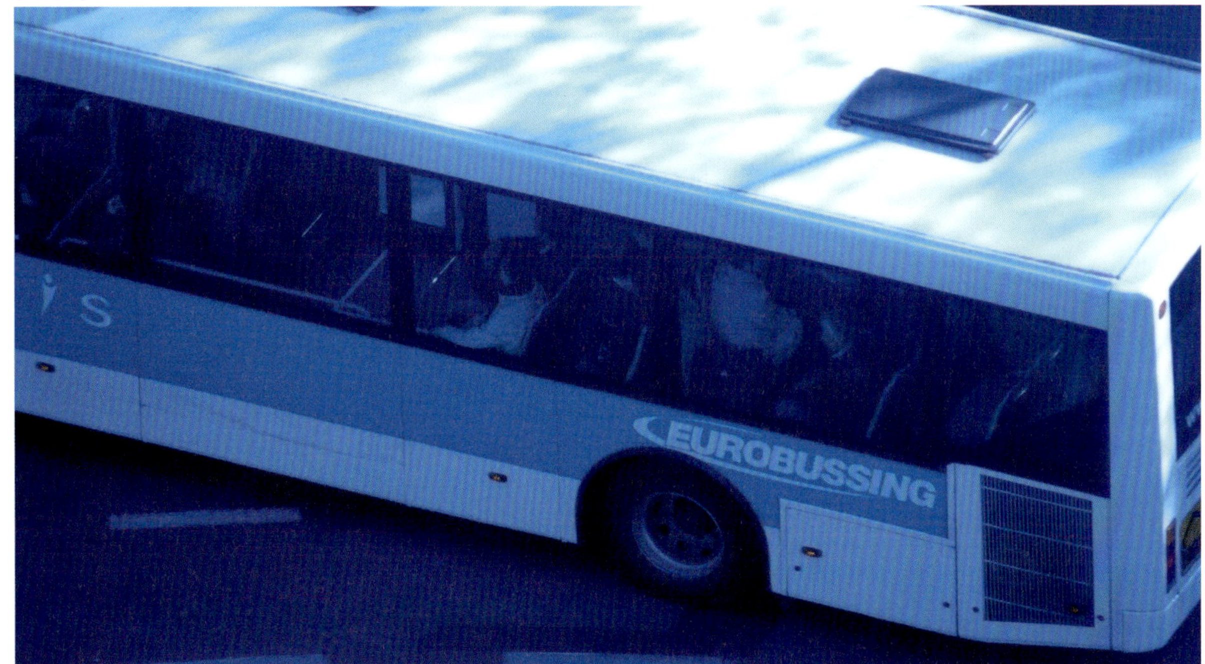

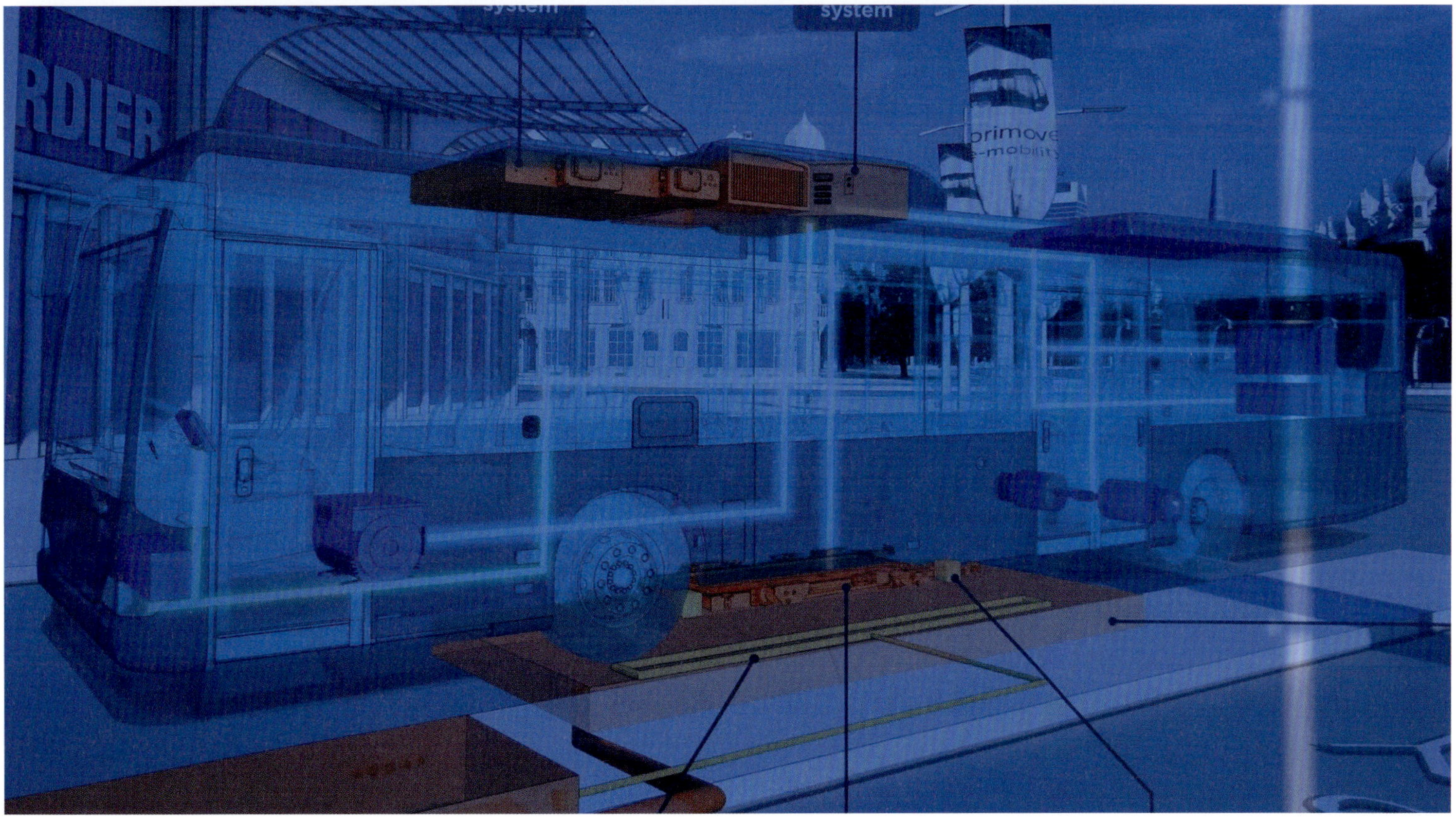

WTC

04:22:12

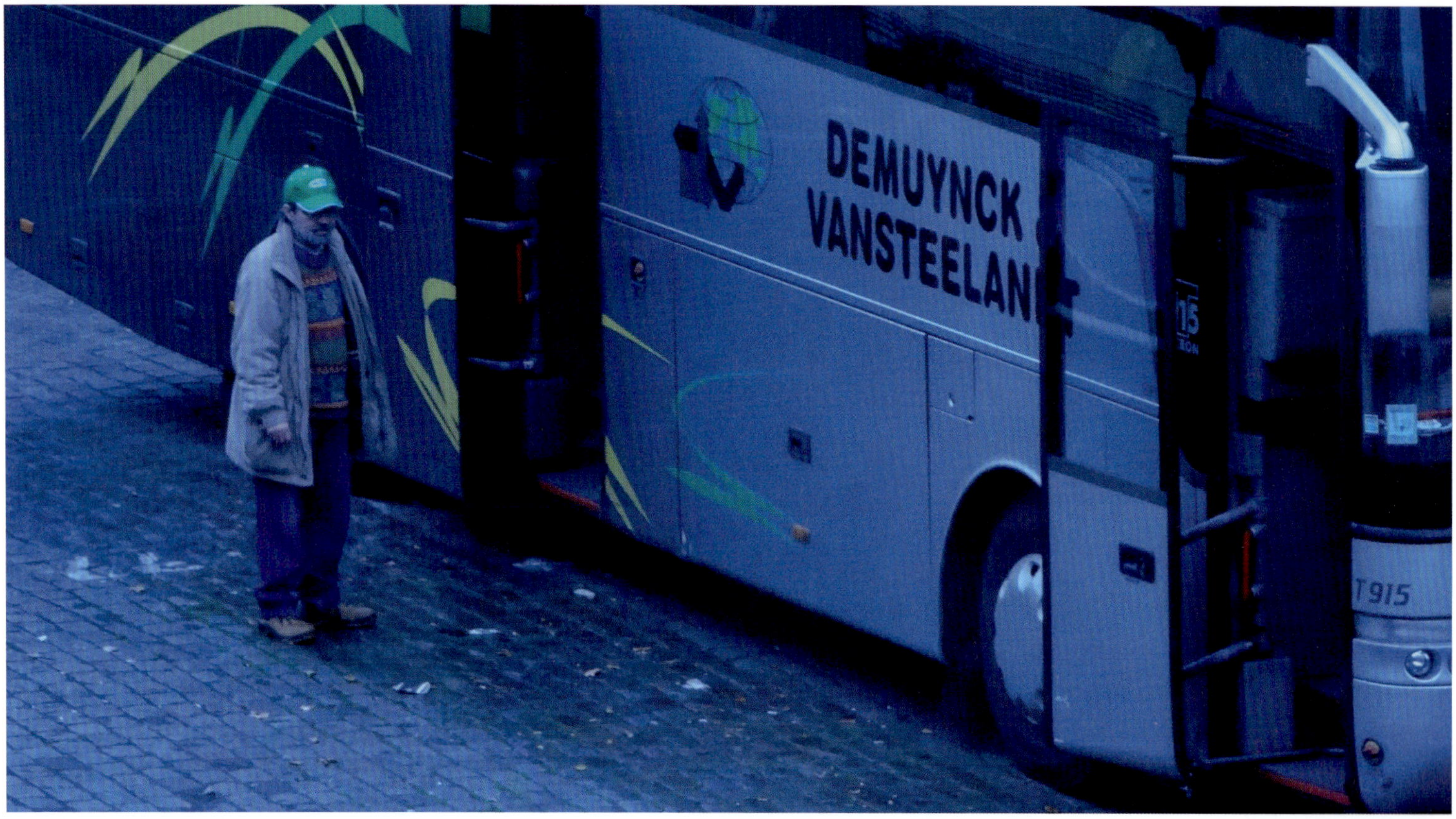

WTC

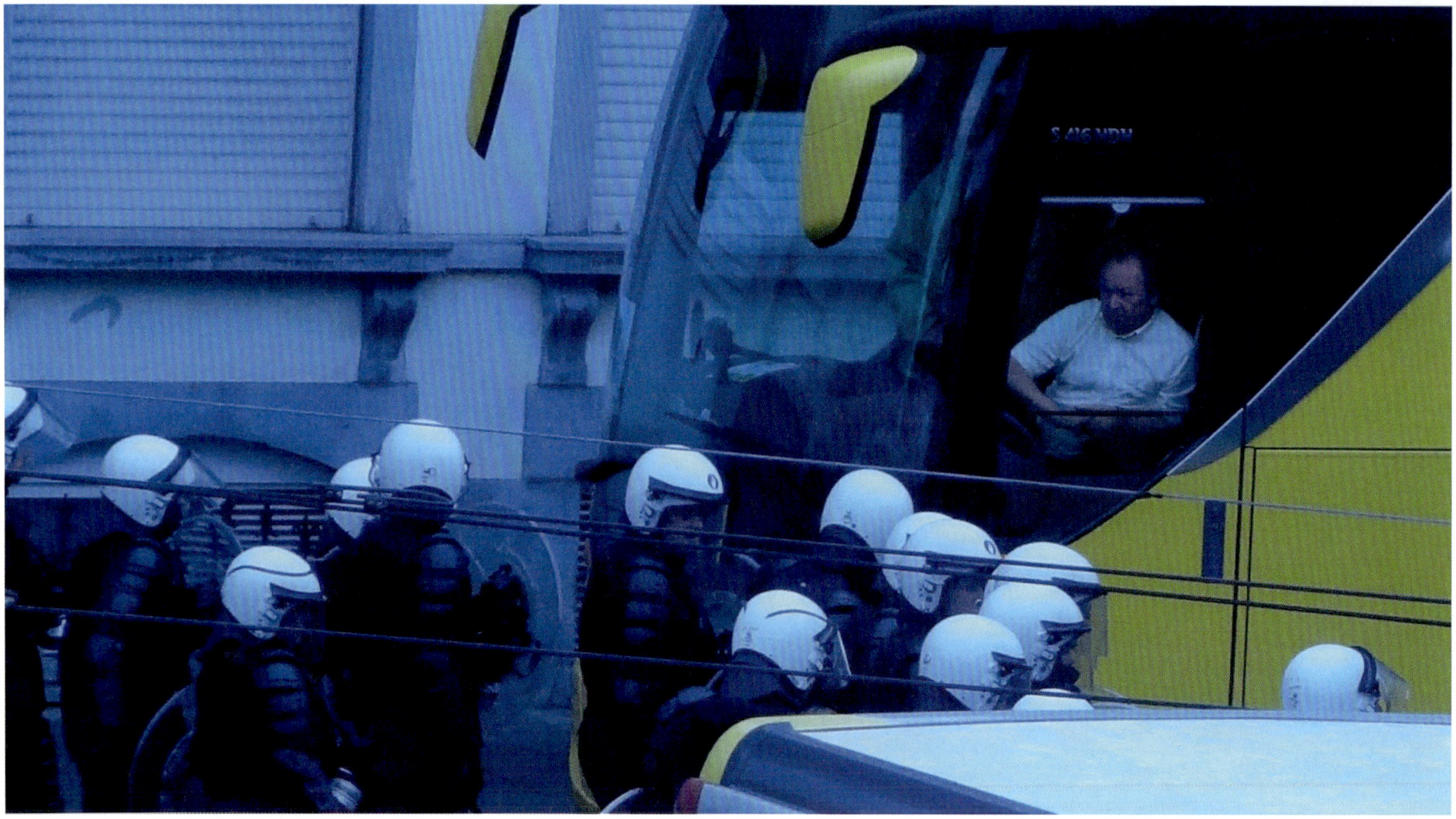

04:32:11

NO STOP
Léonard

DE ZONNESTRAAL
Linden Cars

BUS FAN
BRUSSELS CITY
SHUTTLE
flibco

DE ZONNESTRAAL

WTC

Heidebloem

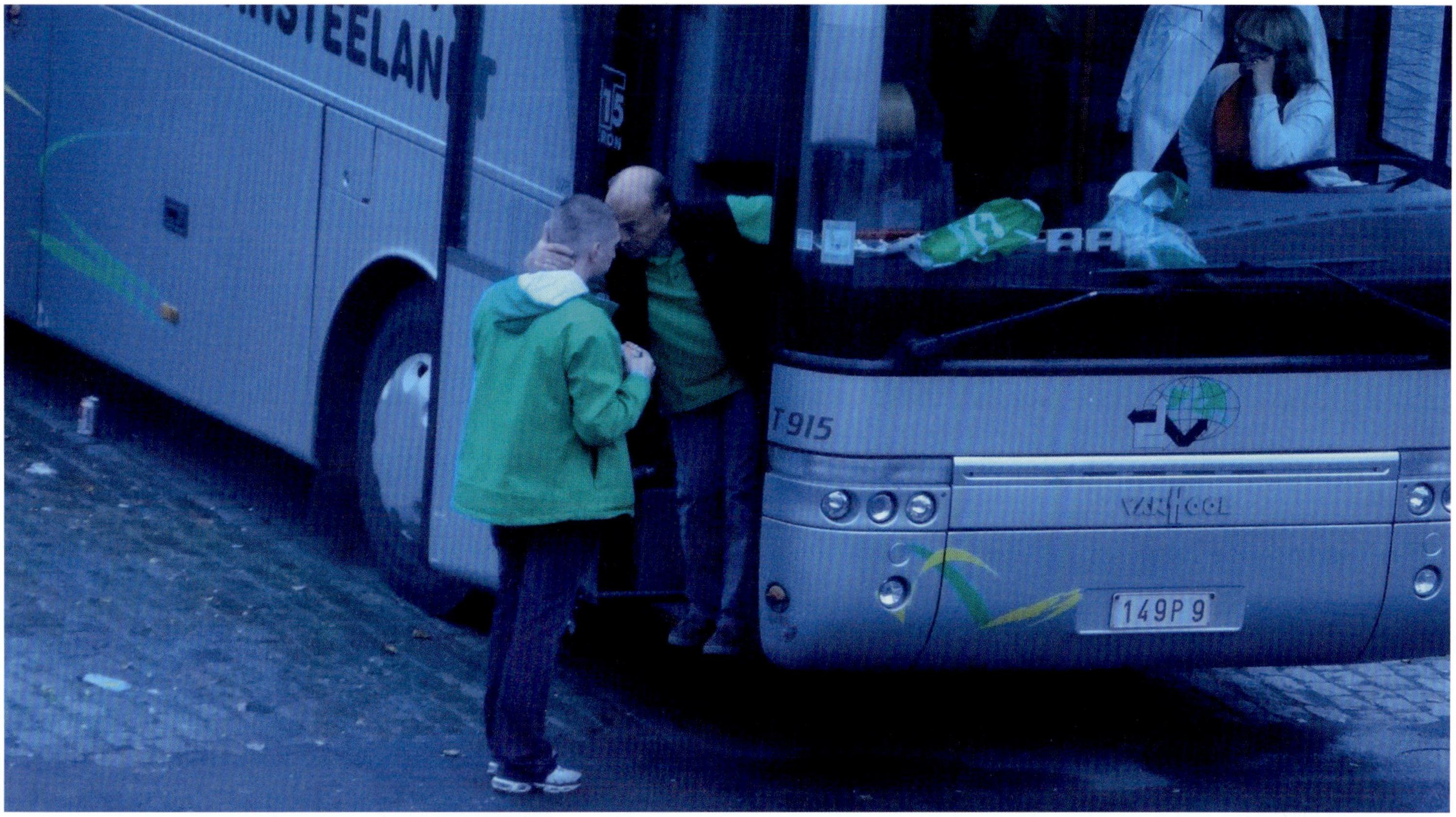

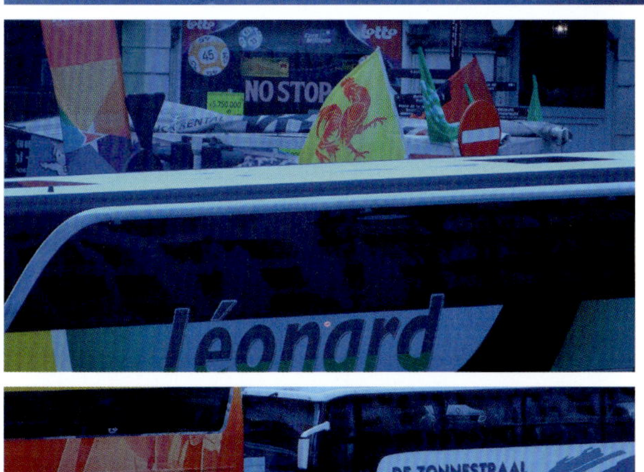

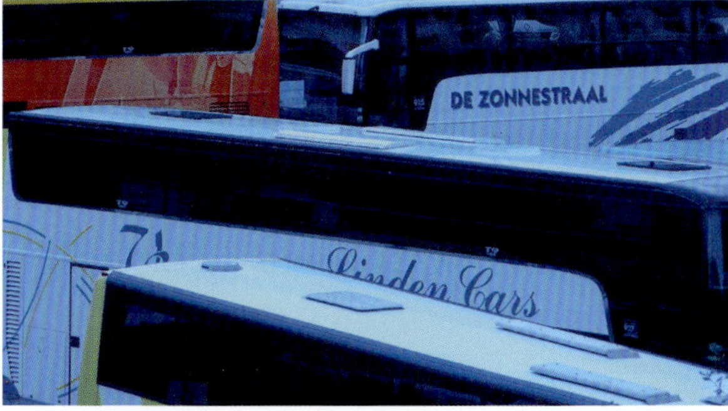

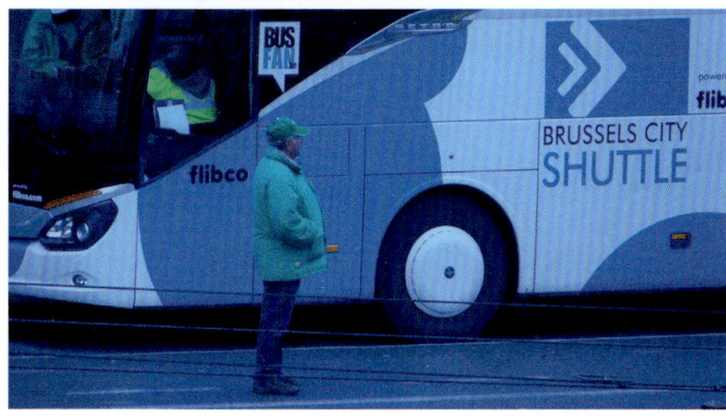

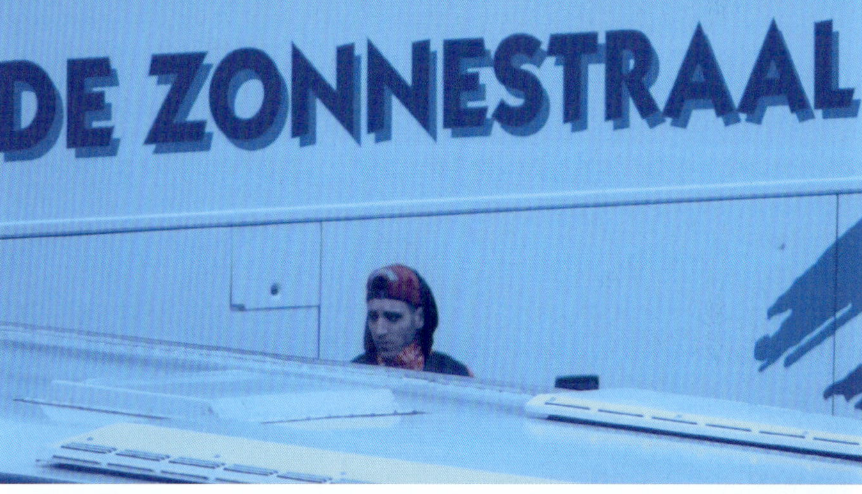

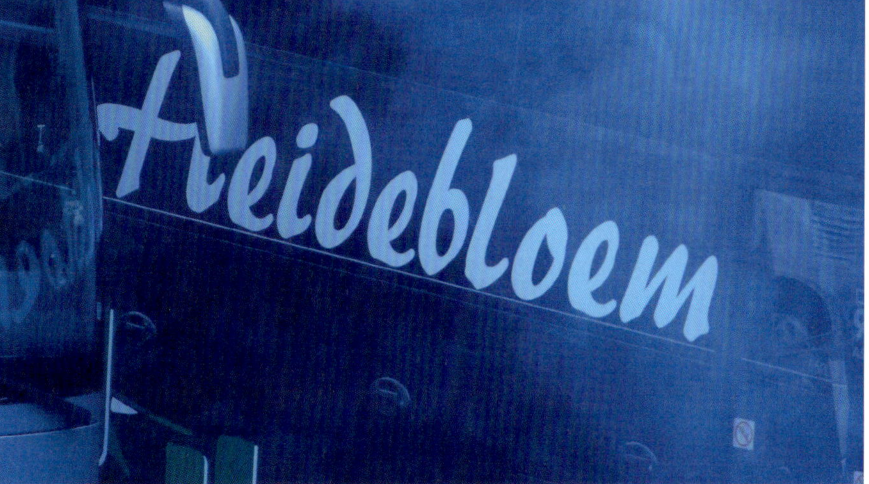

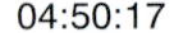
04:50:17

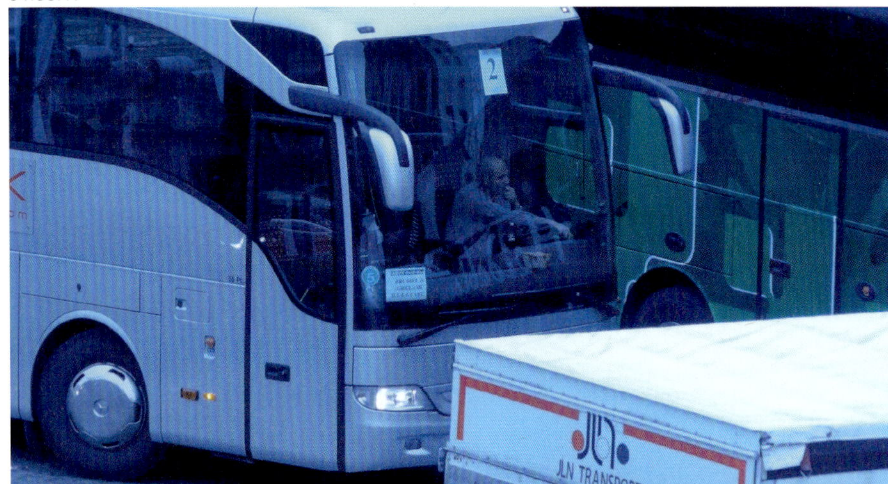

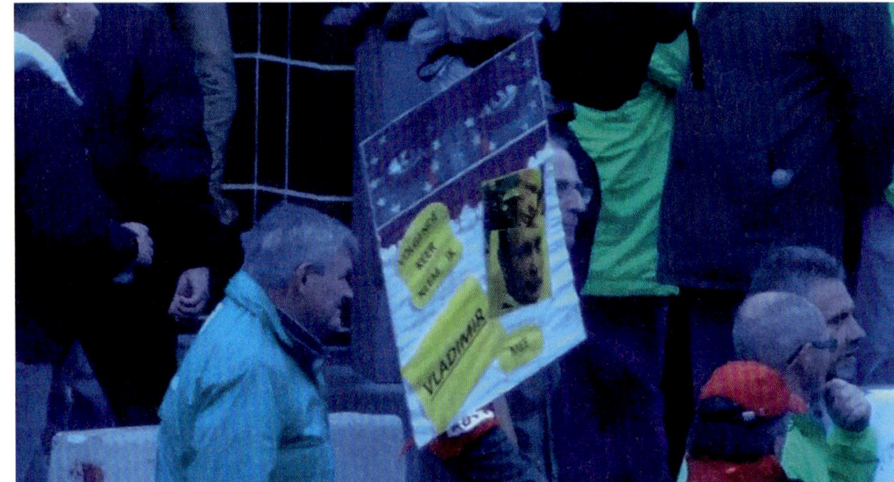

WTC

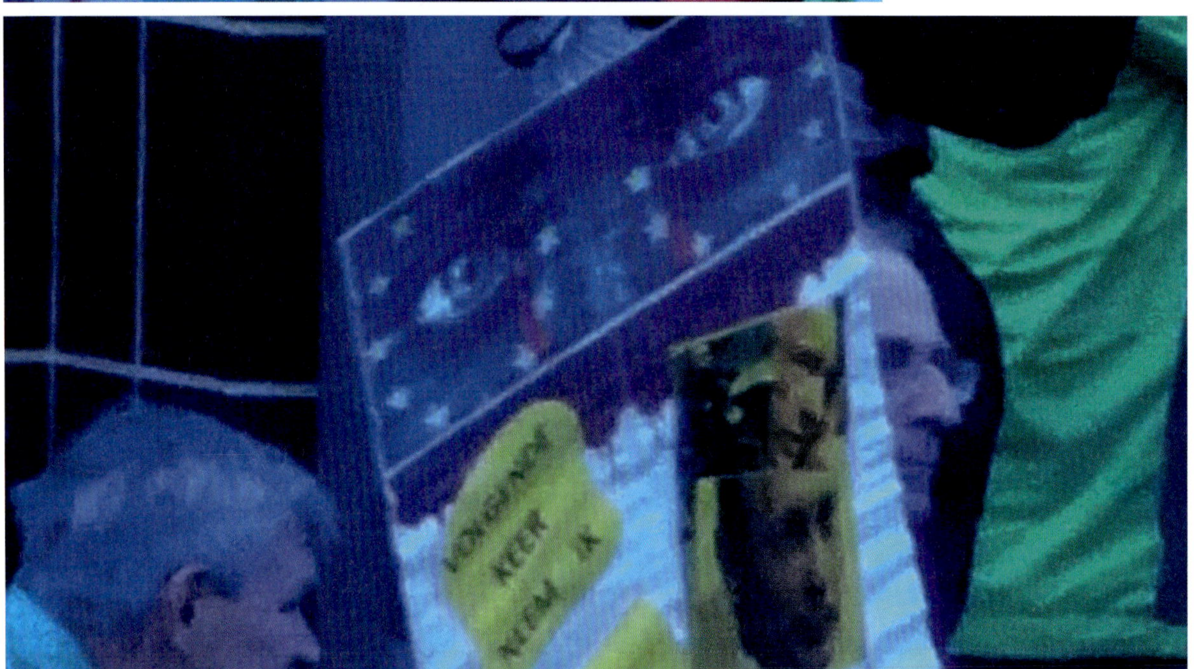

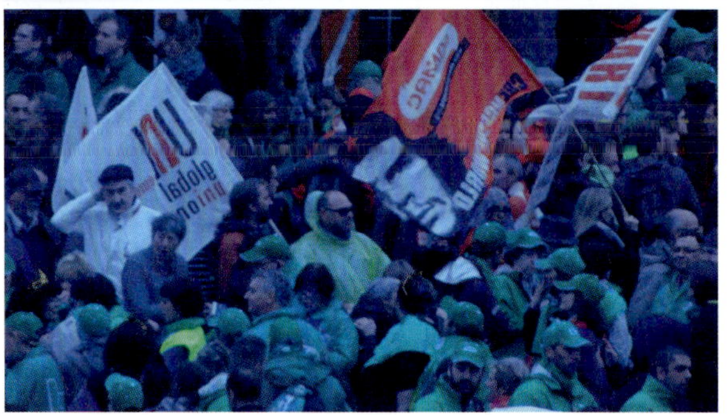

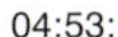

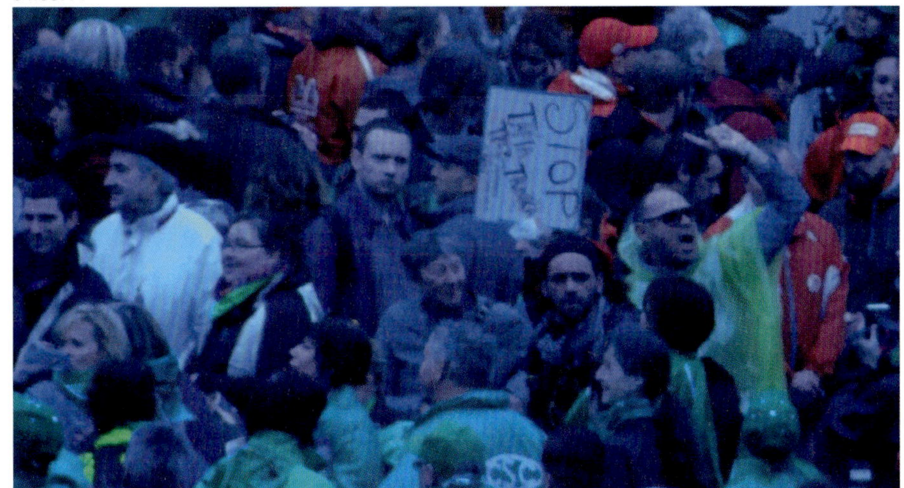

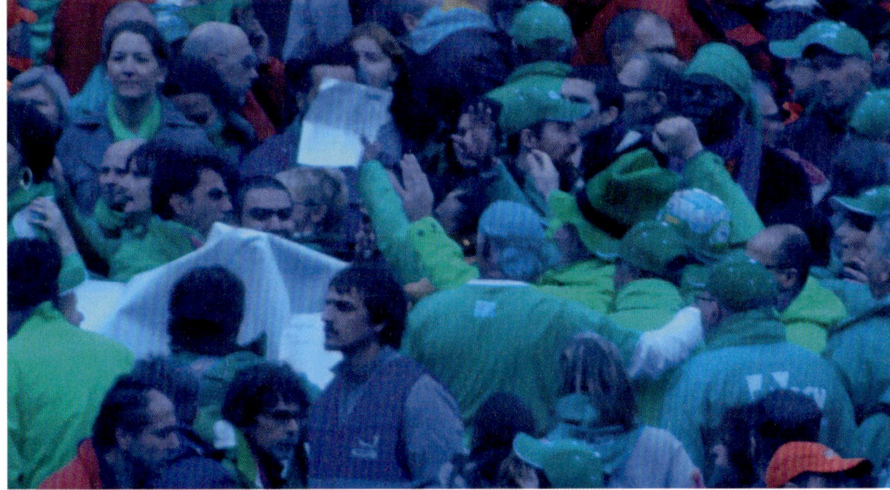

WTC

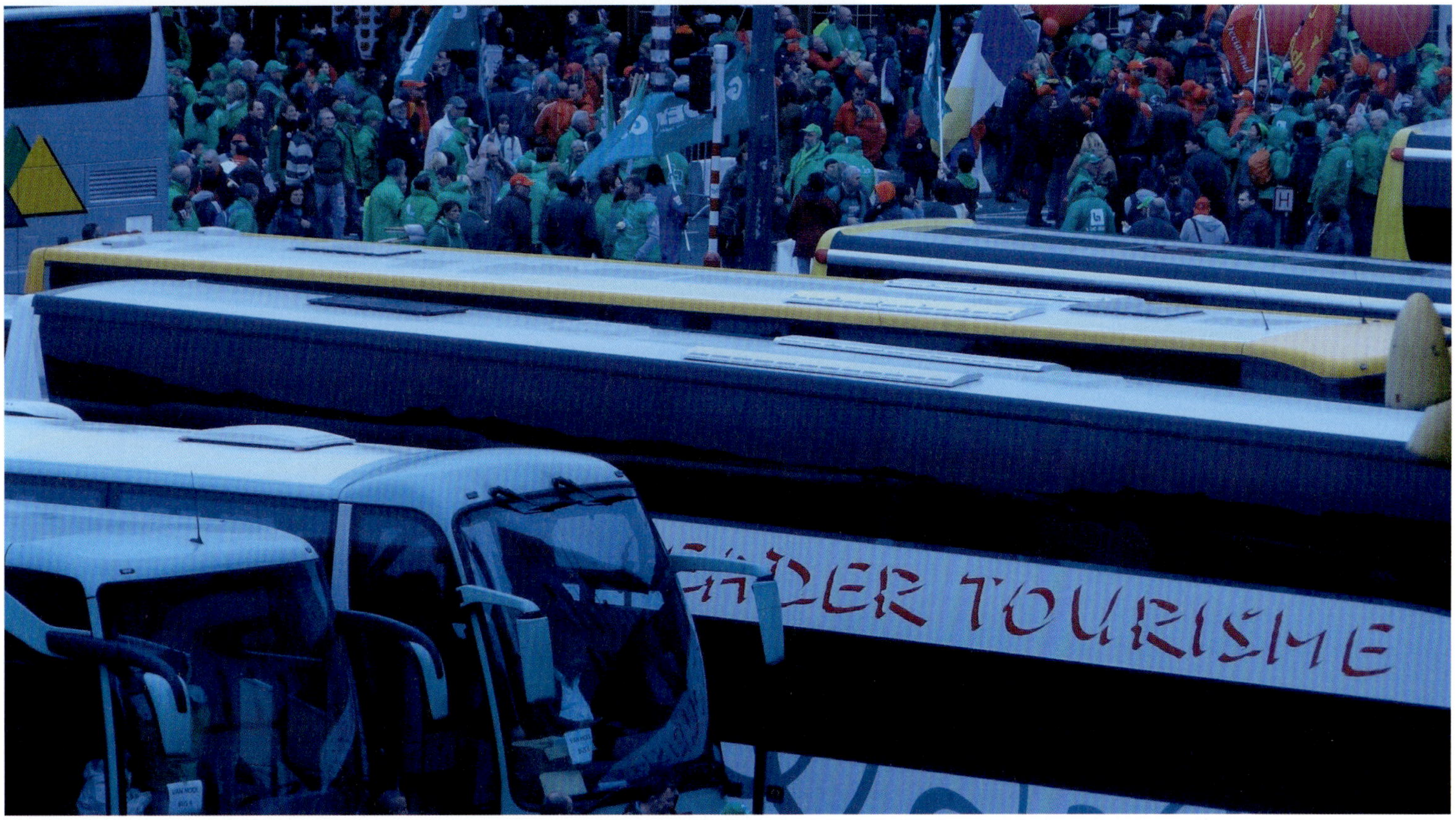

04:55:03

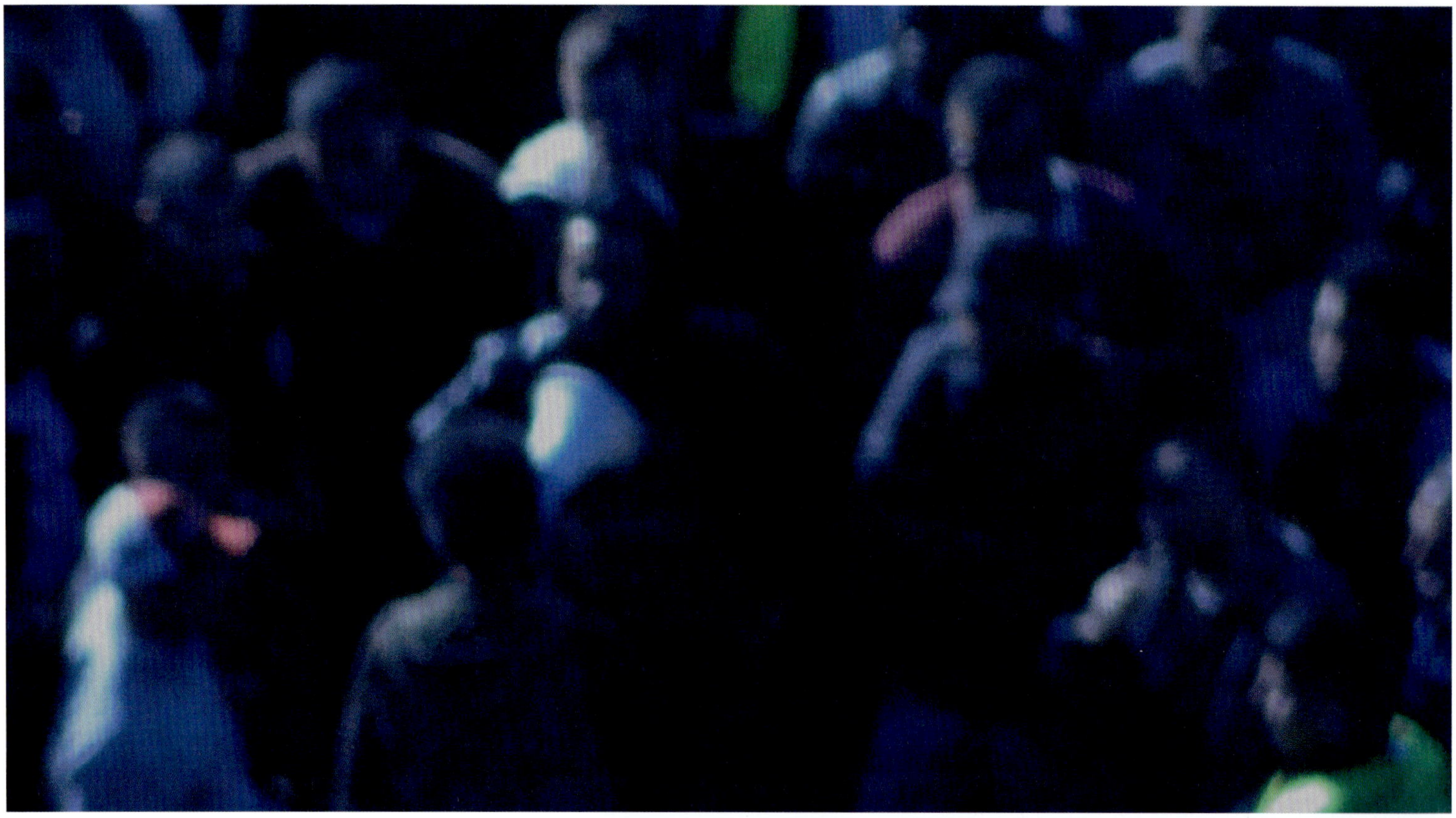

WTC

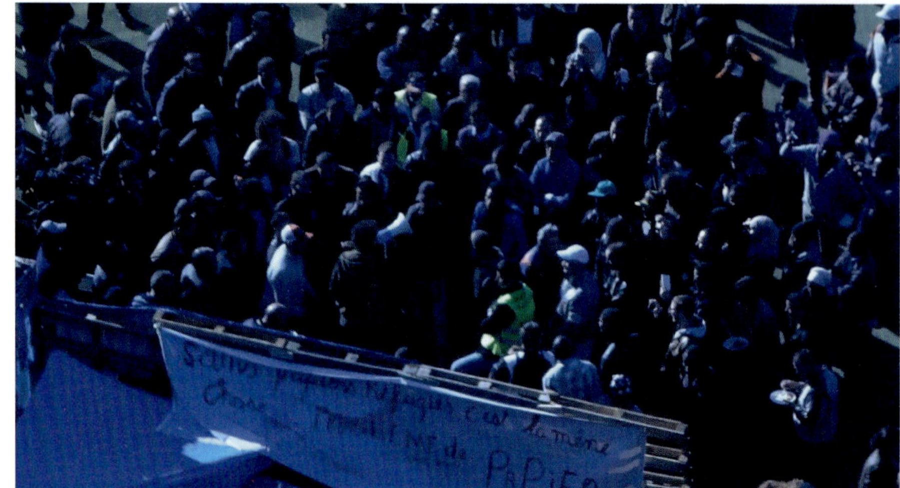

04:56:03

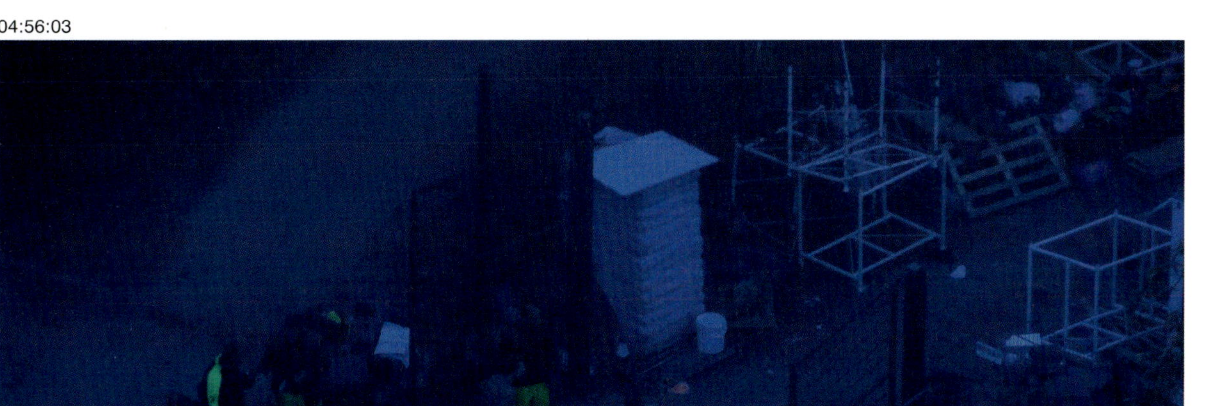

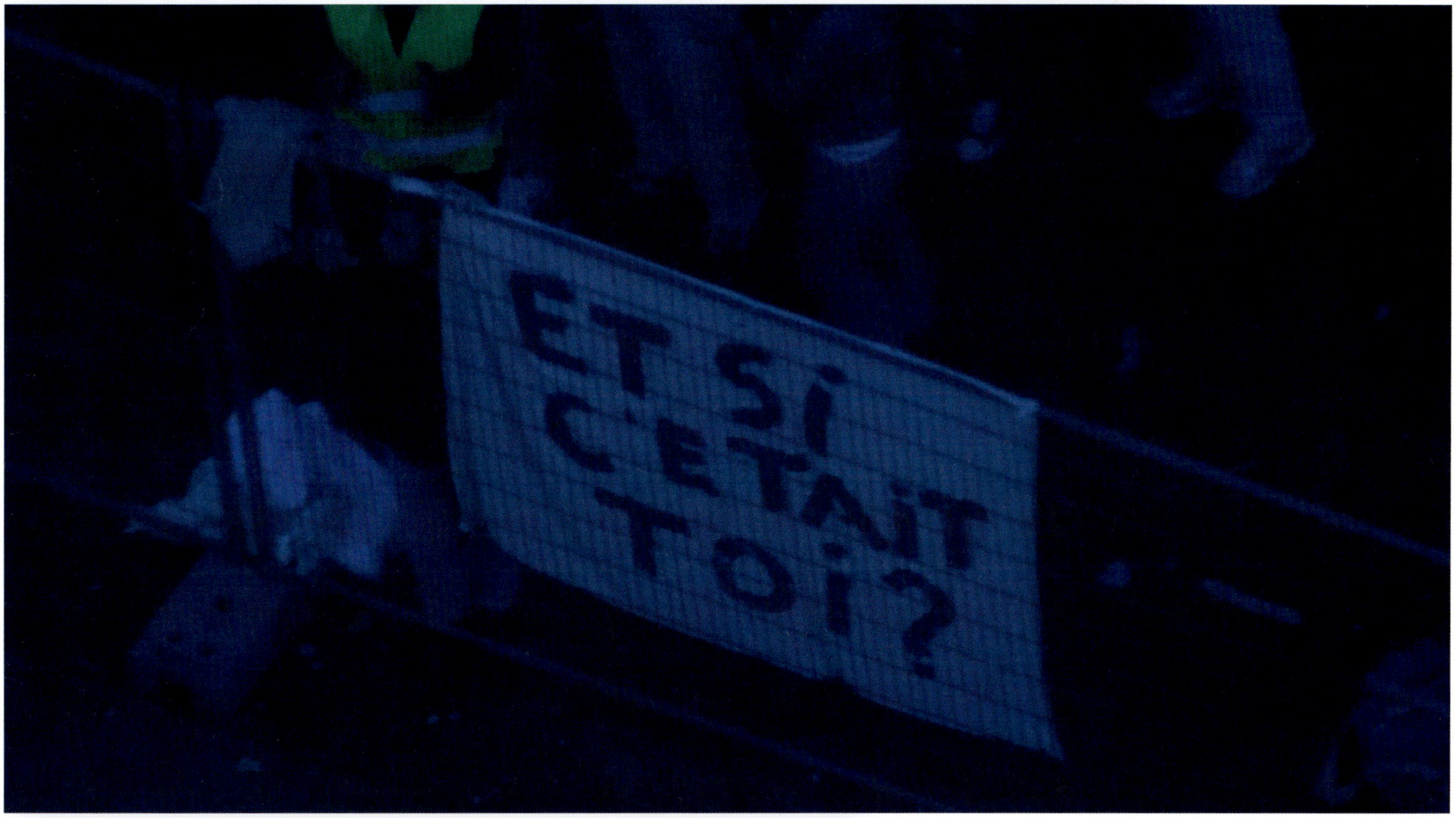

WTC

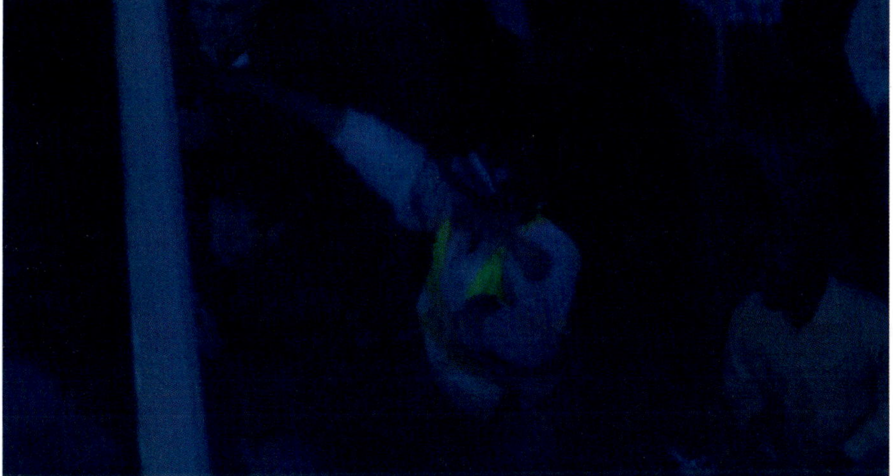

05:01:03

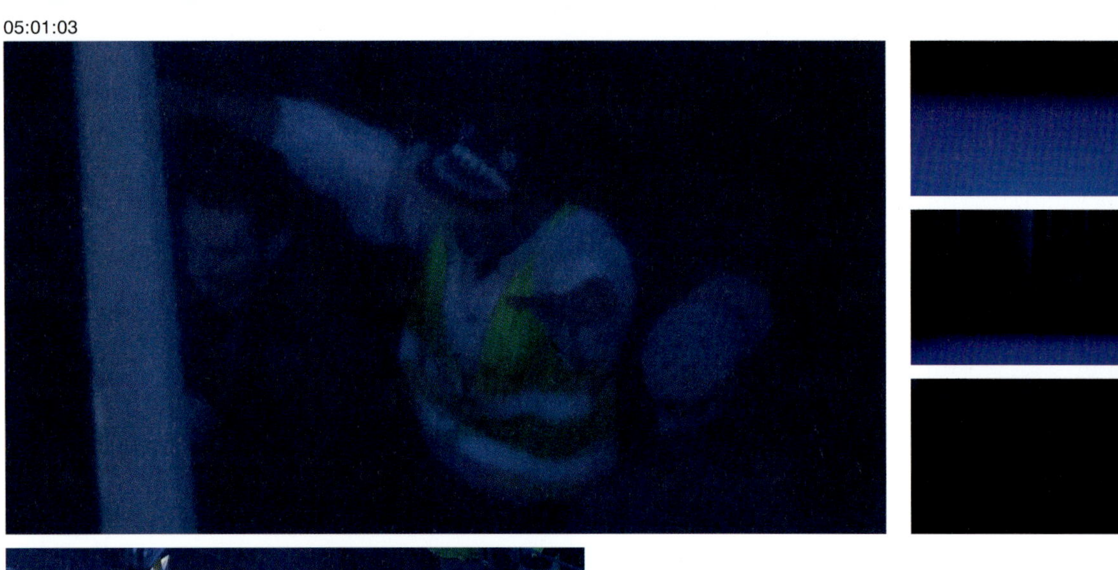

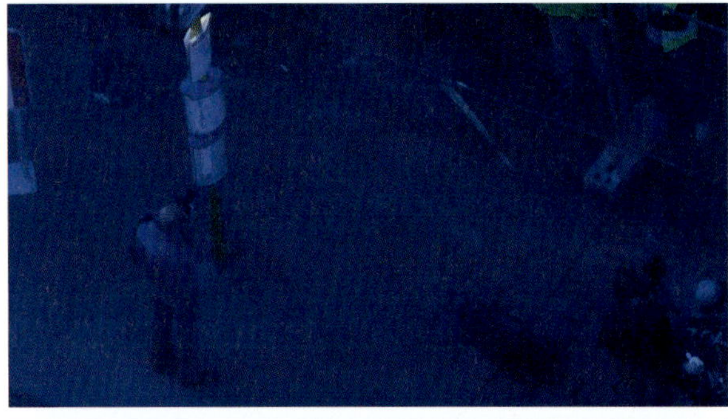

WTC

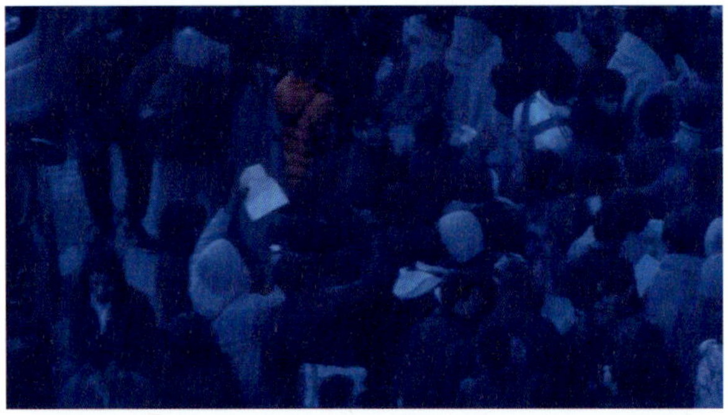

05:37:01

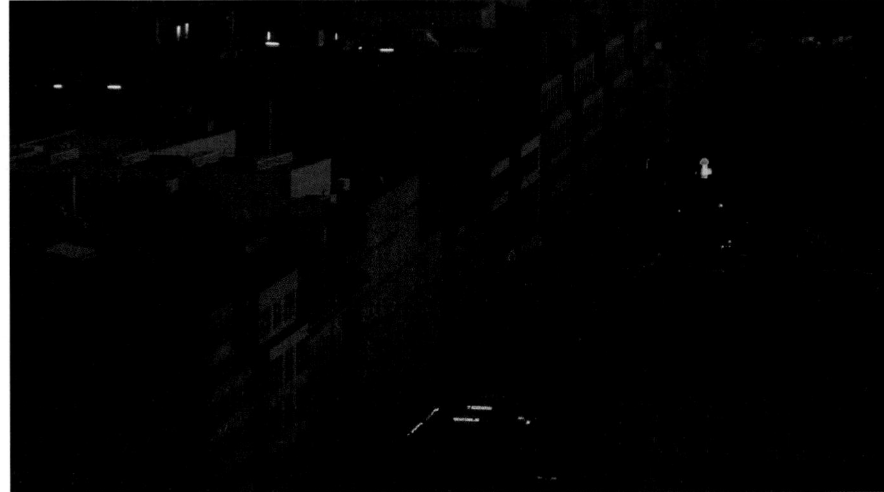

WTC

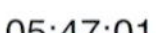
05:47:01

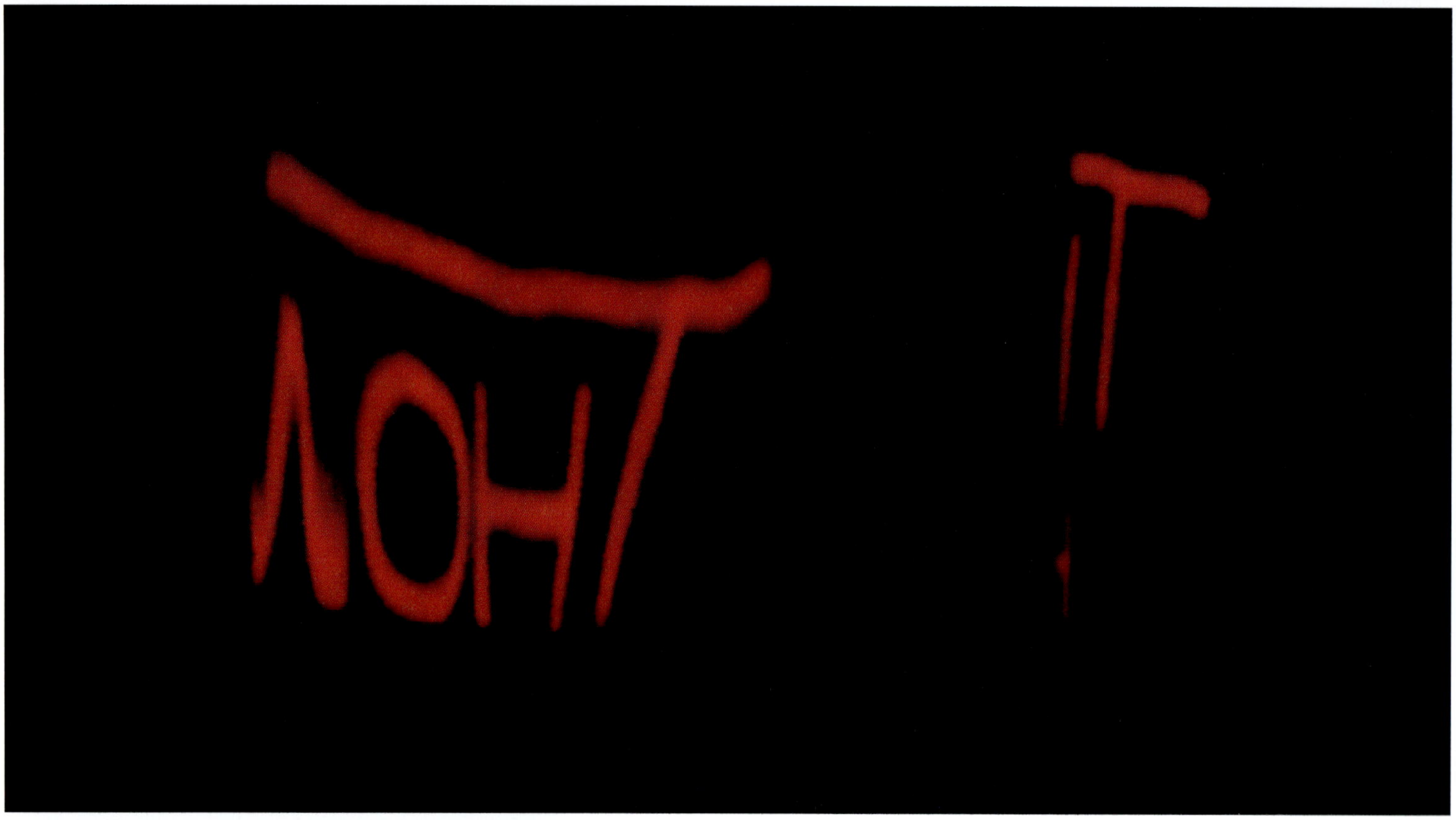

WTC

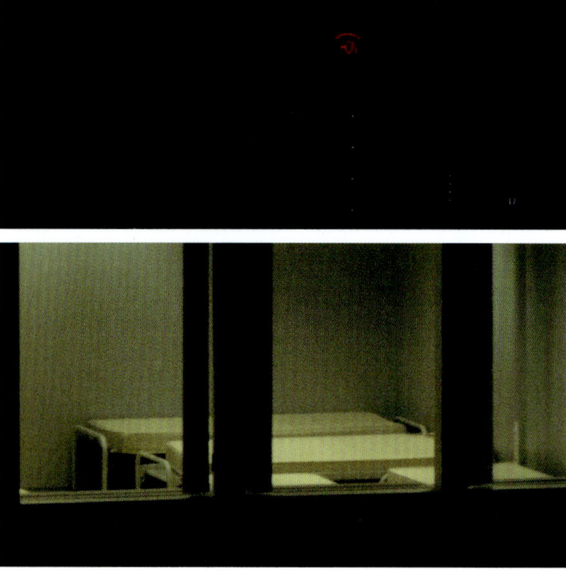

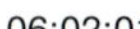
06:02:01

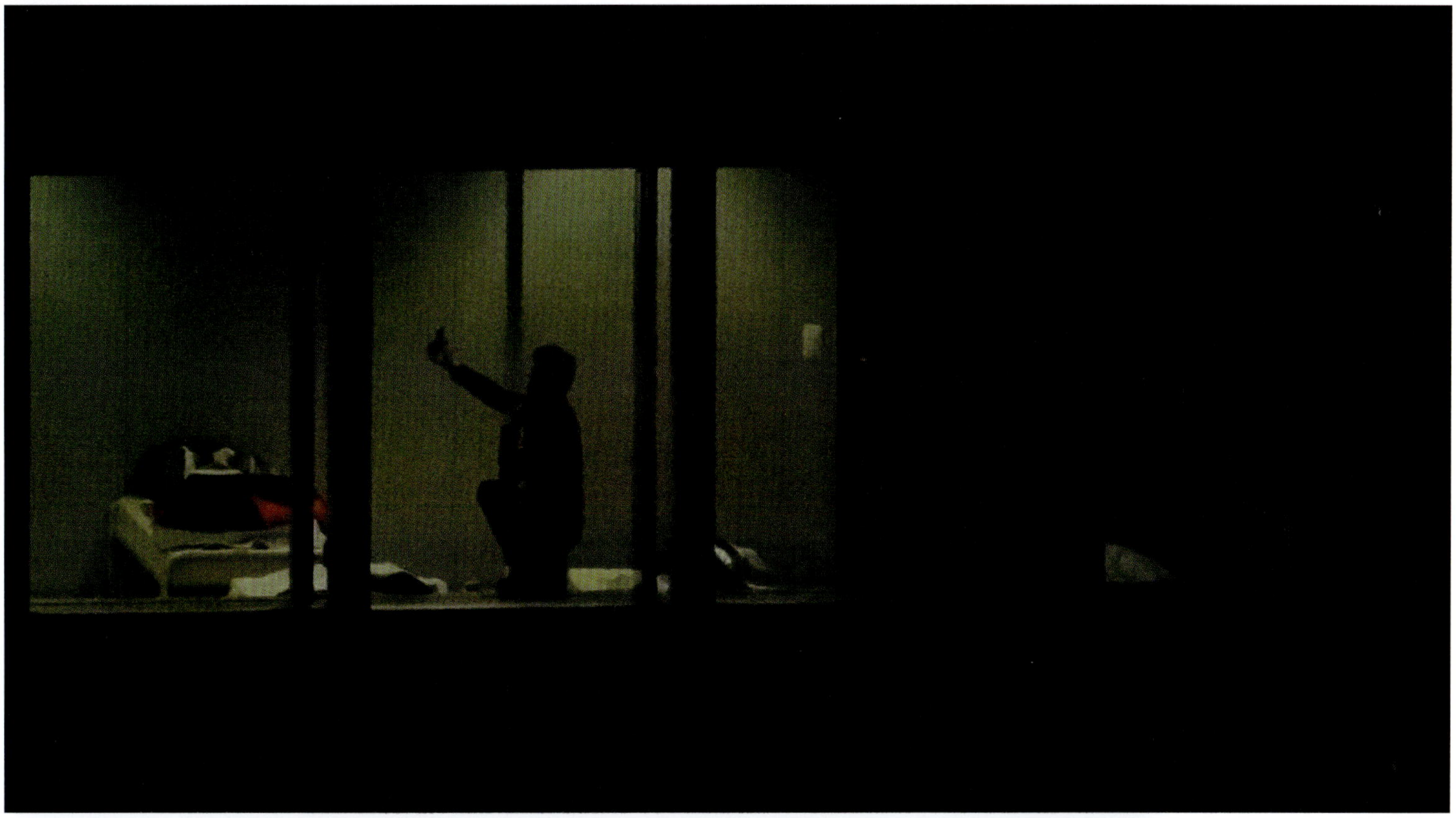

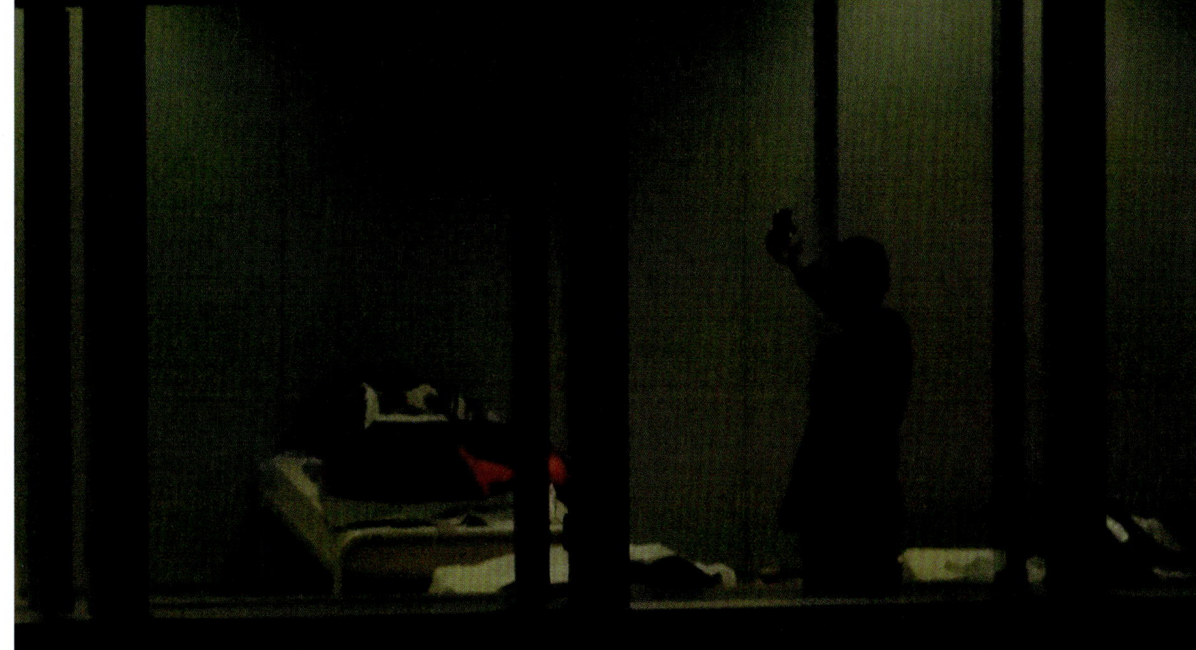

WTC

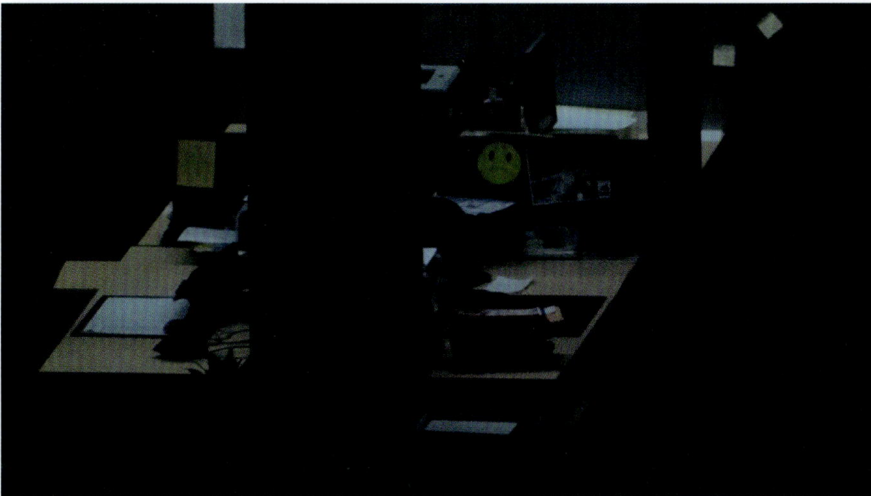

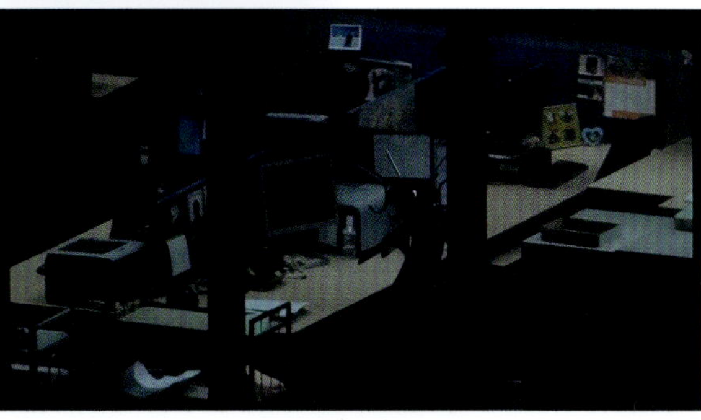

06:23:16

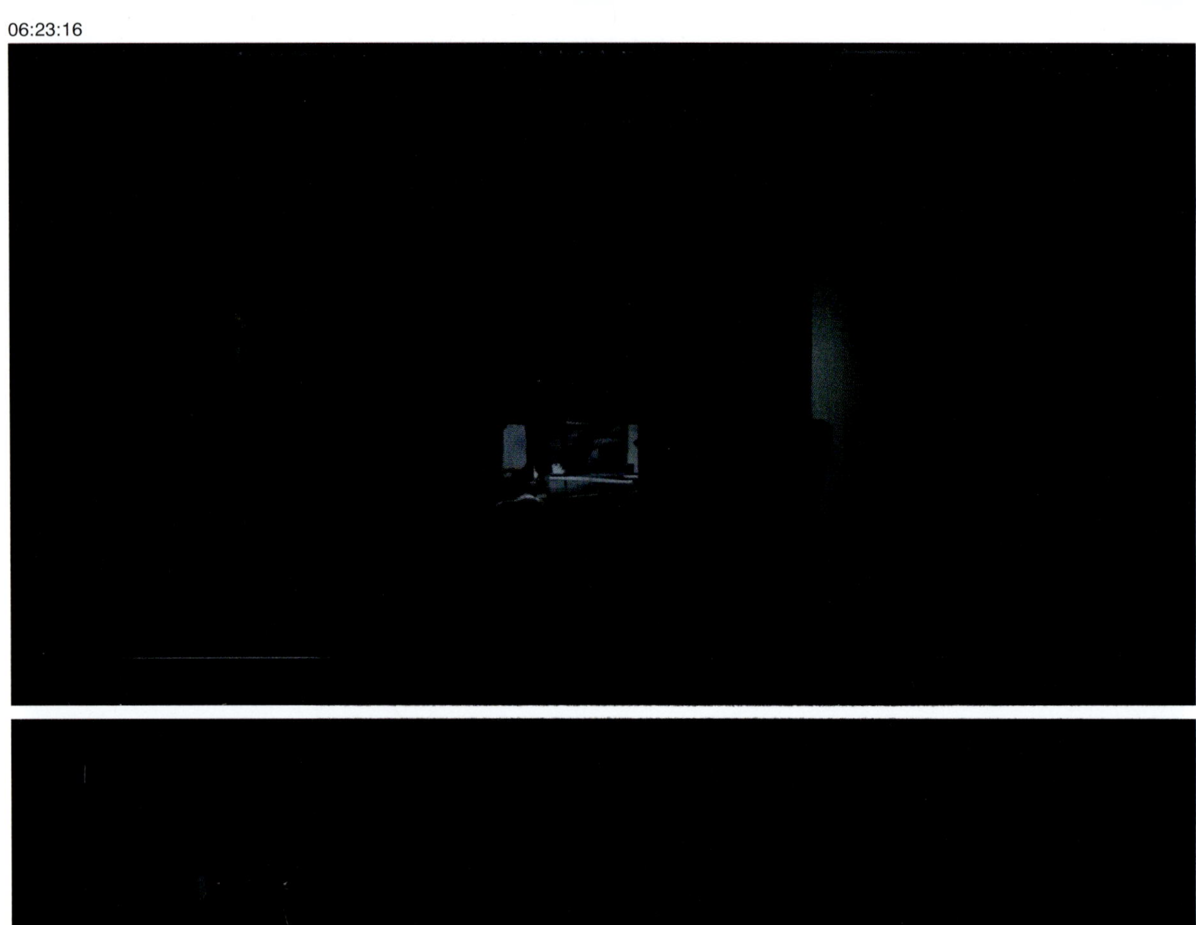

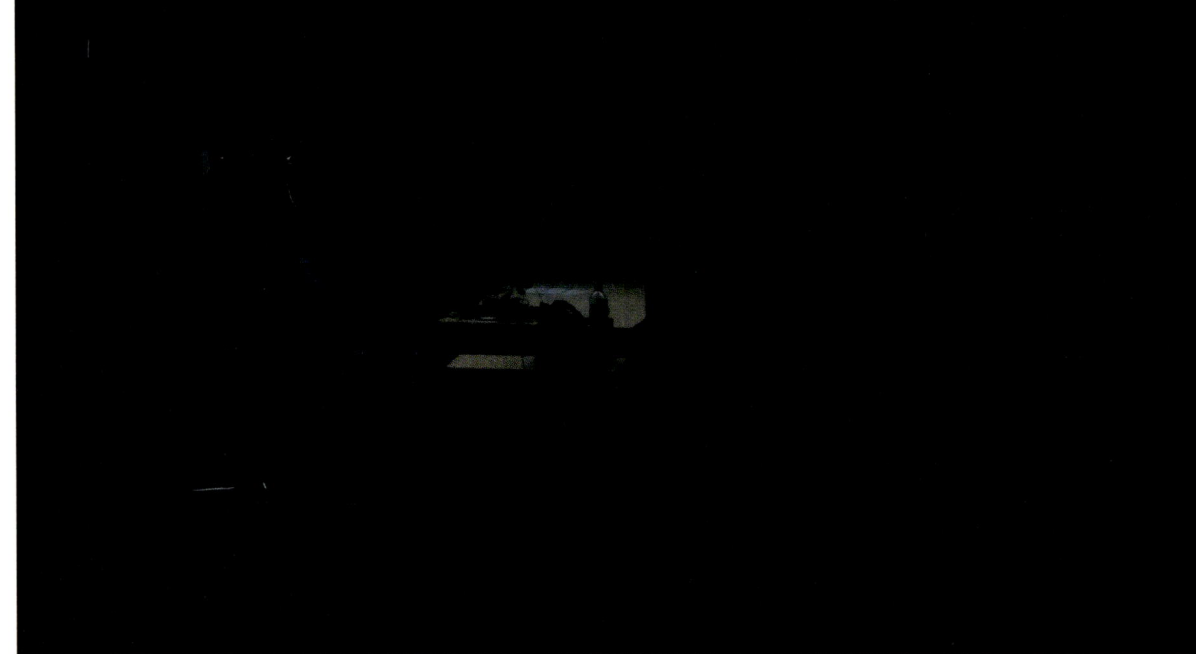

WTC

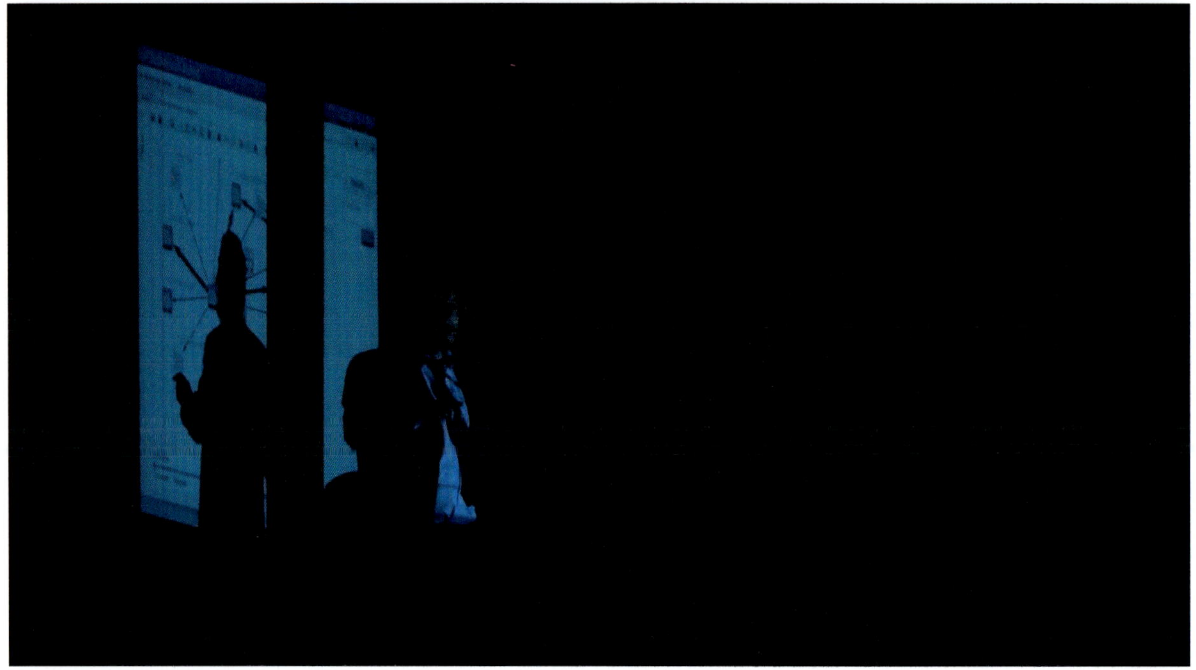

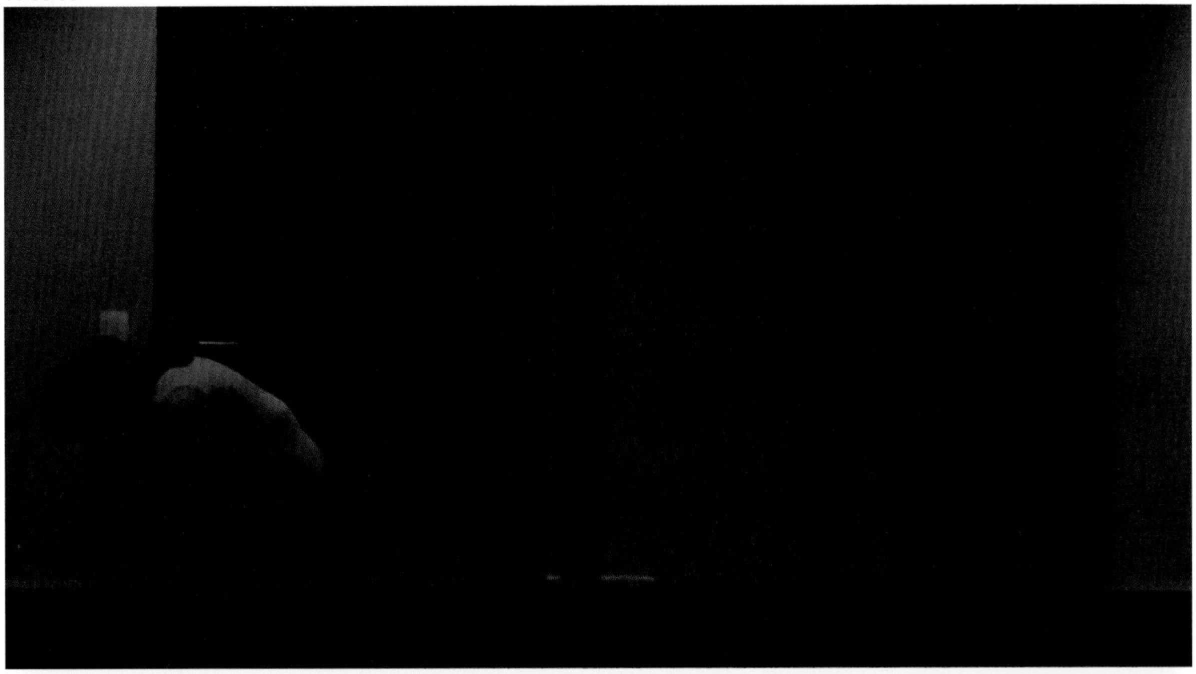

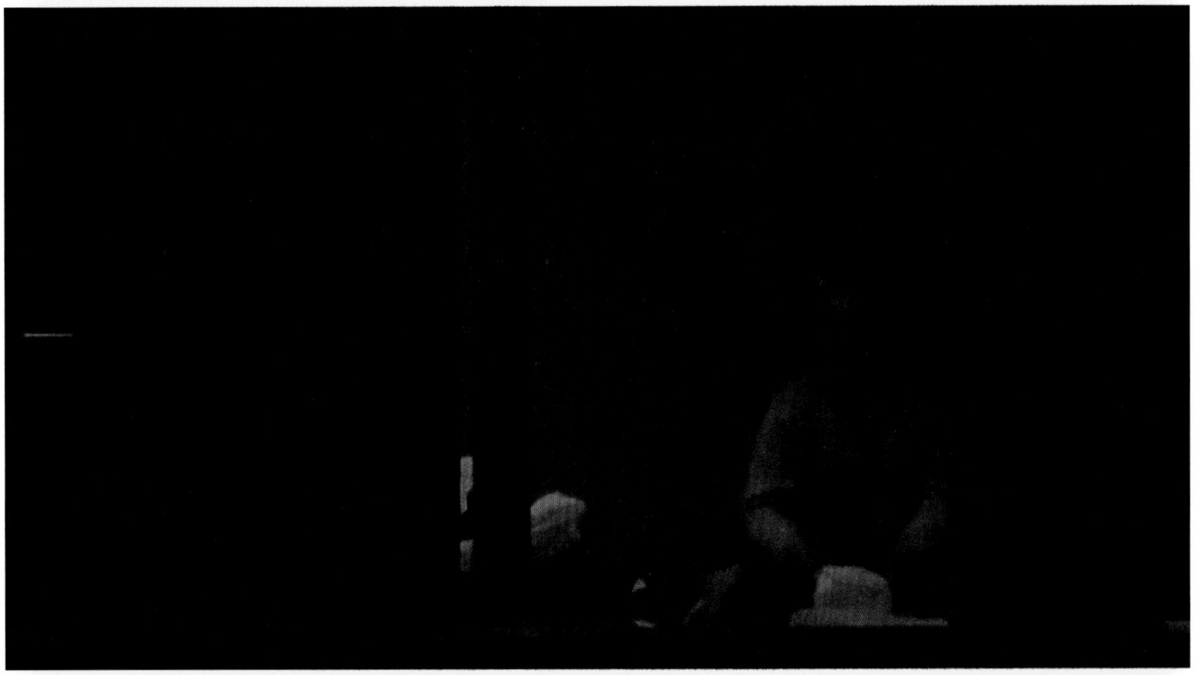

06:38:08

WTC

06:52:21

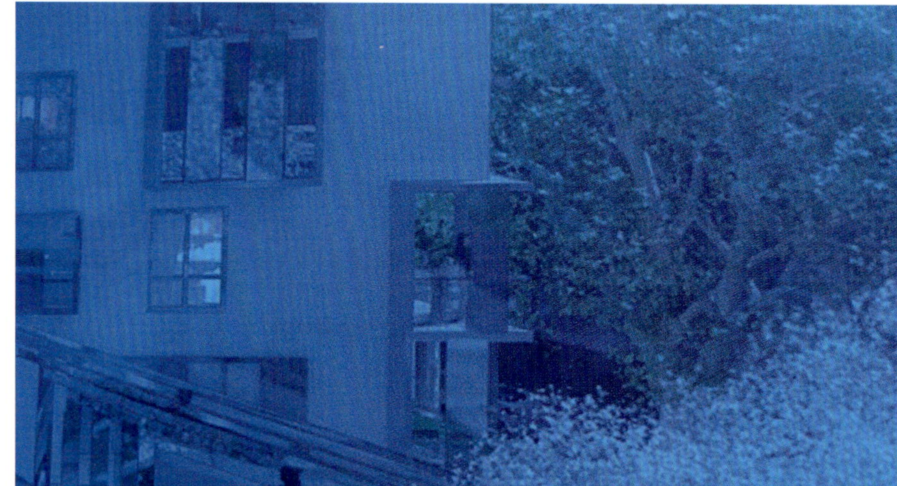

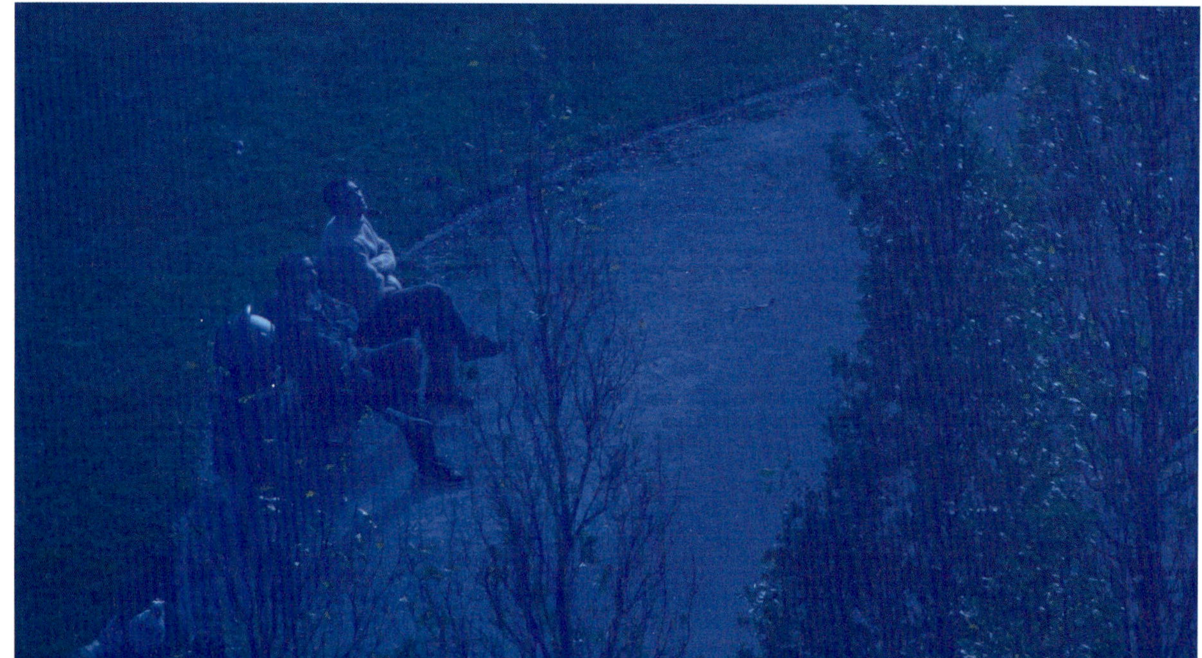

WTC

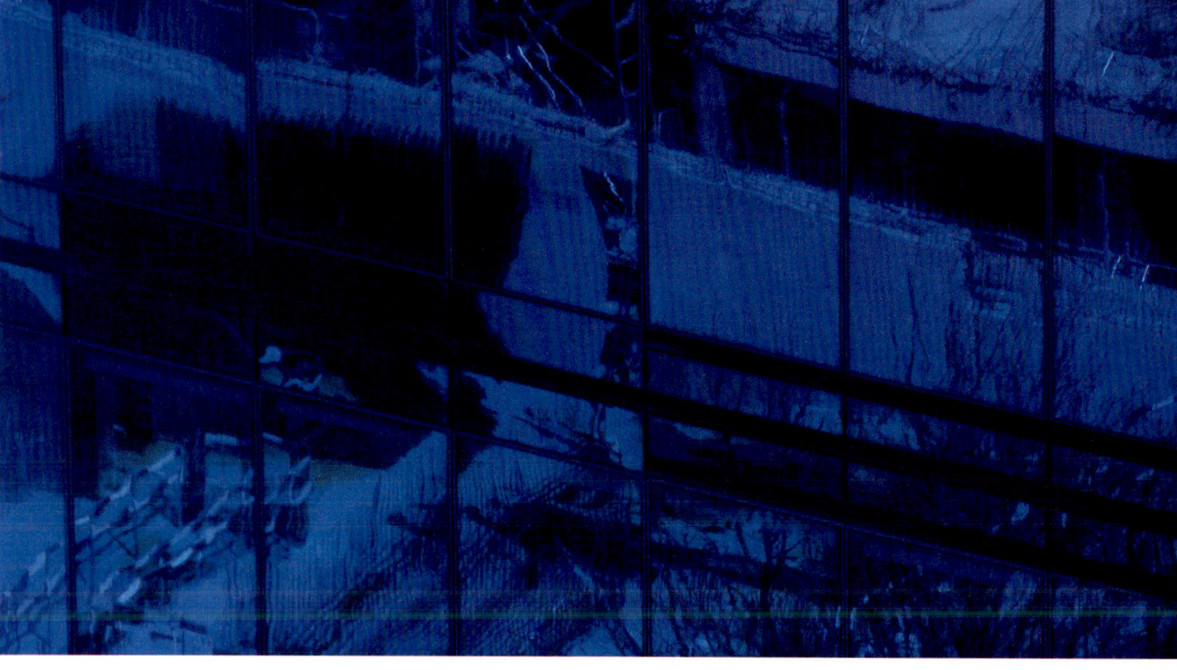

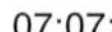

07:07:21

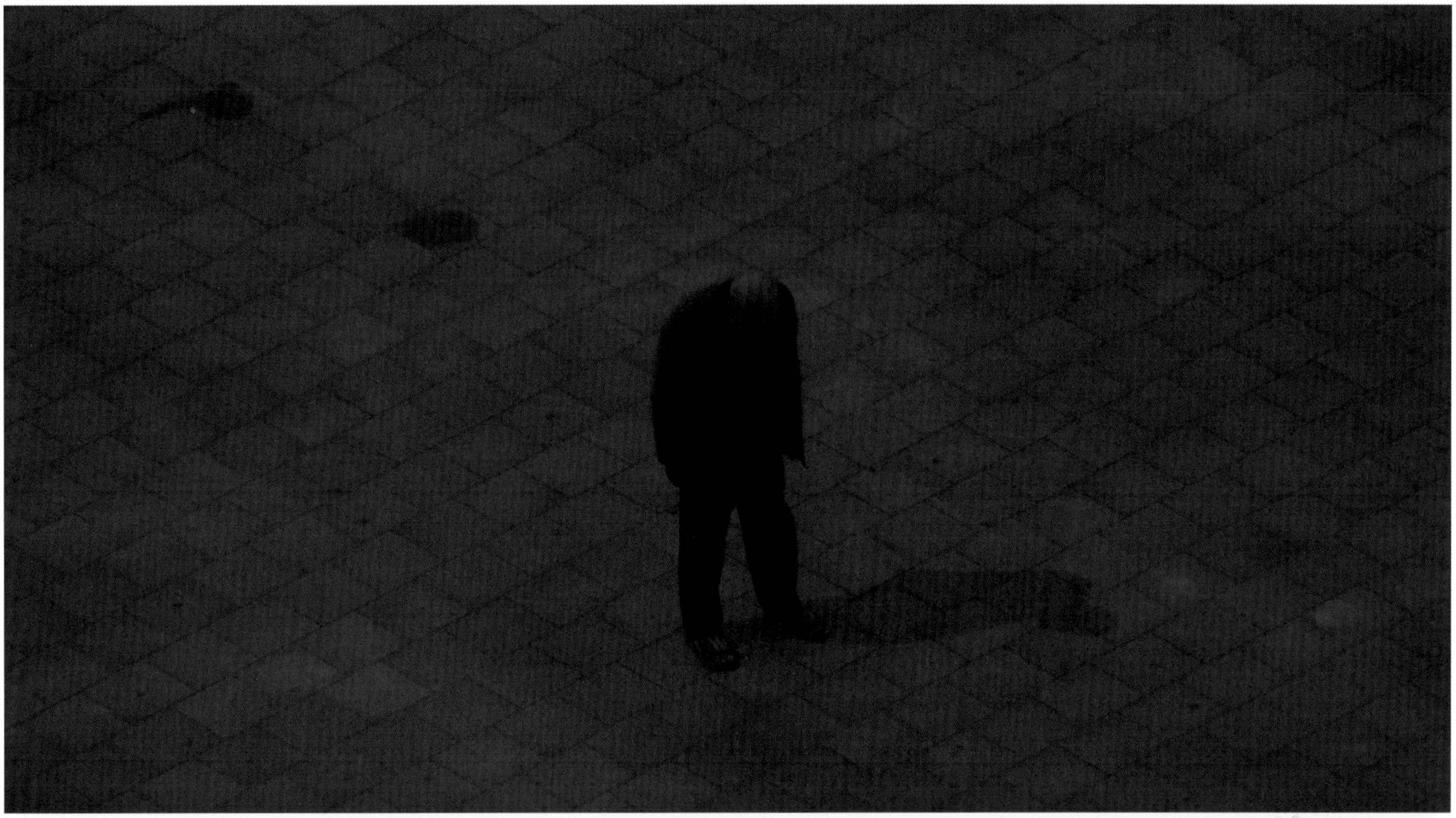

WTC

07:23:00

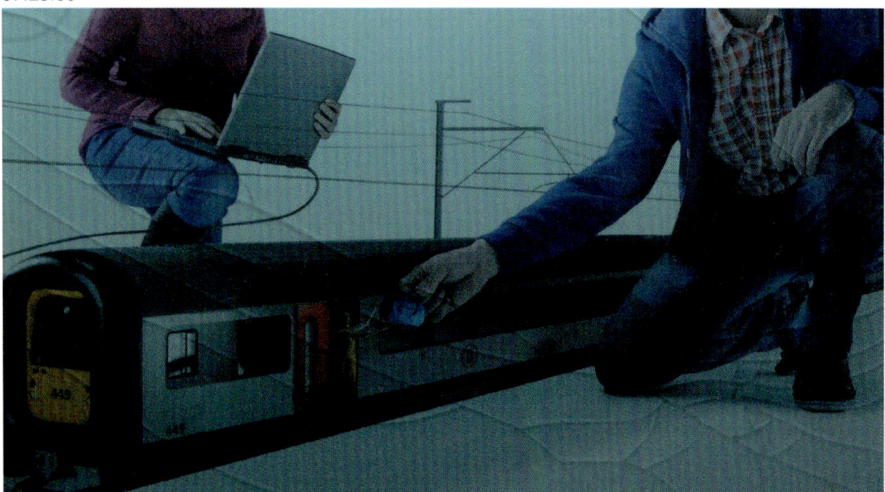

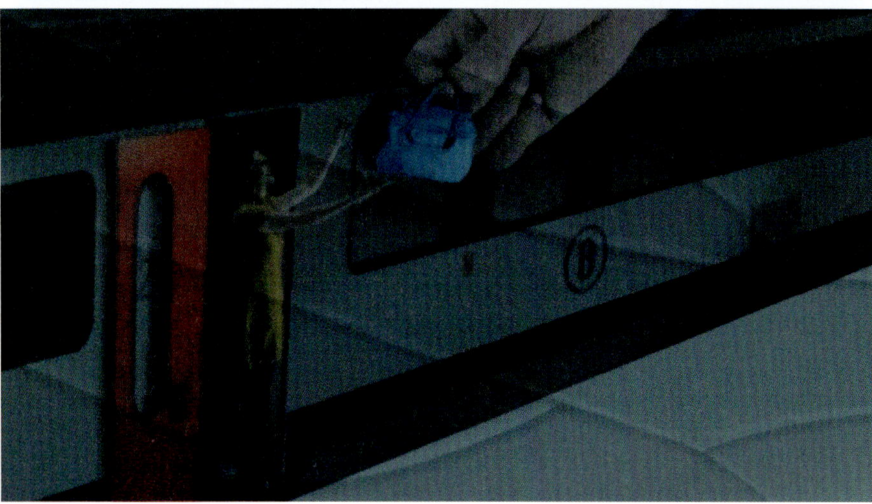

WTC

Chinese Pavilion (2018) video loop 2'38" without sound

EN

Chinese Pavilion is a short video loop in which we see the facades of the eponymous building currently covered in scaffolding. This Chinese Pavilion was commissioned by King Leopold II for the Brussels World's Fair site in the early twentieth century. The architecture of the pavilion, designed by the French architect Alexandre Marcel, can be seen as an Orientalist invention: it is a mixture of chinoiseries and European influences. Leopold II had approached Marcel after seeing his 'Le Tour du Monde', a series of buildings that were to represent the different architectural styles of the world, built during the Paris world exhibition in 1900. Co-funded from resources gathered in the former Congo Free State, this exuberant open-air museum would promote the economic interests of Belgium in China and Japan. The Chinese pavilion was originally set up as a luxury restaurant, and later became a trade museum housing products imported from the Far East as well as Belgian products destined for export. The renovations of this building have been postponed until at least 2021.

FR

Chinese Pavilion est une courte boucle vidéo où l'on contemple les murs extérieurs du « pavillon chinois », alors recouverts d'échafaudages. Ce pavillon d'exposition se trouve dans le quartier du « Heysel » : il résulte d'une commande du roi belge Léopold II à l'occasion de l'Exposition universelle de Bruxelles au début du XXe siècle. Dessiné par l'architecte français Alexandre Marcel, il peut être vu comme une fantaisie orientaliste, mélangeant des « chinoiseries » à des influences européennes. Léopold II avait fait appel à Marcel après avoir vu son « Tour du Monde », une série de bâtiments construits pour l'Exposition universelle de 1900 à Paris, visant à représenter les différents styles architecturaux autour du monde. Financé en partie par des ressources puisées dans ce qu'on appelait alors État indépendant du Congo, cet extravagant musée en plein air entendait développer les intérêts économiques belges en Chine et au Japon. Initialement conçu pour abriter un restaurant gastronomique, le pavillon chinois accueillit par la suite un musée témoignant du commerce avec l'Extrême-Orient avec des collections de biens importés comme de l'artisanat belge destiné à l'export. Les rénovations prévues pour ce bâtiment ont été repoussées à l'année 2021 au plus tôt.

NL

De videoloop *Chinese Pavilion* toont het Chinees paviljoen dat in steigers getooid is. Dit paviljoen werd begin twintigste eeuw gebouwd, in opdracht van de toenmalige Belgische koning Leopold II voor het wereldtentoonstellingsgebied van Brussel. De architectuur van het paviljoen, ontworpen door de Franse architect Alexandre Marcel, kan gezien worden als een oriëntalistisch bedenksel: het is een mengeling van chinoiserieën en Europese invloeden. Leopold II had Marcel benaderd na het zien van zijn 'Le Tour du Monde', een reeks gebouwen die de verschillende bouwstijlen van de wereld zouden weergeven, gebouwd voor de wereldtentoonstelling in Parijs in 1900. Het Chinees paviljoen, mede gefinancierd met inkomsten uit de voormalige Congo-Vrijstaat, werd gebouwd met de bedoeling de economische belangen van België in China en Japan te behartigen. Oorspronkelijk moest het paviljoen dienen als luxe-restaurant, maar het werd uiteindelijk gebruikt als museum voor producten uit het Verre Oosten die bestemd waren voor export naar Europa. De renovatie van dit gebouw is nog tot minstens 2021 uitgesteld.

00:00:00

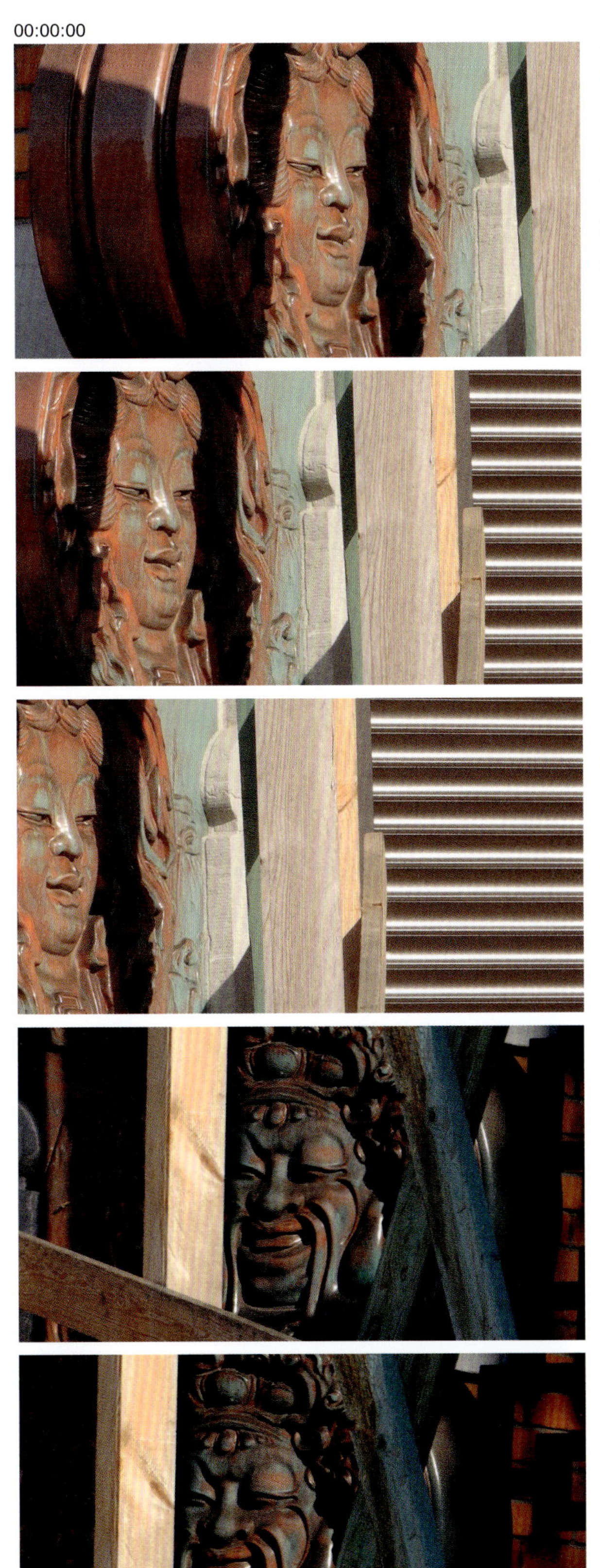

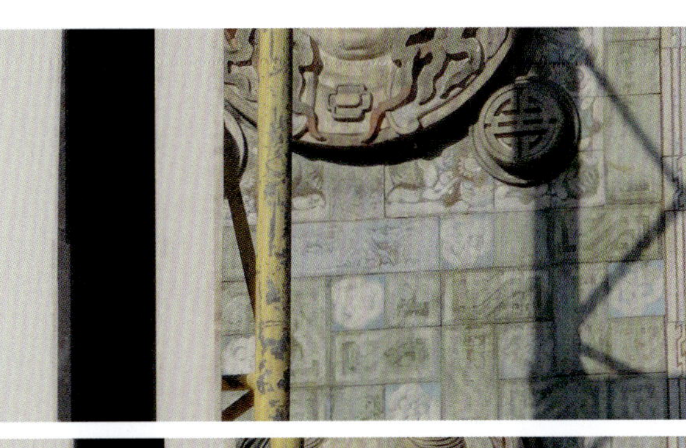

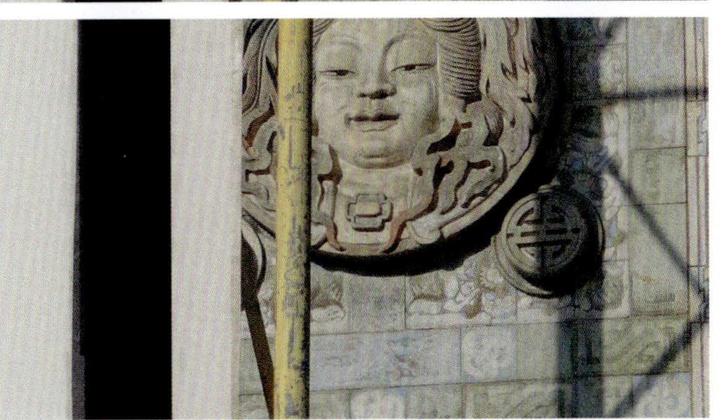

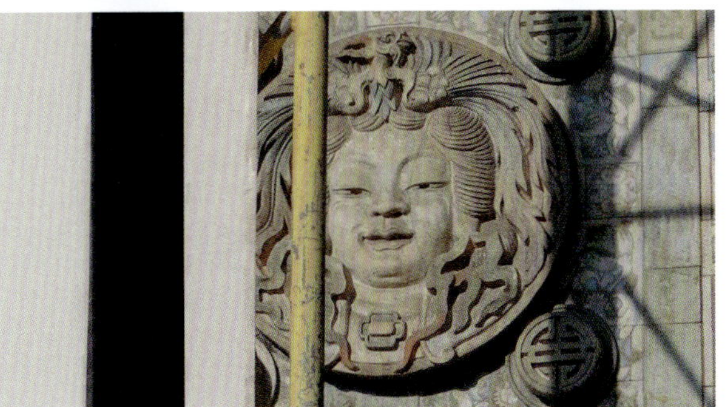

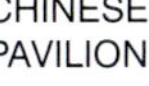

CHINESE
PAVILION

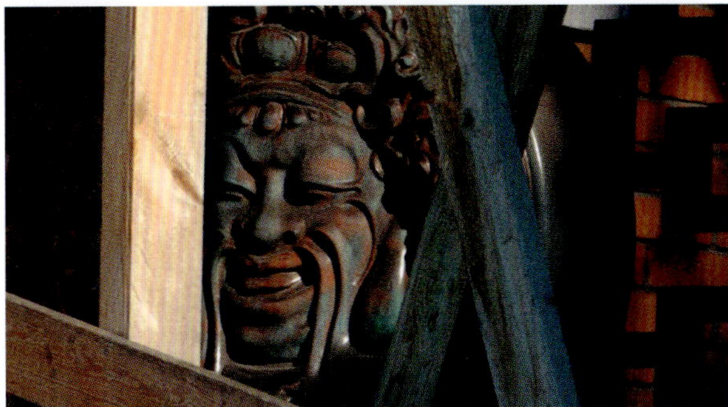

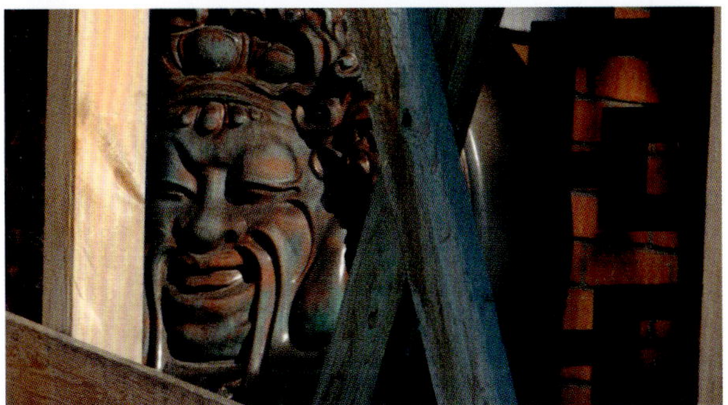

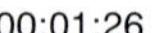

00:01:26

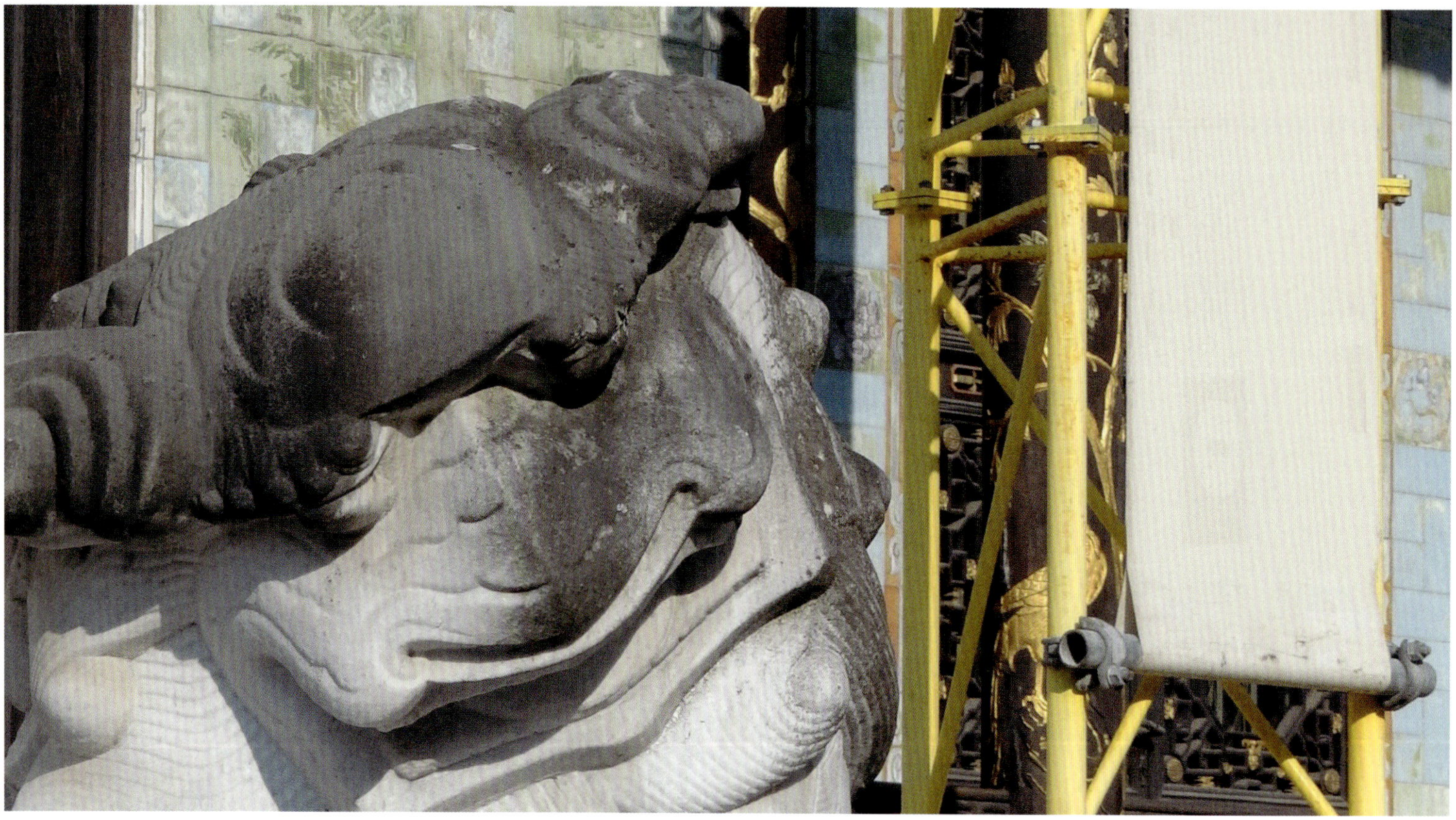

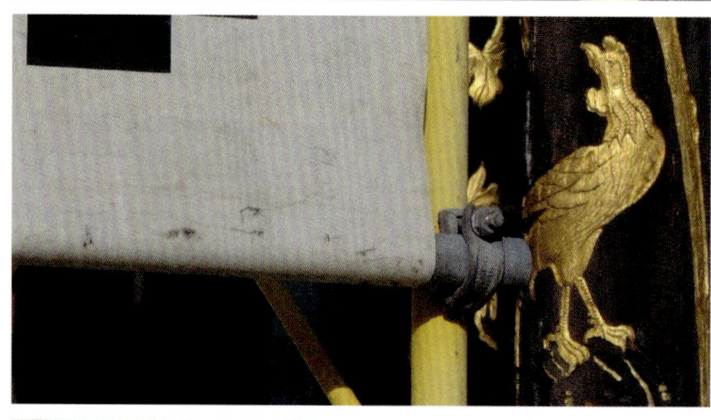

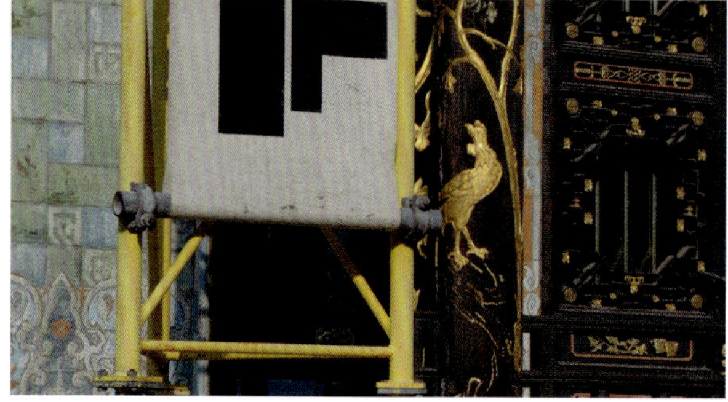

CHINESE
PAVILION

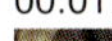
00:01:49

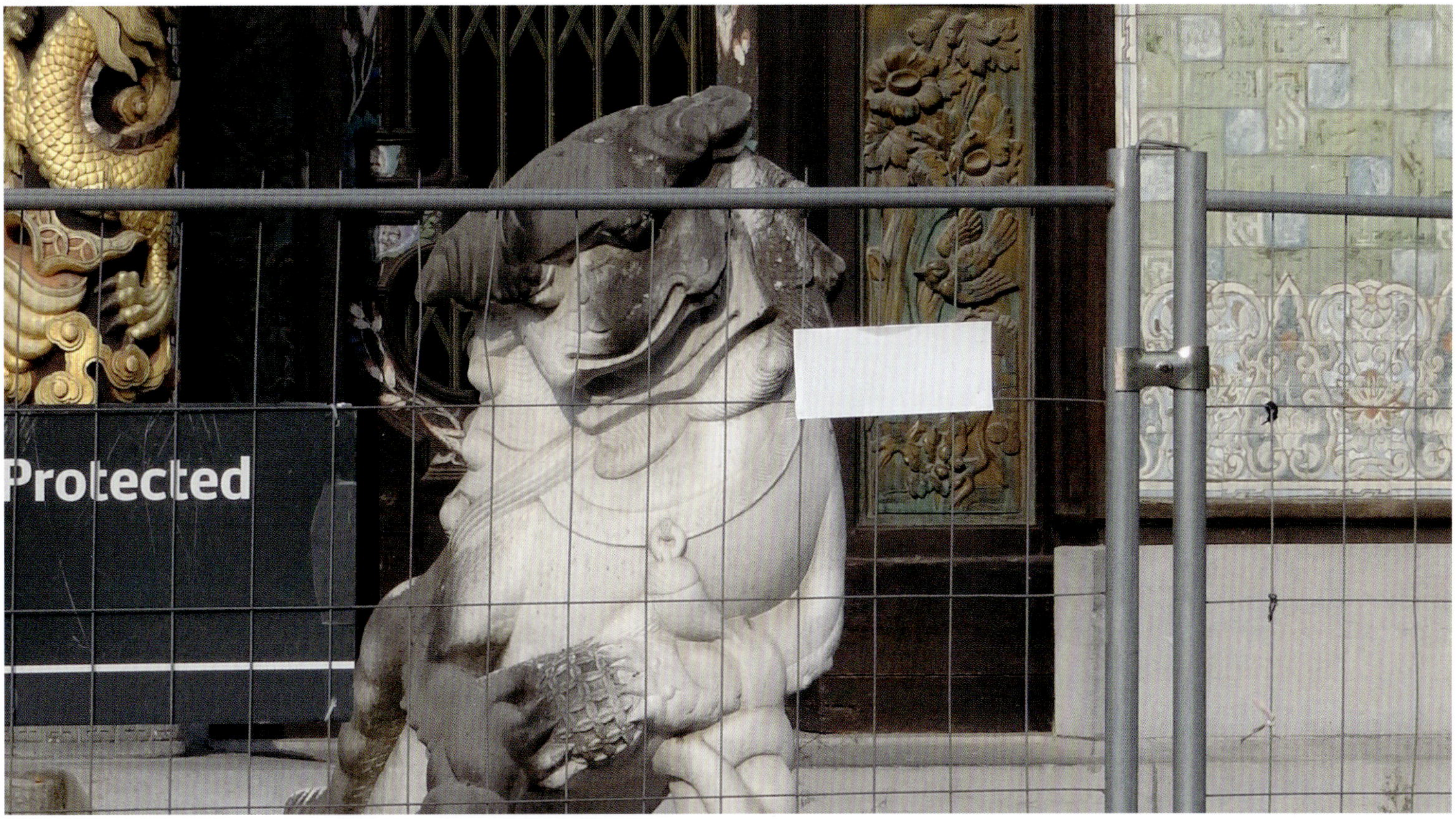

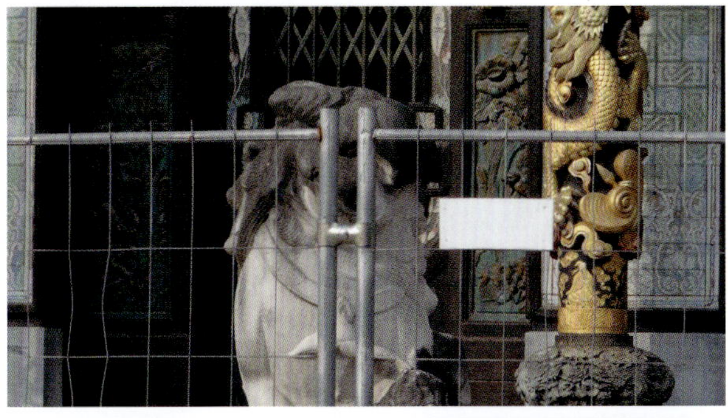

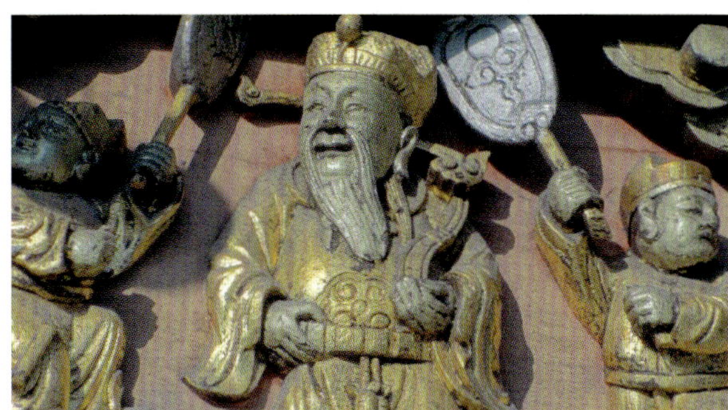

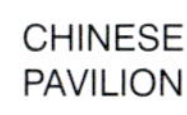
CHINESE
PAVILION

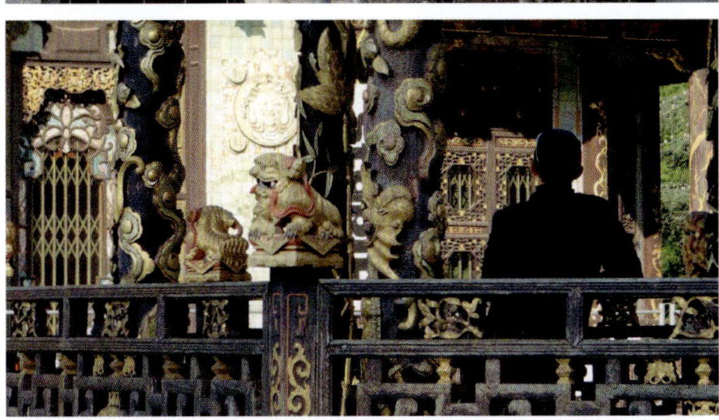

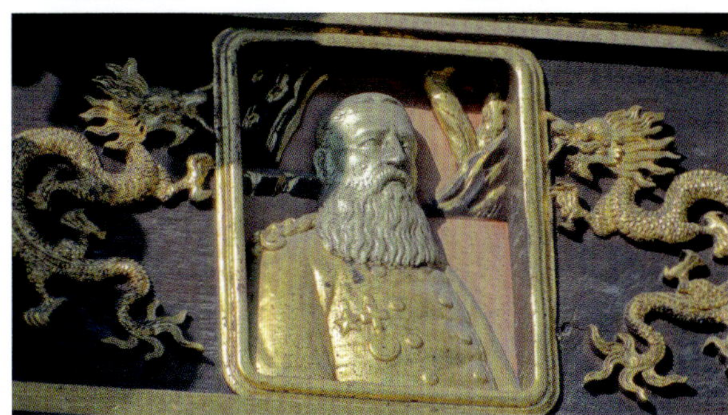

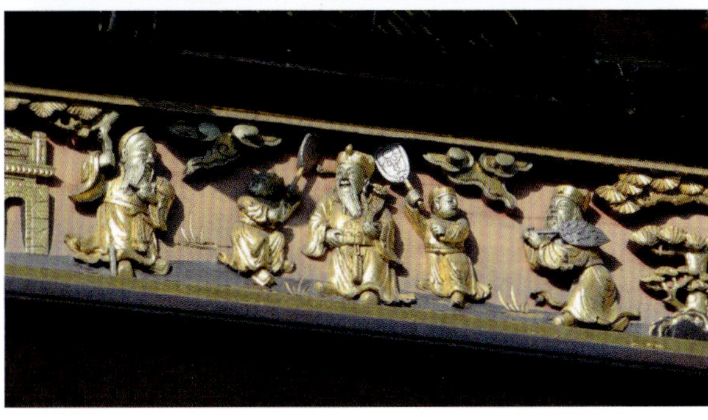

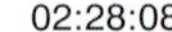
02:28:08

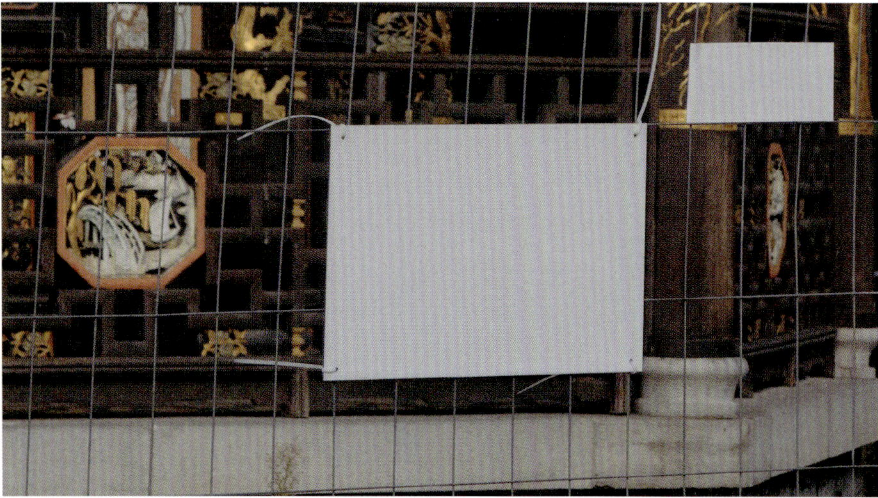

CHINESE
PAVILION

Mall of Europe (2018)

video 26'50"
sound by:
Maxime
Rouquart

EN

In her video *Mall of Europe,* Emma van der Put reflects on the 'Heysel/Heizel', the Brussels World's Fair site where the acclaimed Expo '58 was held. This world exhibition was a forerunner and a tribute to the new, modernist ideas of progress and projected an image of a future in which the rise of a consumer society would fulfil the promises of the good life for all. Echoes of these ideas can be found in the still inhabited modernist 'Model Neighbourhood' which was presented at the World's Fair of 1958, giving the public an example of a modern way of living. *Mall of Europe* places these ideals alongside the imperfections of the historical present. Current plans for the modernization of the Brussels World's Fair area, including the construction of the shopping center 'Mall of Europe', will again add a new chapter to the visualizations of the future. The stories of linear thinking about progress are juxtaposed with the complex and layered nature of the contemporary moment; the image is confronted with reality.

FR

Dans sa vidéo *Mall of Europe,* Emma van der Put mène une réflexion sur le quartier du « Heysel » qui abrita les expositions universelles bruxelloises et notamment l'illustre Expo '58. Avant-gardiste, cette foire mettait à l'honneur les nouvelles idées modernistes et progressistes, projetant une image du futur où l'avènement de la société de consommation permettrait à chacun de vivre dans le meilleur des mondes. Ces idées trouvent leur écho dans le quartier moderniste — encore inhabité aujourd'hui — présenté à l'Exposition universelle de 1958, une « Cité modèle » censée illustrer auprès du public un mode de vie véritablement moderne. L'œuvre vidéo *Mall of Europe* recontextualise un tel idéal par rapport aux imperfections du temps présent. Les plans actuels en vue de la modernisation du quartier des expositions de Bruxelles incluent la construction d'un centre commercial nommé « Mall of Europe » : l'occasion d'ajouter un nouveau chapitre aux visions, prévisions ou prévisualisations de l'avenir. L'artiste juxtapose des narrations linéaires glorifiant le progrès et d'autres relayant la complexité du moment contemporain multipliant les niveaux de signification — l'image est confrontée à la réalité.

NL

In *Mall of Europe* reflecteert Emma van der Put op de 'Heizel', het wereldtentoonstellingsgebied van Brussel waar de veelgeprezen Expo '58 werd gehouden. Deze wereldtentoonstelling was een schoolvoorbeeld van het modernistisch vooruitgangsdenken en projecteerde een hoopvol beeld van een toekomst waarin de opkomst van een consumptiemaatschappij de levenskwaliteit voor iedereen zou verhogen. Echo's van deze ideeën zijn terug te vinden in de nog steeds bewoonde modernistische 'Modelwijk' die op de wereldtentoonstelling van 1958 werd getoond om het publiek een voorbeeld te geven van een nieuwe manier van leven. *Mall of Europe* plaatst deze idealen naast de huidige plannen voor de modernisering van het gebied. De bouw van het winkelcentrum 'Mall of Europe' en de geplande renovaties van de Modelwijk, zullen wederom een nieuwe laag toevoegen bovenop voorgaande visualisaties van de toekomst. Het lineaire vooruitgangsdenken komt tegenover het complexe en gelaagde karakter van de huidige tijd te staan; het beeld wordt geconfronteerd met de werkelijkheid.

00:00:00

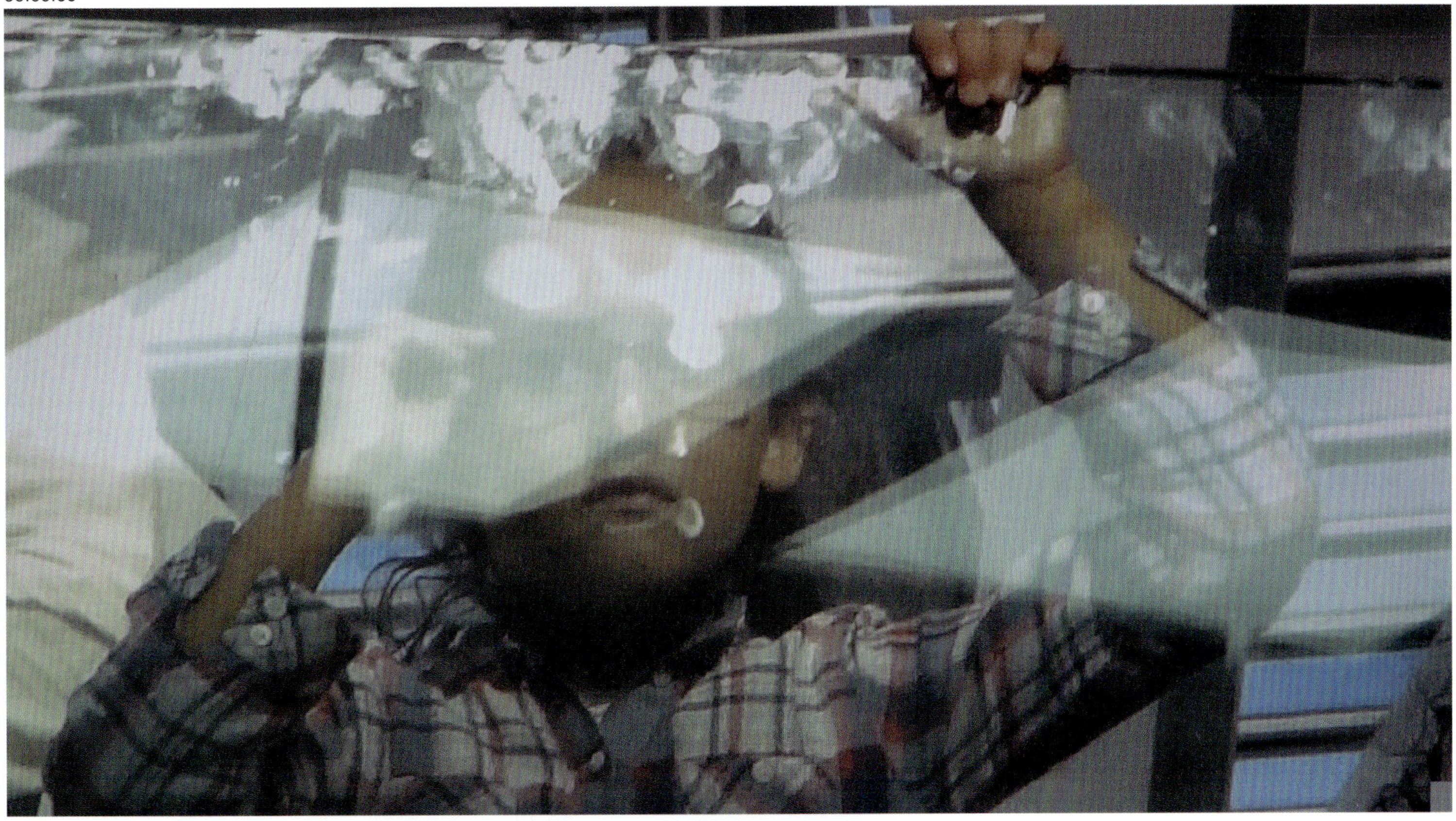

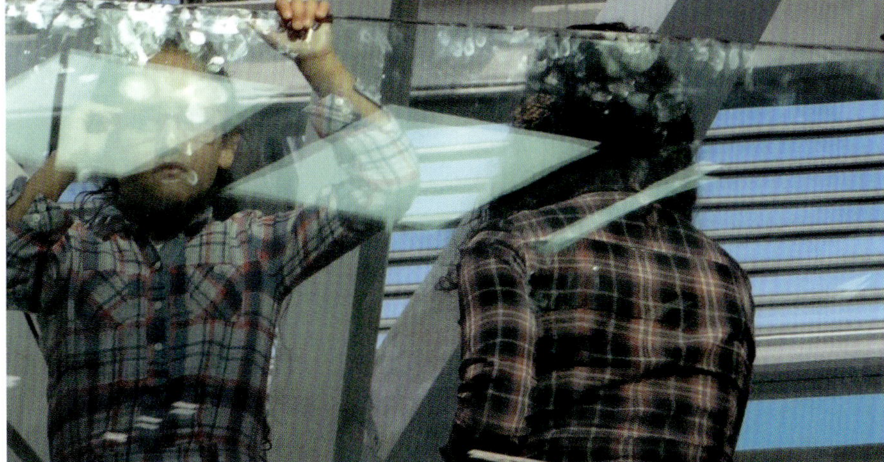

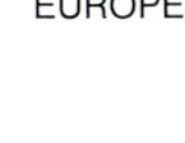

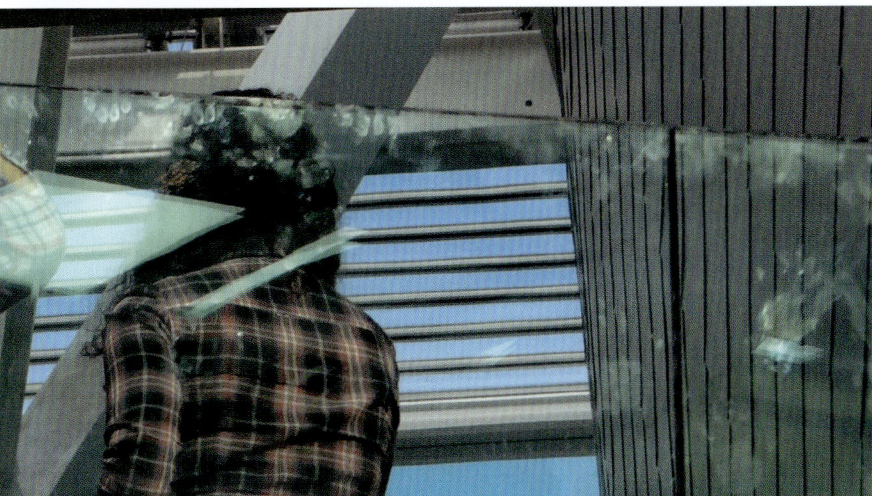

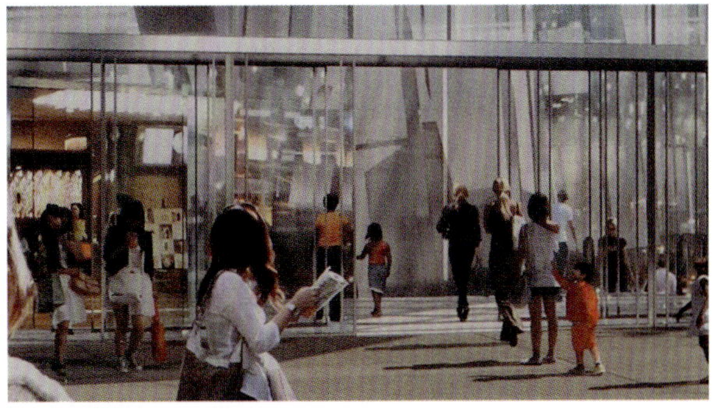

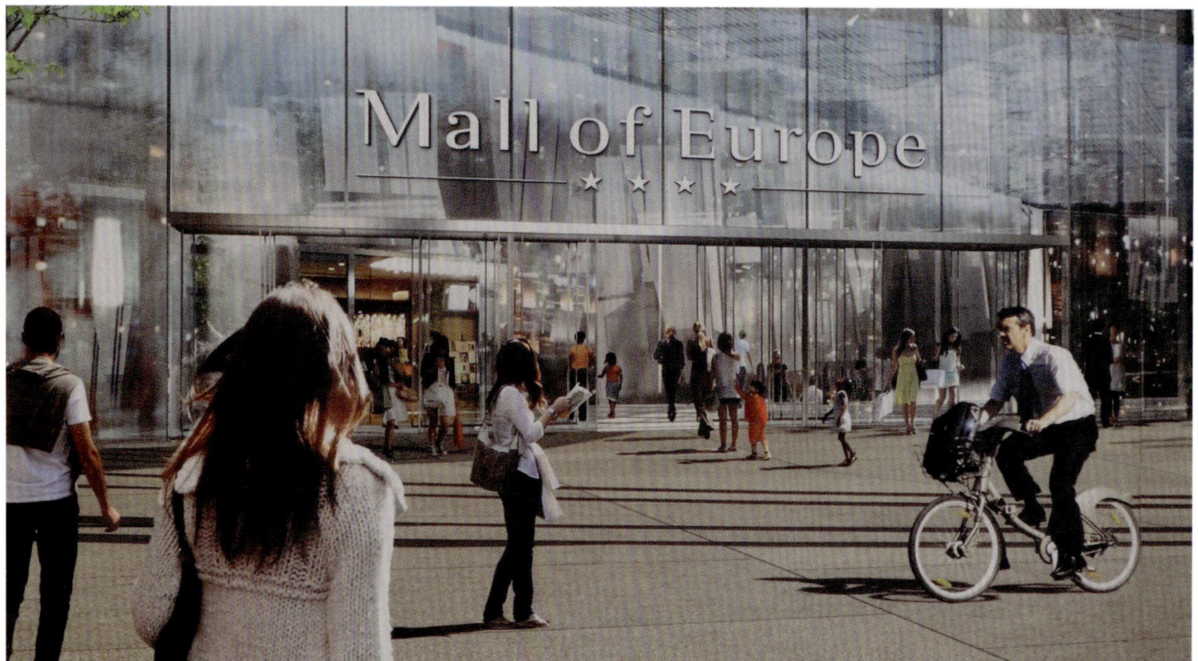
Mall of Europe

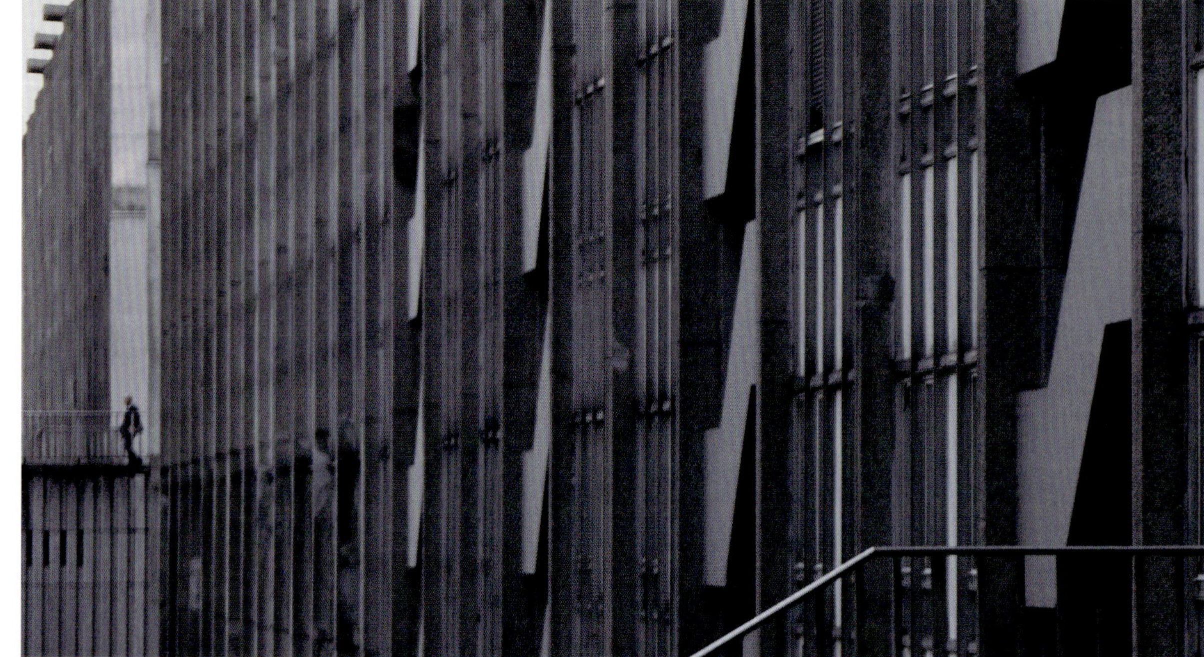

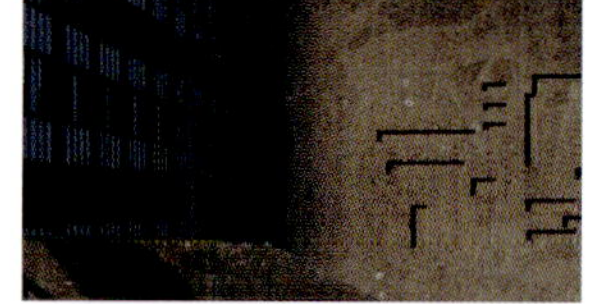

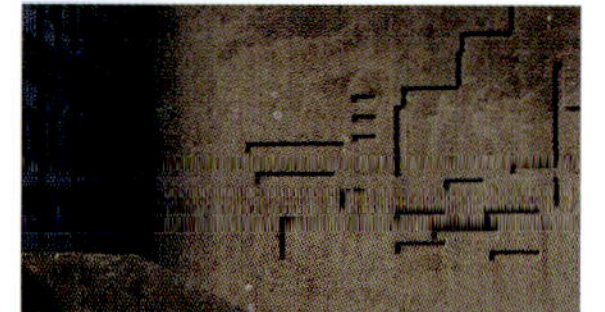

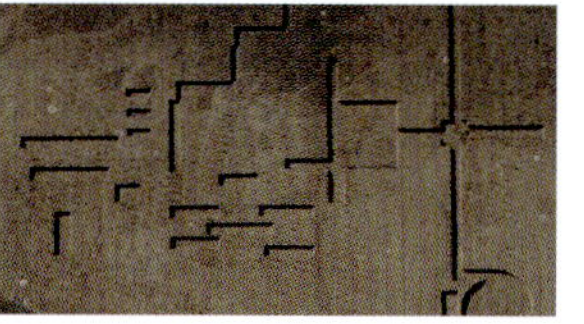

01:59:13

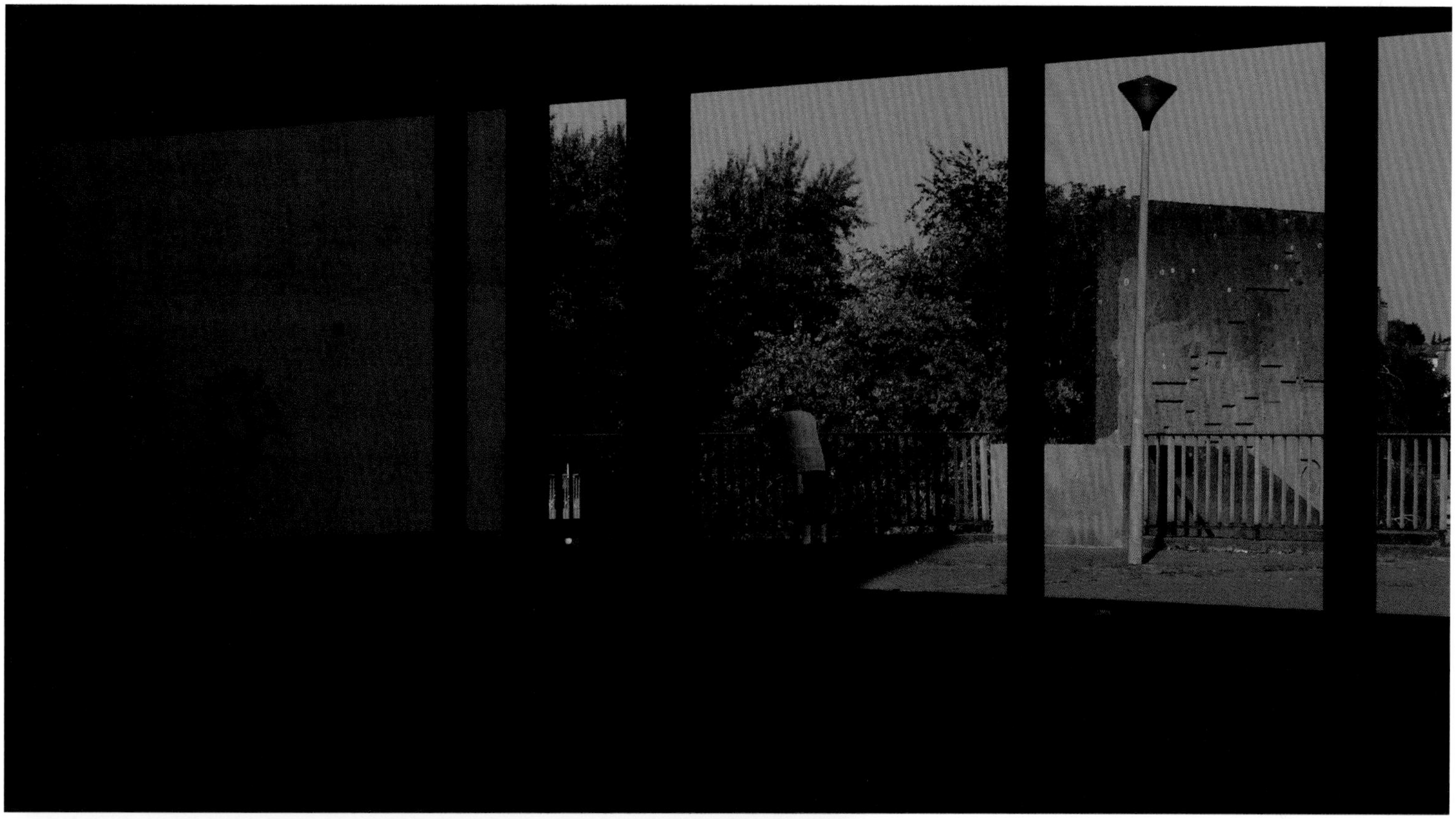

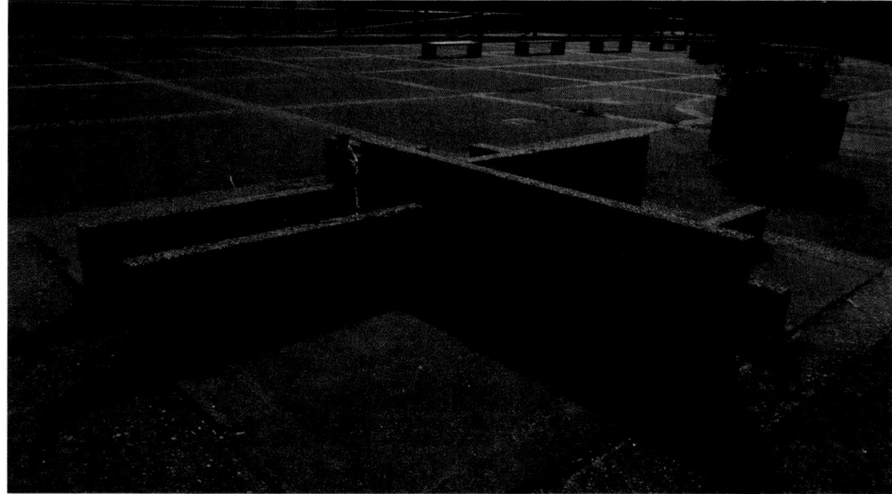

02:26:06

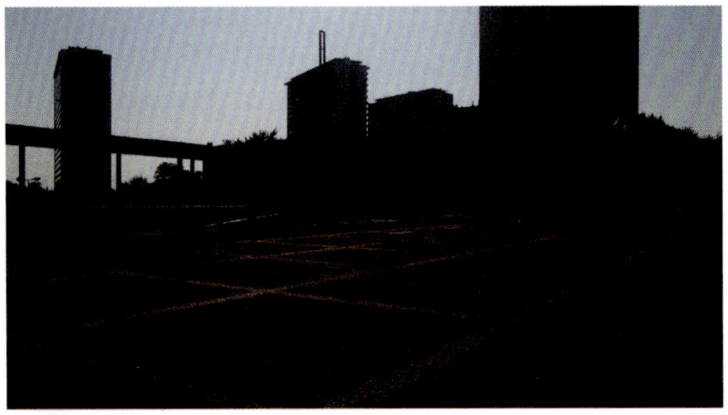

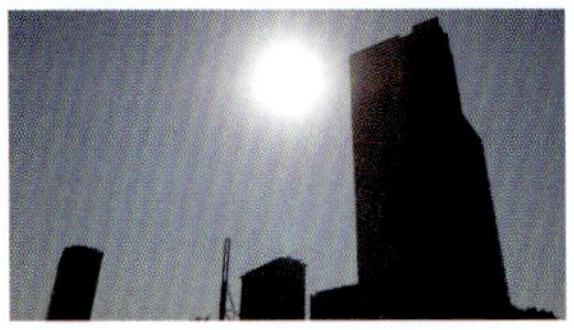

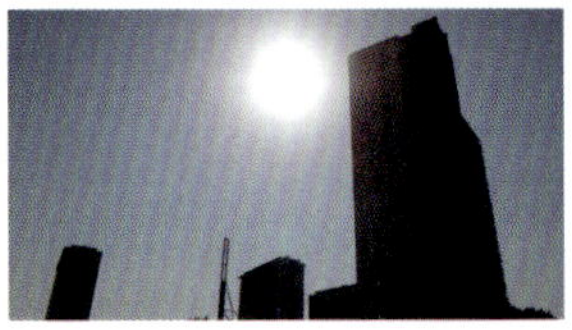

MALL
OF
EUROPE

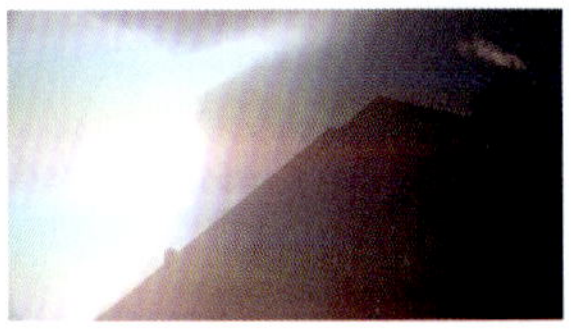

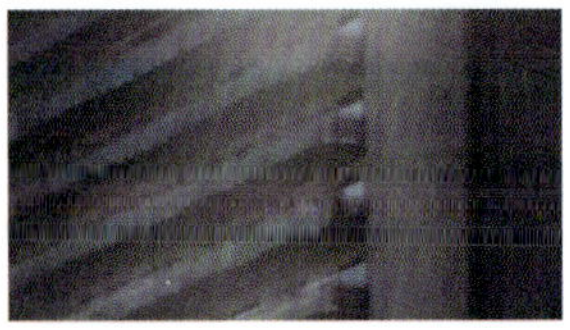

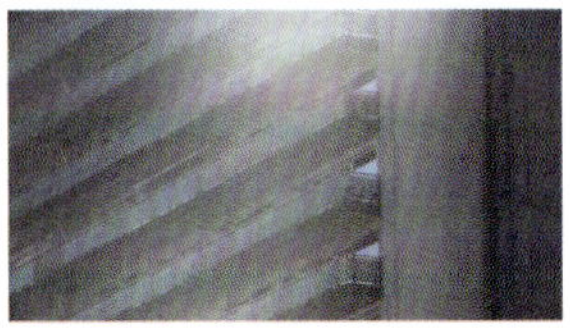

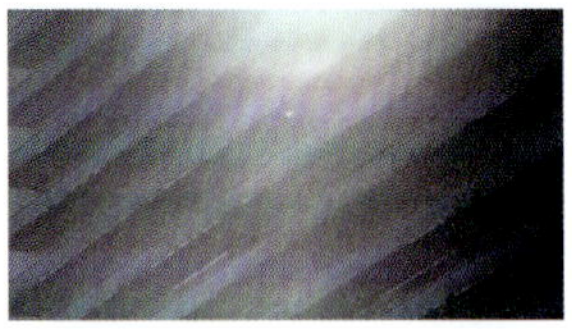

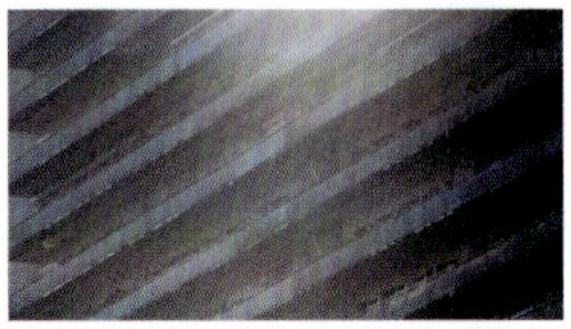

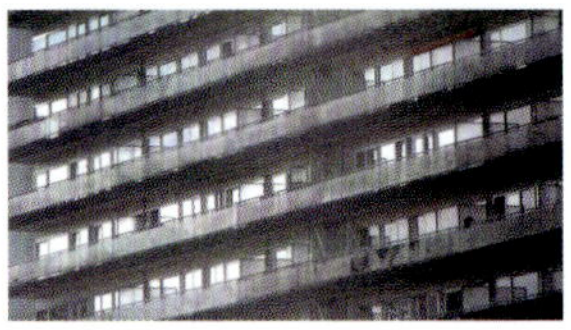

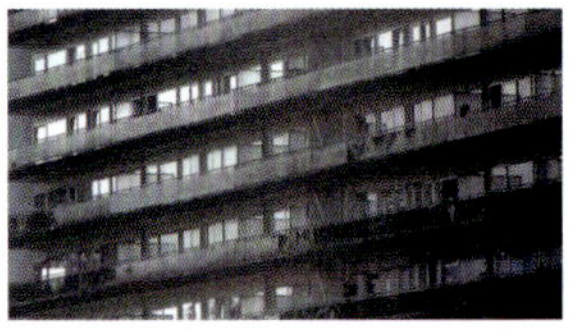

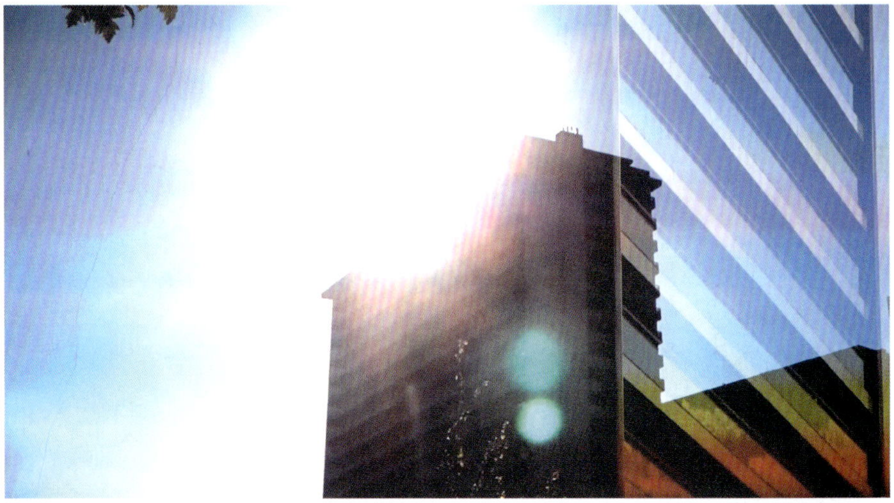

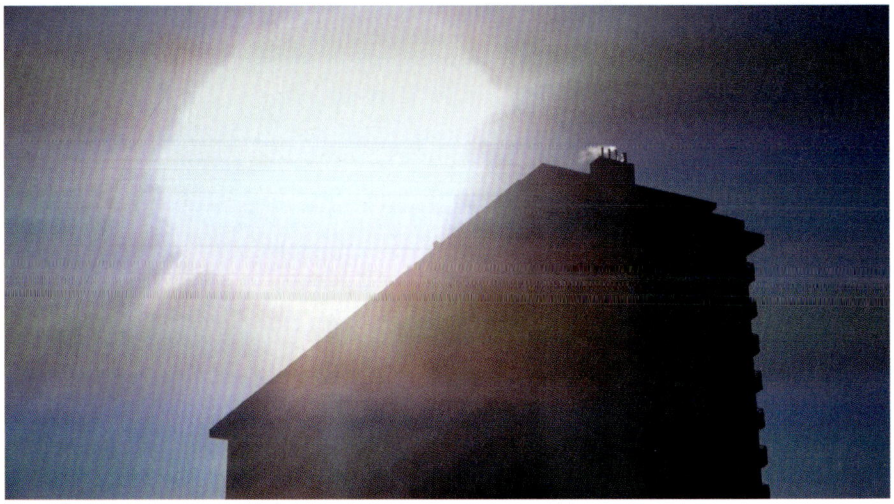

MALL
OF
EUROPE

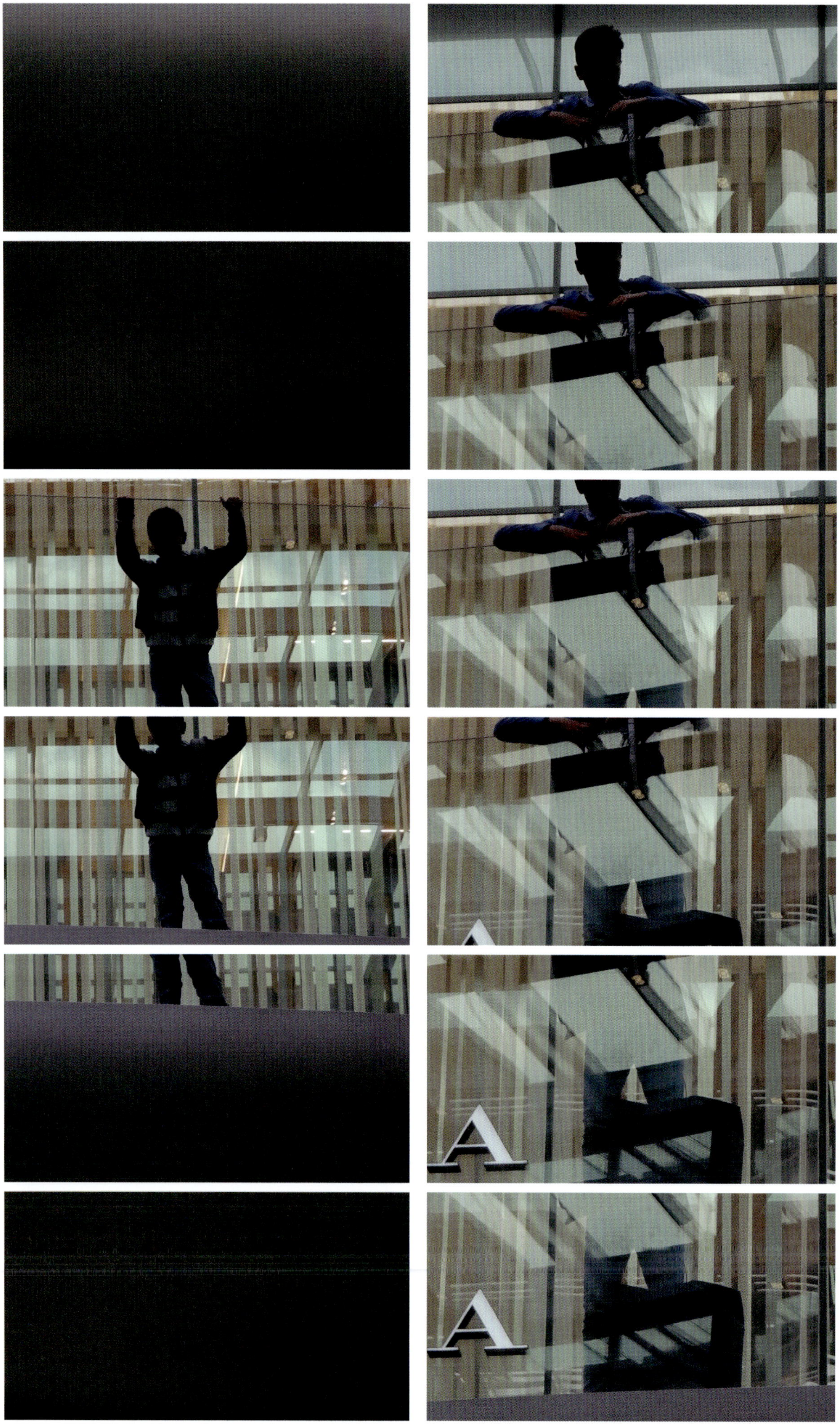

MALL
OF
EUROPE

04:17:16

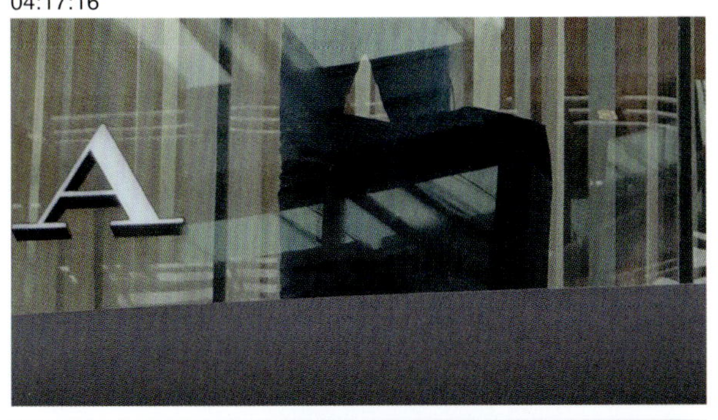

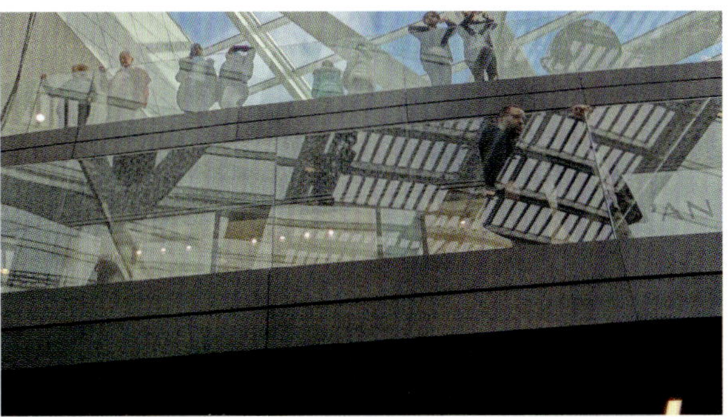

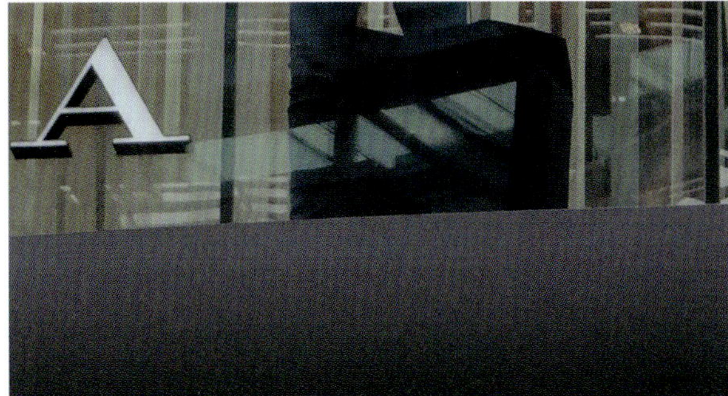

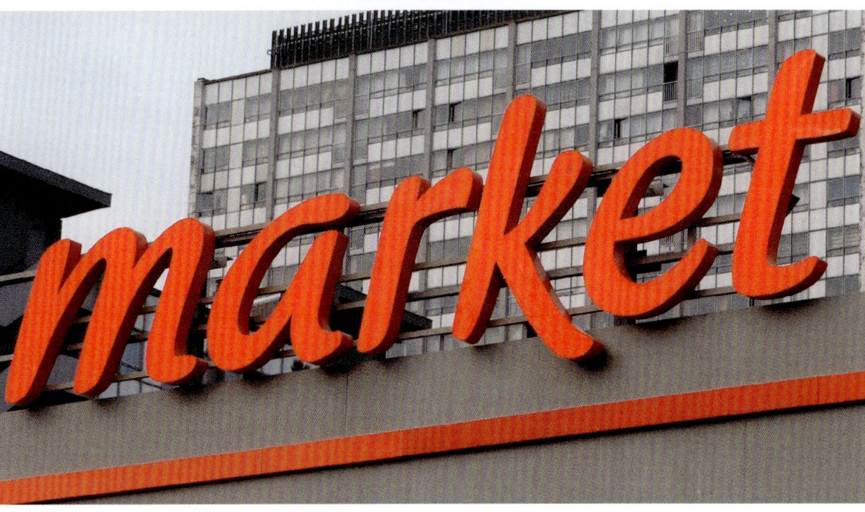

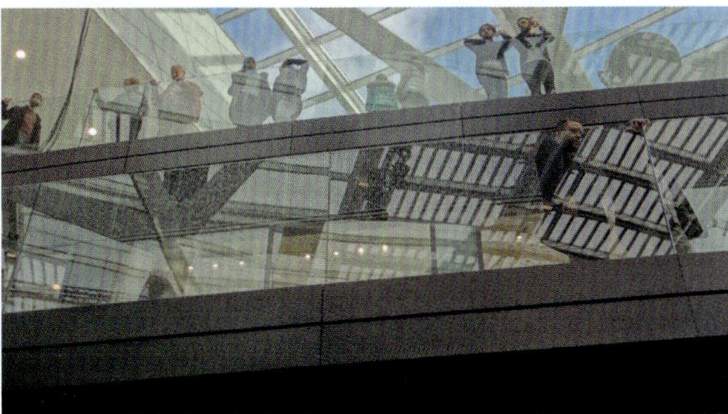

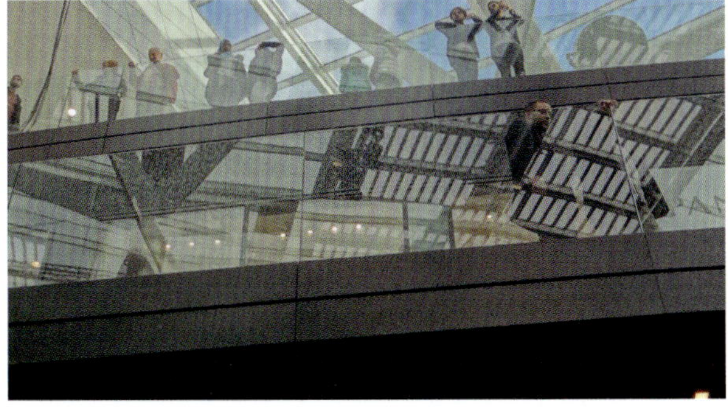

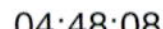
04:48:08

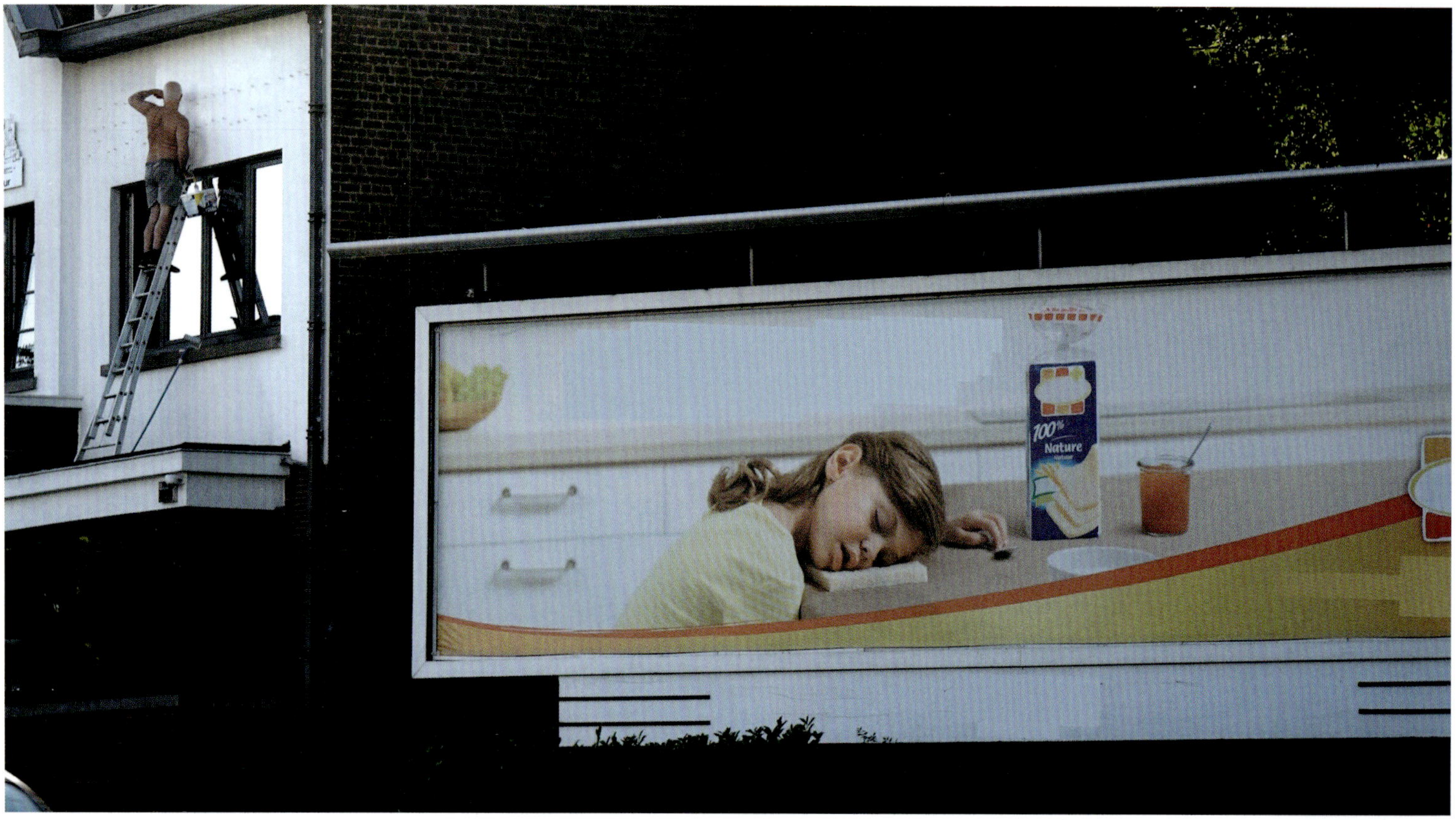

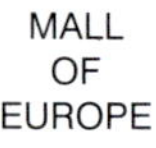
MALL
OF
EUROPE

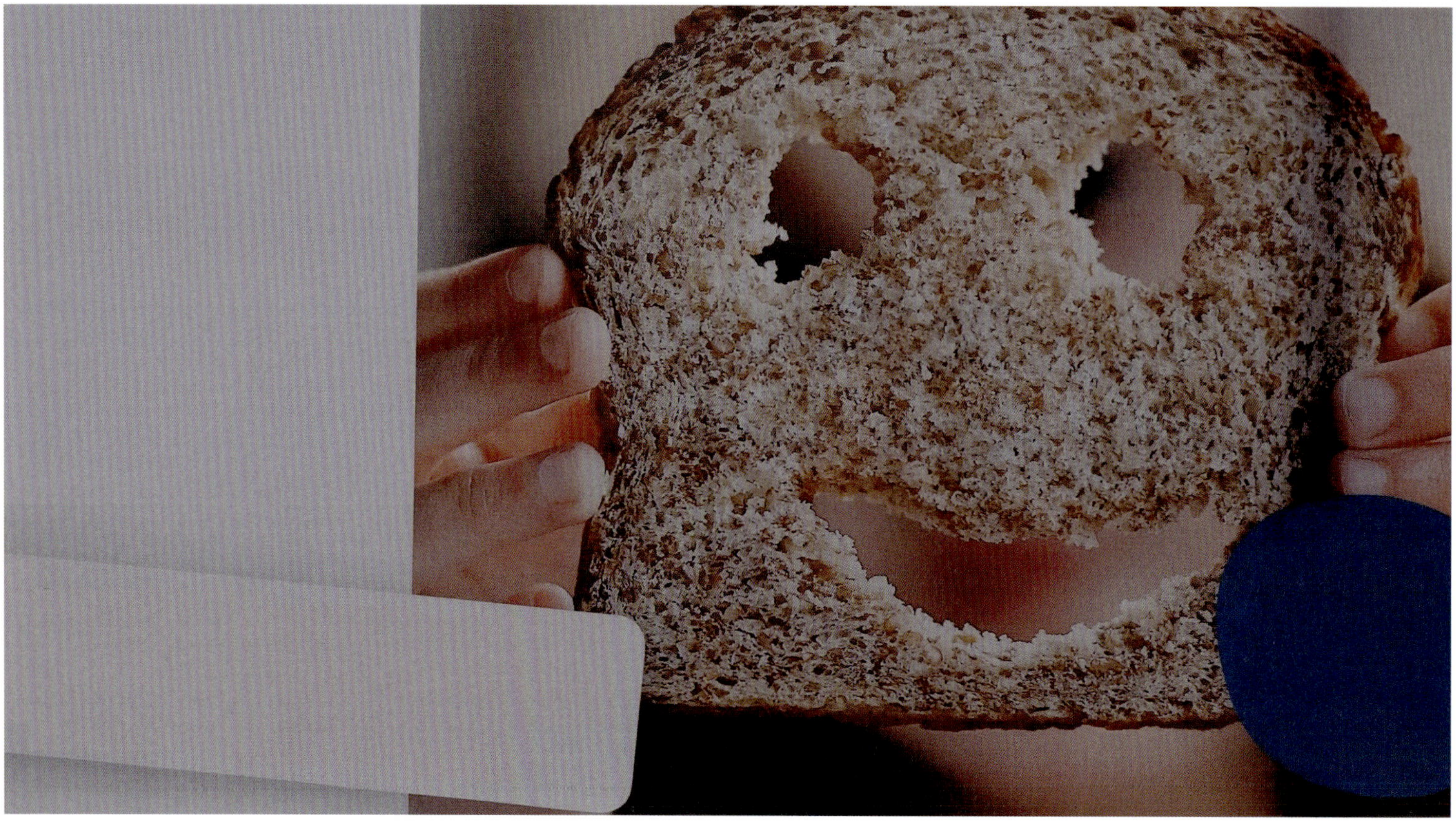

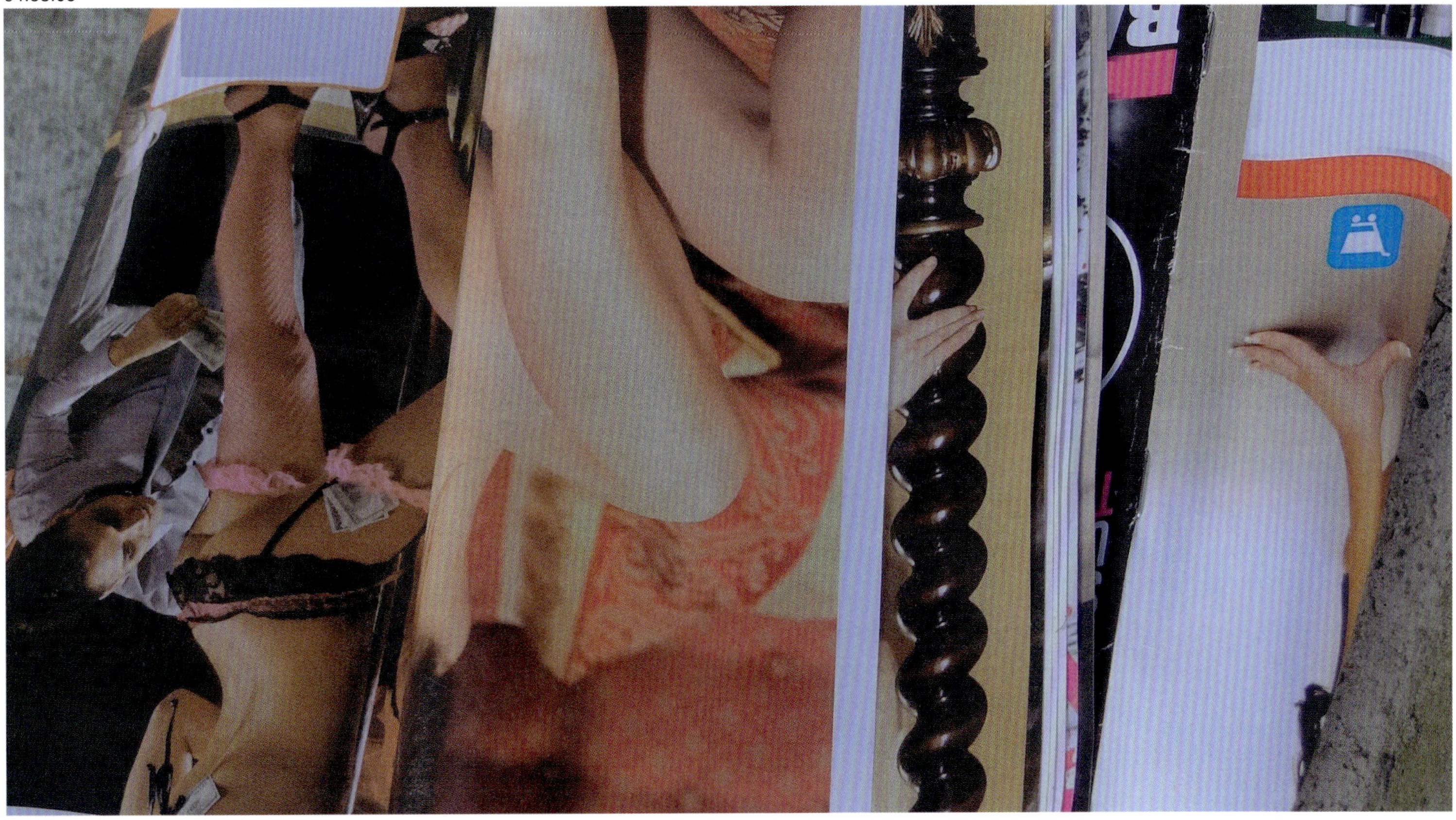

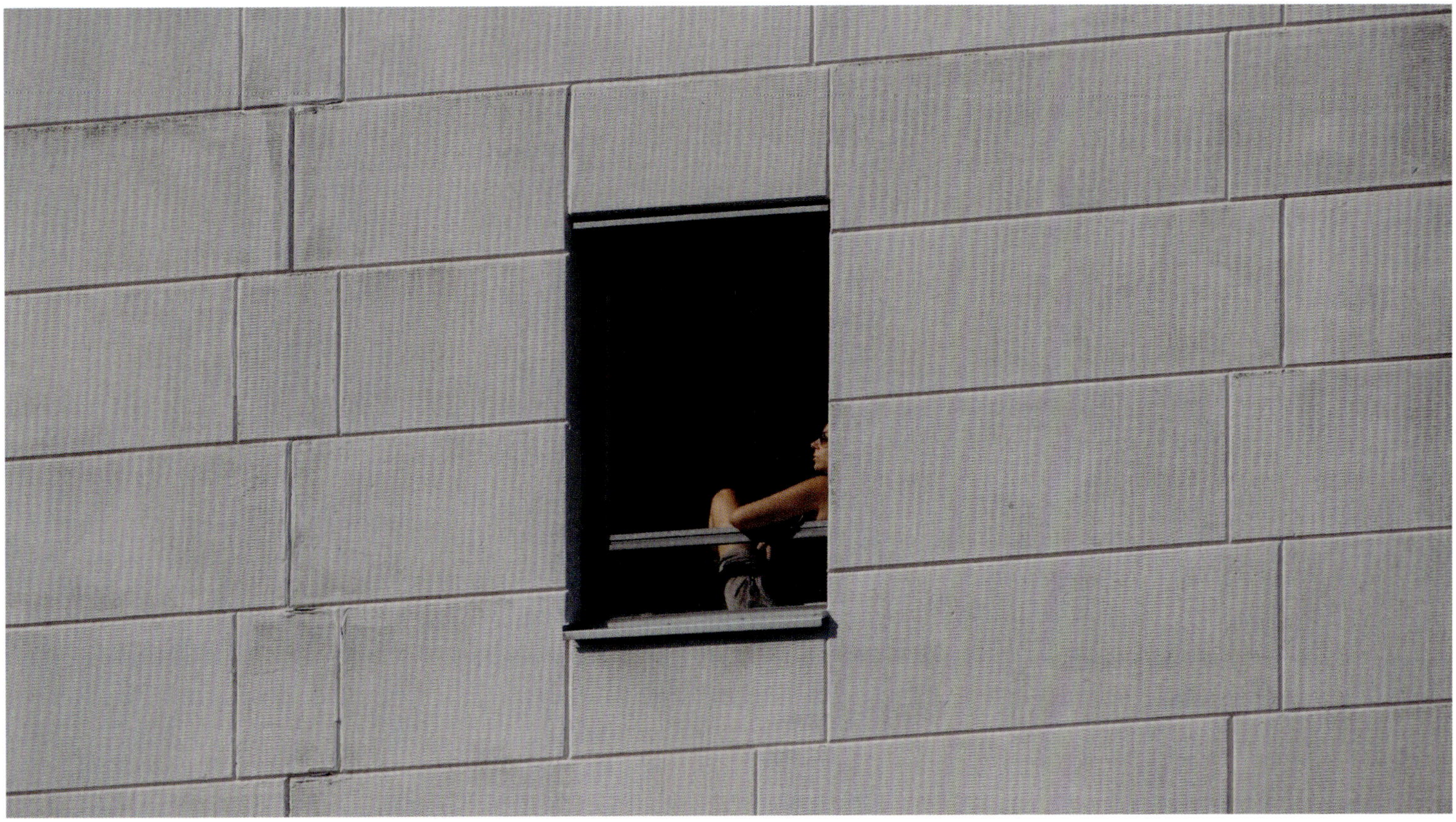

04:58:06

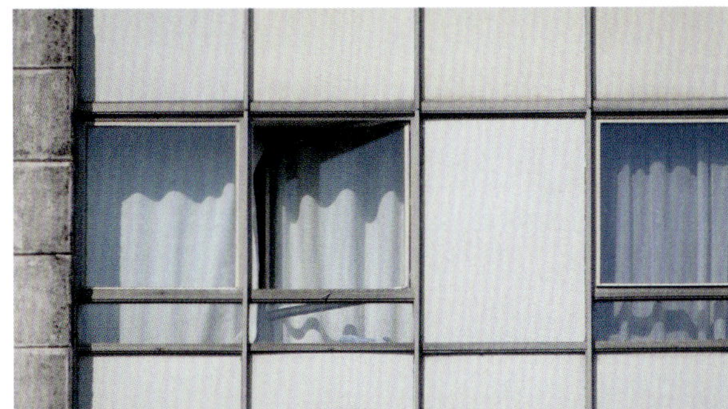

MALL
OF
EUROPE

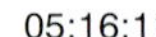
05:16:11

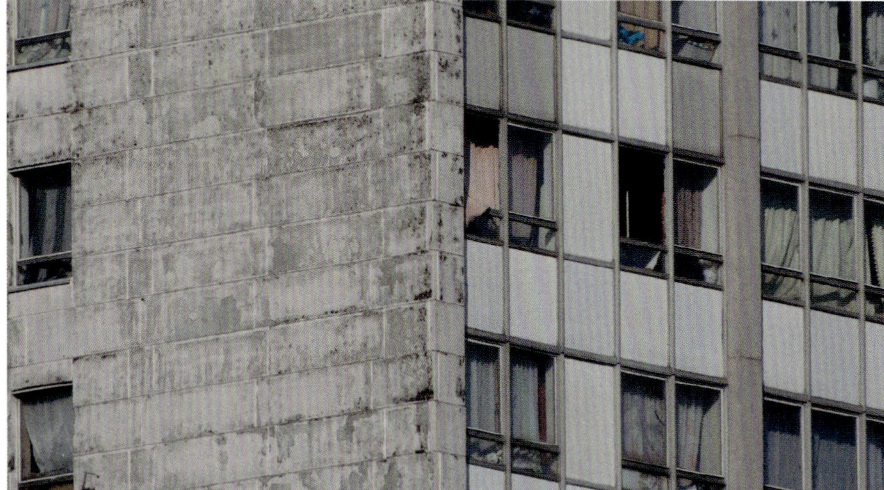

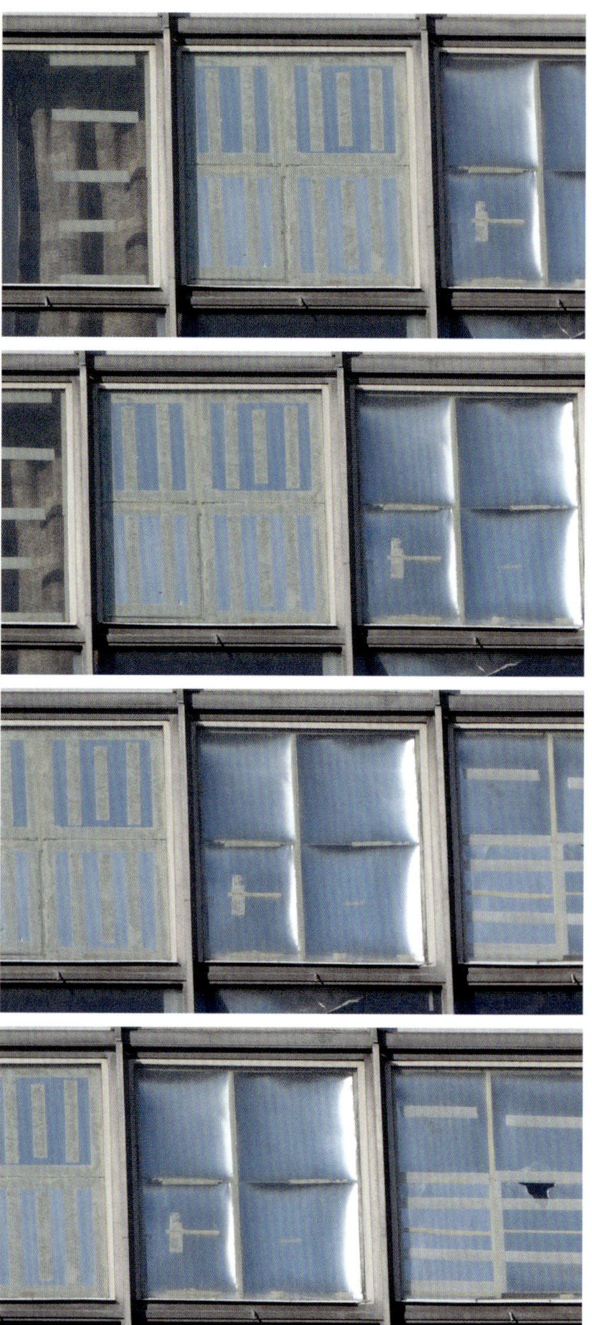

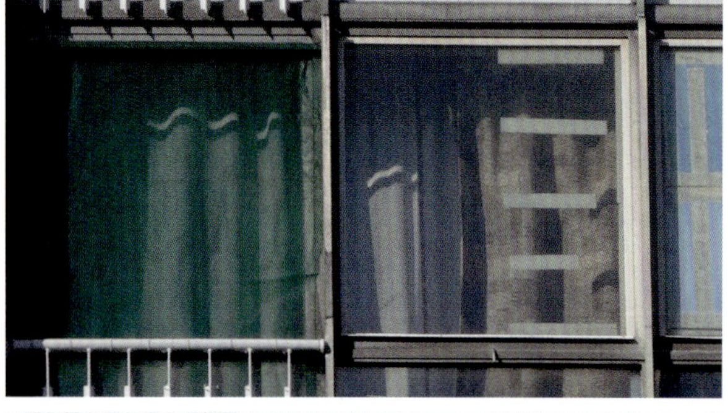

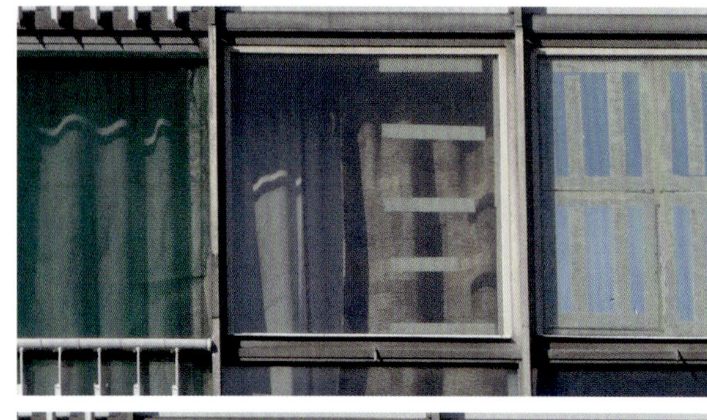

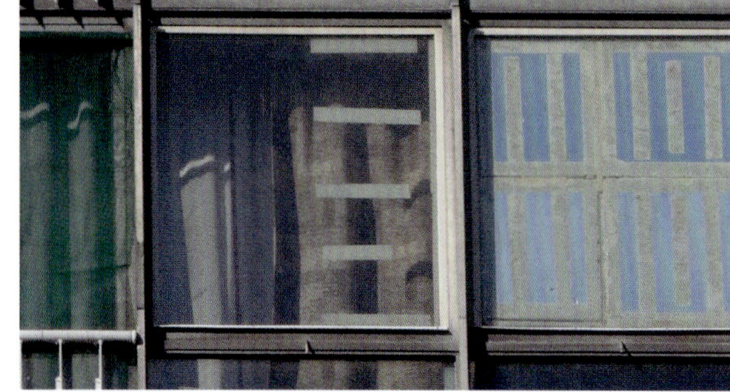

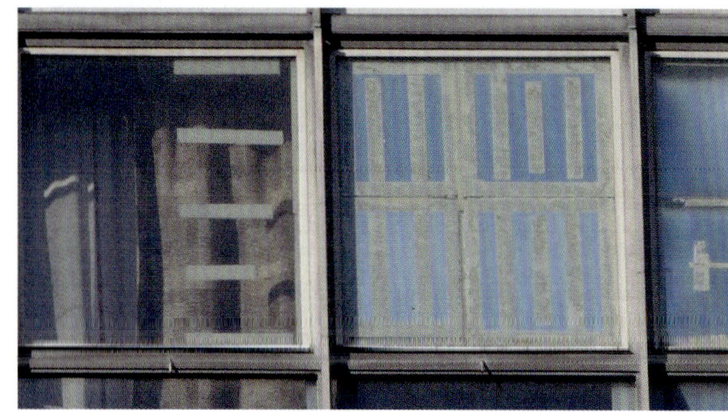

05:49:18

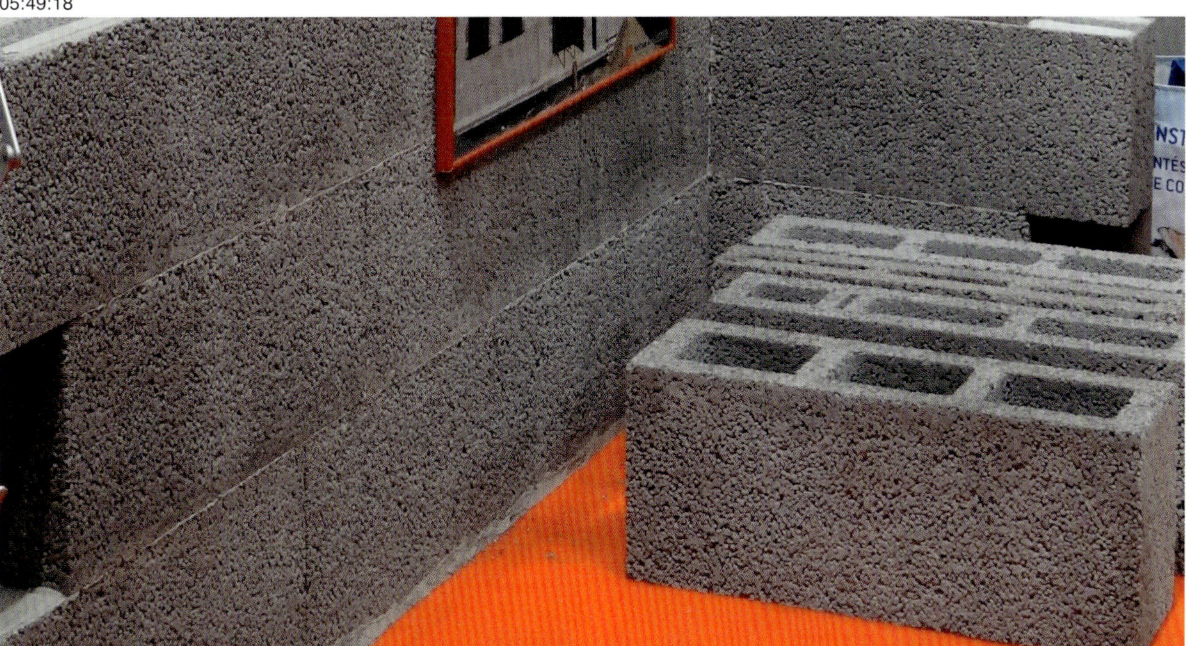

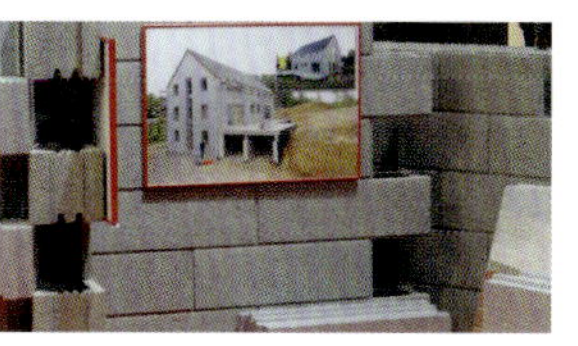

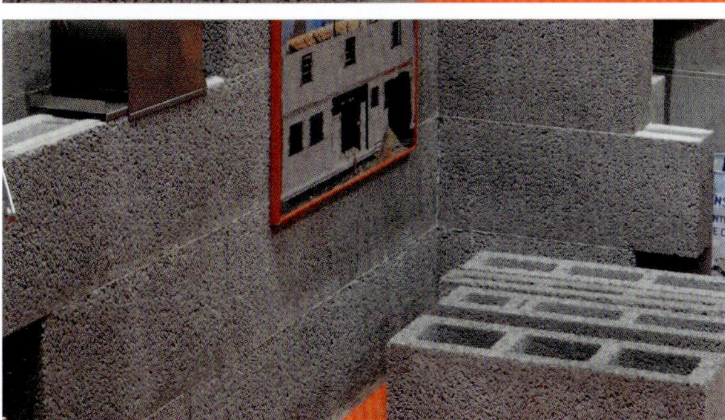

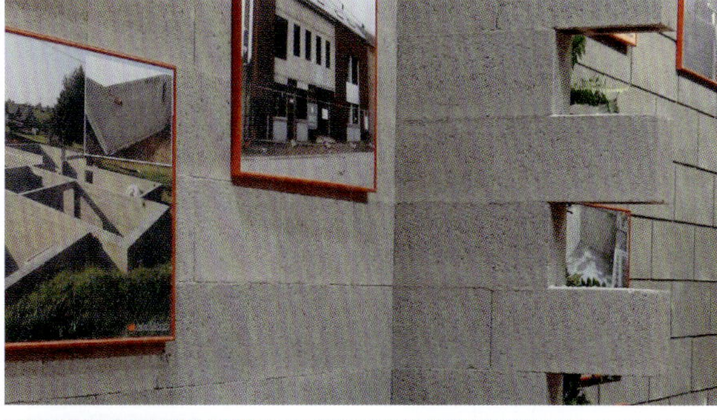

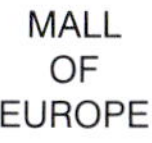

MALL
OF
EUROPE

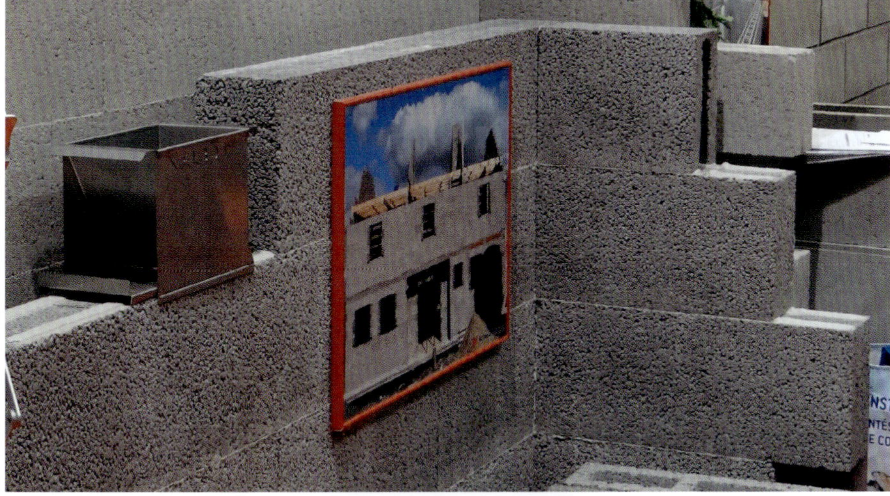

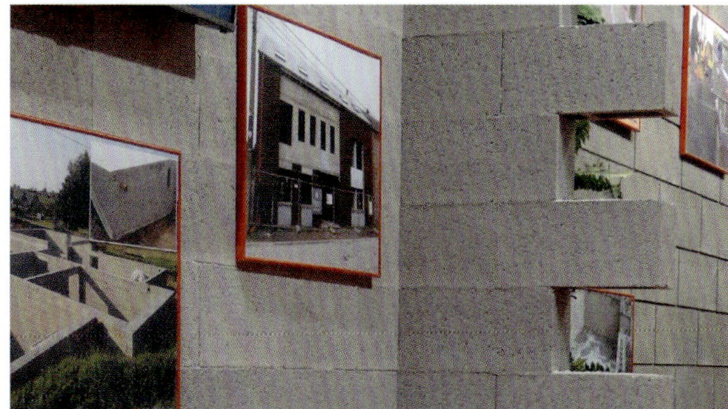

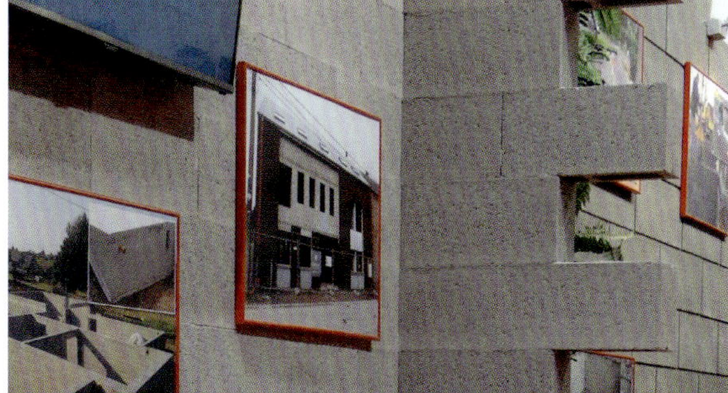

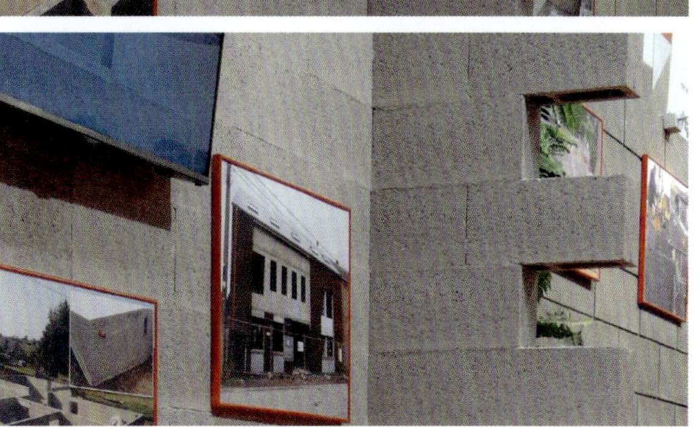

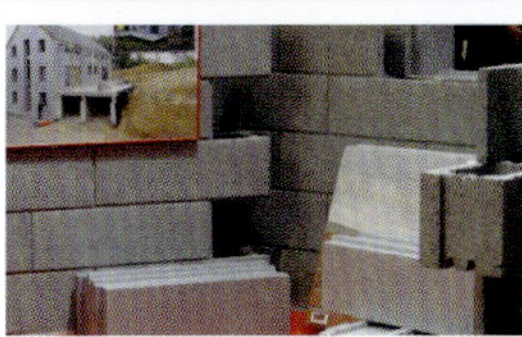

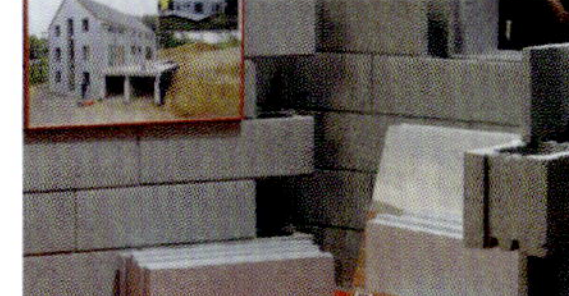

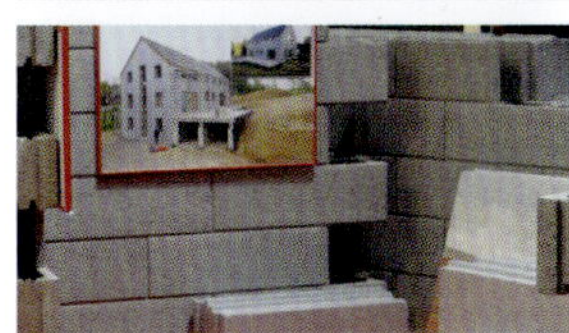

06:43:09

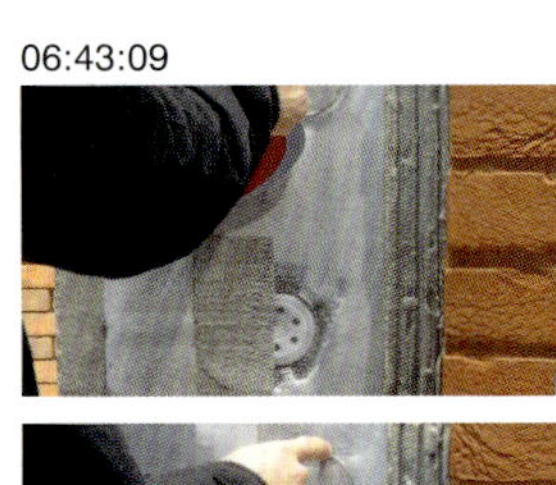

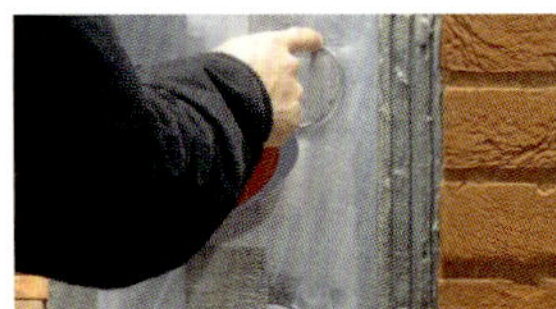

MALL
OF
EUROPE

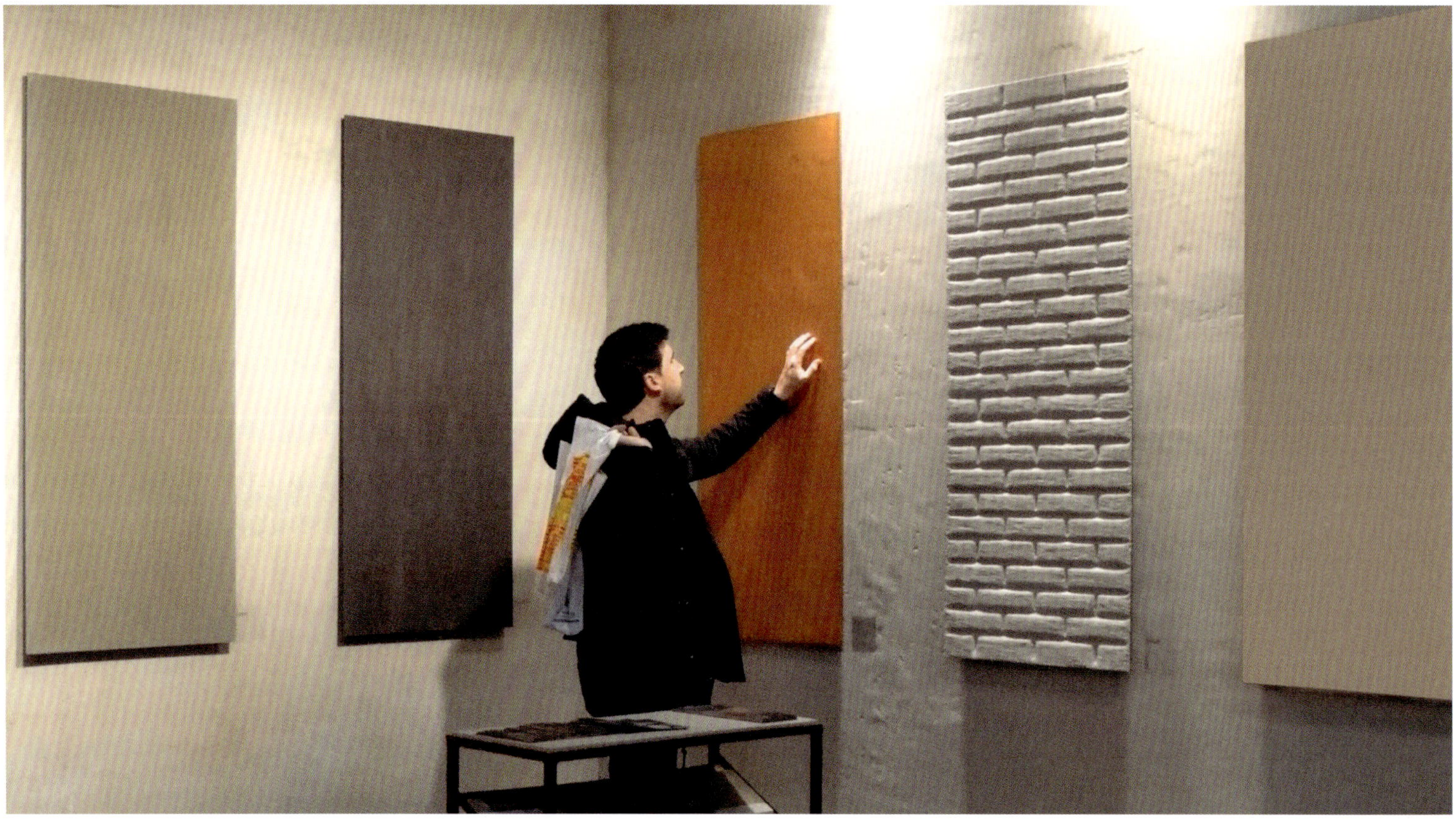

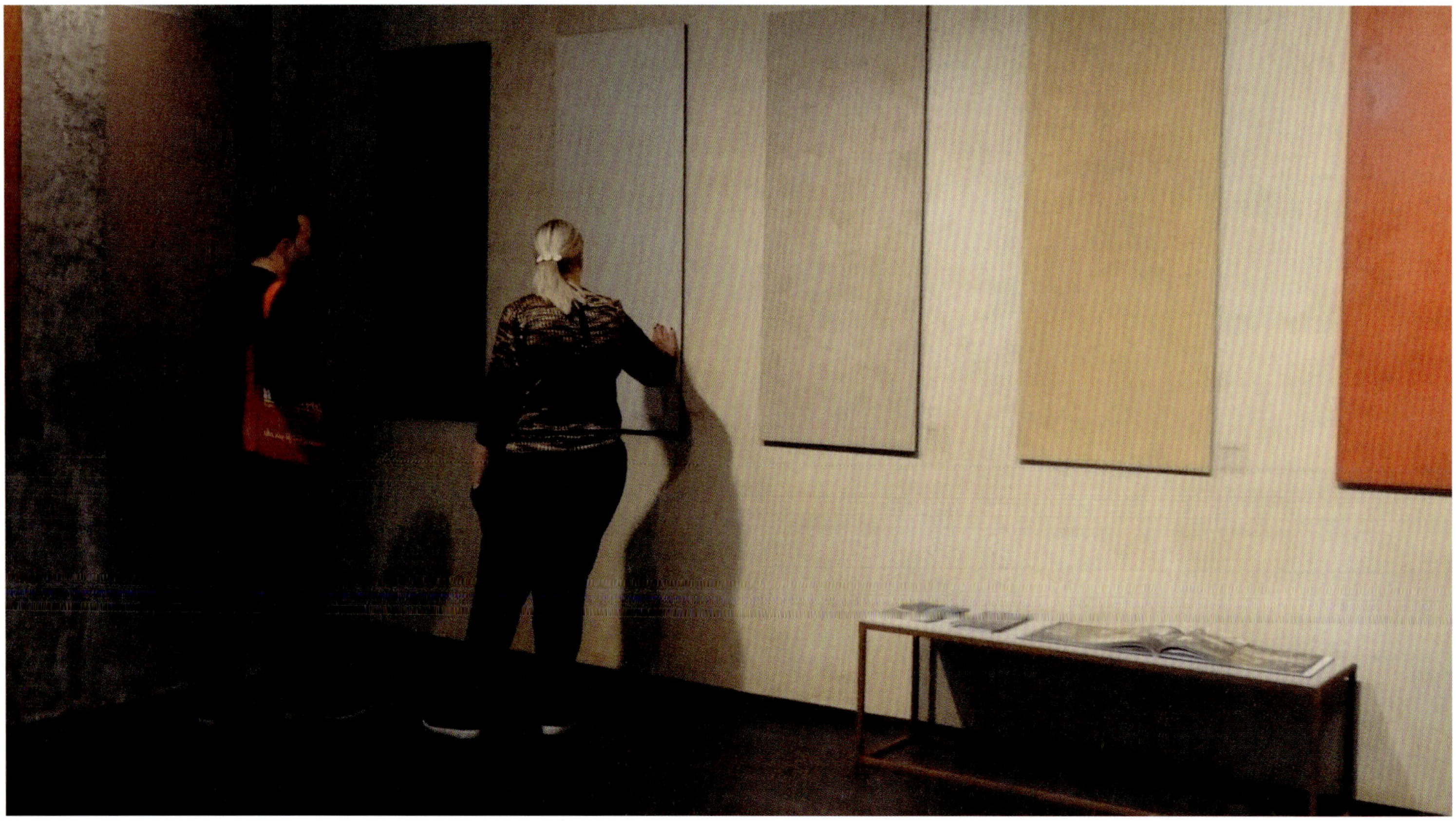

07:11:03

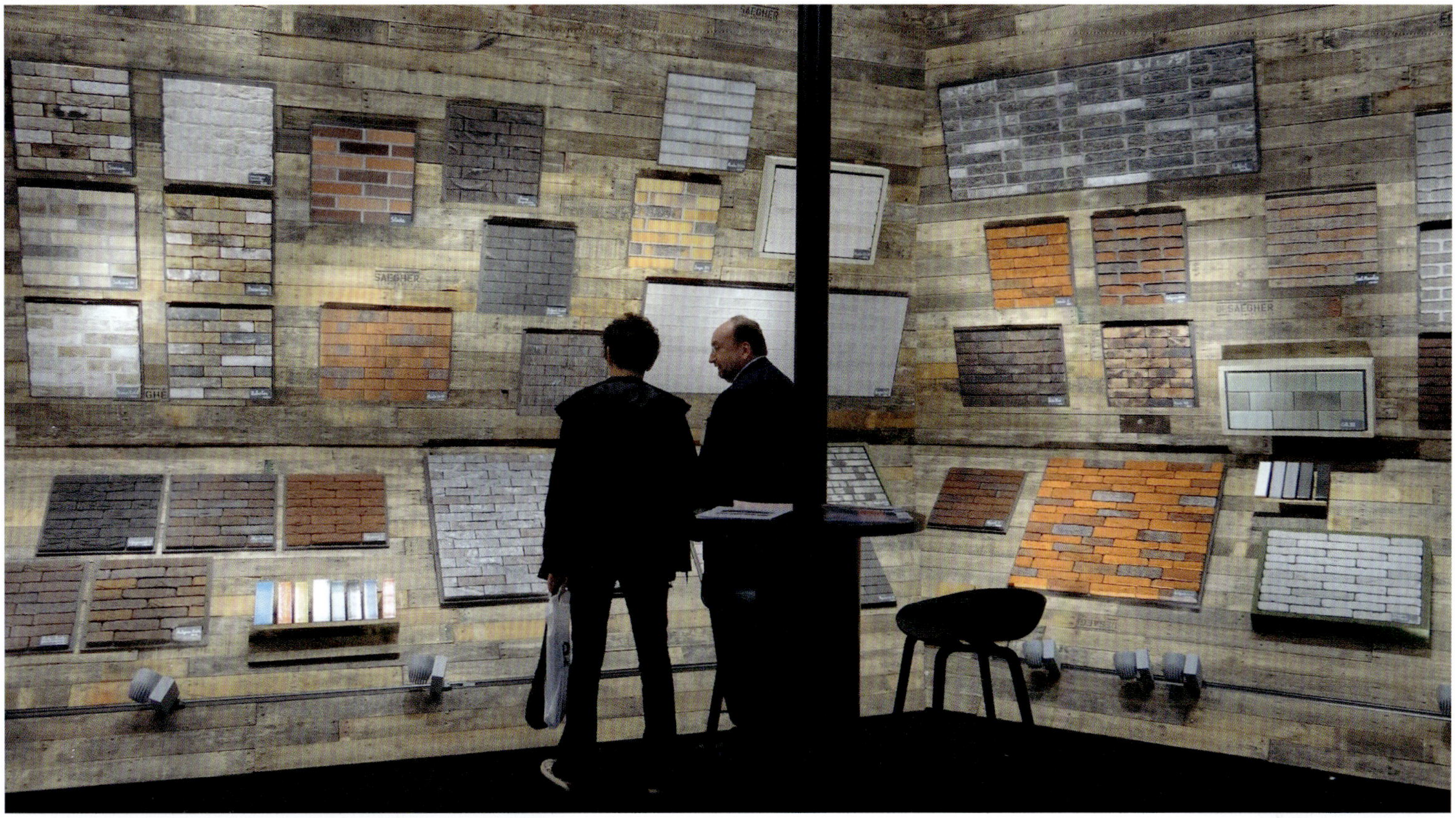

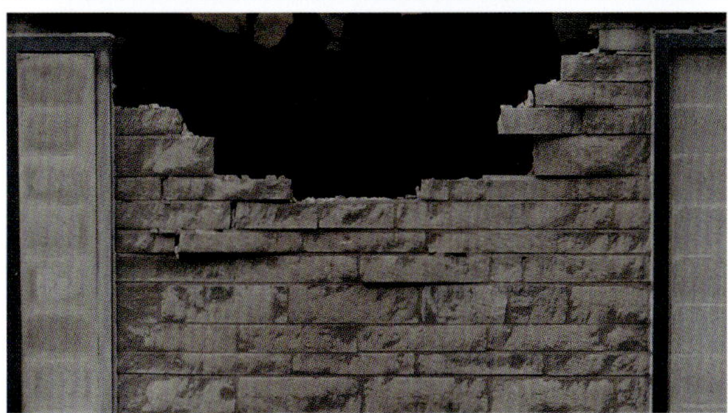

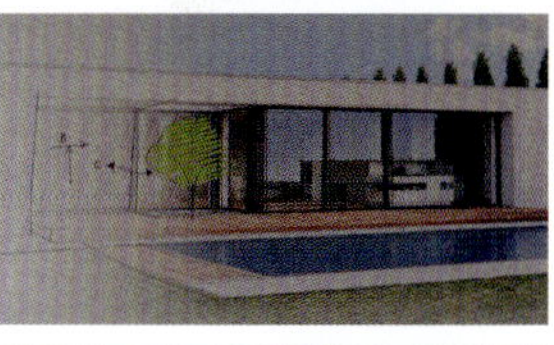

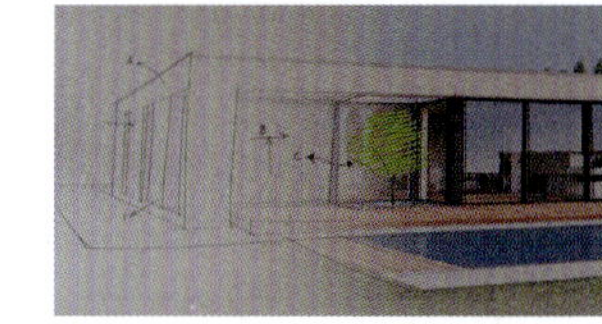

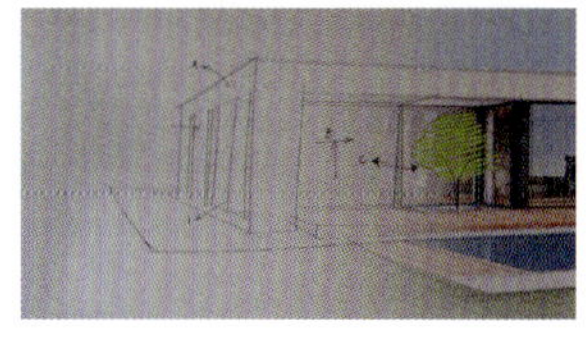

MALL
OF
EUROPE

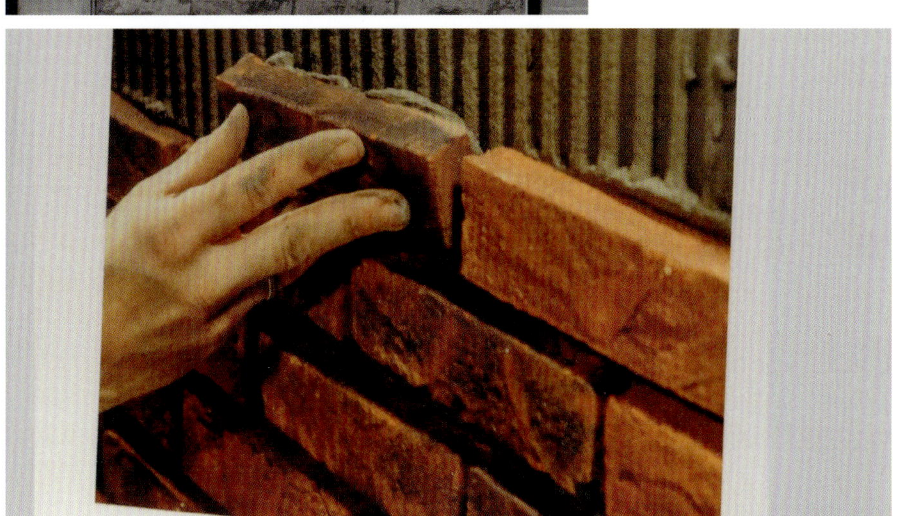

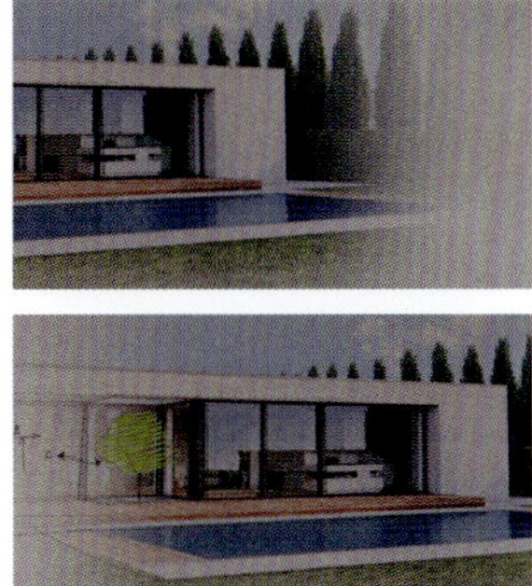

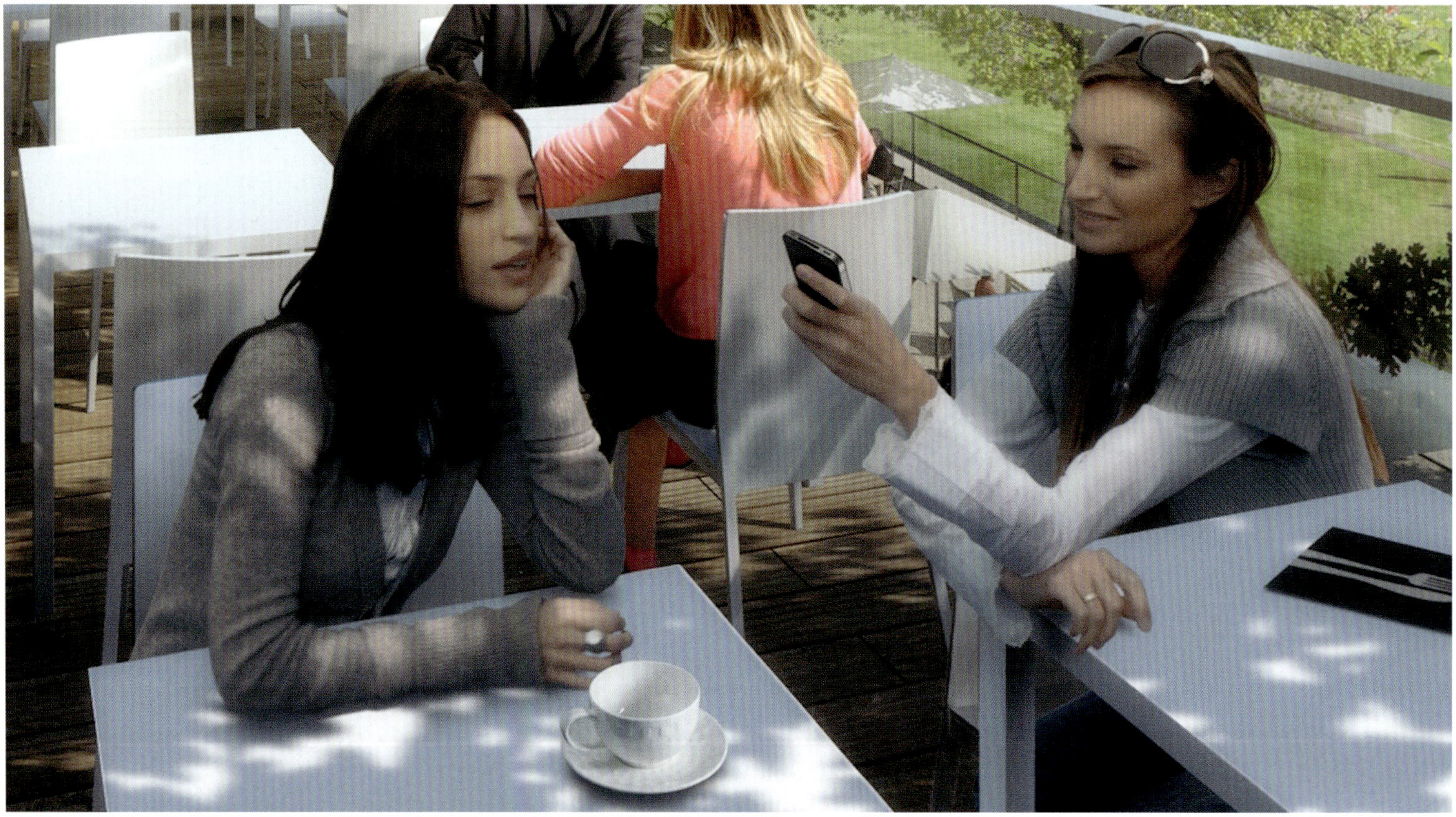

08:22:12

MALL
OF
EUROPE

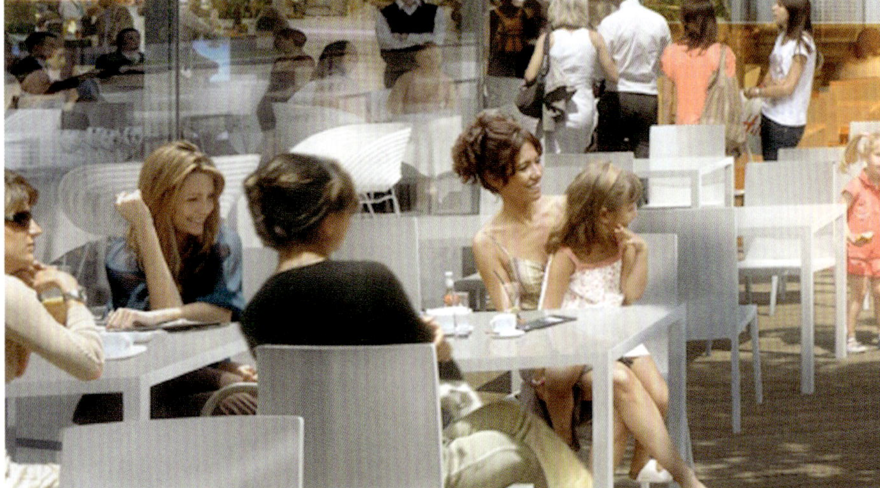

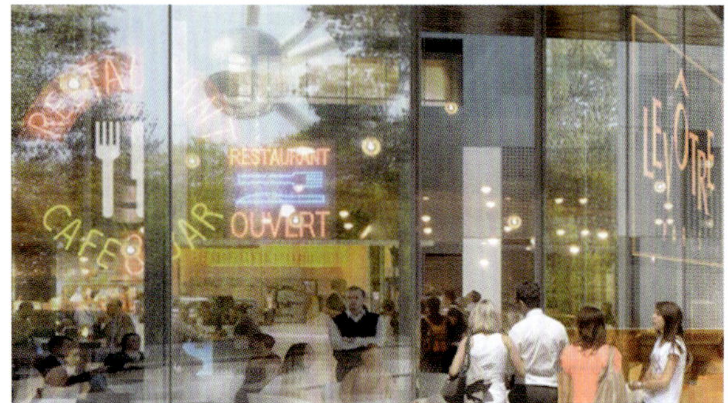

08:53:00

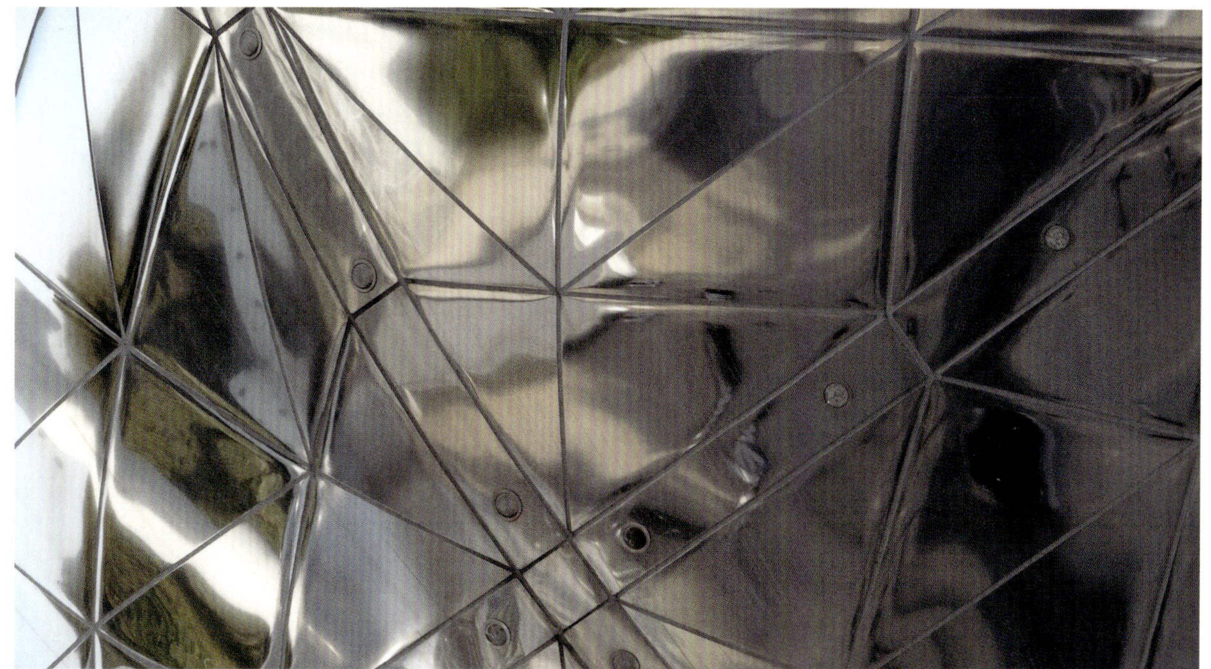

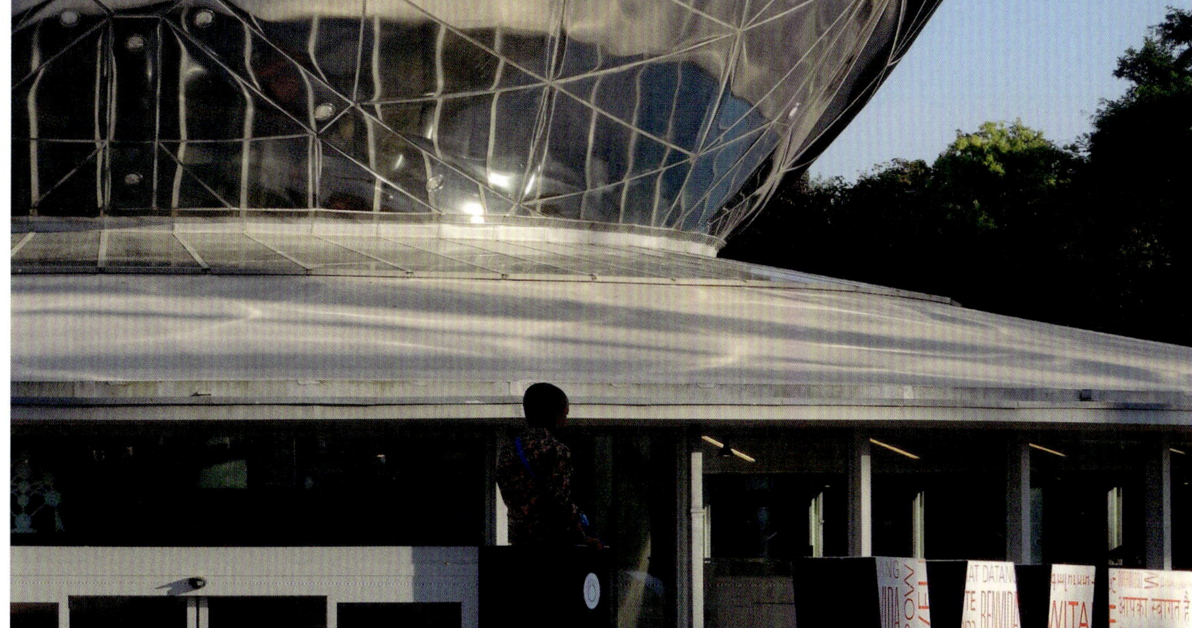

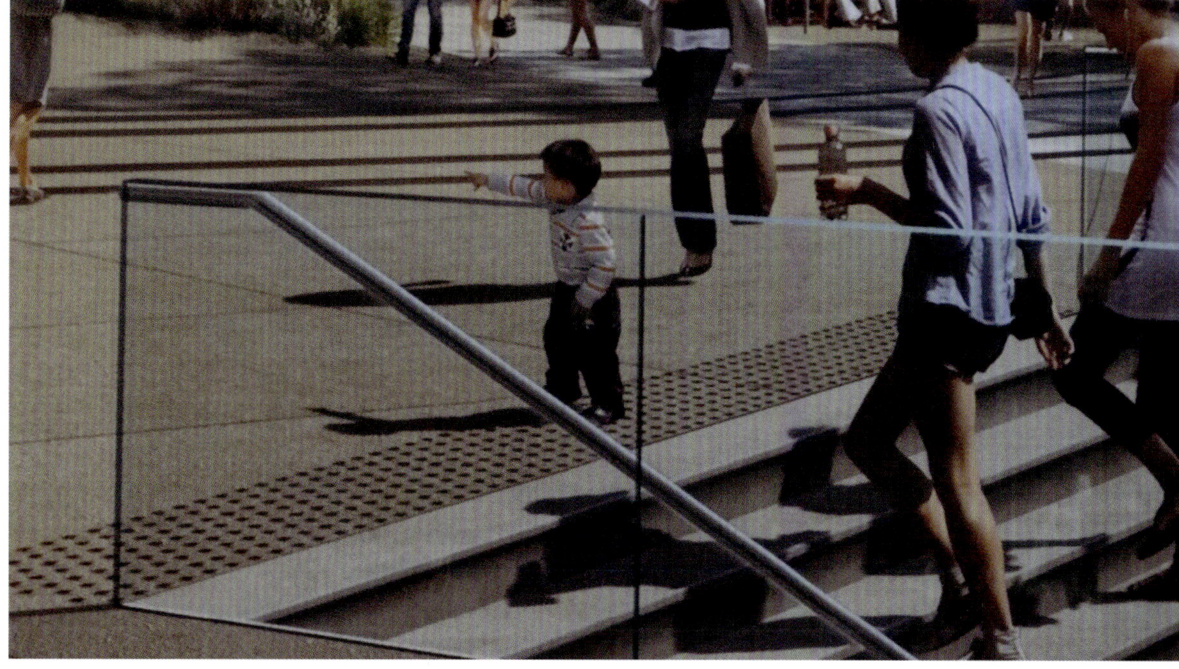

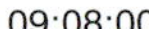

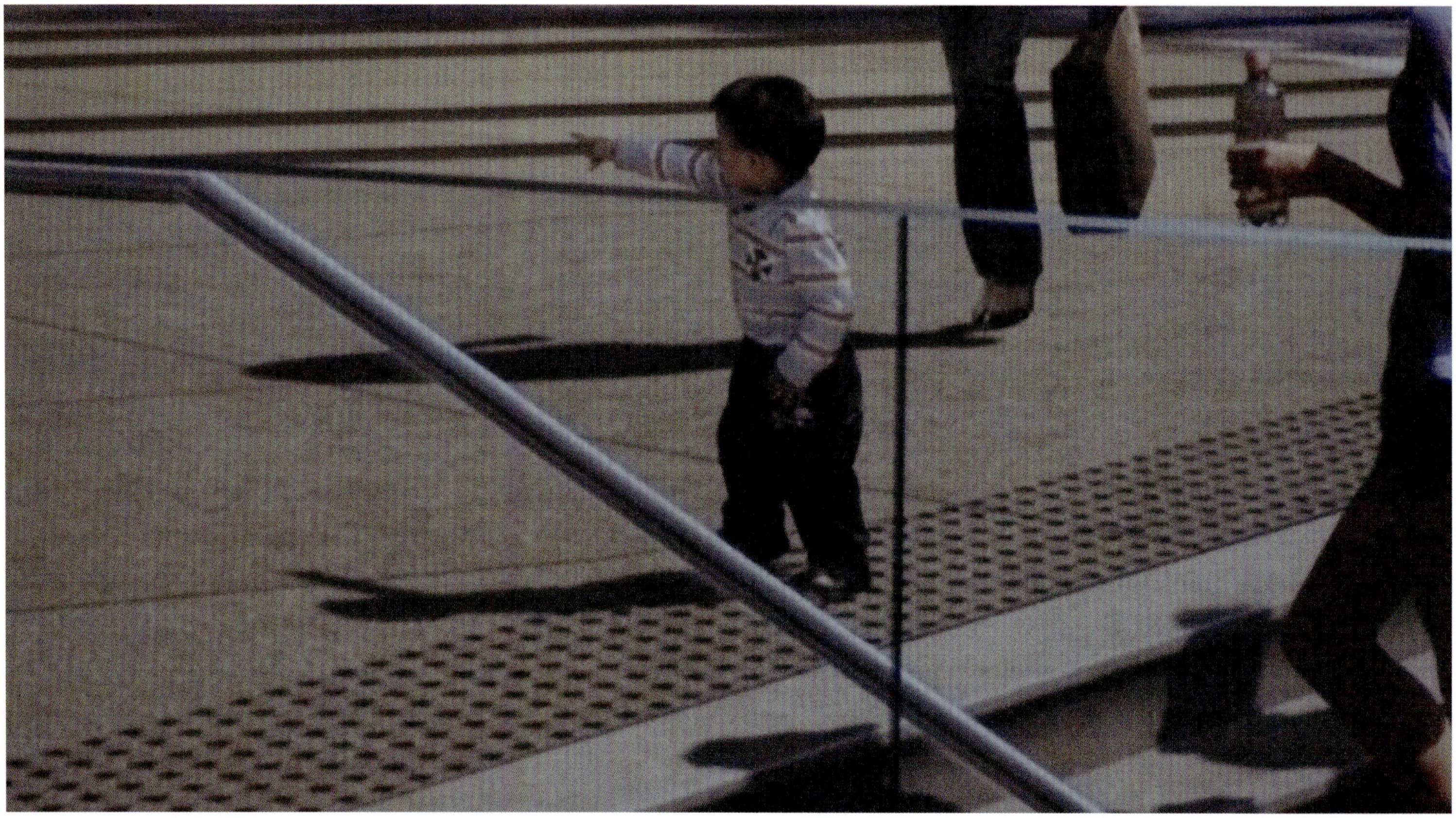

MALL
OF
EUROPE

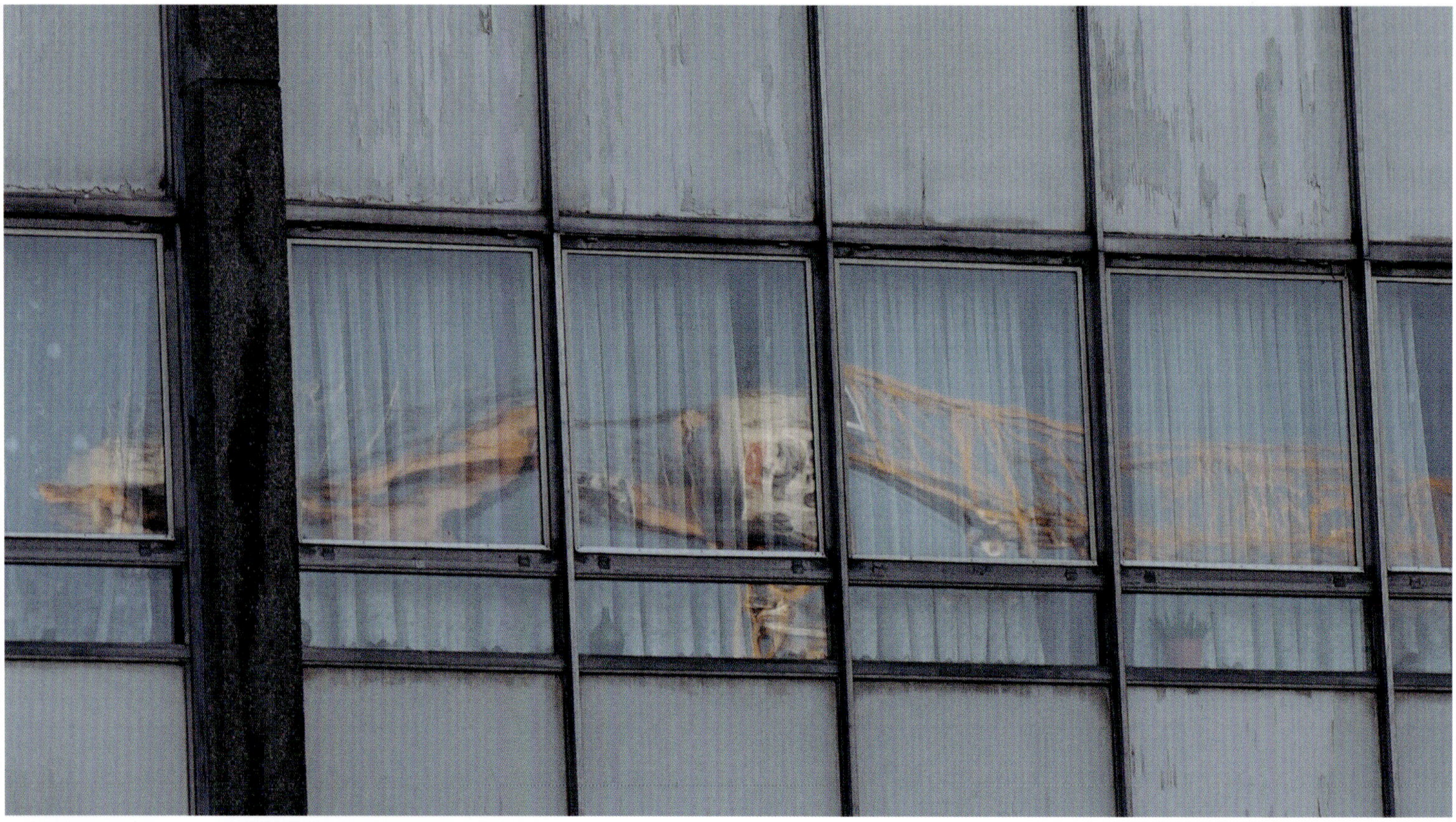

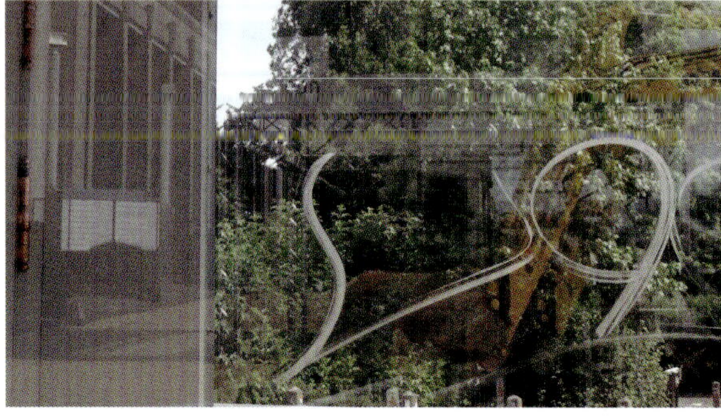

09:28:06

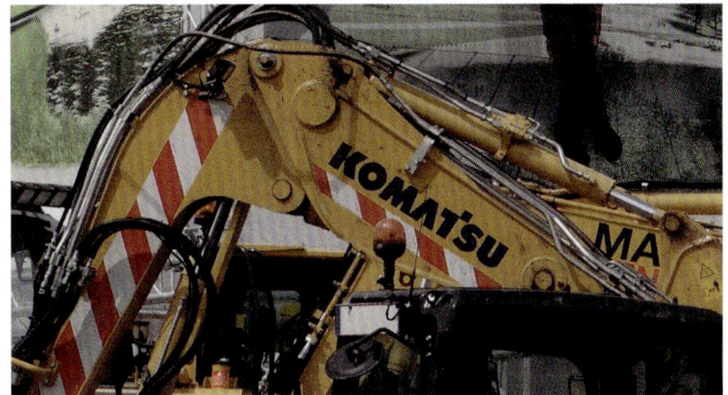

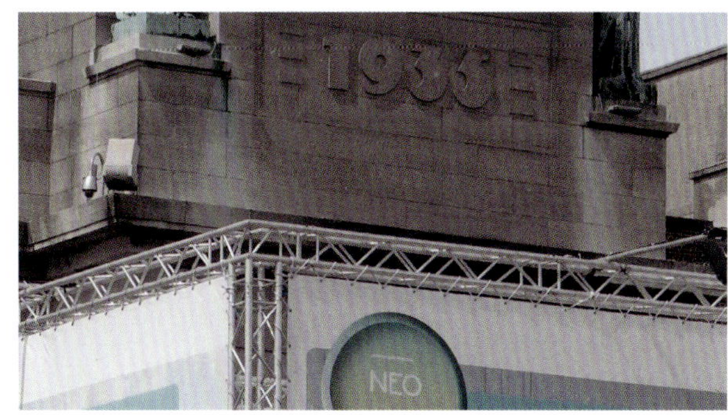

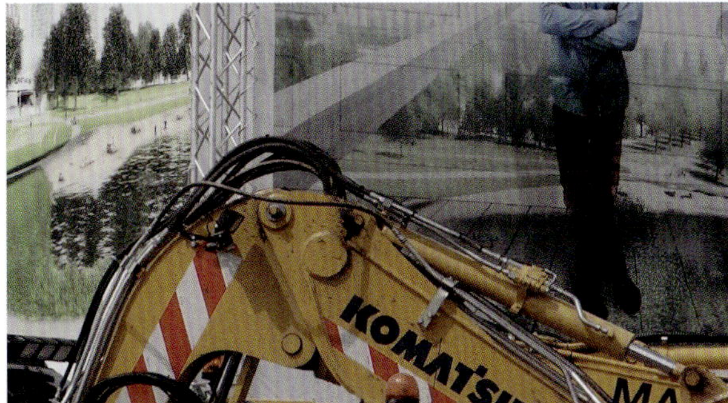

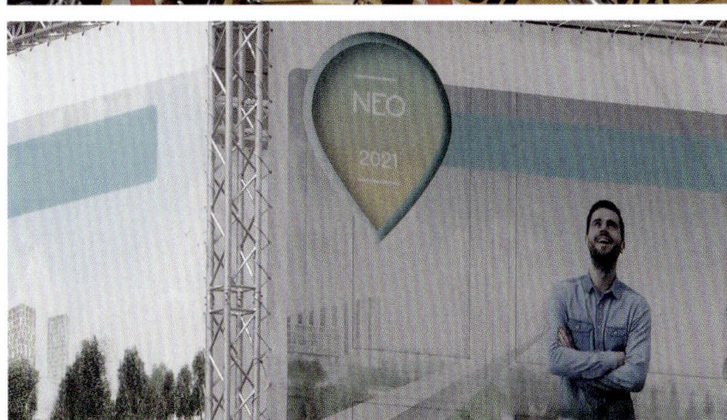

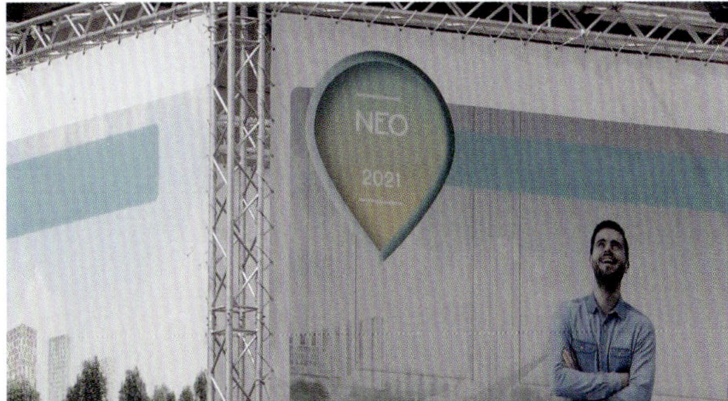

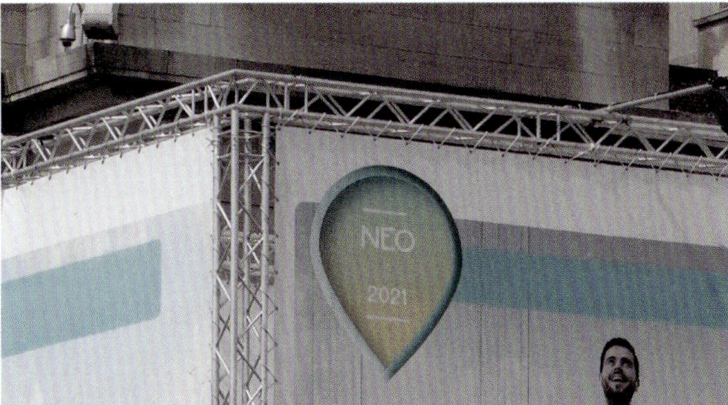

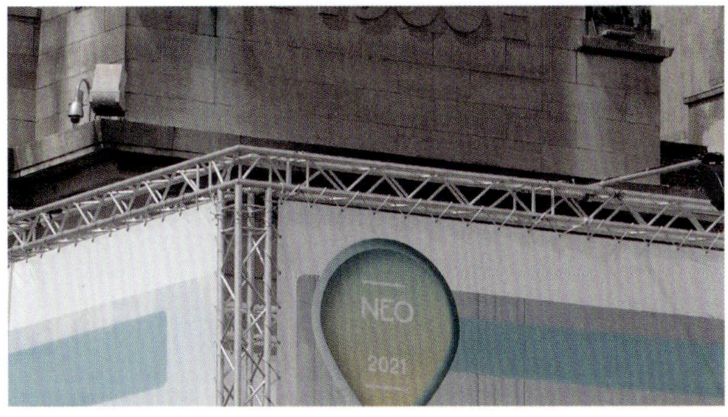

MALL
OF
EUROPE

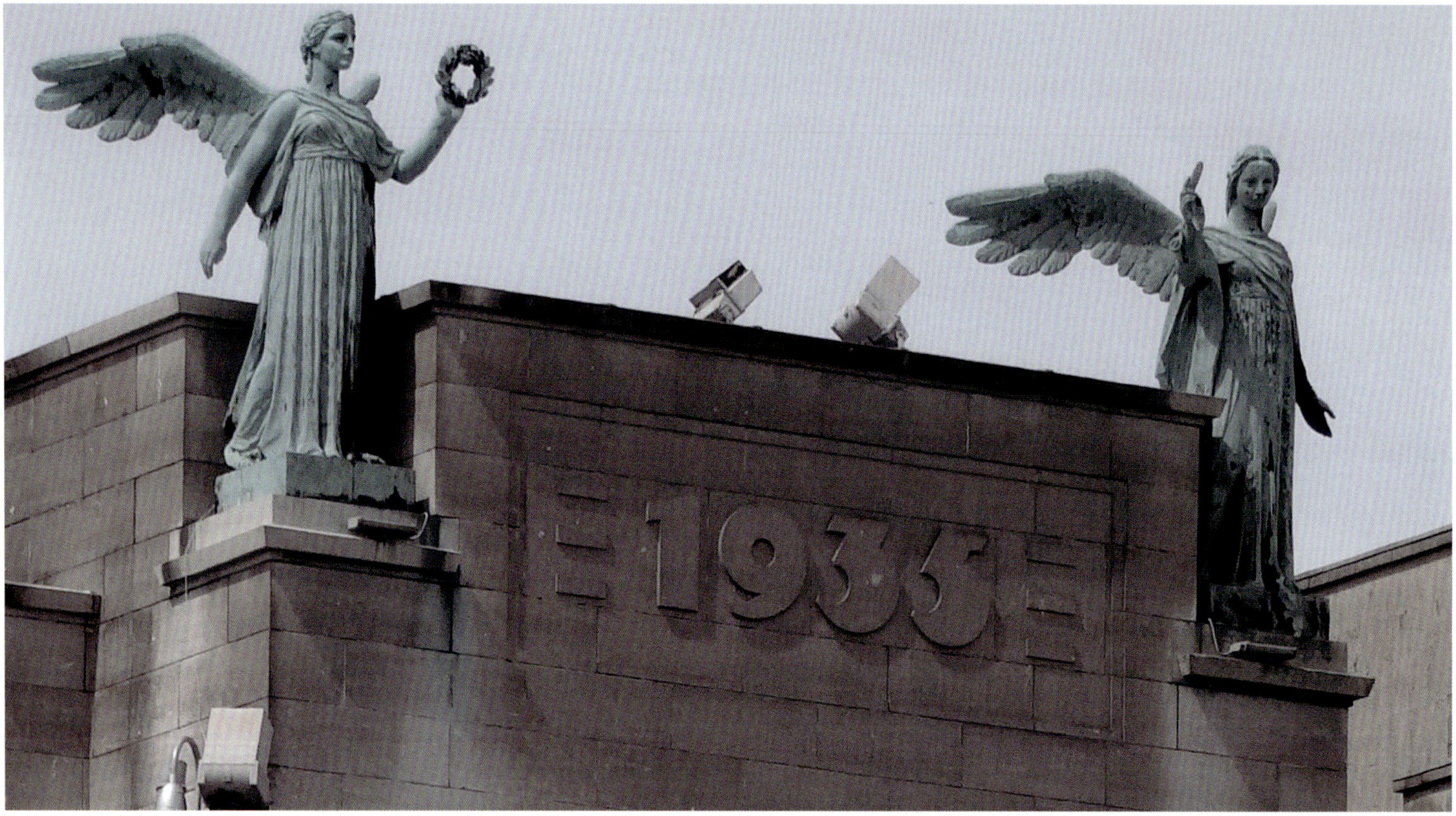

10:21:18

MALL
OF
EUROPE

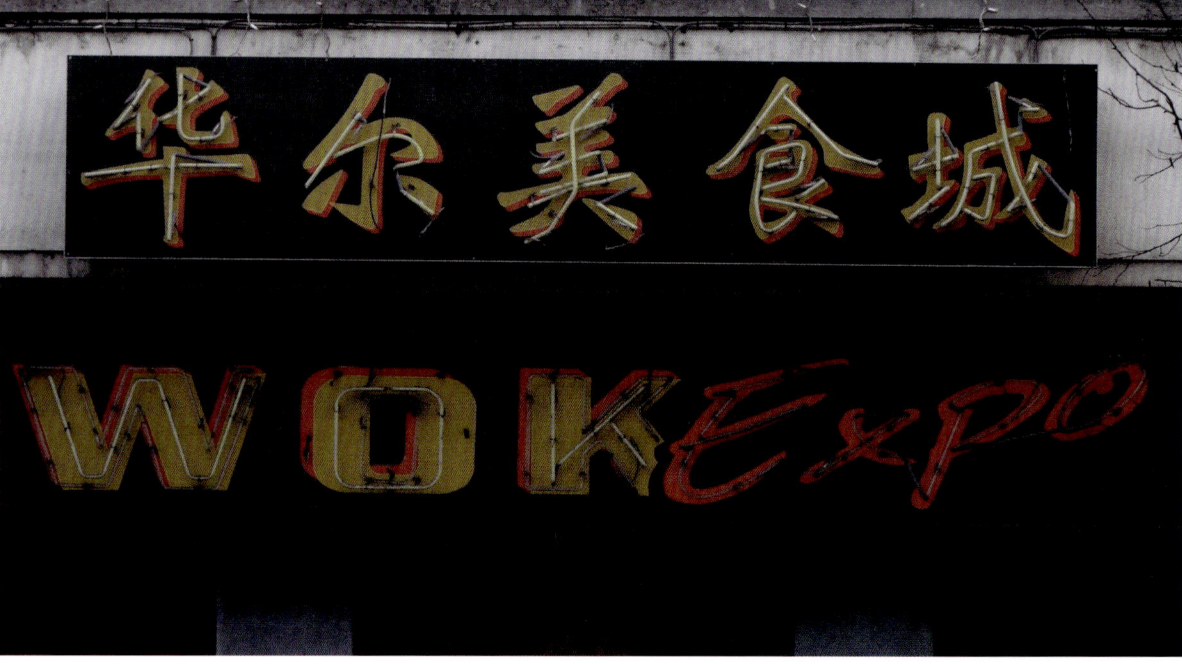

10:36:10

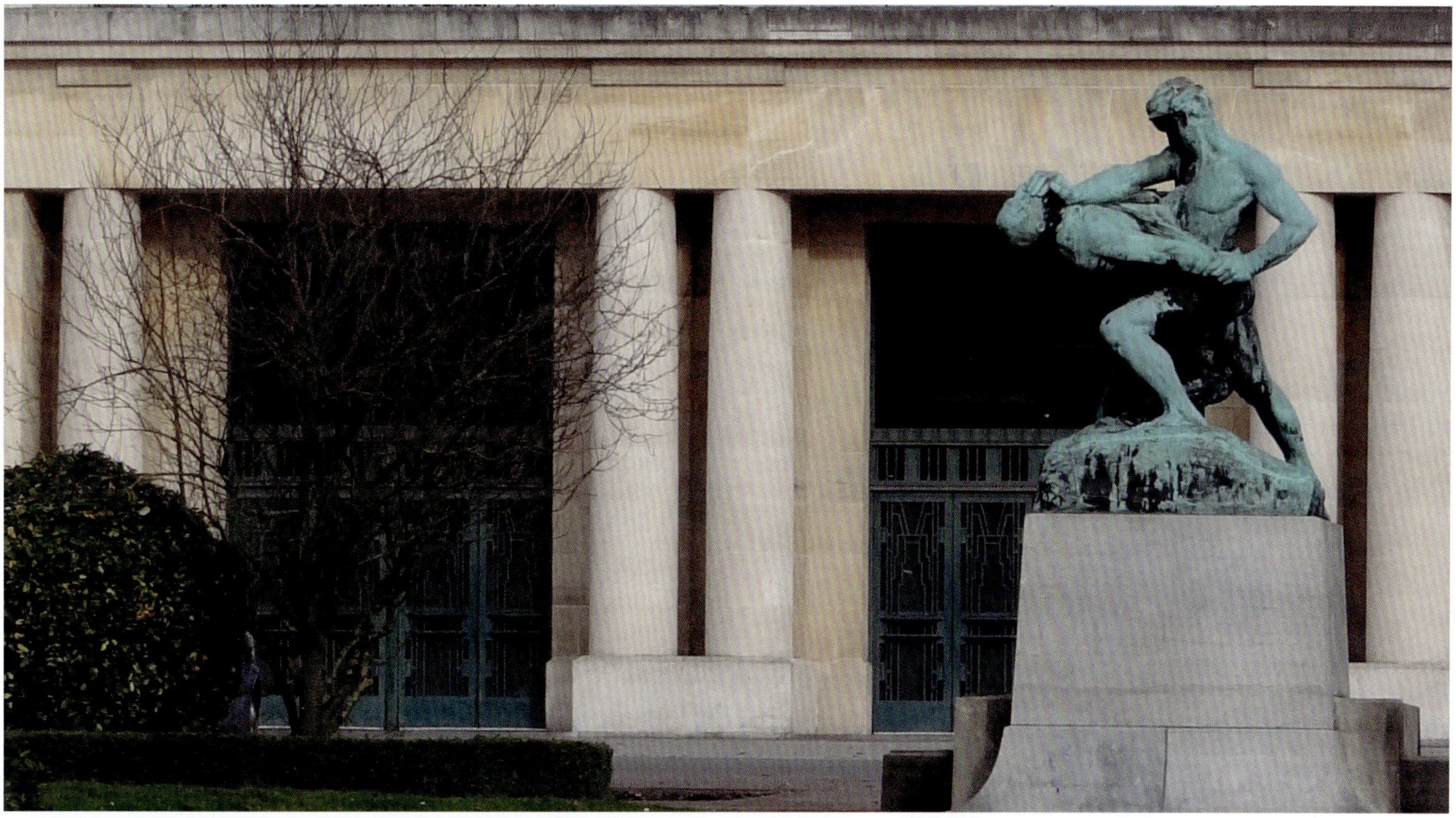

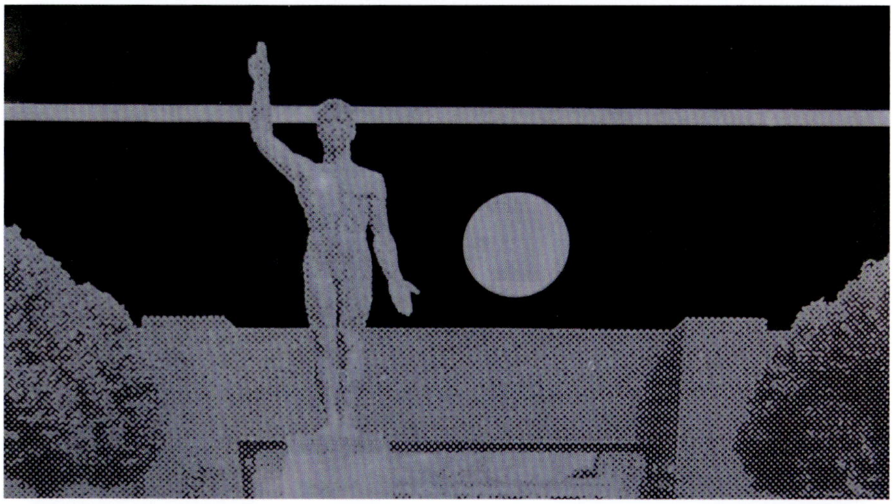

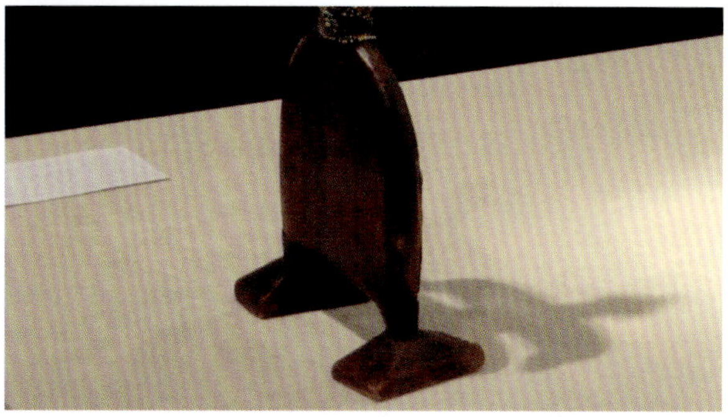

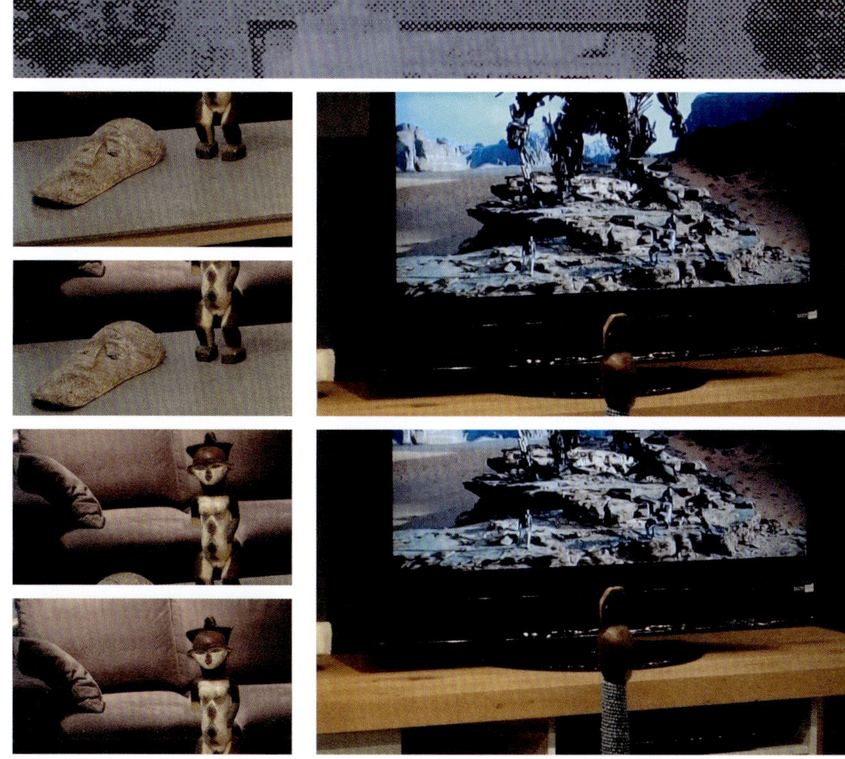

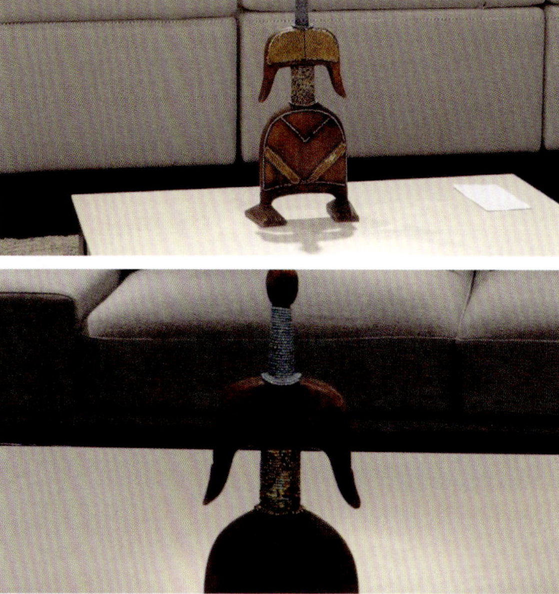

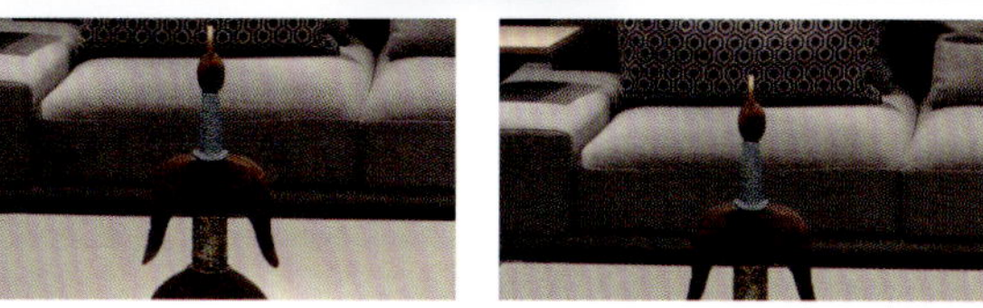

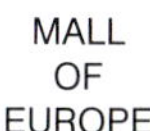

MALL
OF
EUROPE

12:24:00

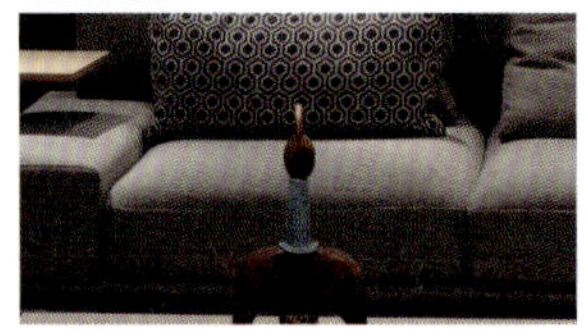

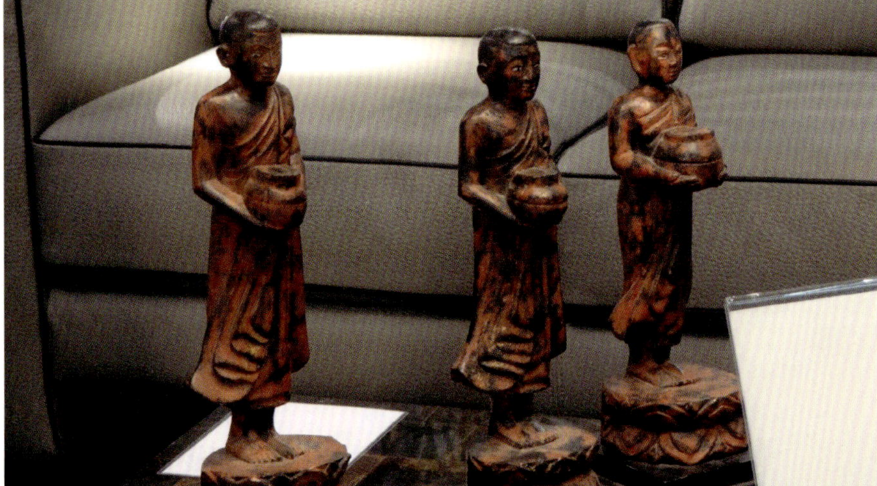

MALL
OF
EUROPE

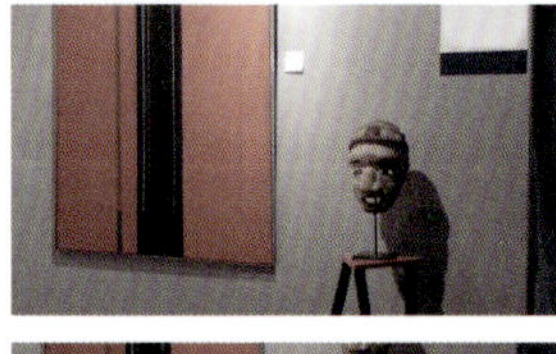

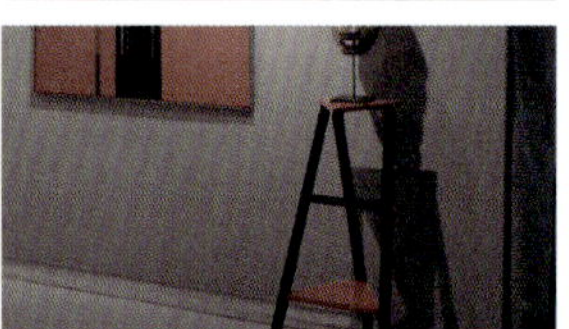

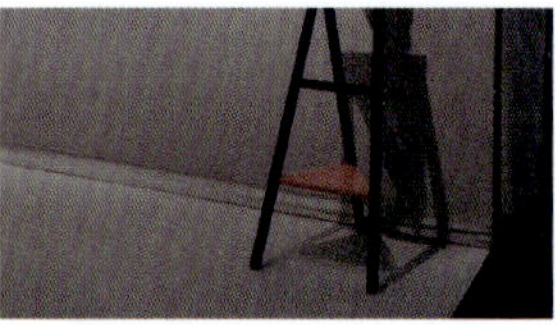

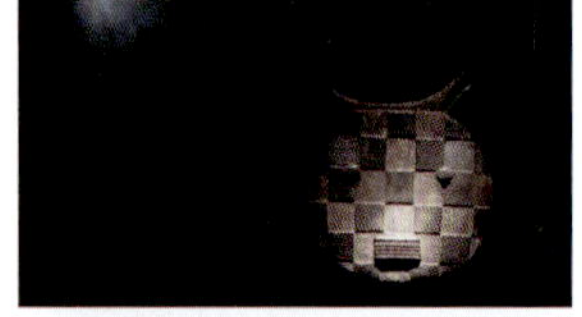

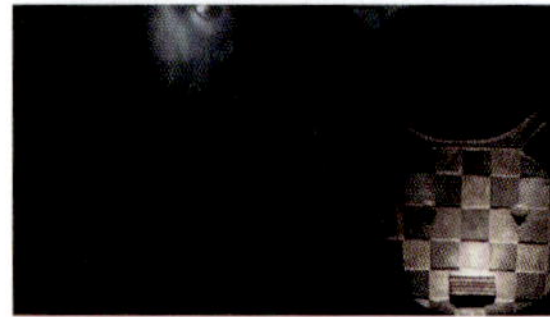

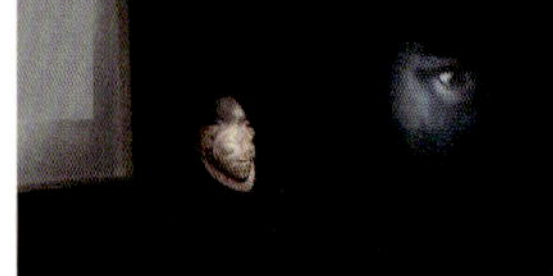

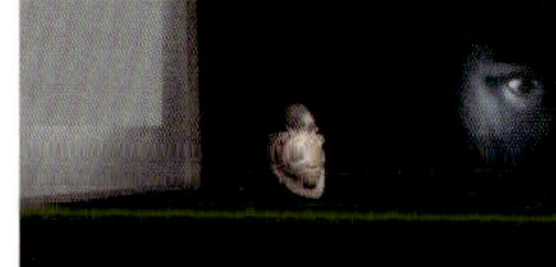

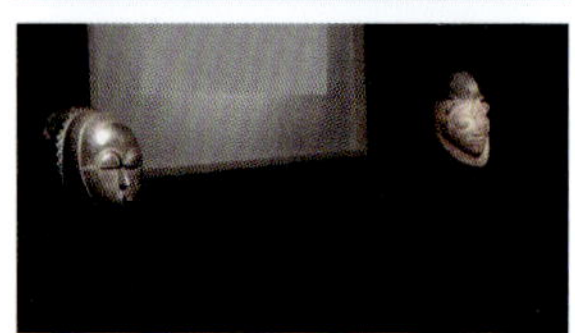

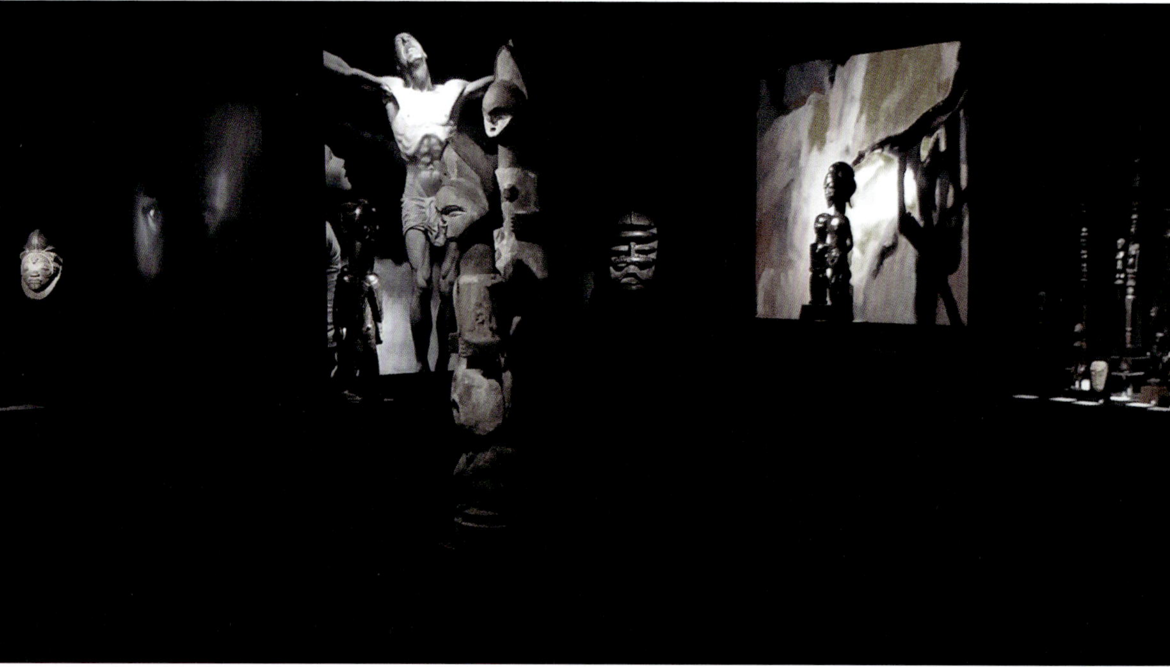

14:06:16

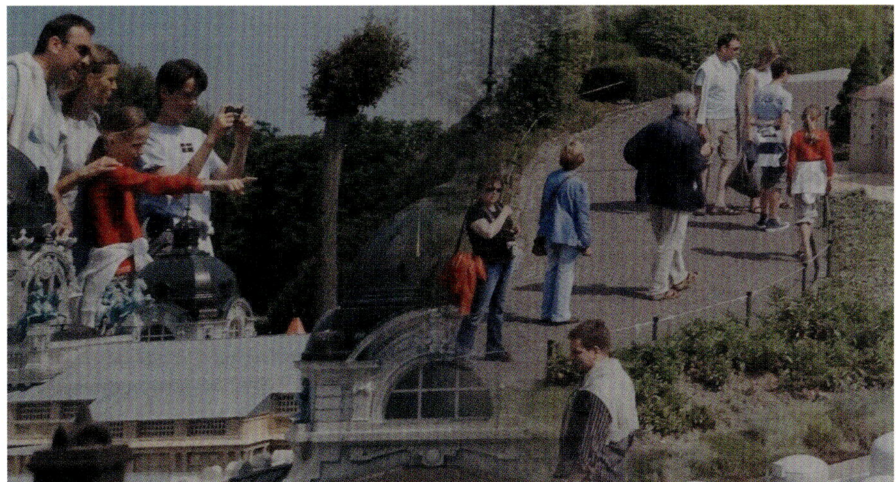

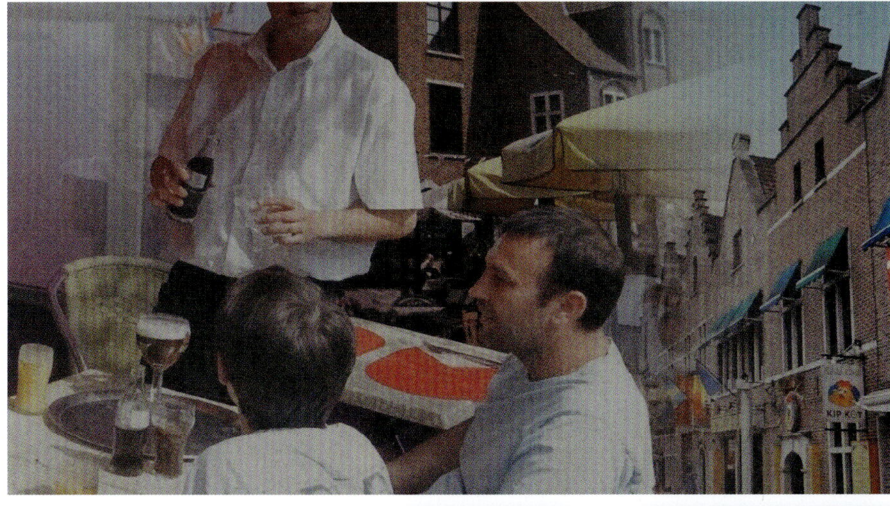

MALL
OF
EUROPE

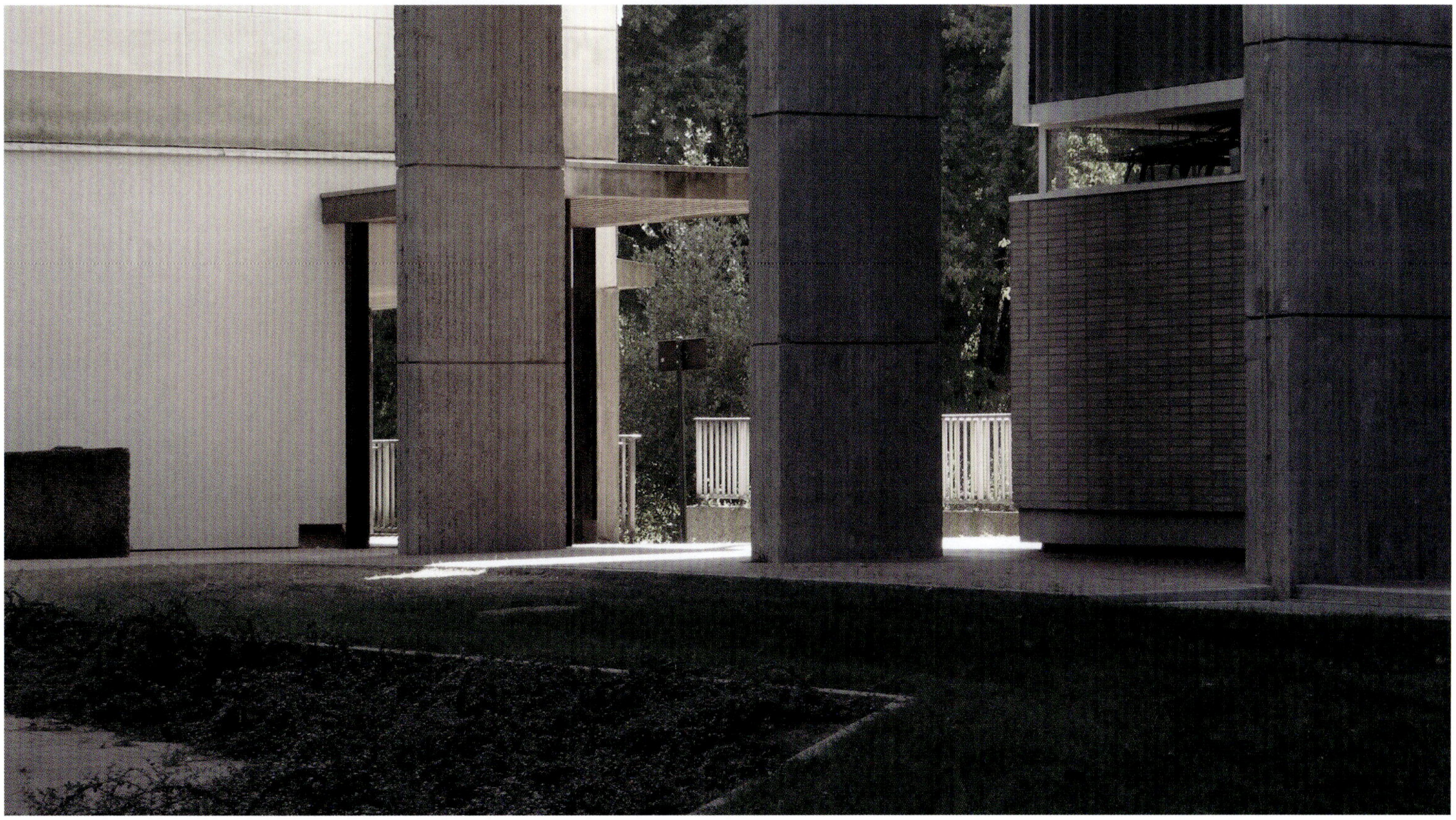

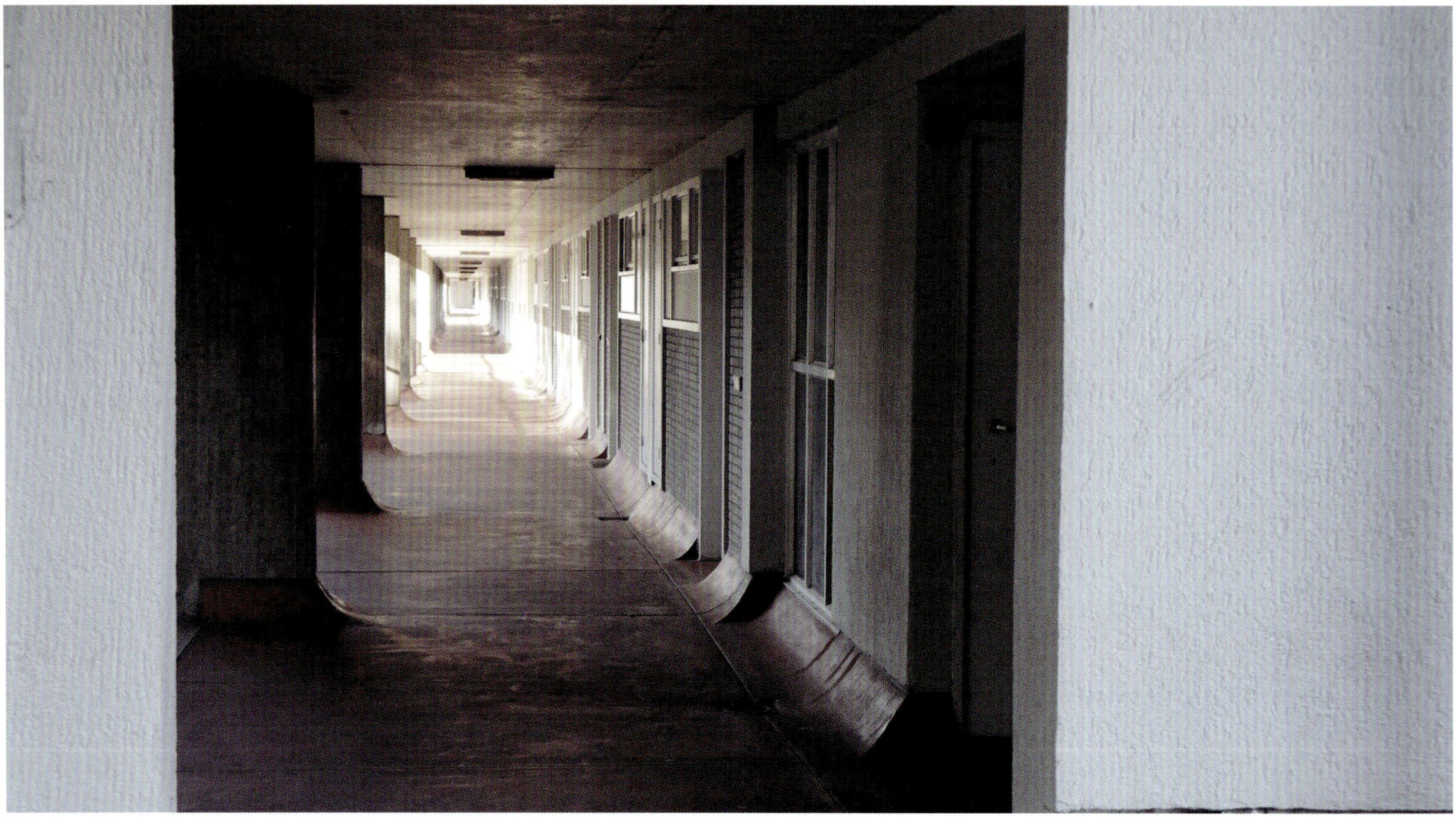

14:33:07

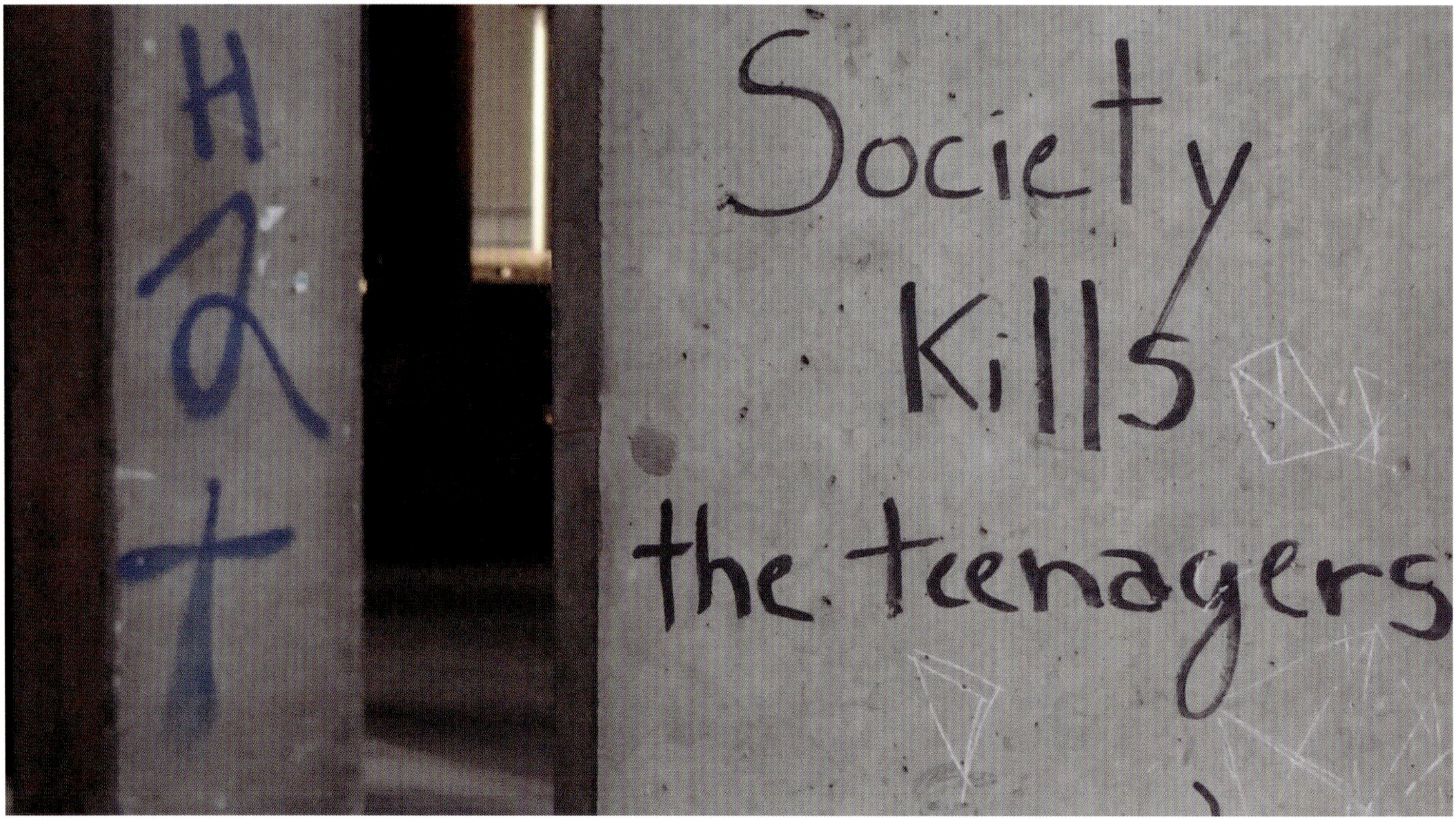

15:14:16

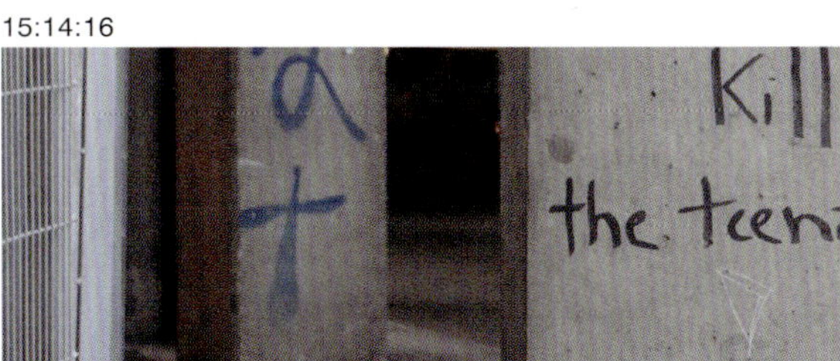

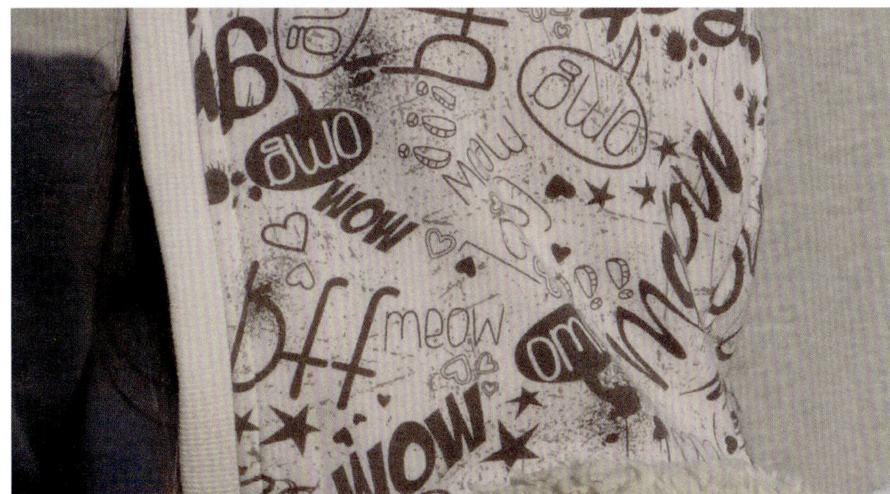

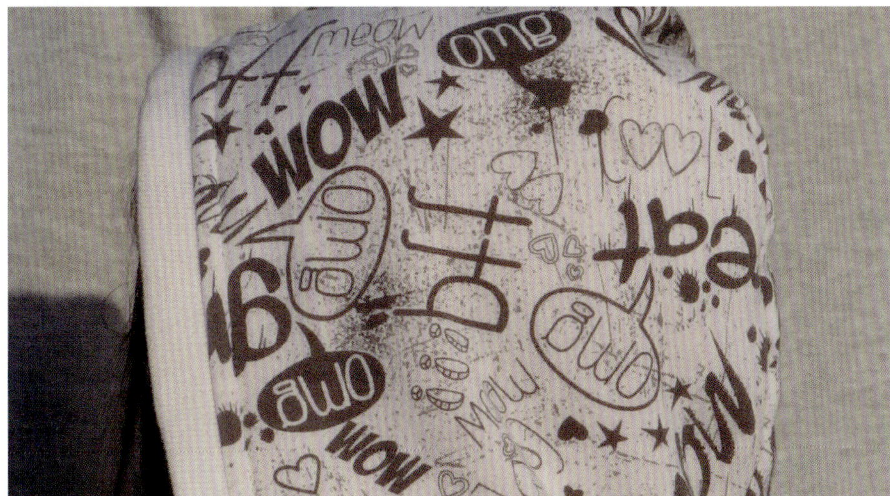

MALL
OF
EUROPE

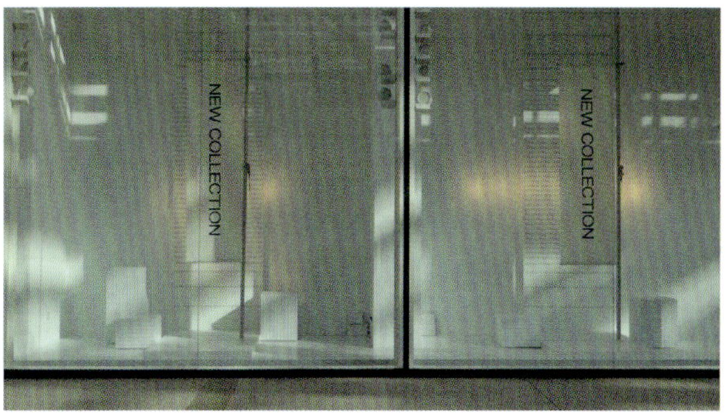

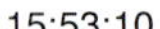

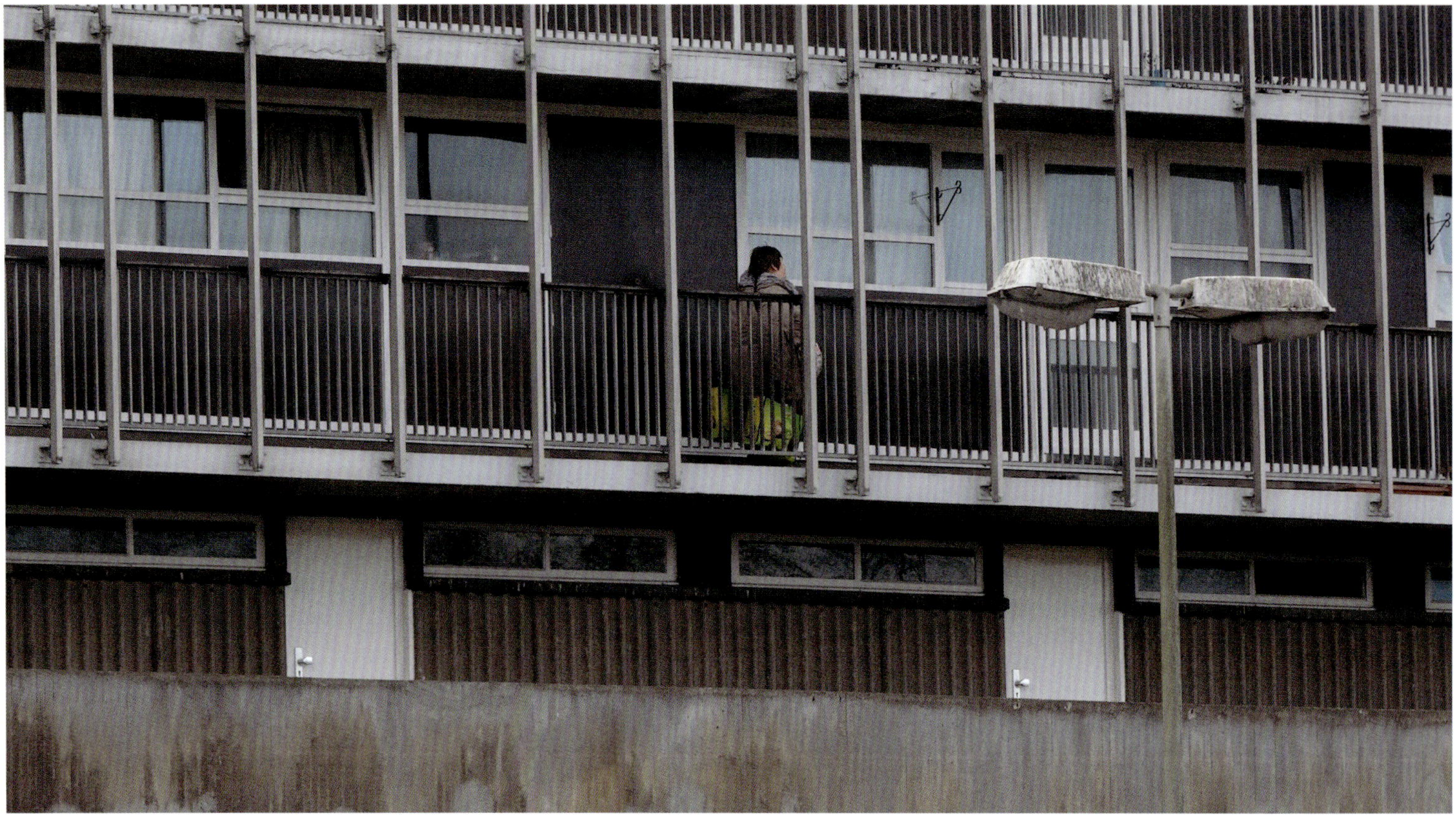

15:53:10

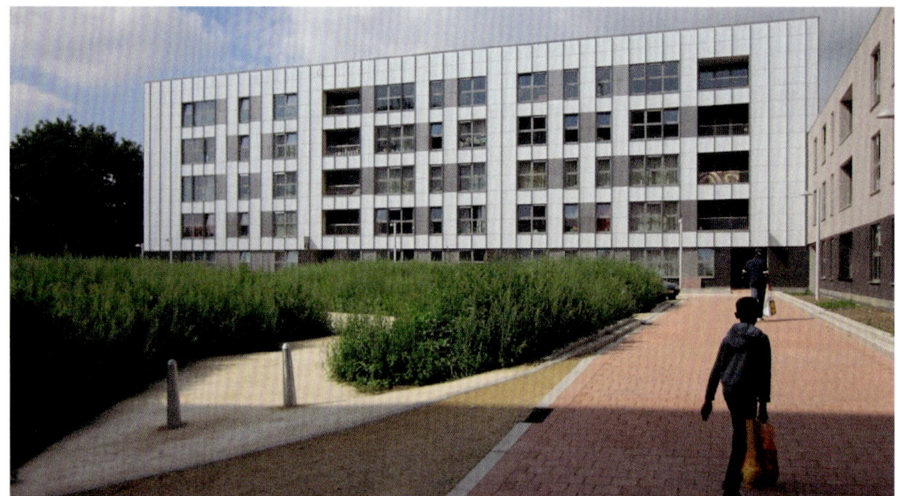

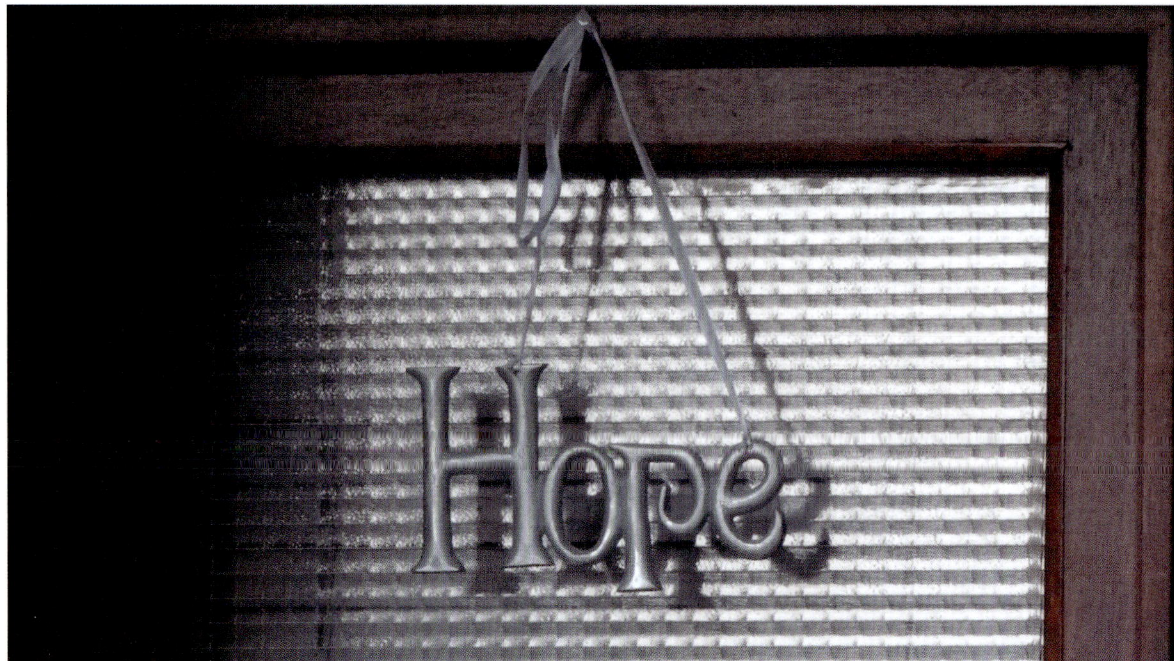

16:15:21

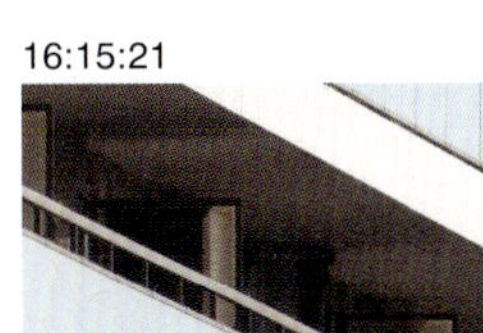
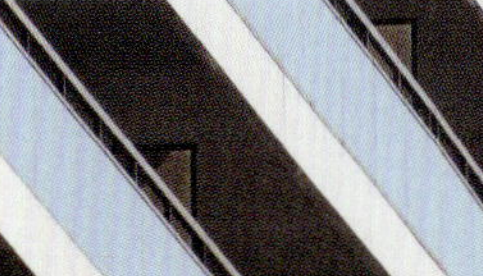
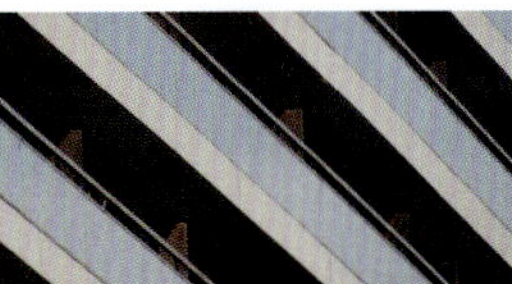
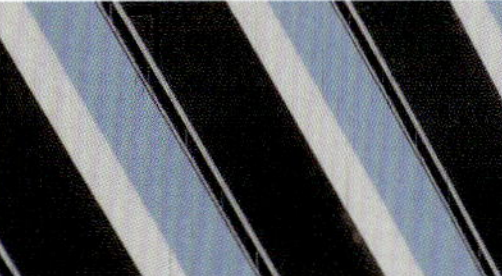
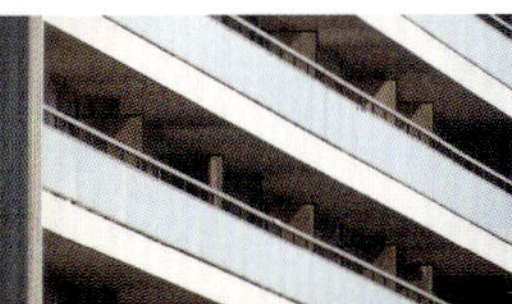
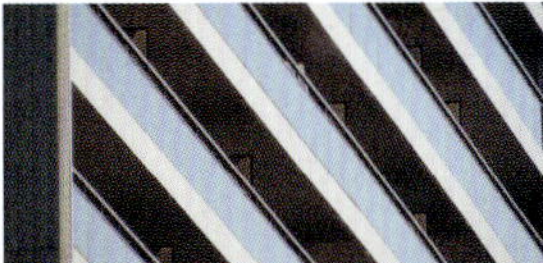
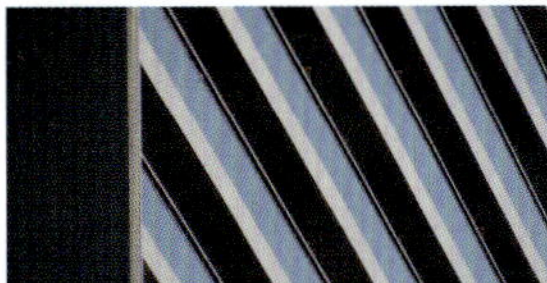
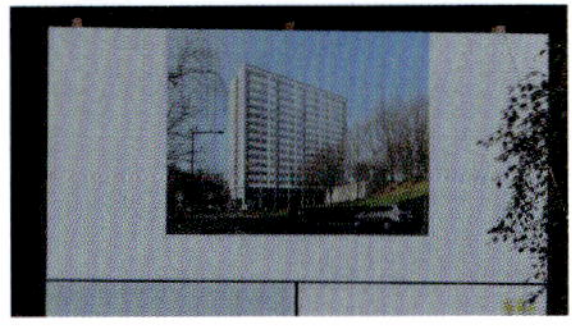

MALL
OF
EUROPE

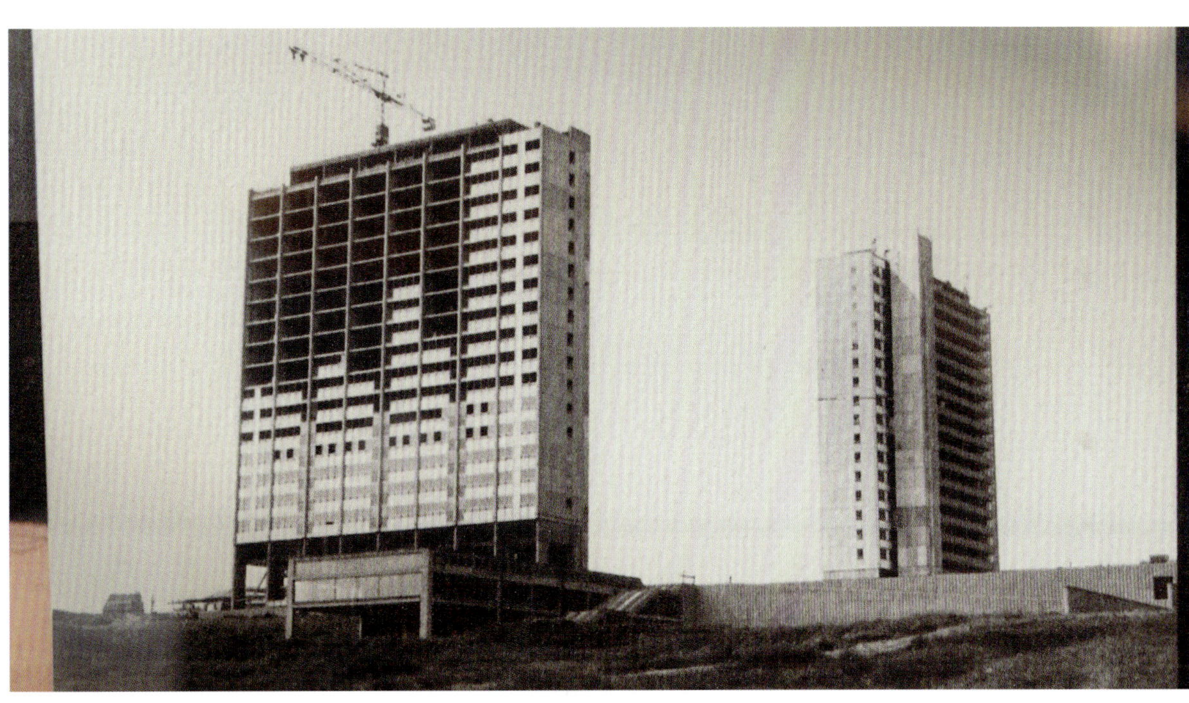

16:56:23

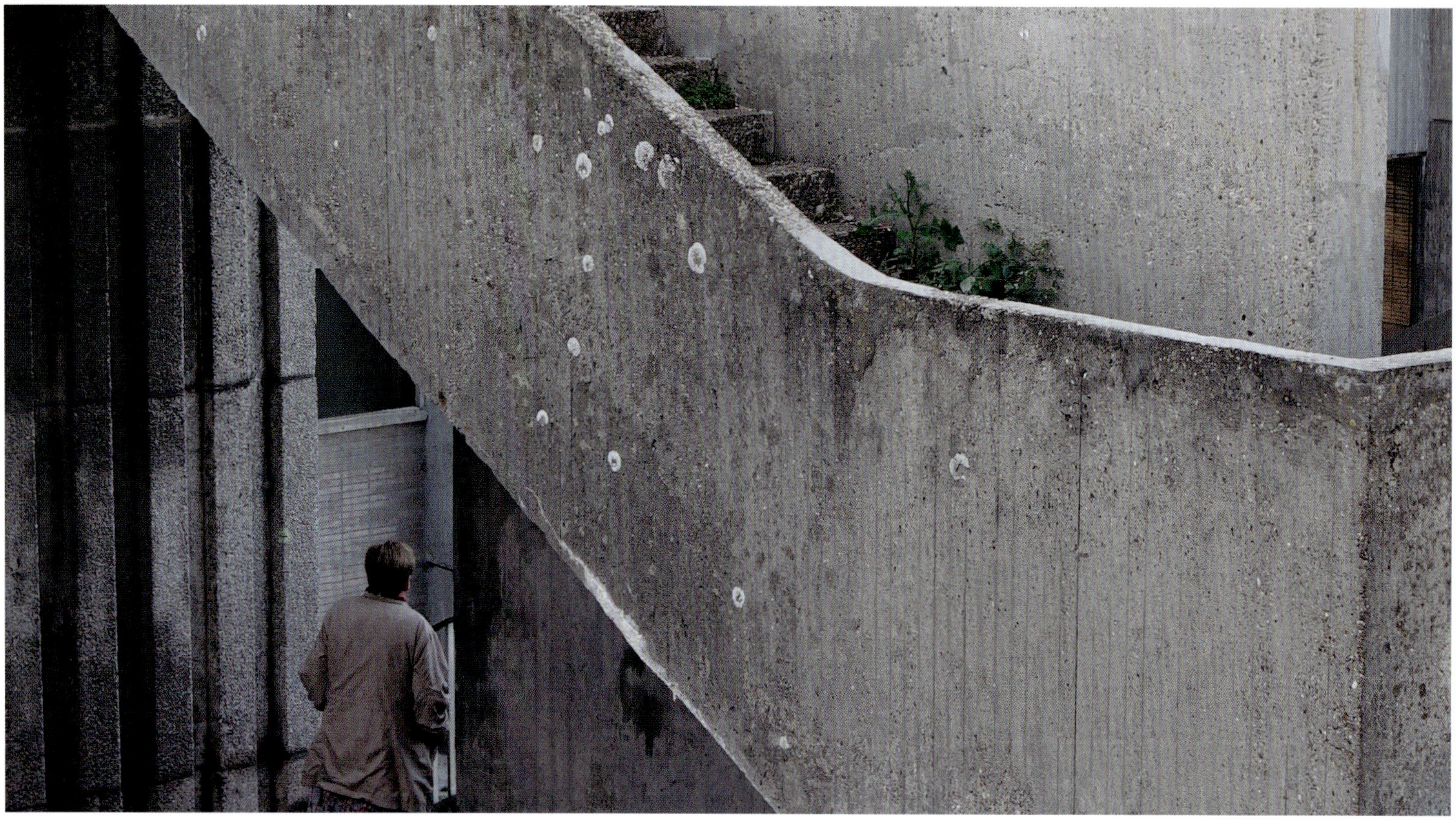

MALL
OF
EUROPE

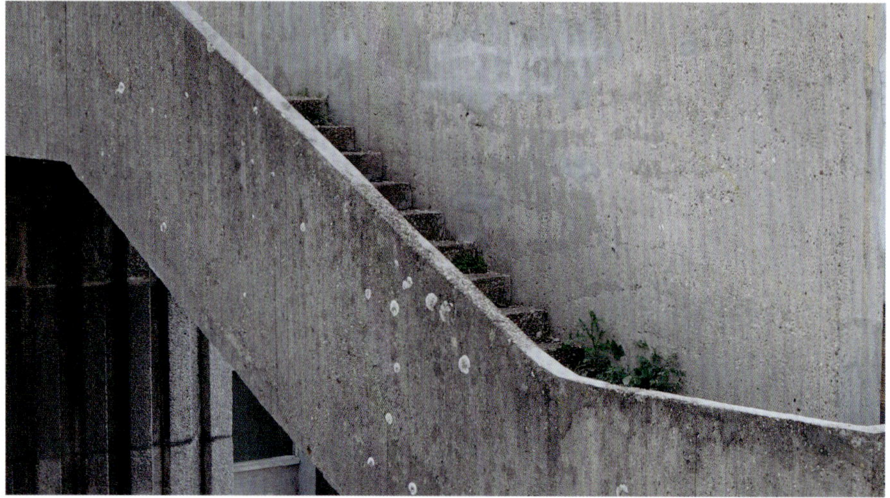

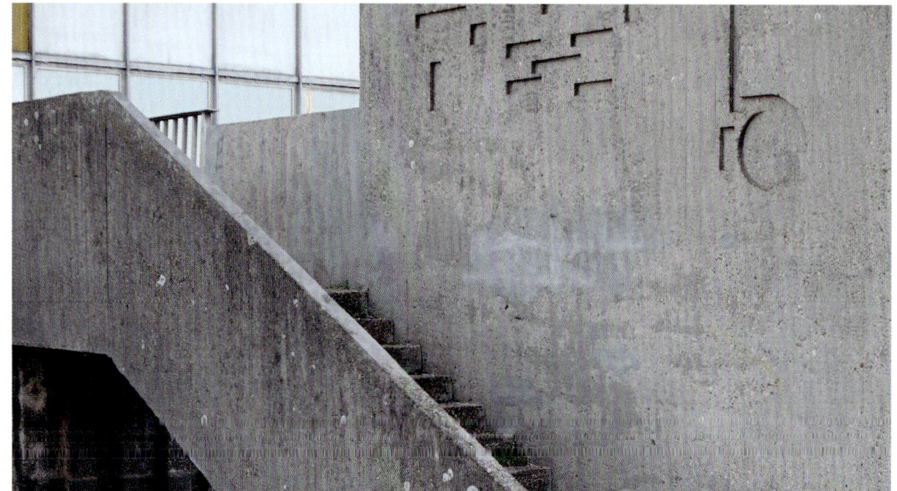

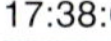
17:38:03

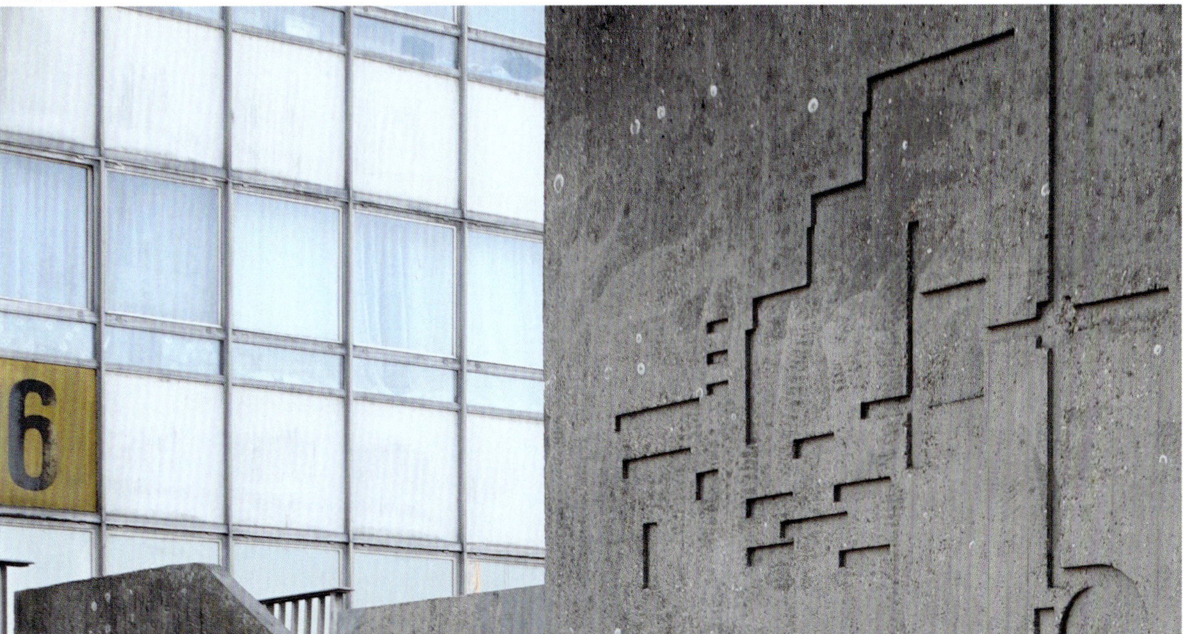

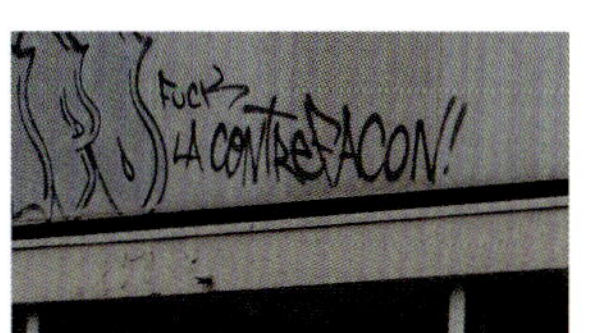

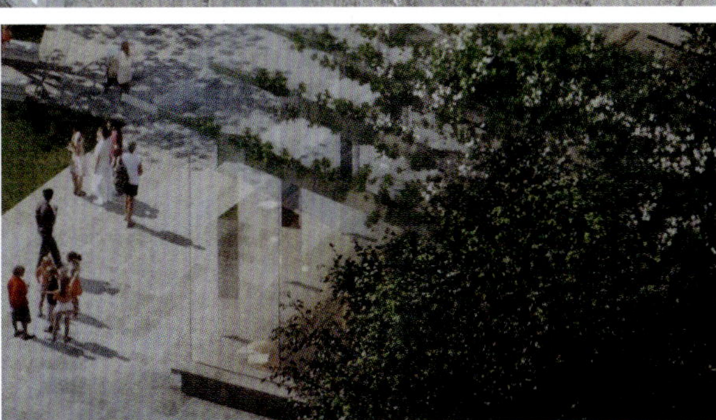

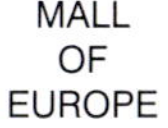
MALL
OF
EUROPE

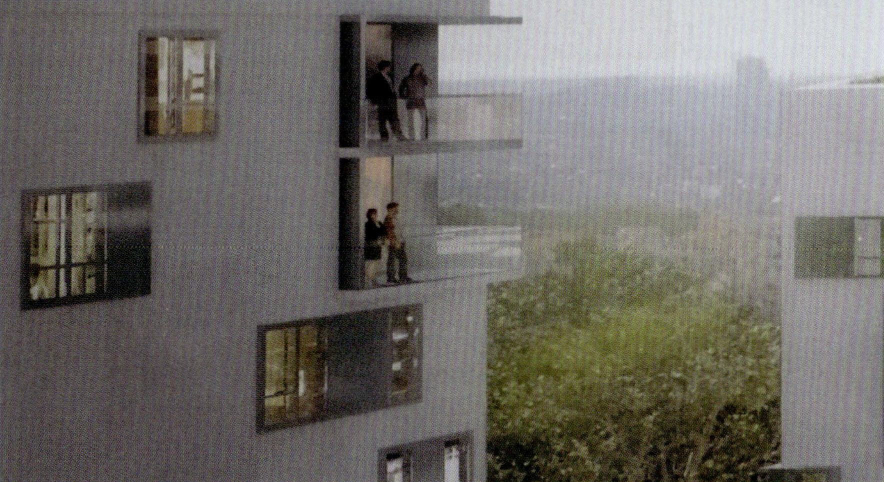

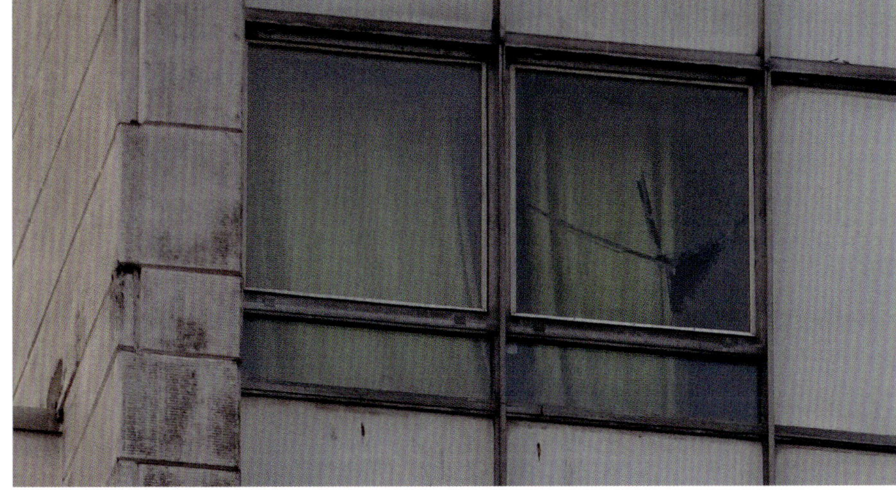

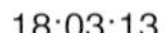
18:03:13

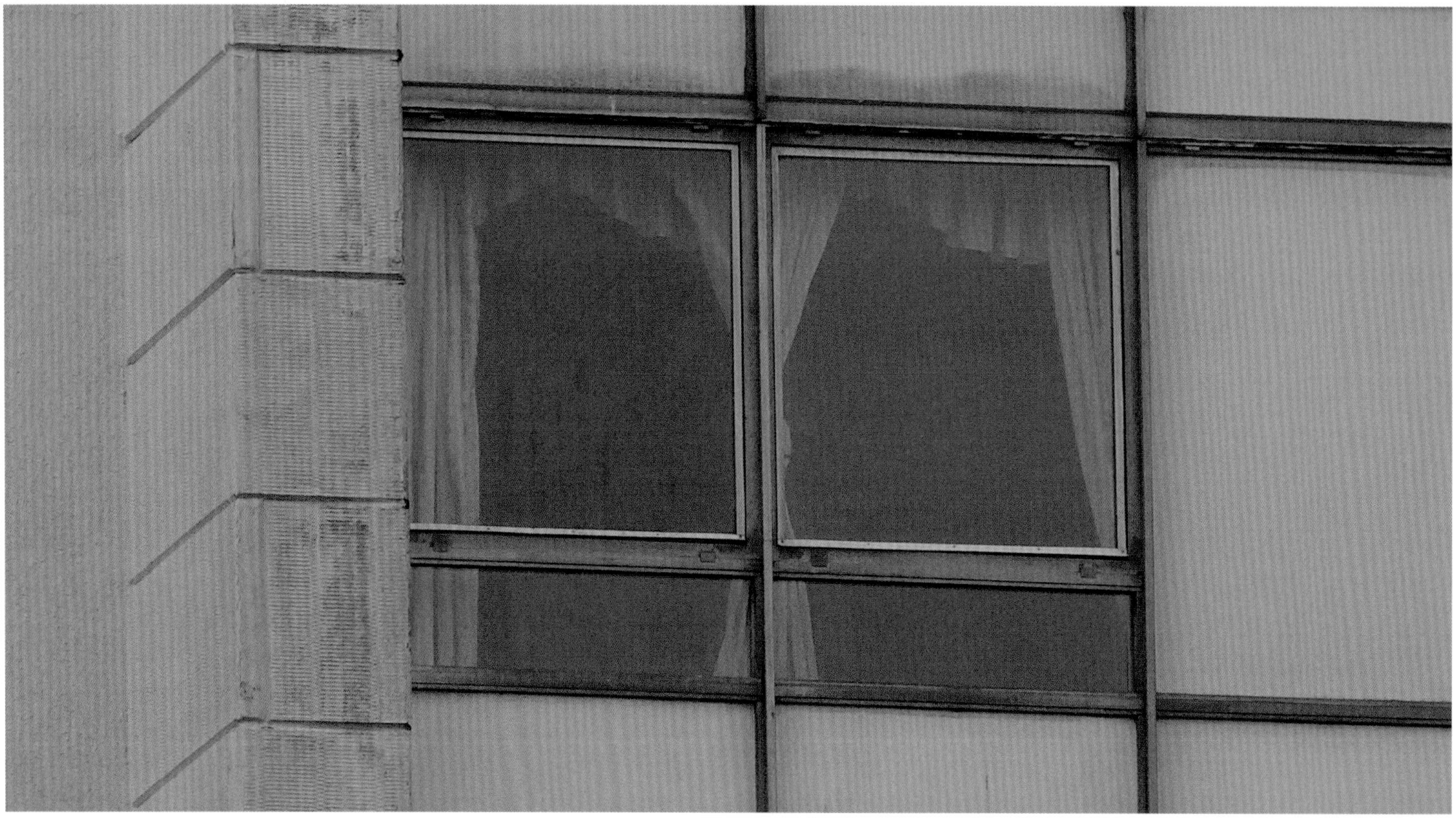

MALL
OF
EUROPE

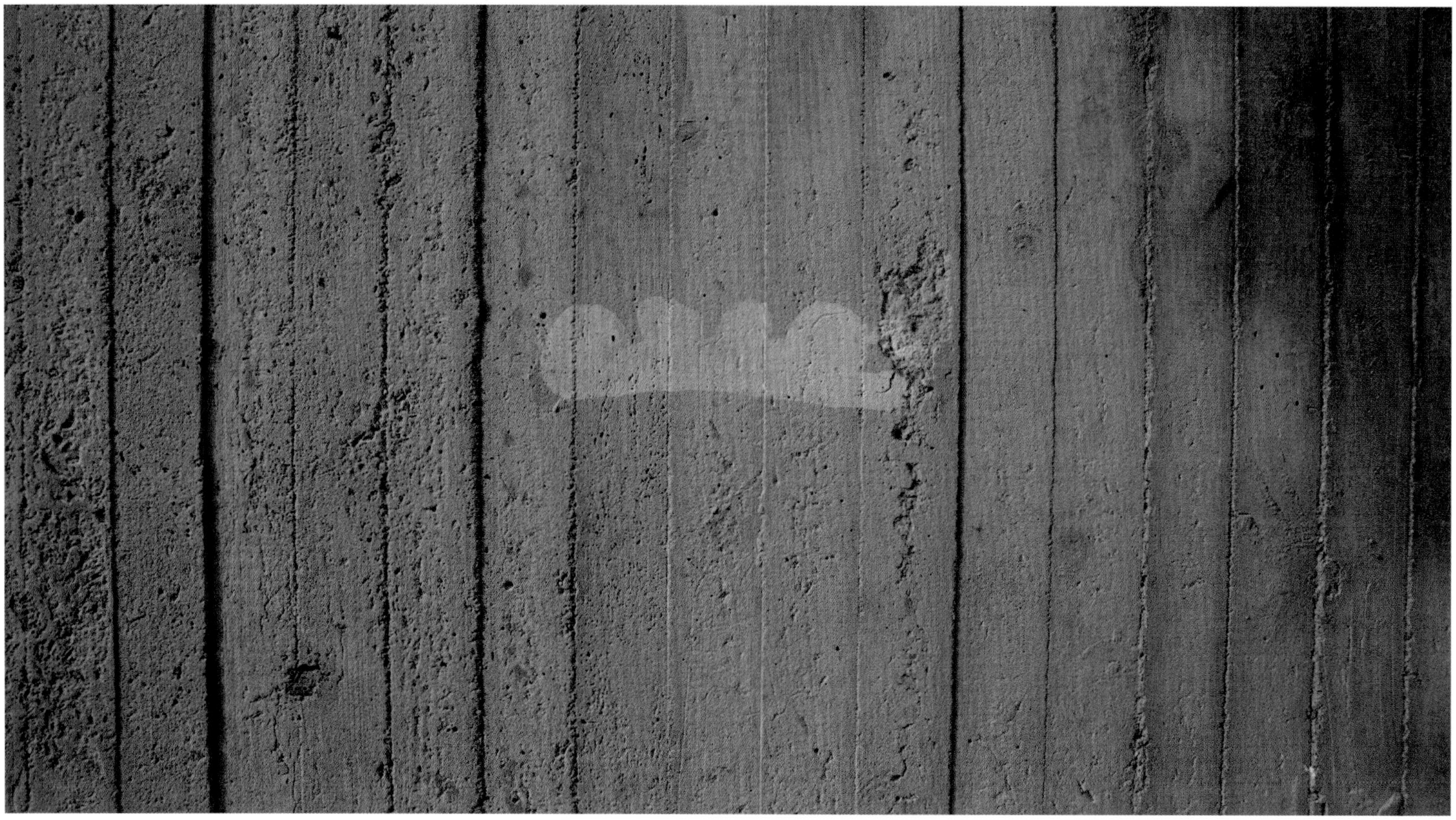

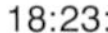
18:23:13

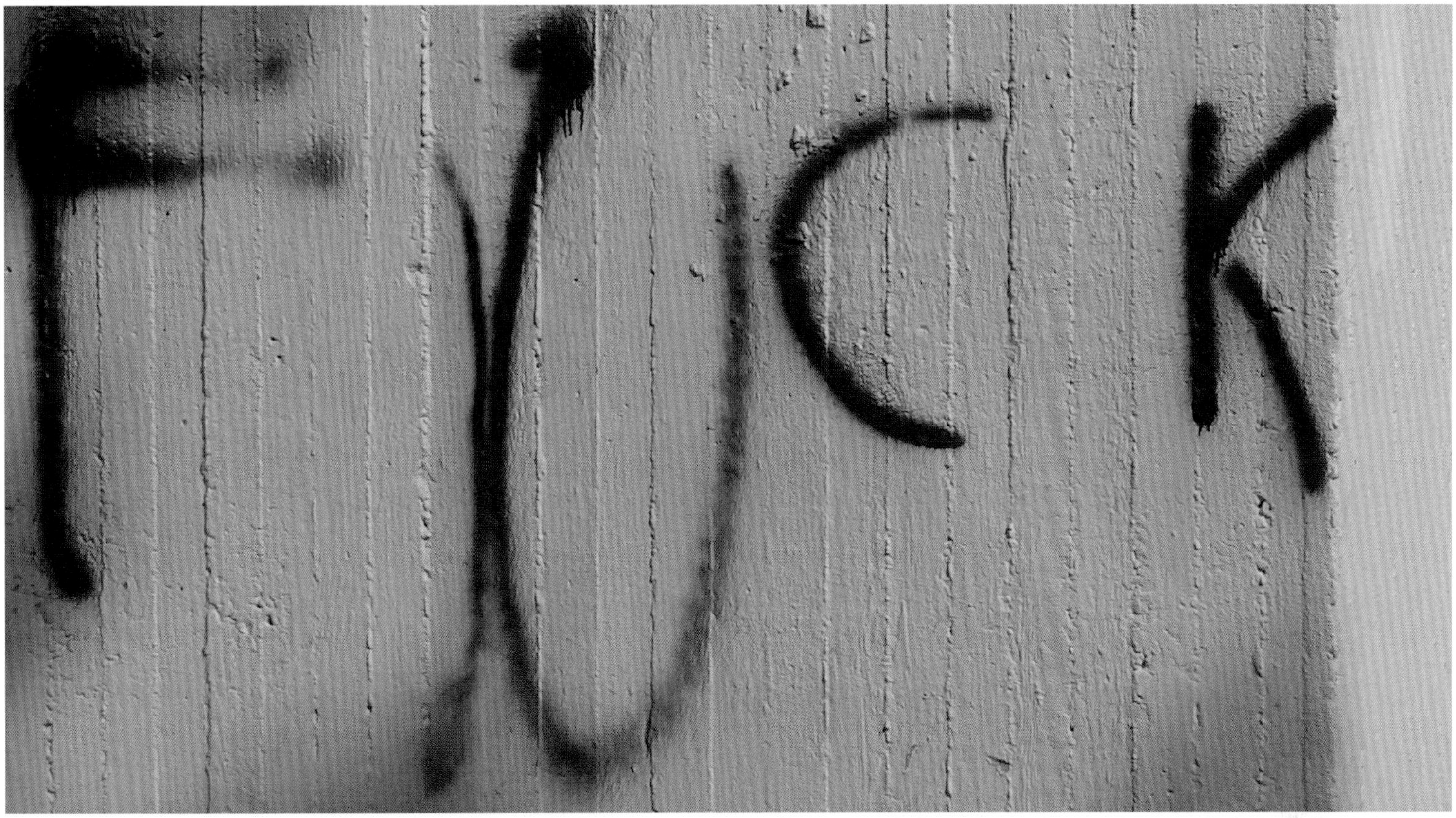

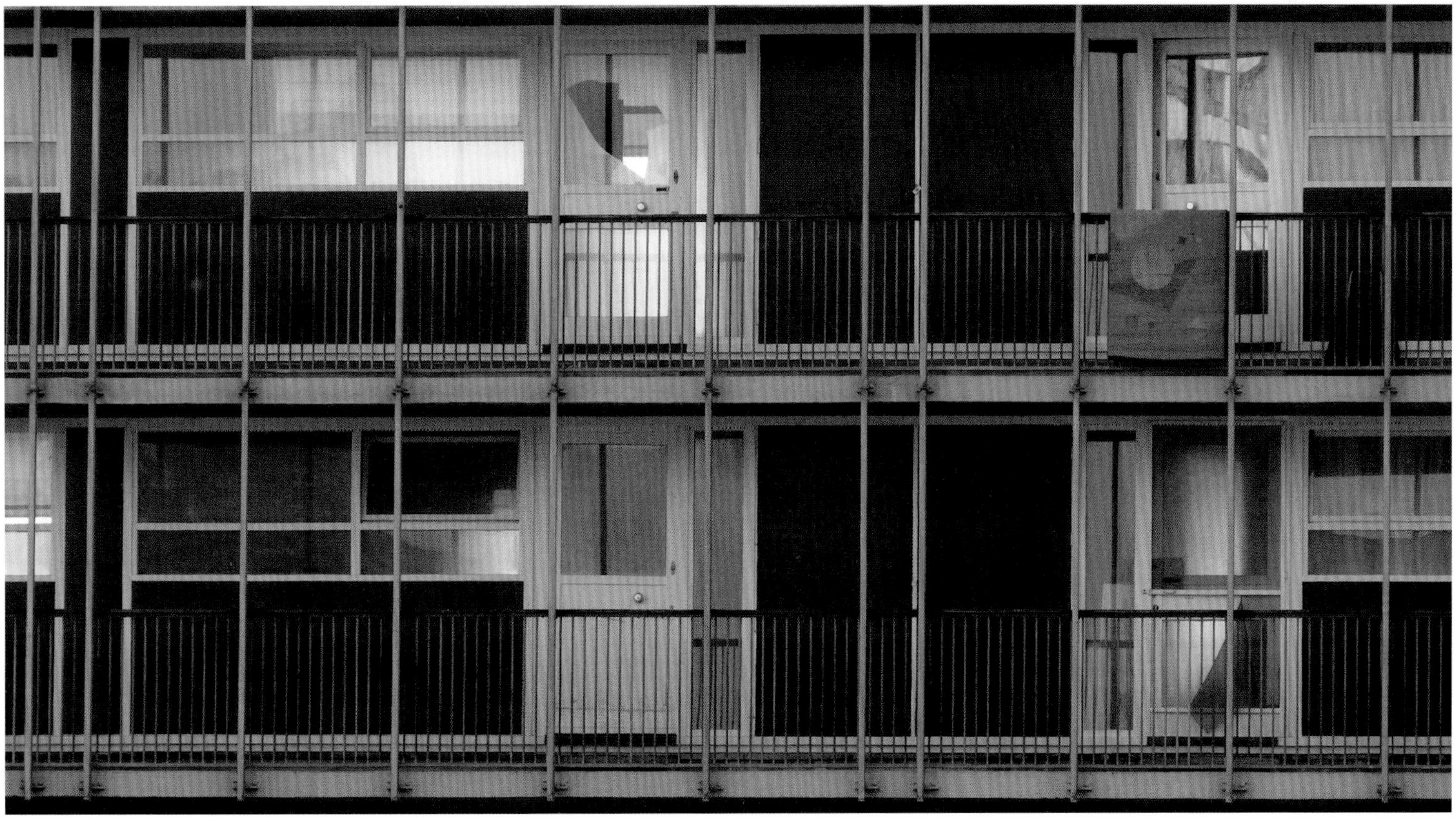

18:38:12

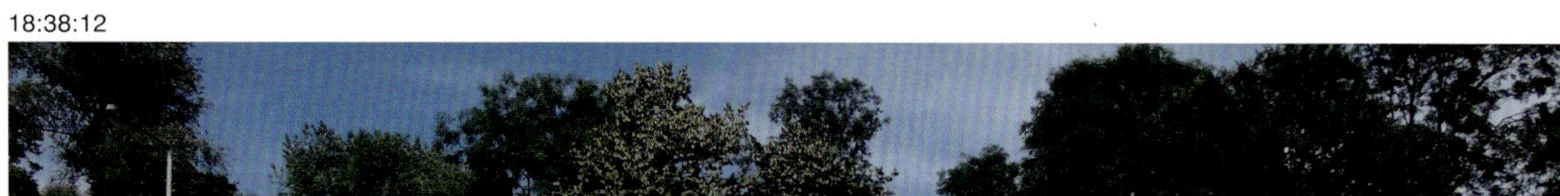

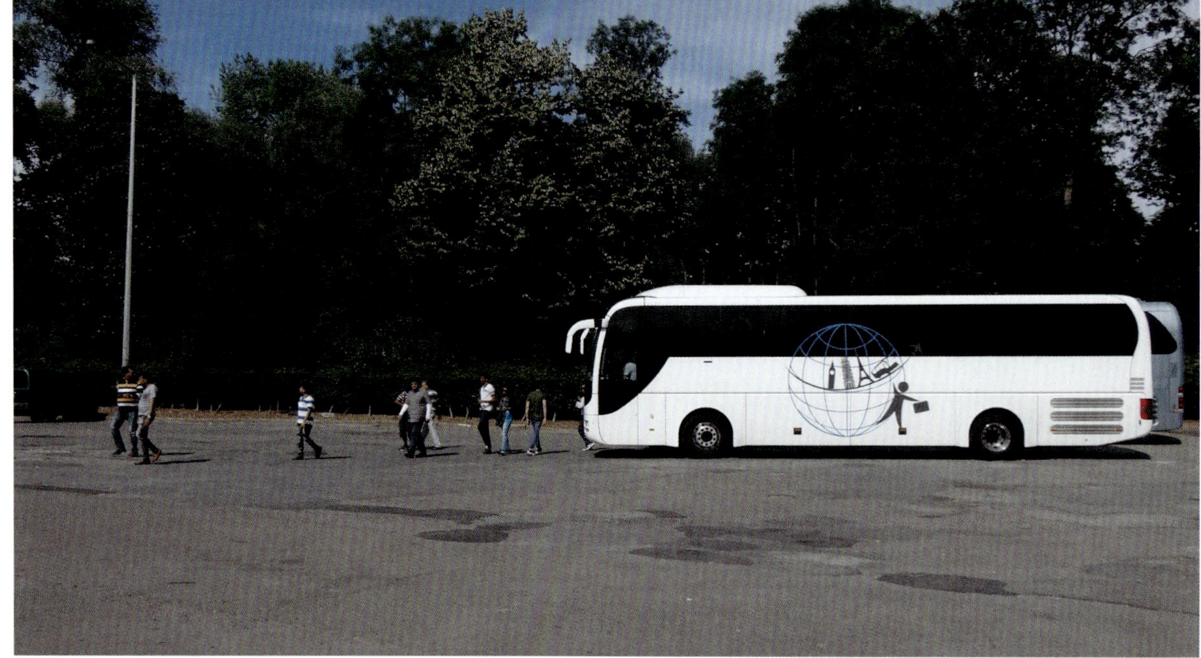

MALL
OF
EUROPE

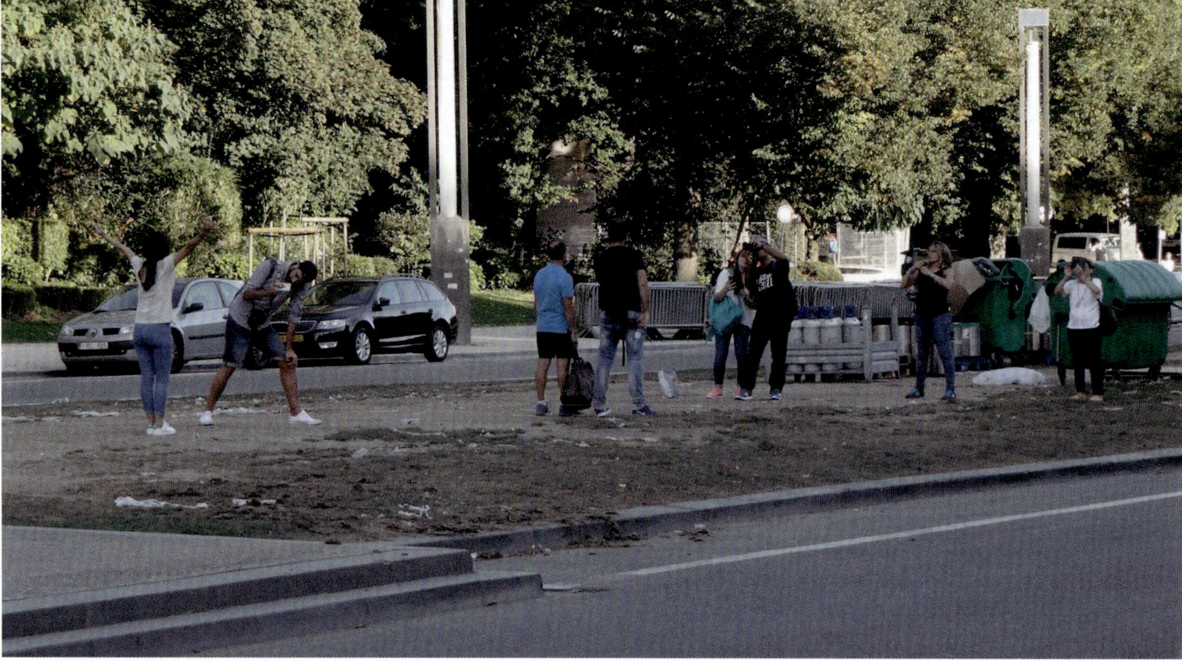

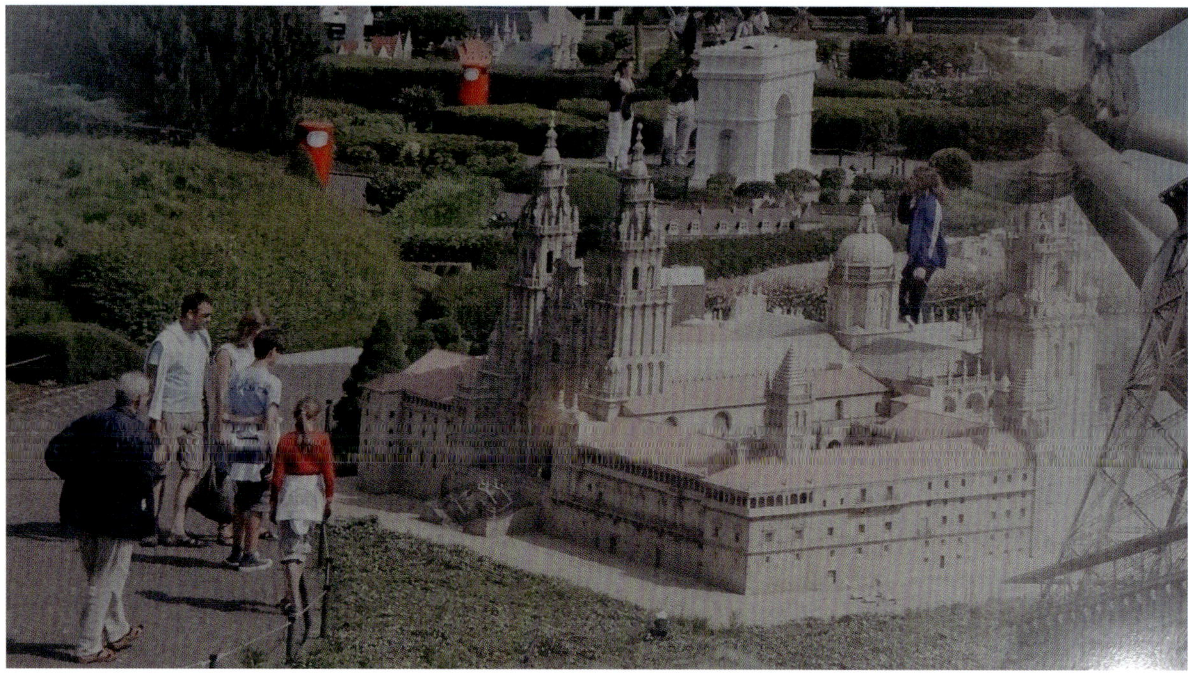

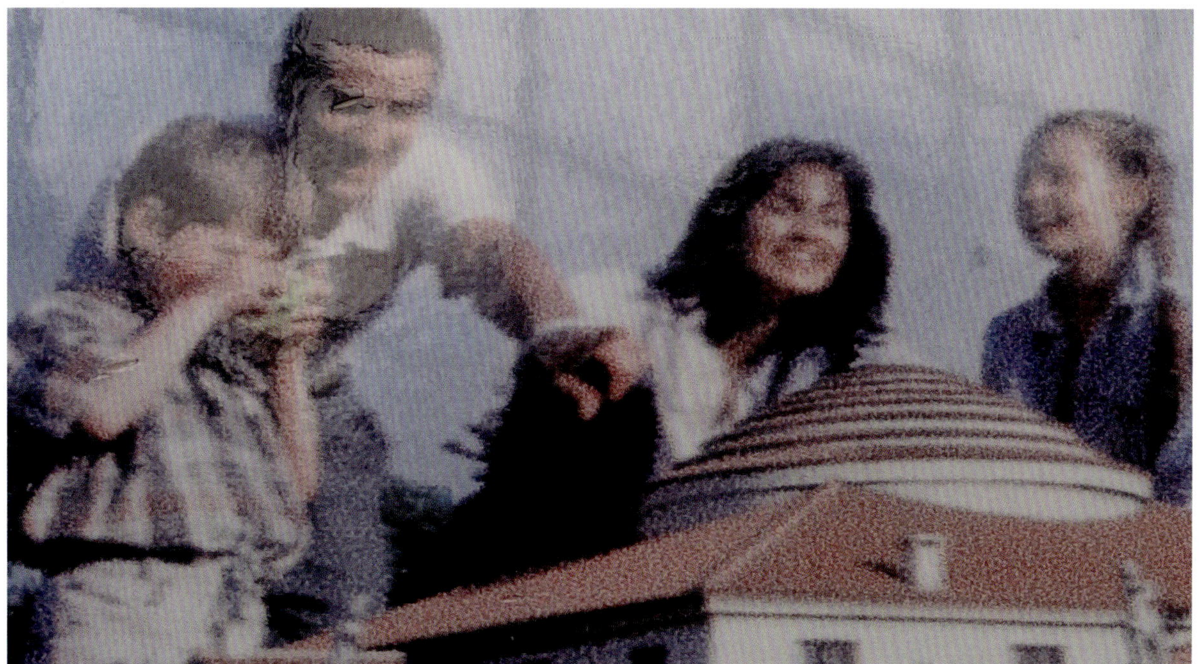

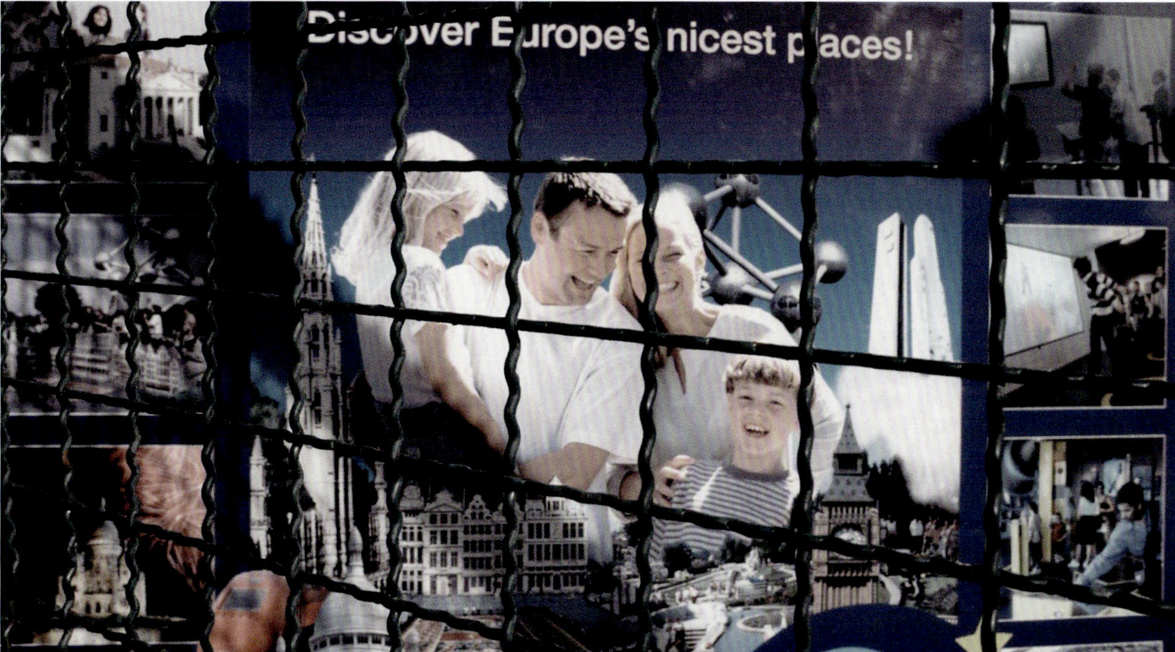

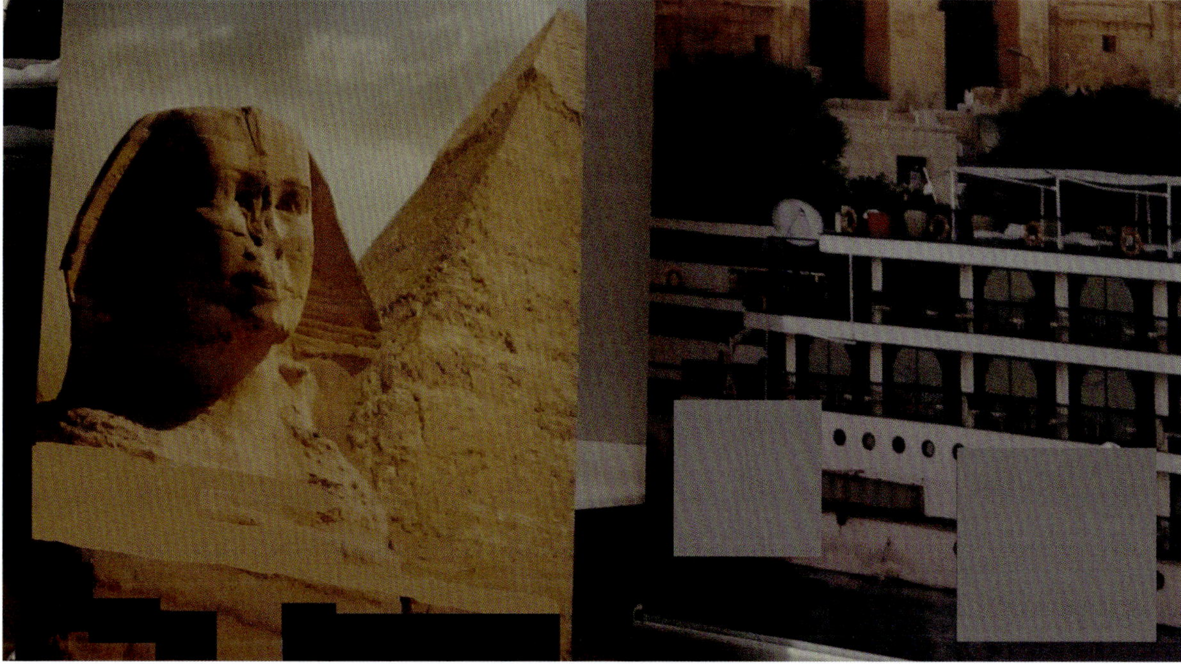

MALL OF EUROPE

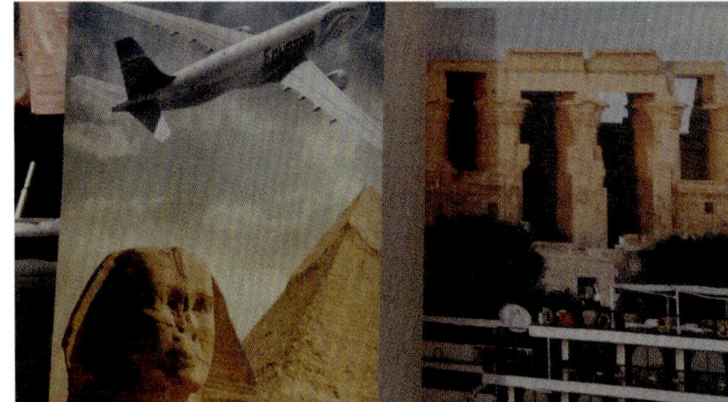

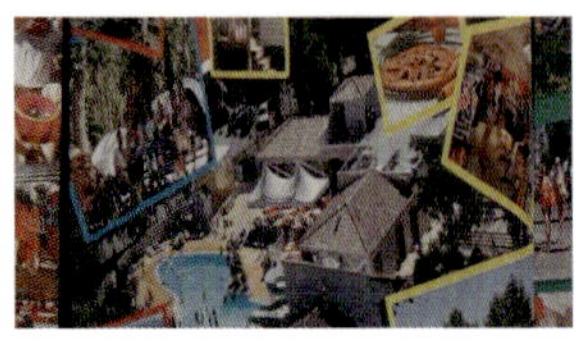

MALL
OF
EUROPE

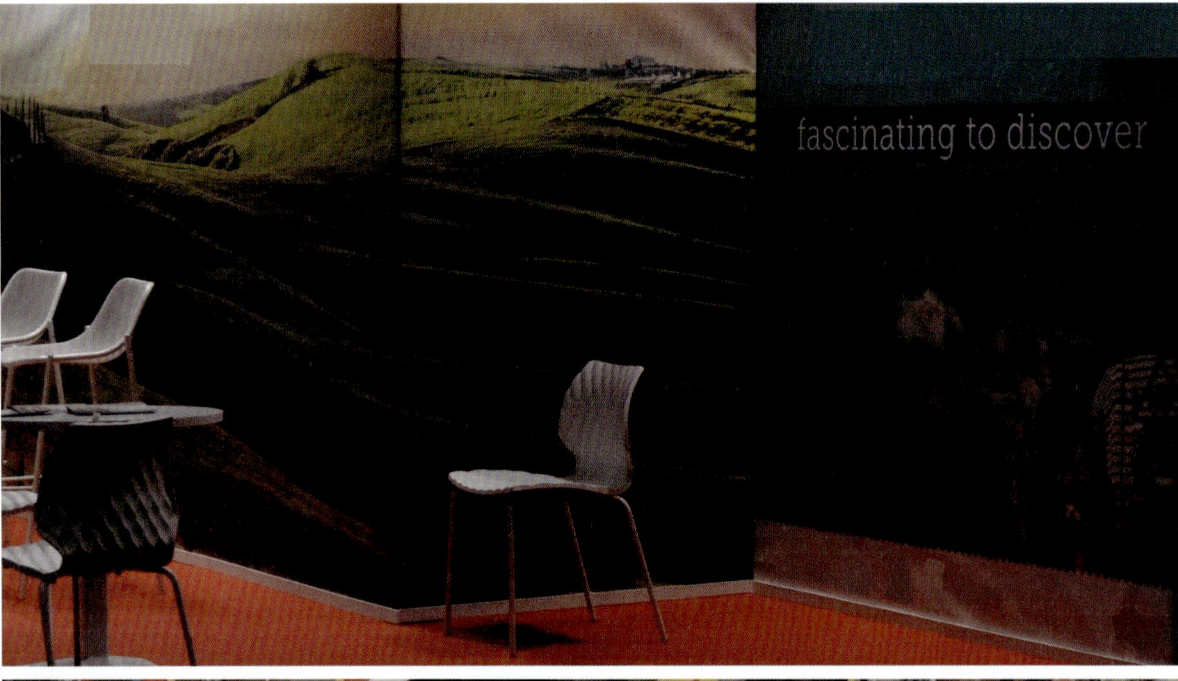

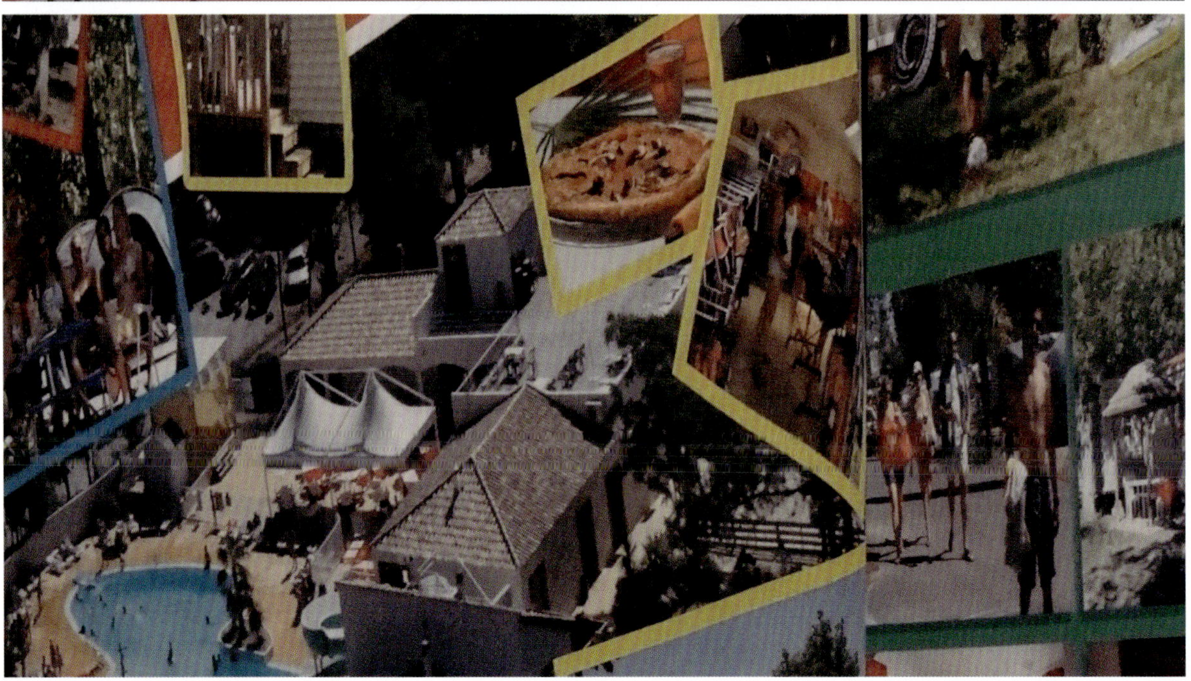

20:48:22

The Experience

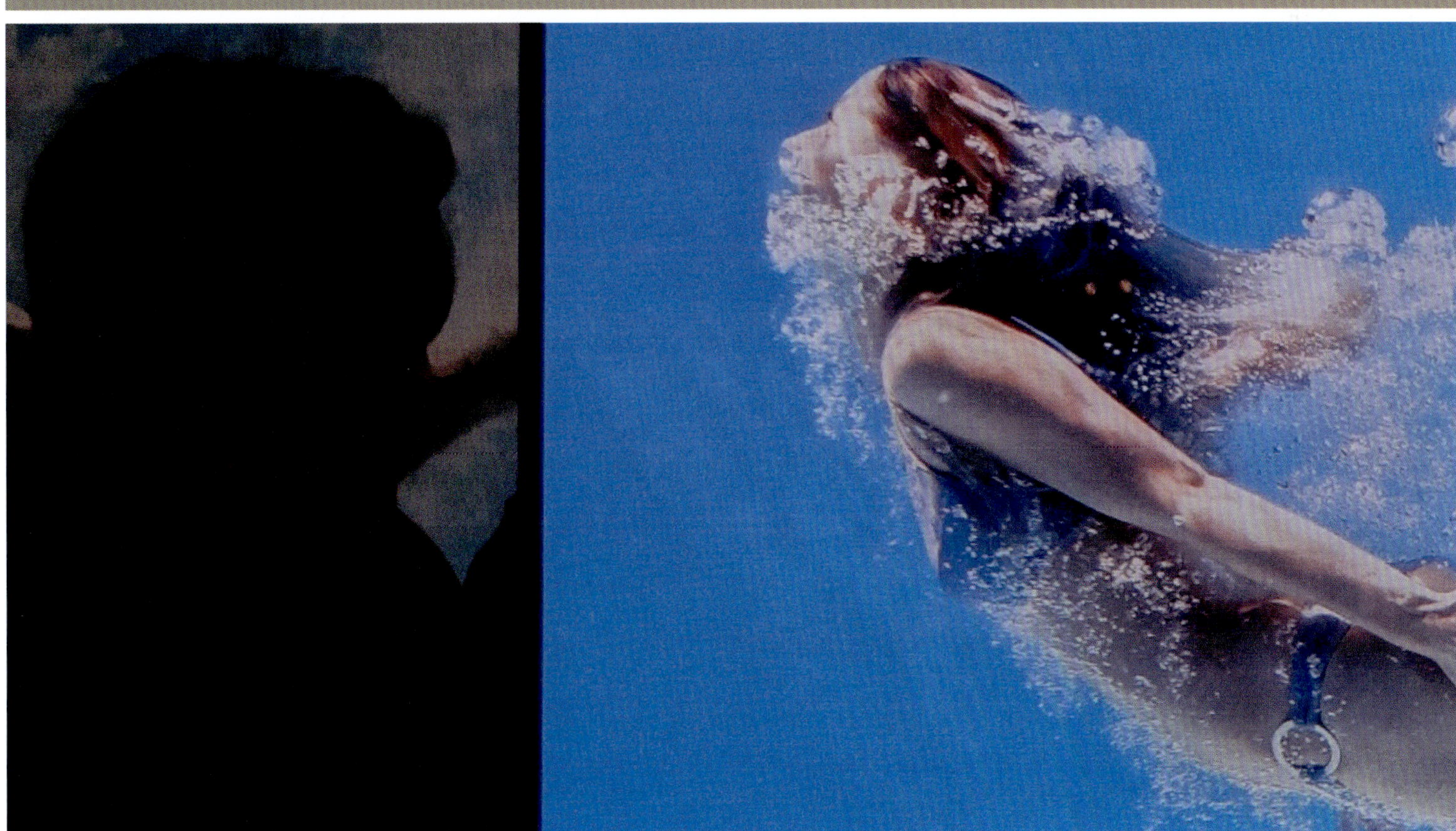

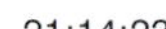

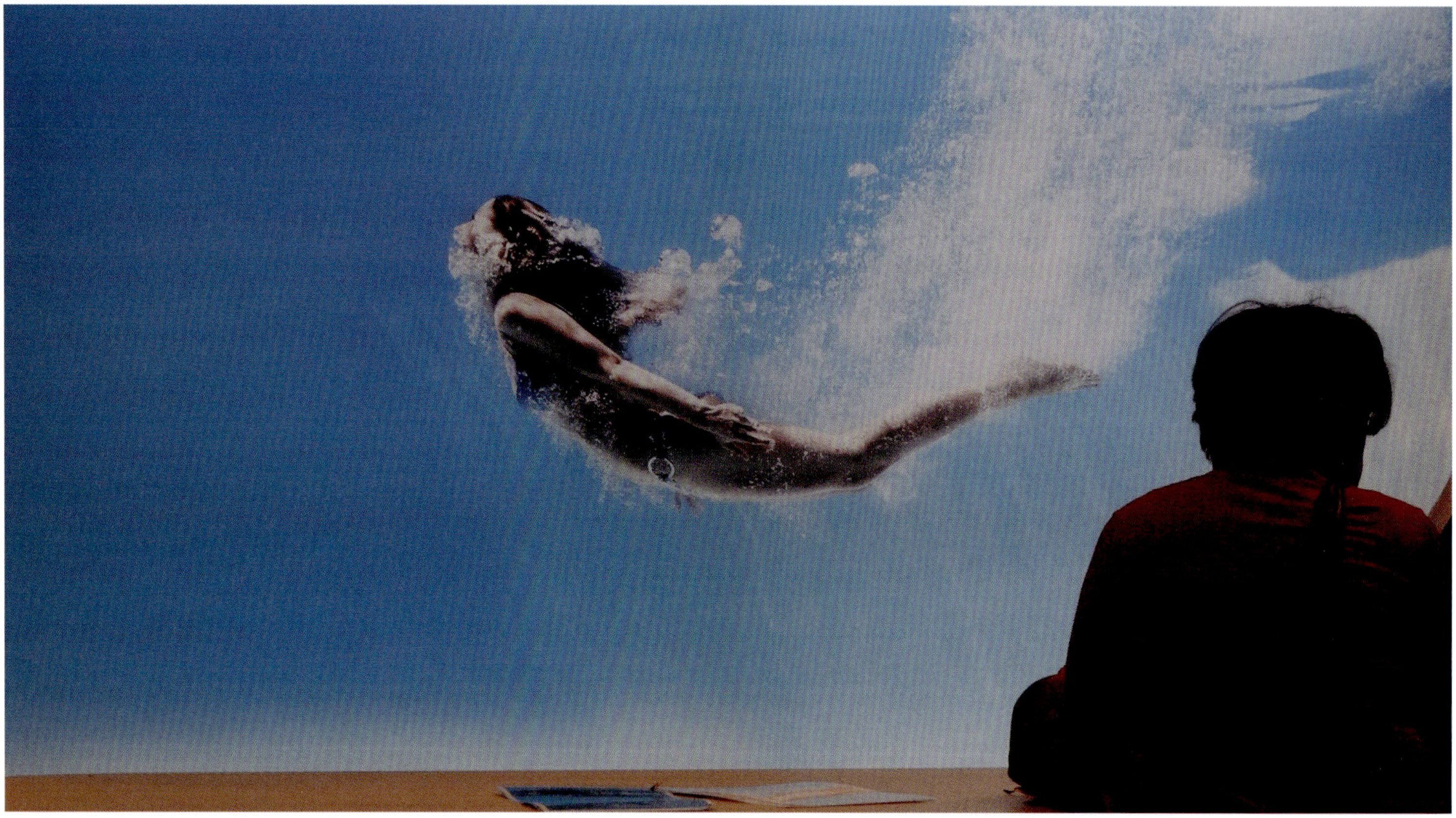

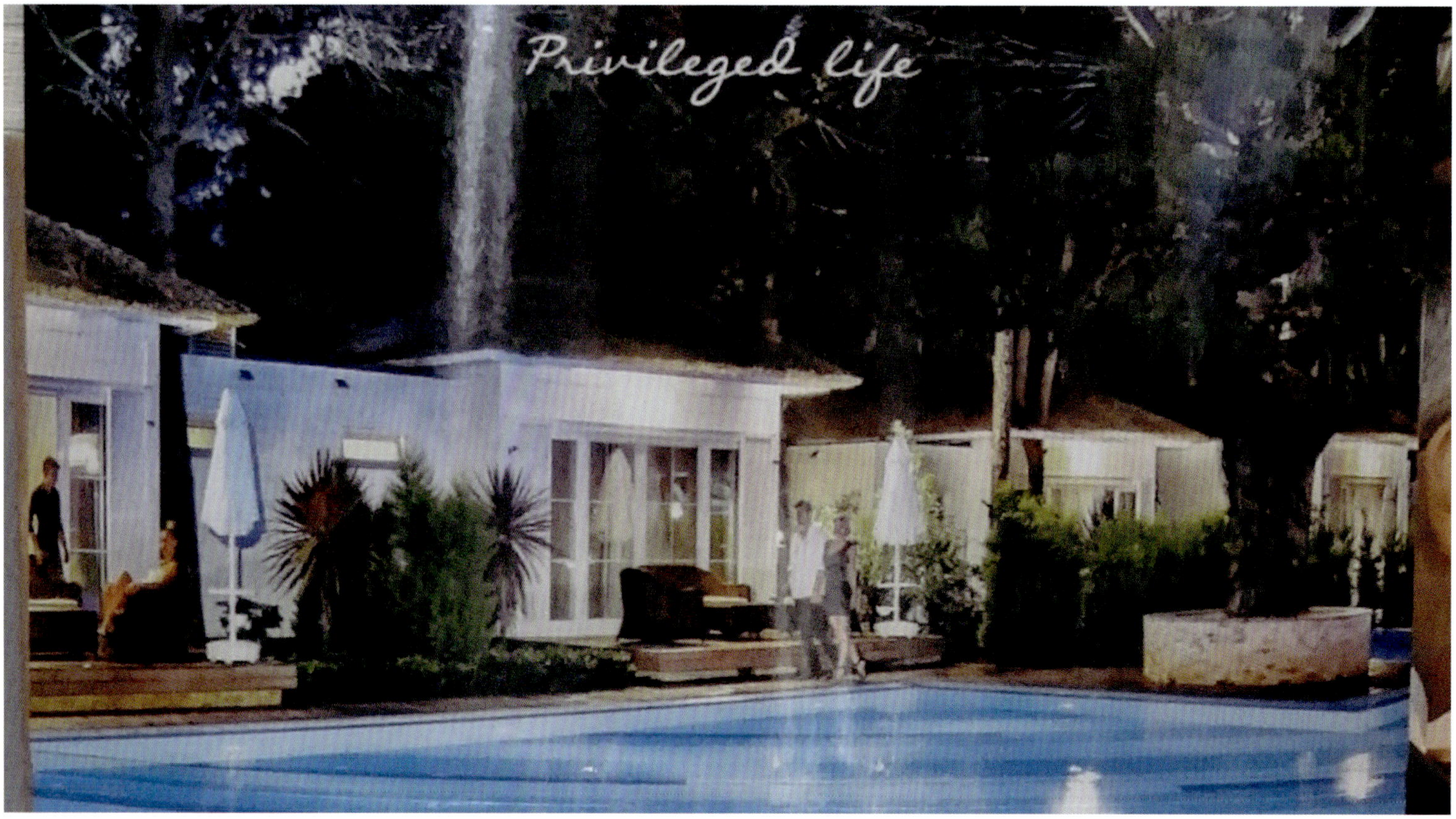

Privileged life

21:35:17

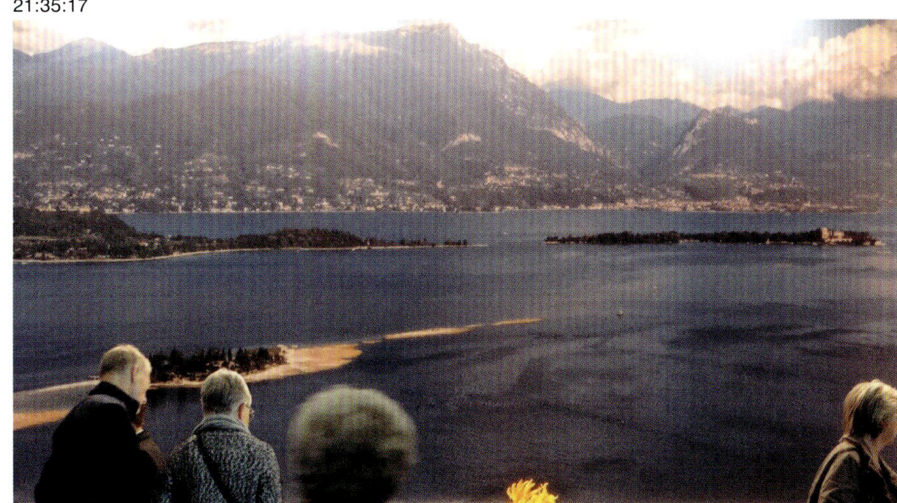

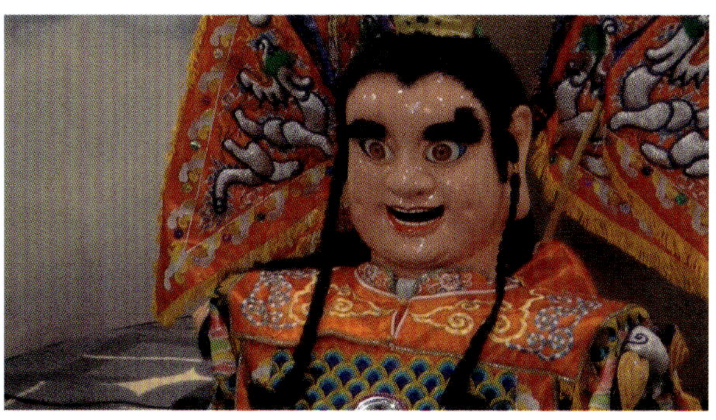

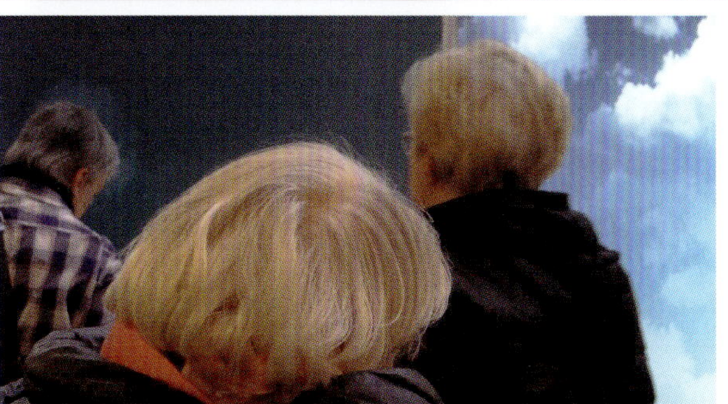

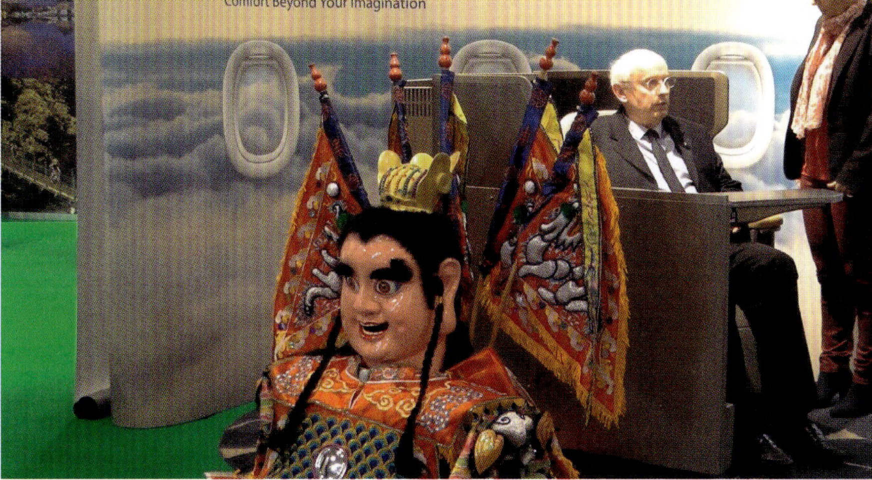

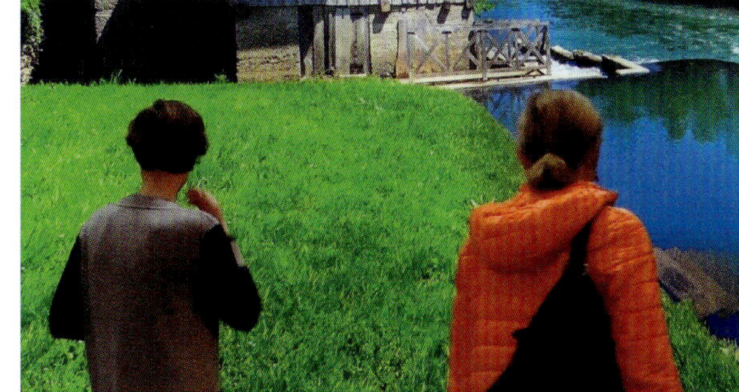

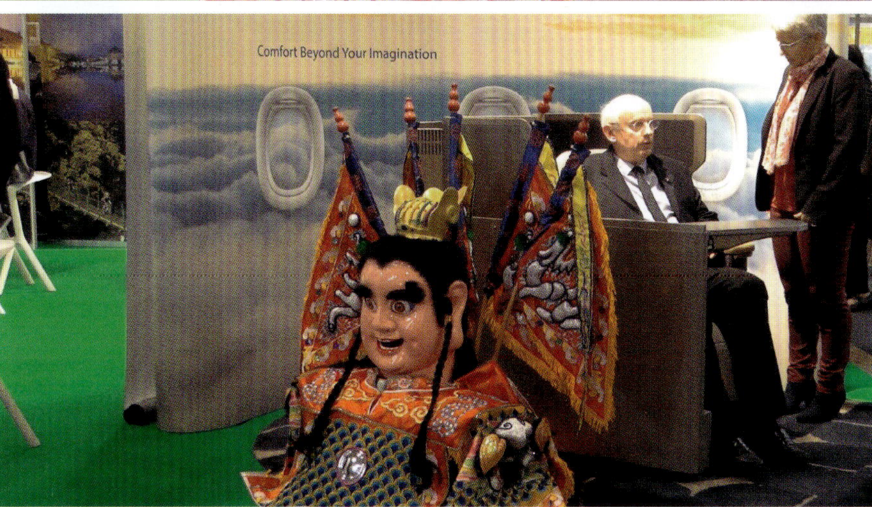

MALL
OF
EUROPE

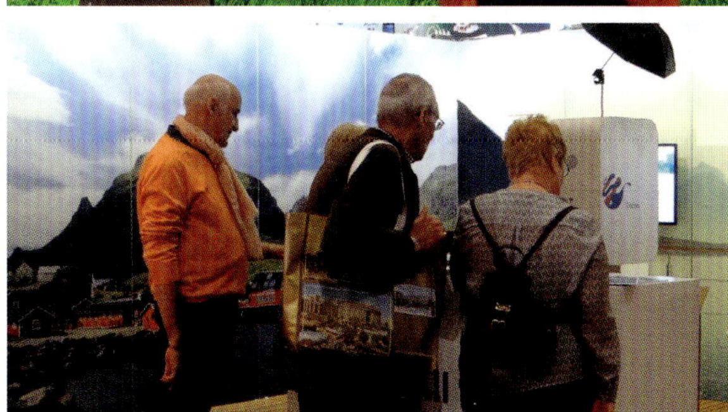

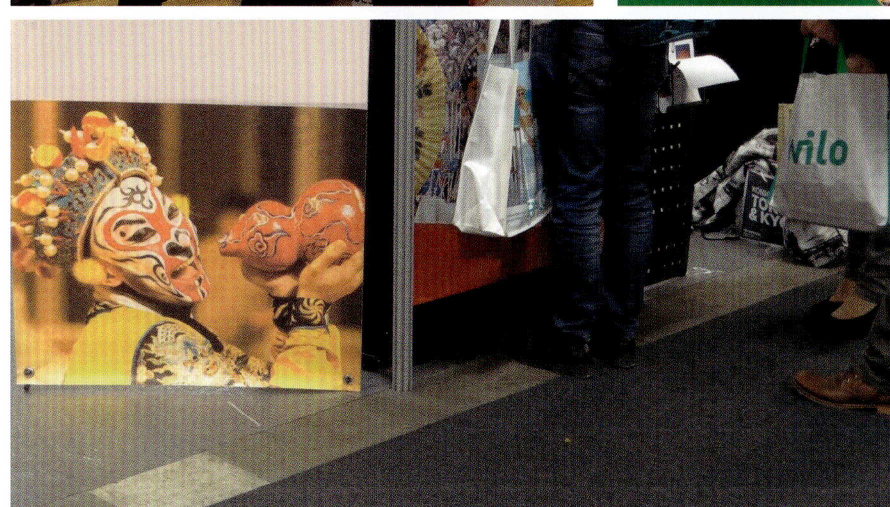

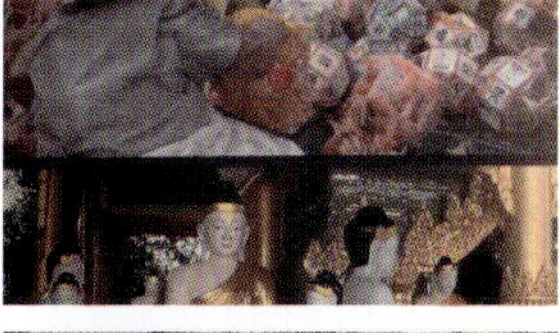

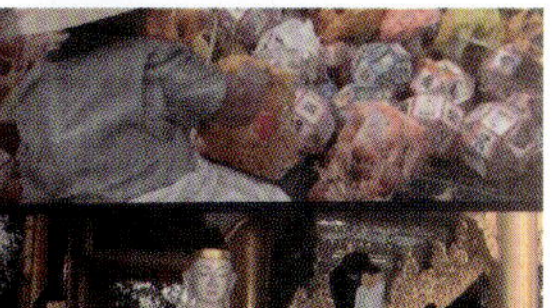

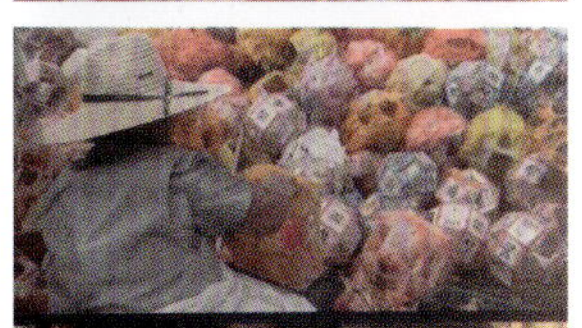

23:22:03

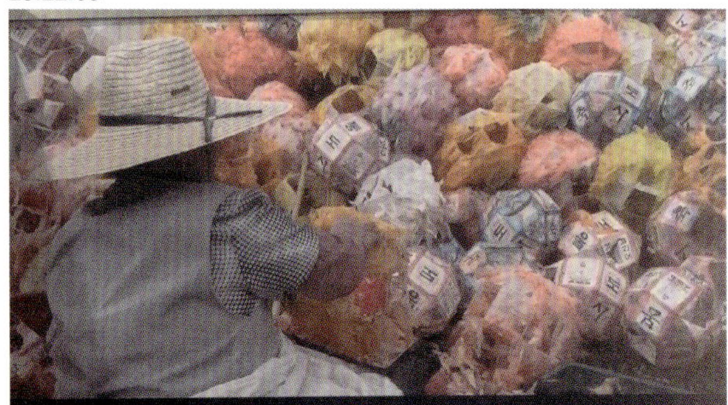

MALL
OF
EUROPE

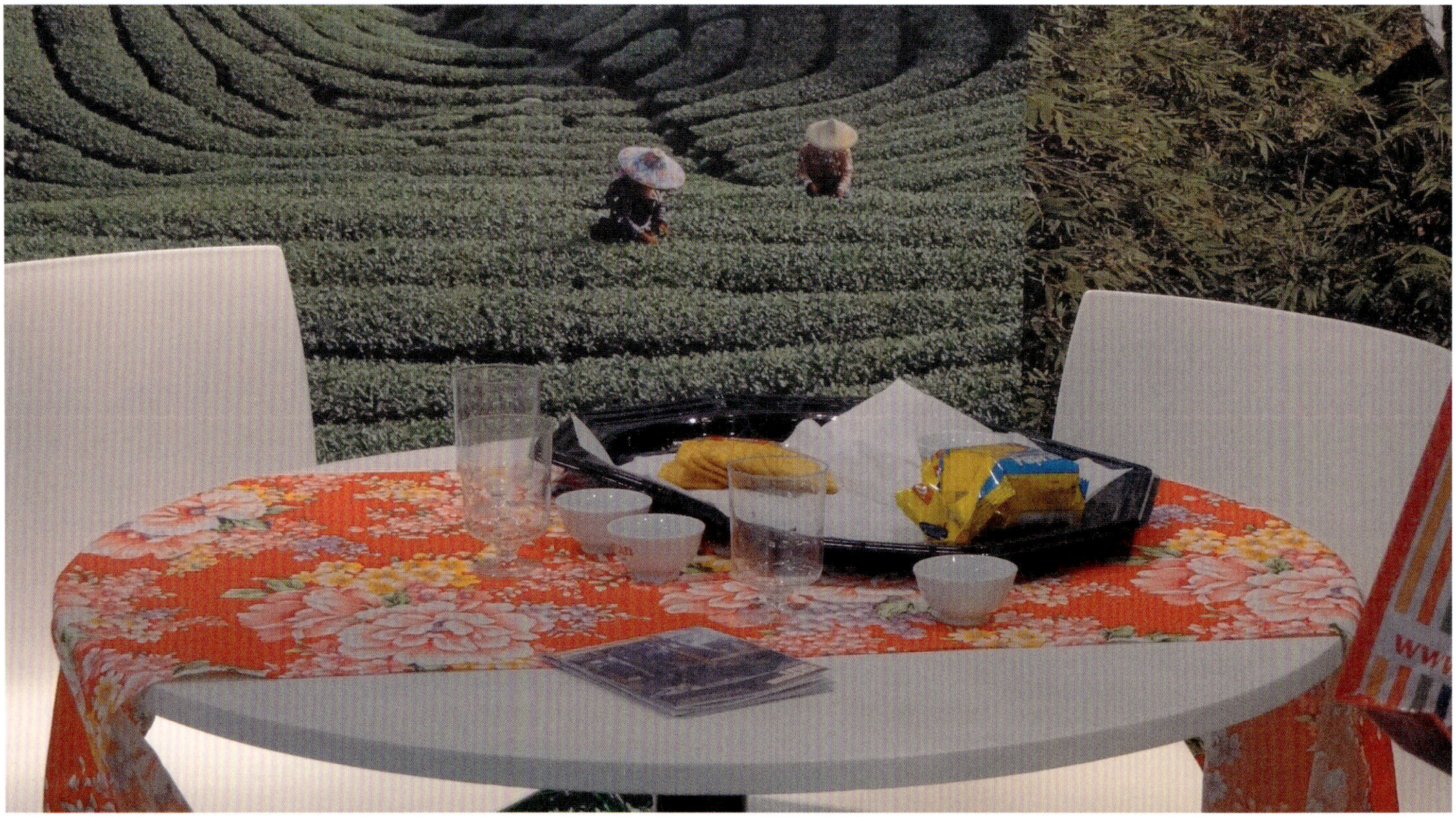

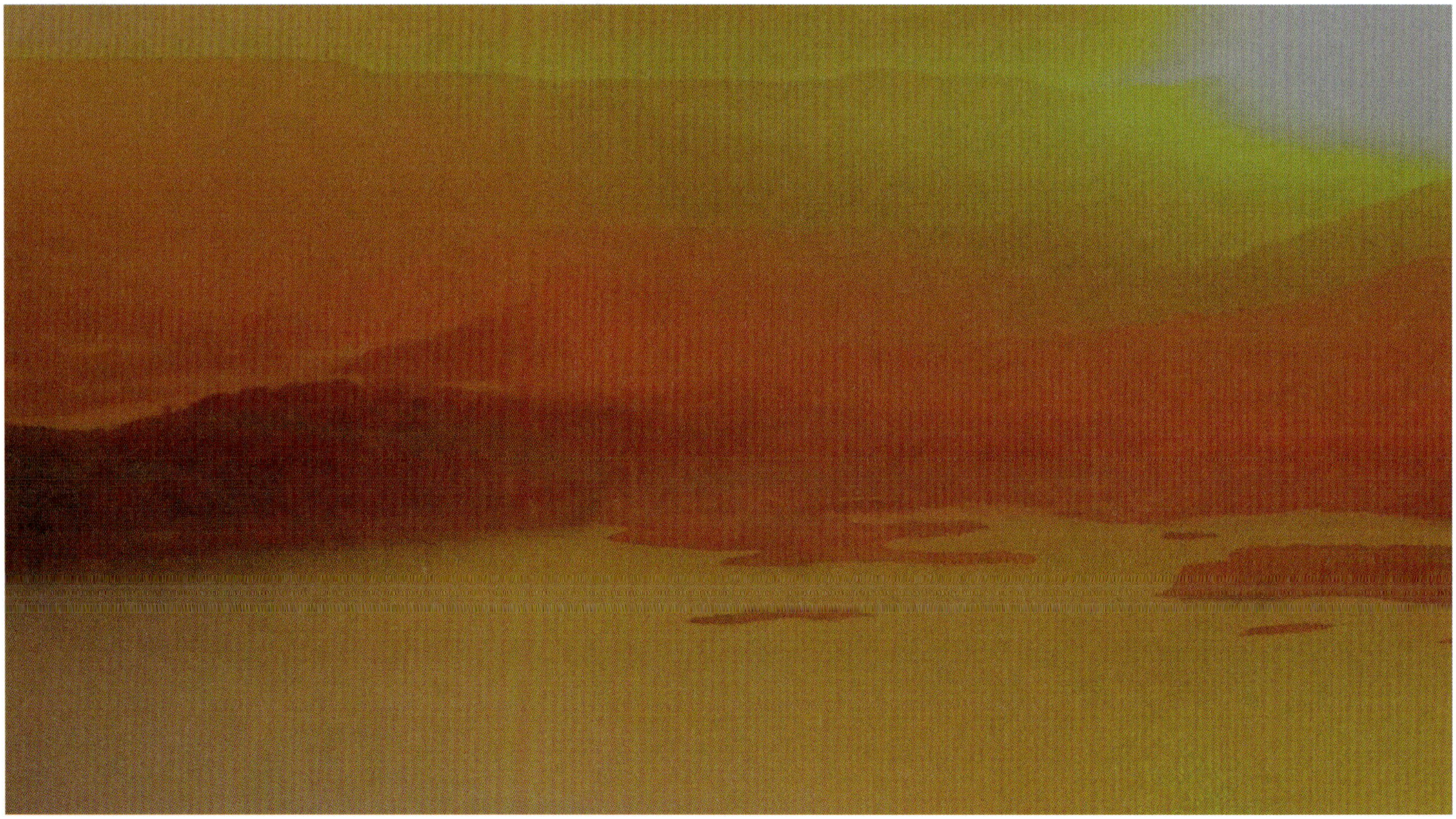

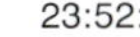

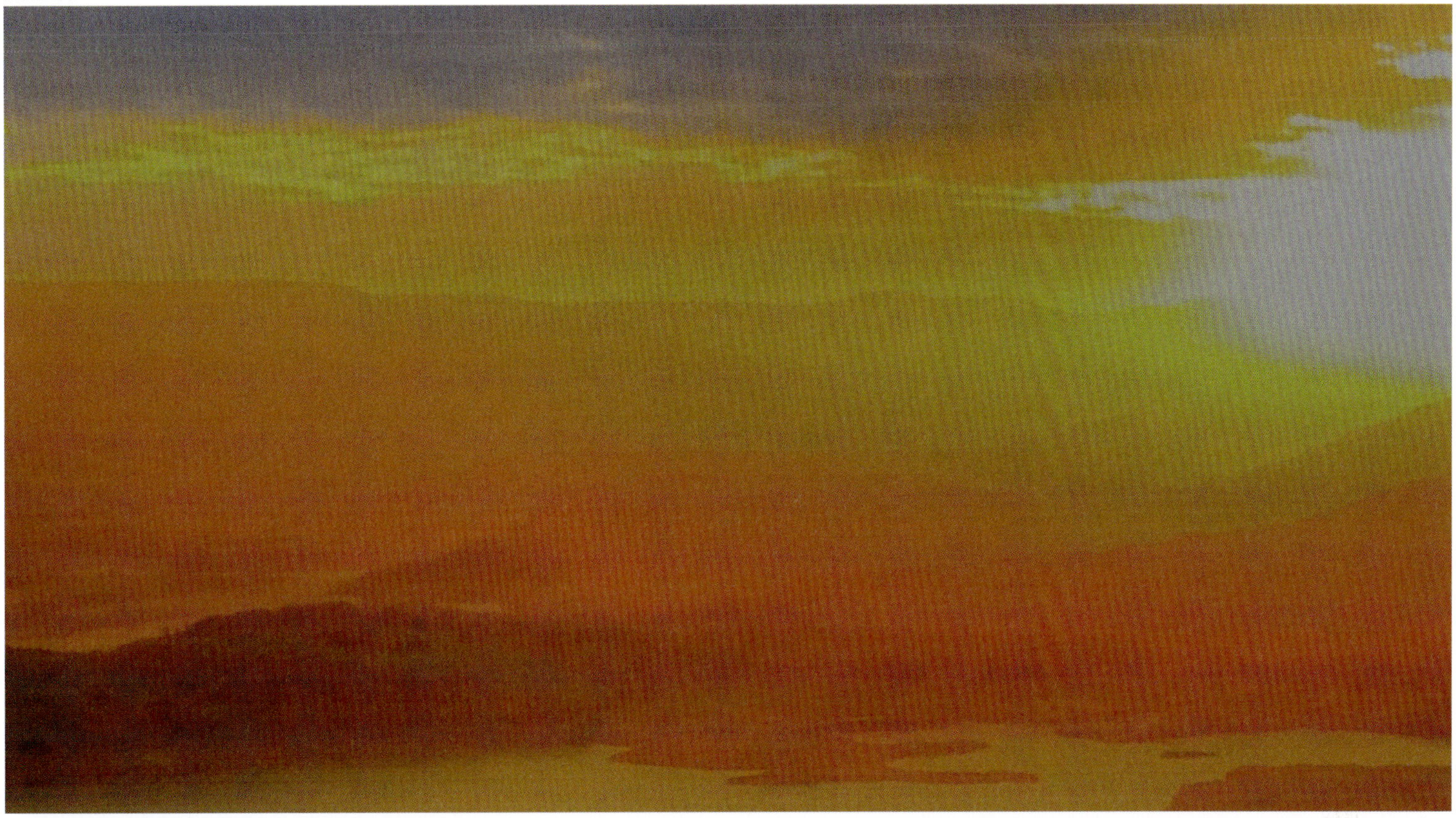

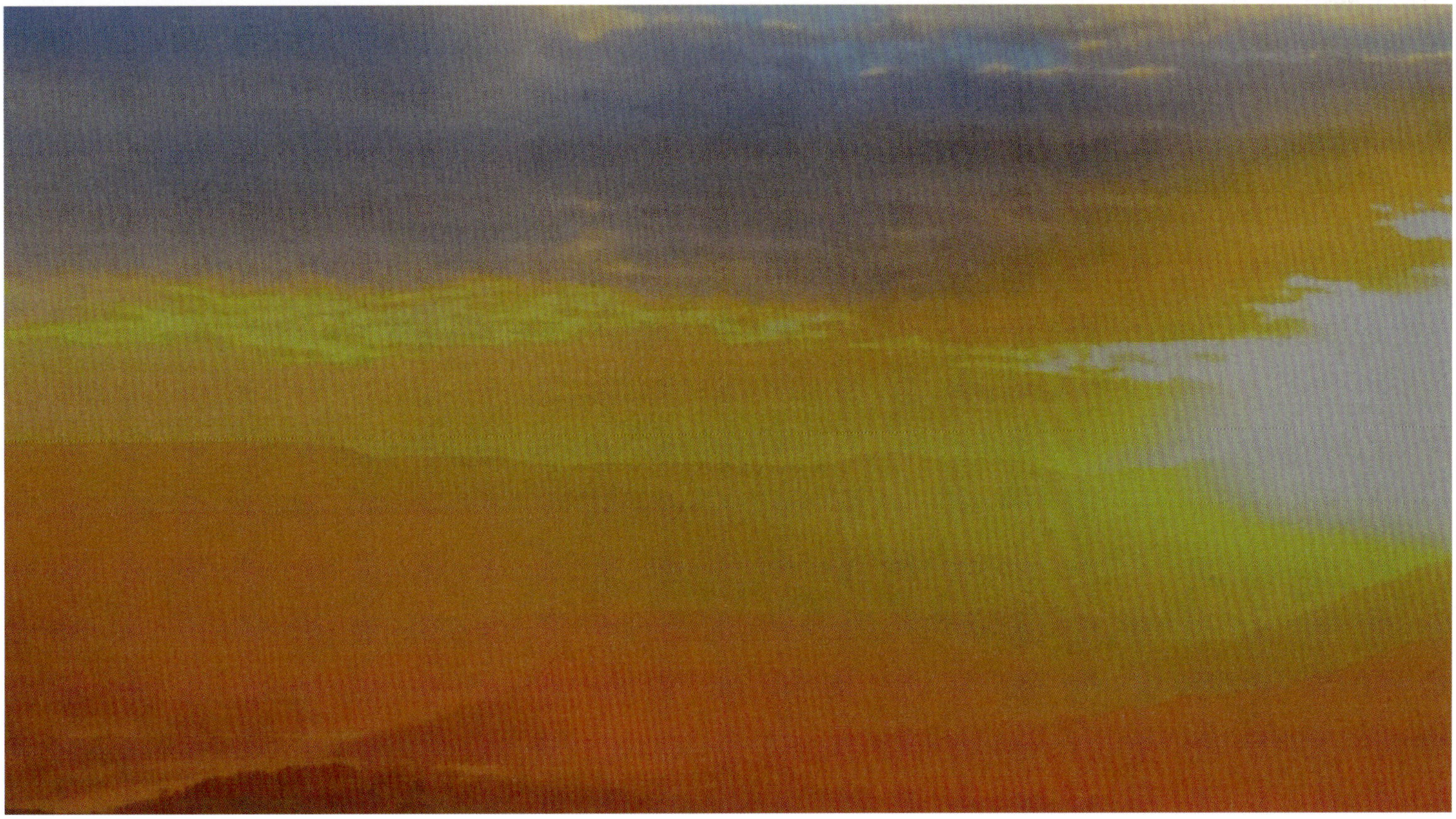

MALL
OF
EUROPE

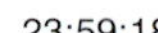
23:59:18

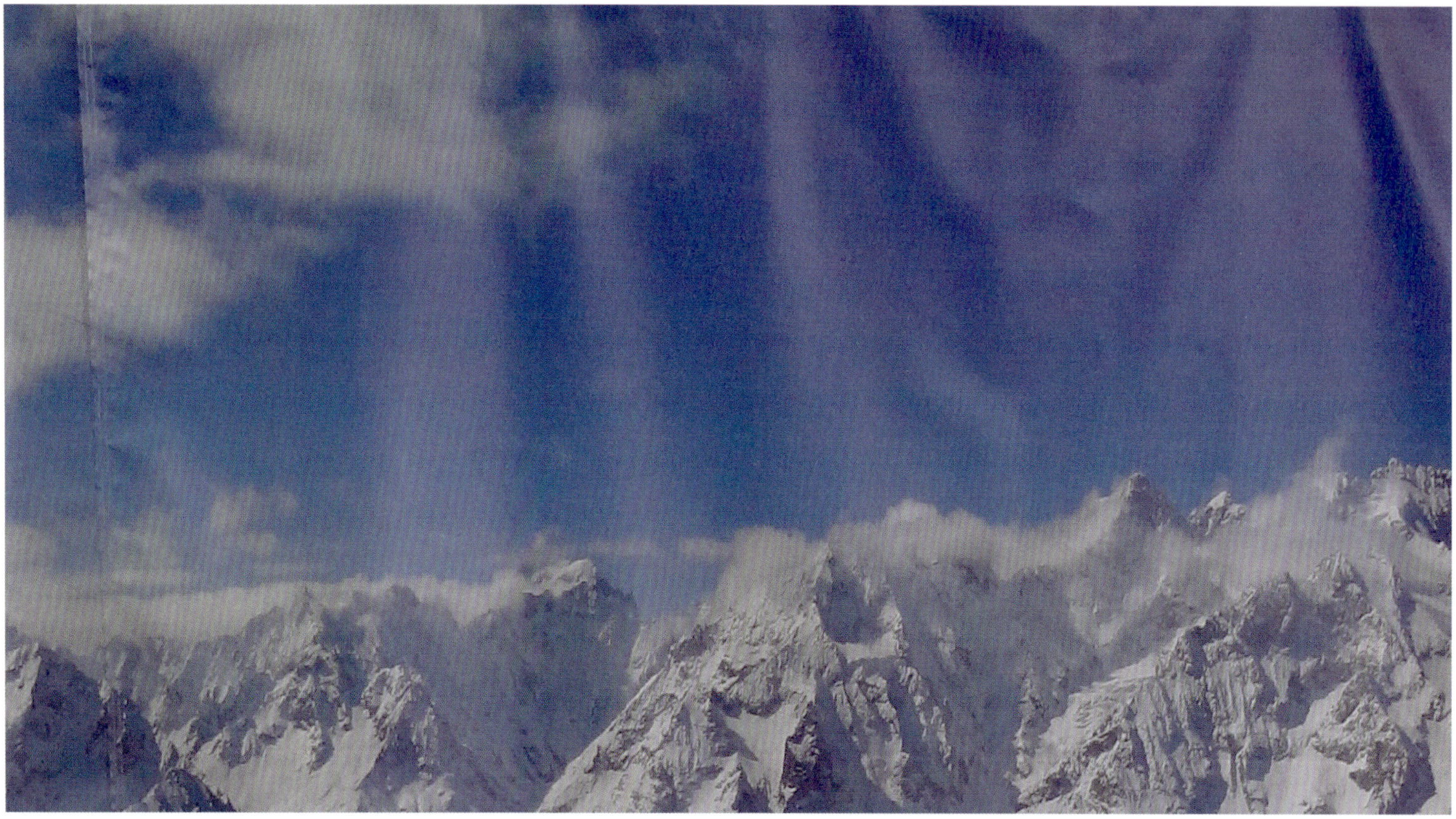

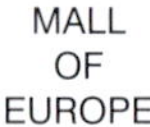
MALL
OF
EUROPE

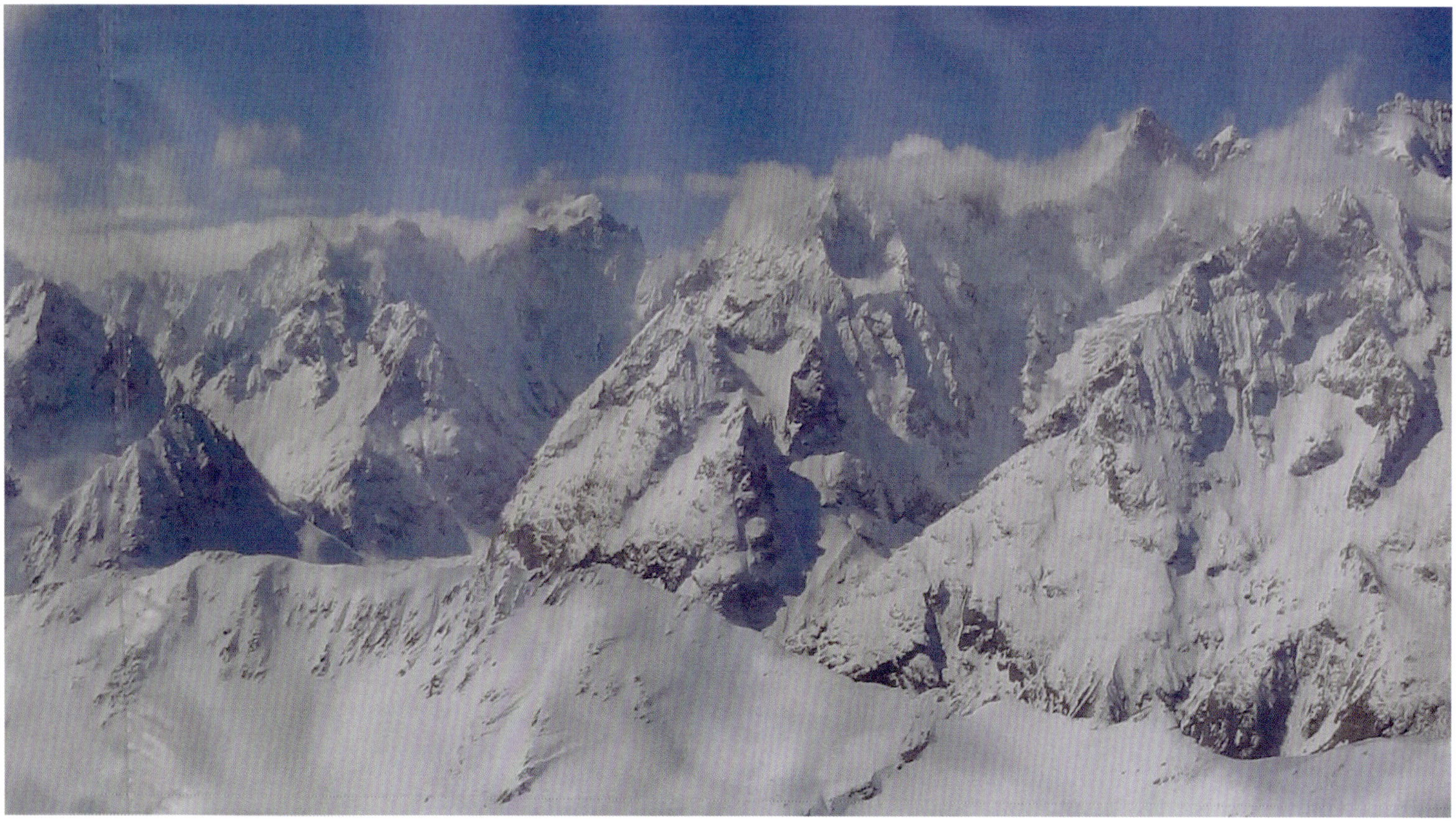

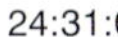

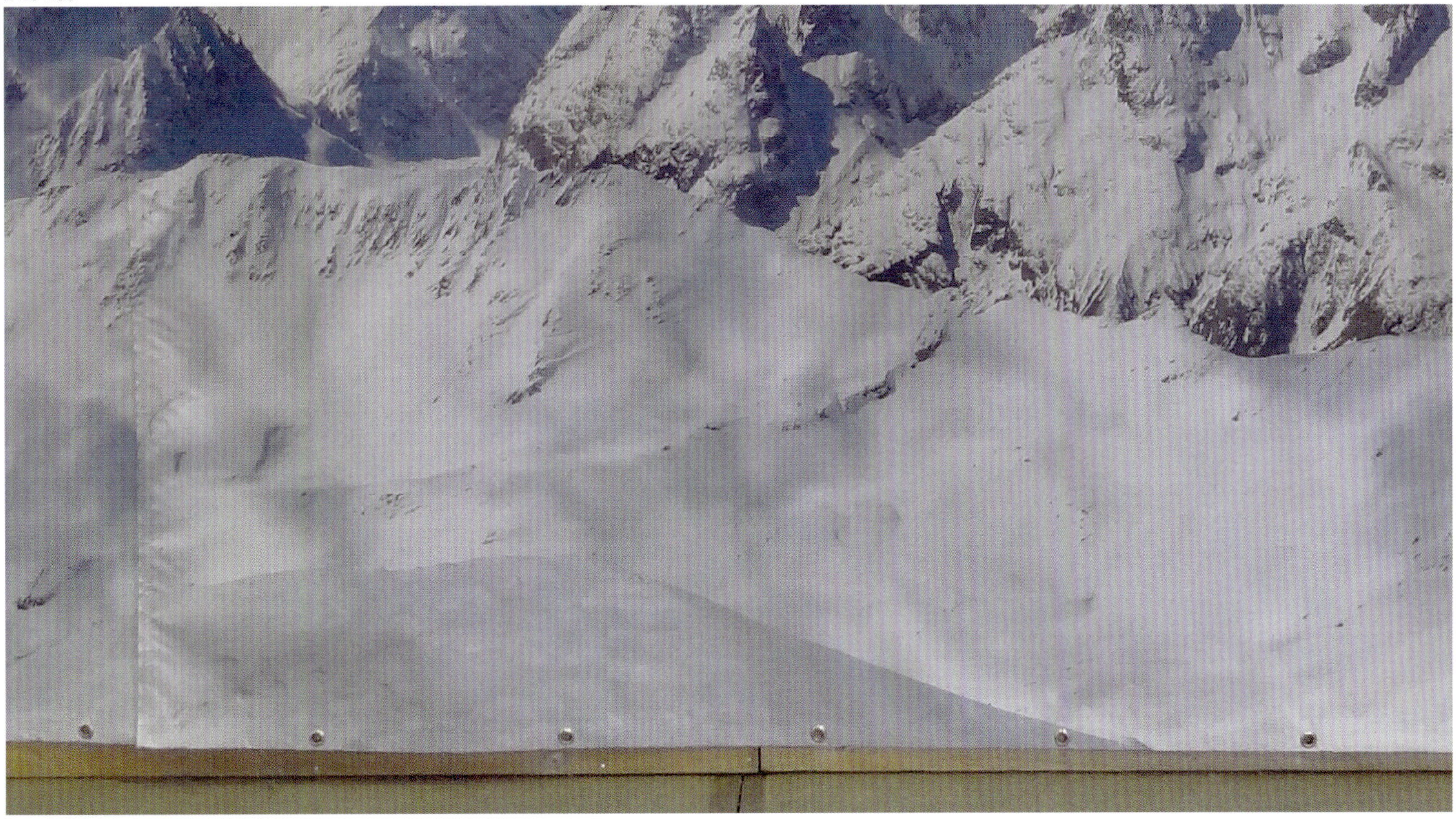

24:31:03

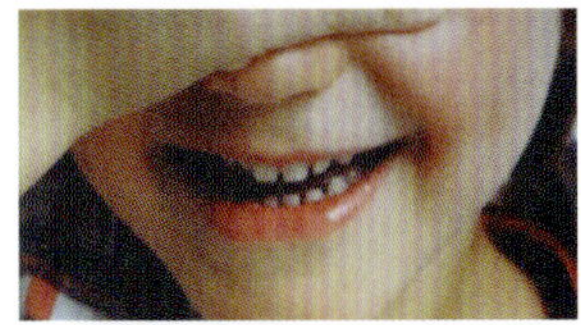

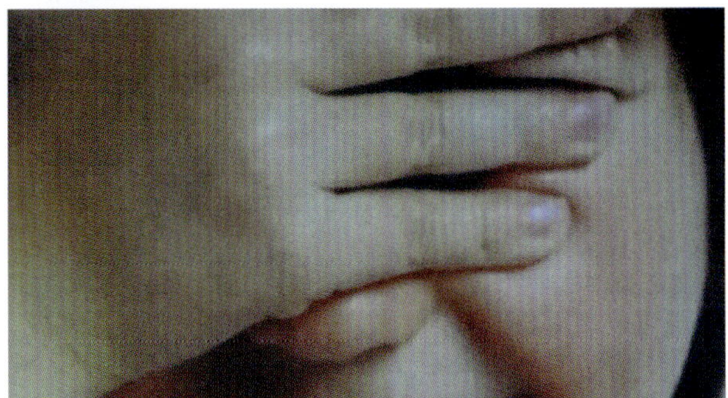

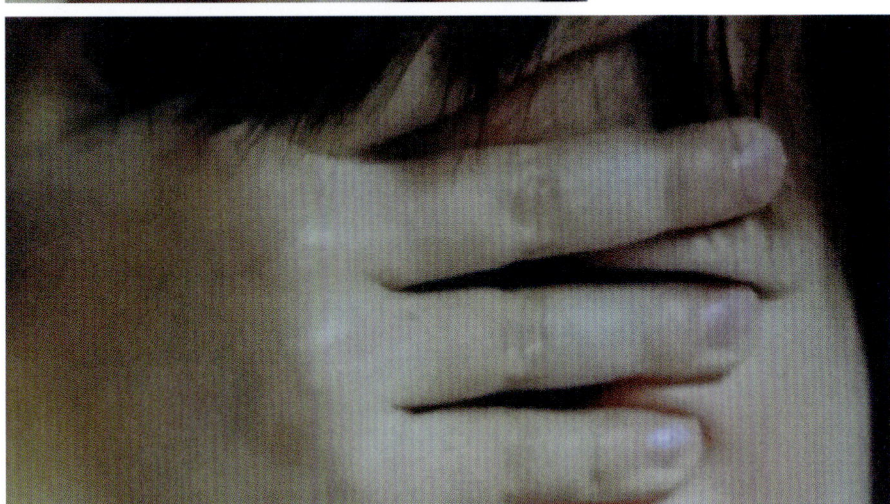

MALL
OF
EUROPE

25:19:18

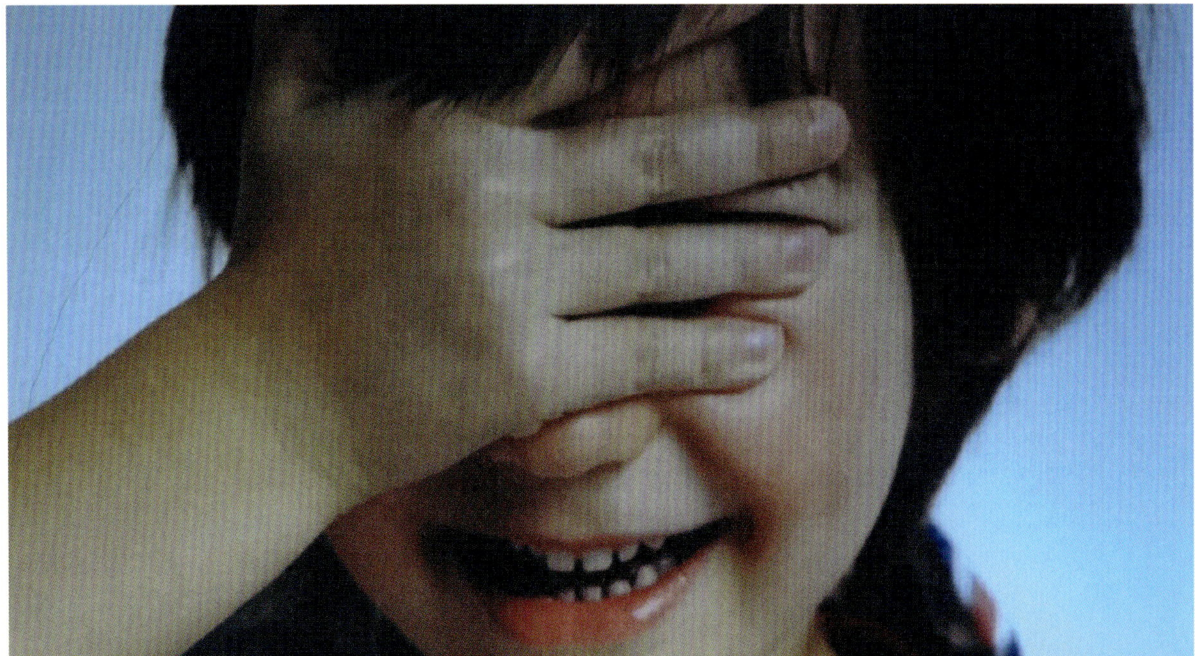

MALL
OF
EUROPE

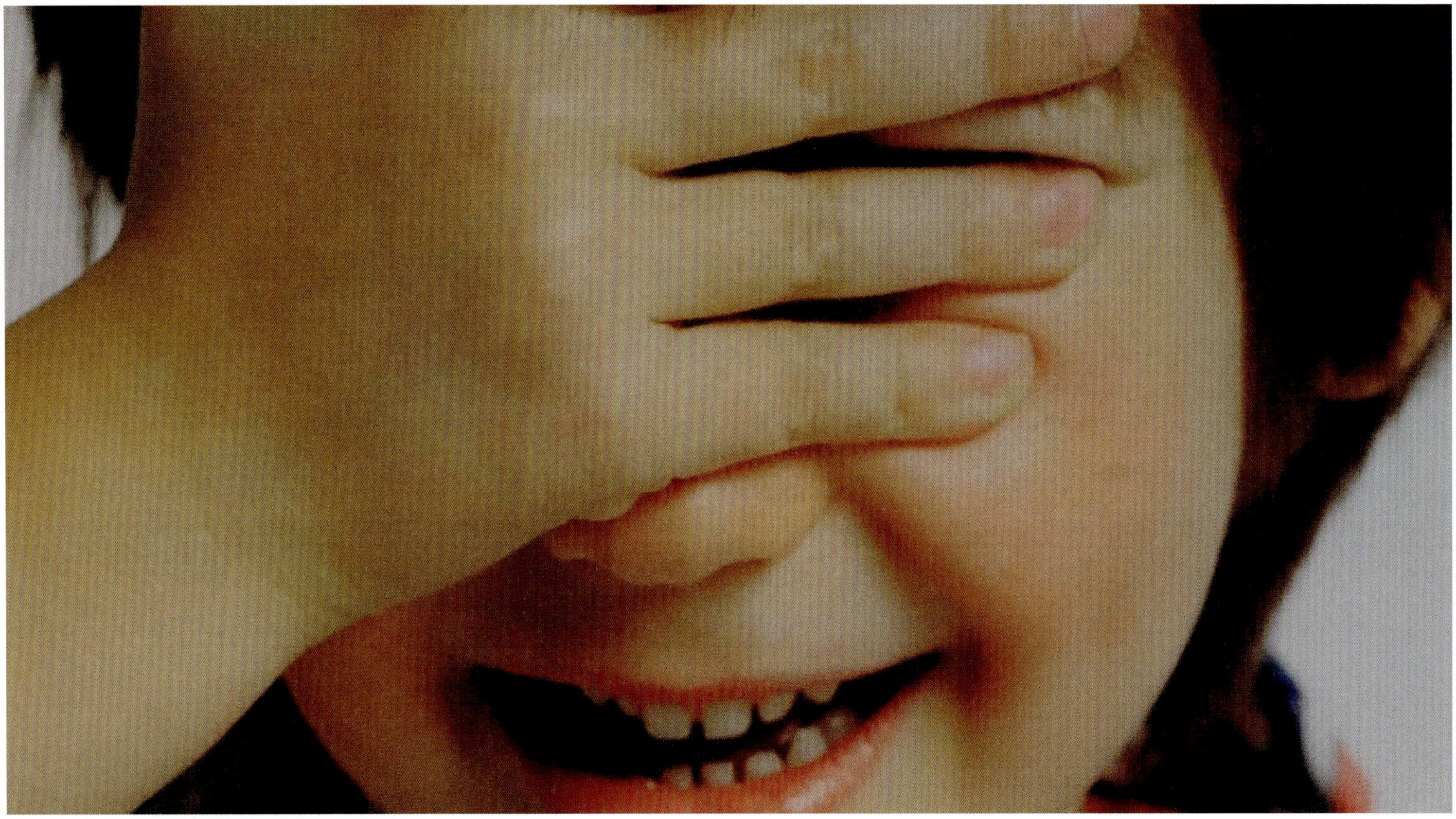

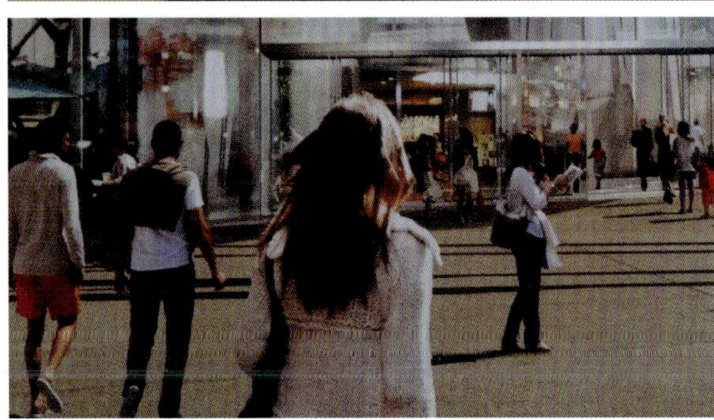

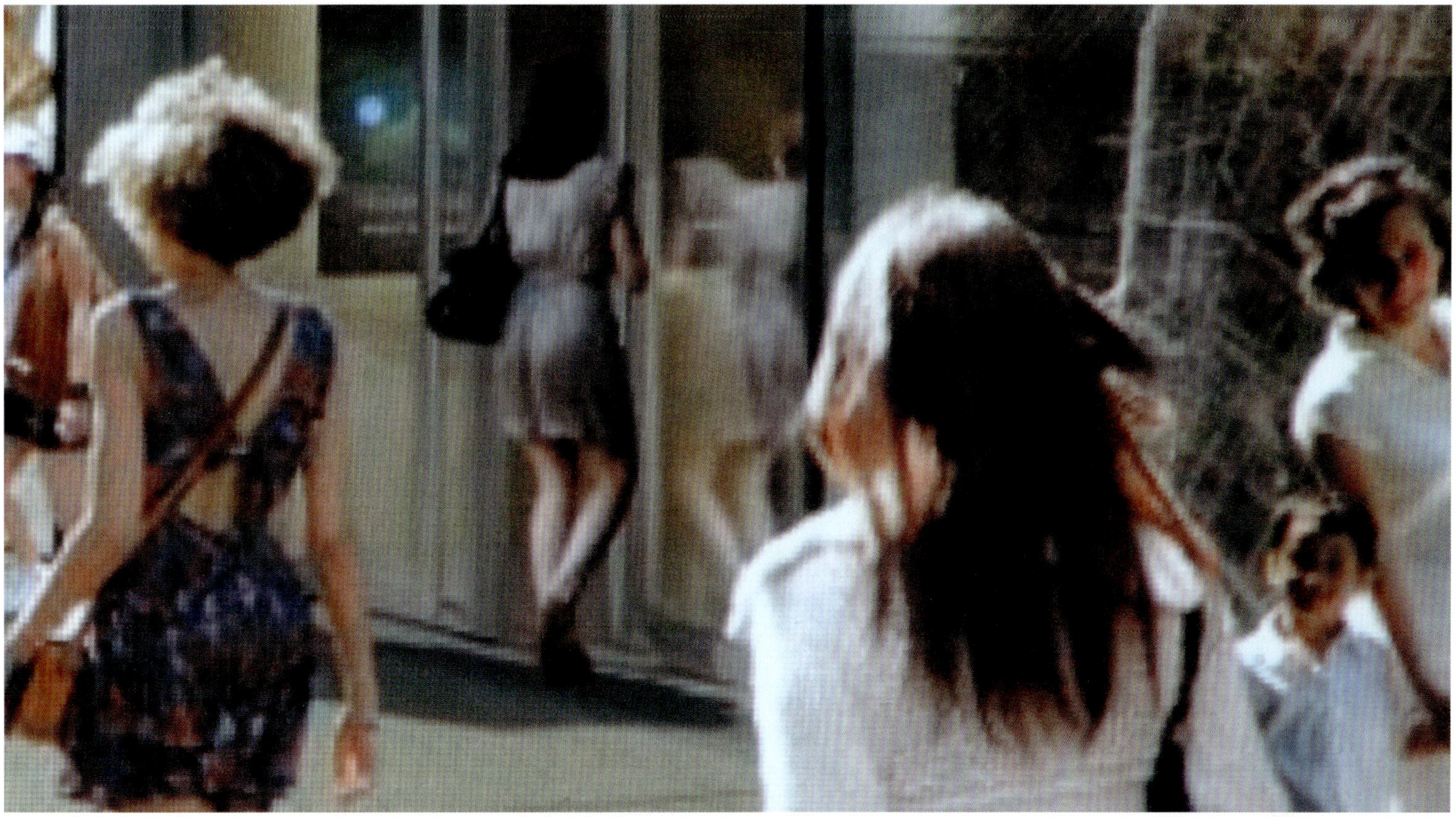

25:40:16

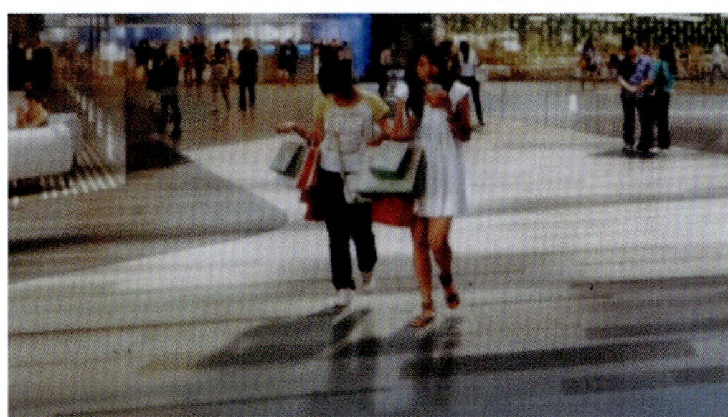

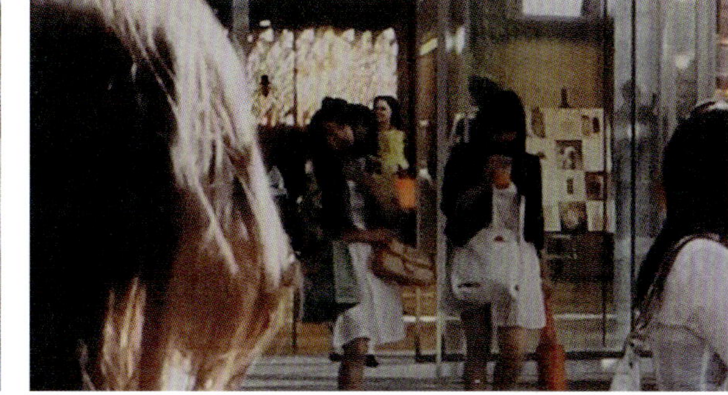

MALL
OF
EUROPE

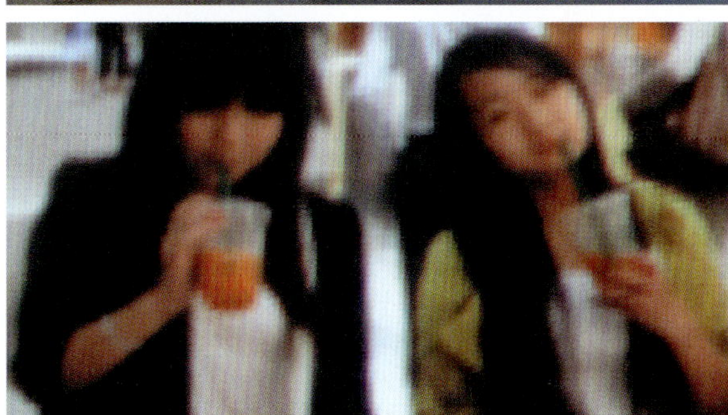

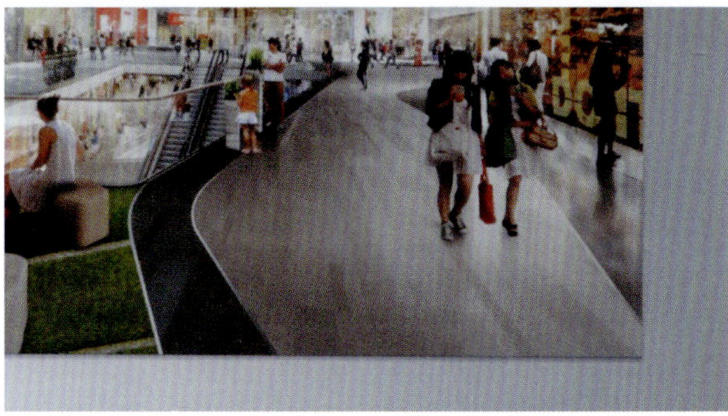

26:14:23

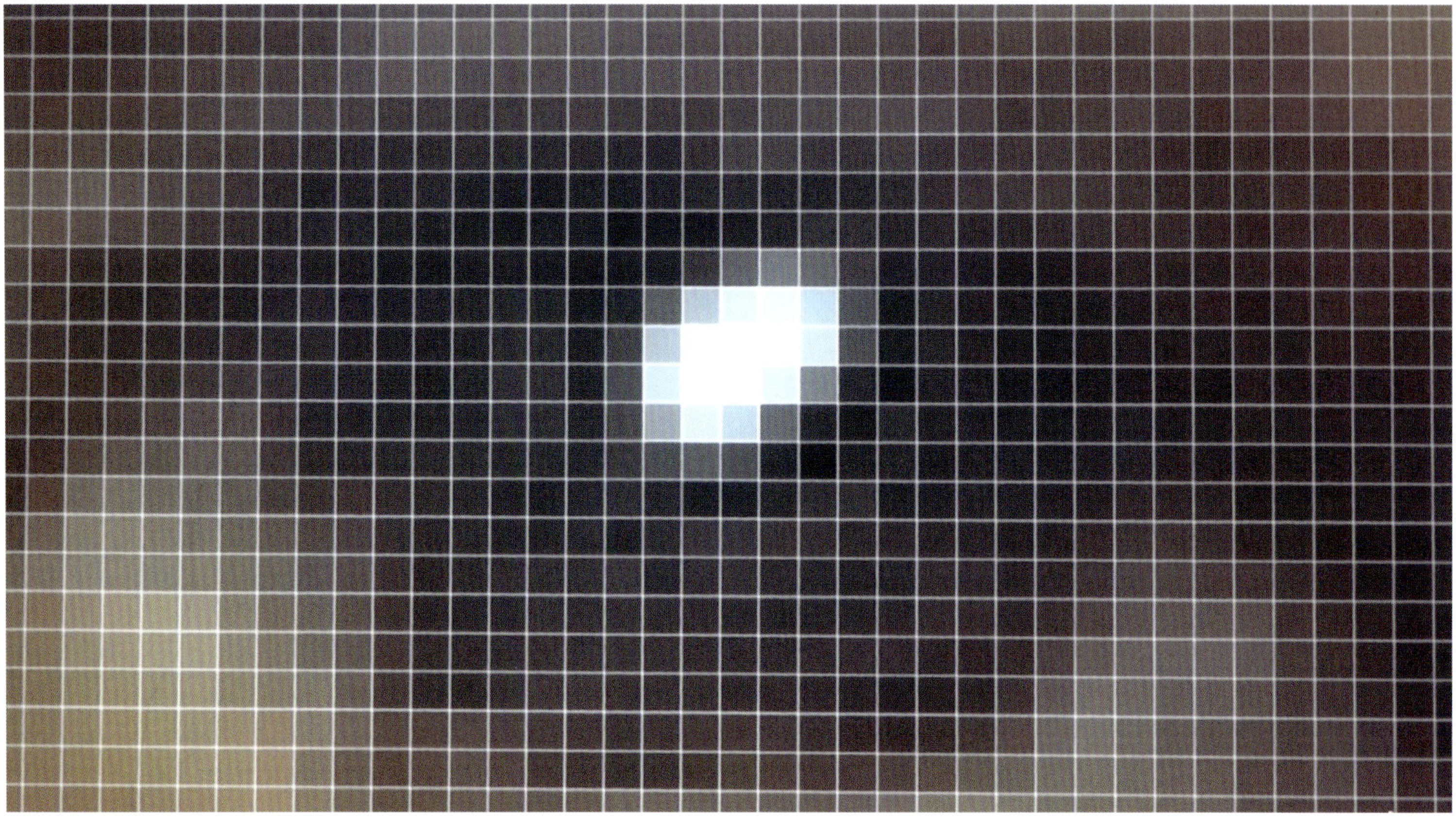

MALL
OF
EUROPE

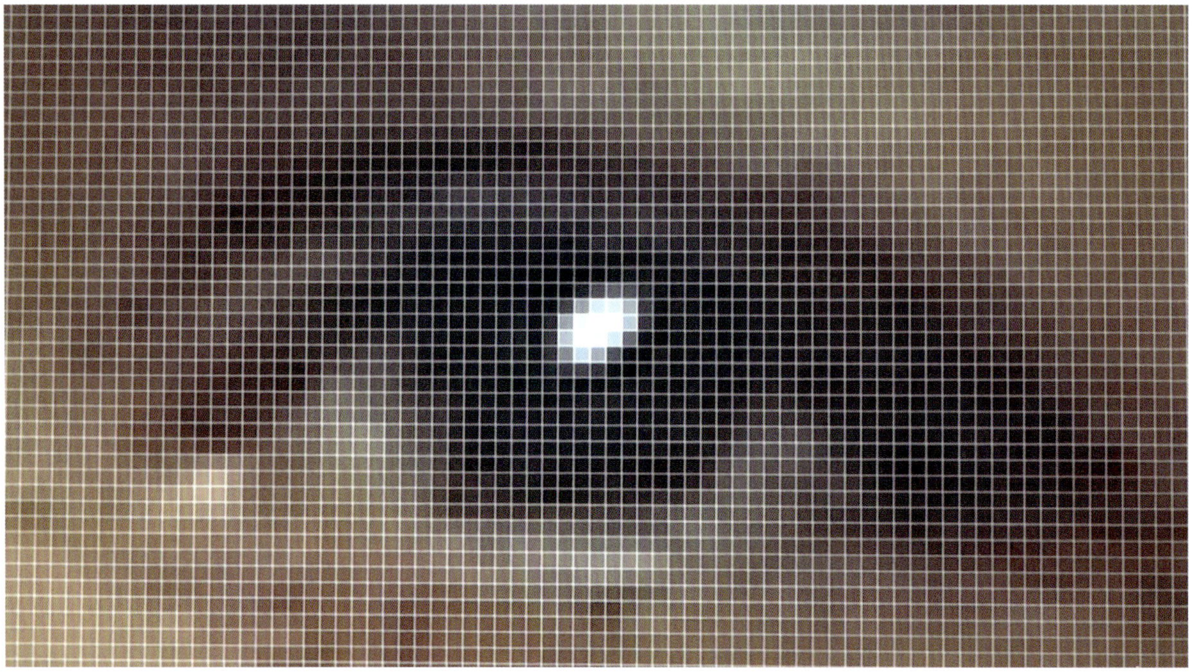

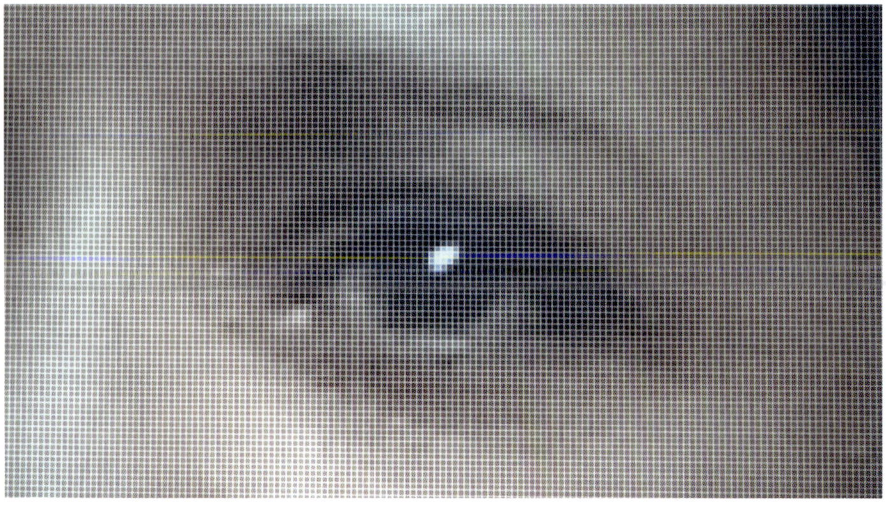

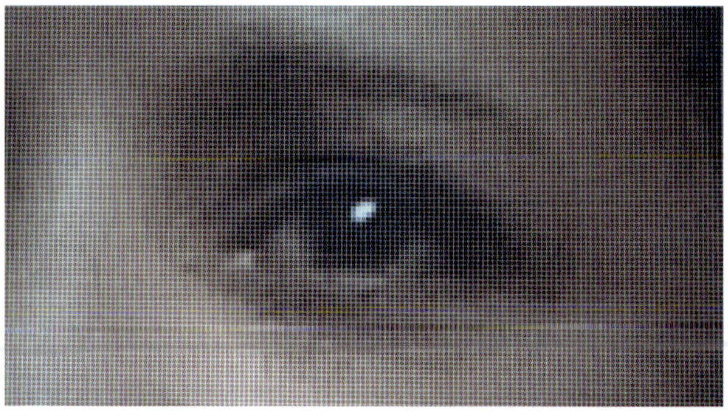

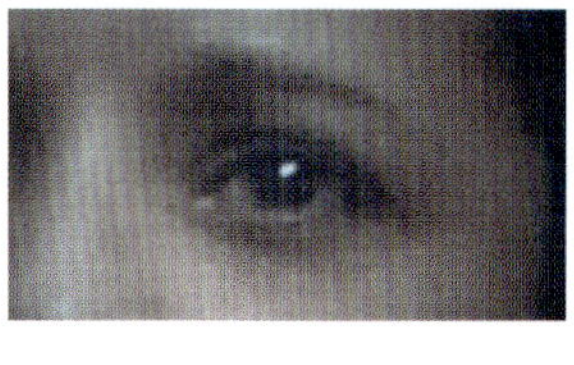

26:36:03

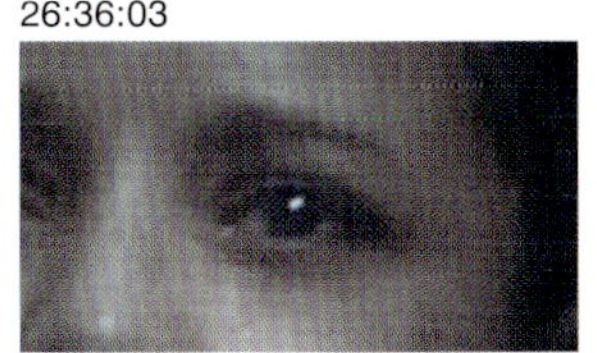

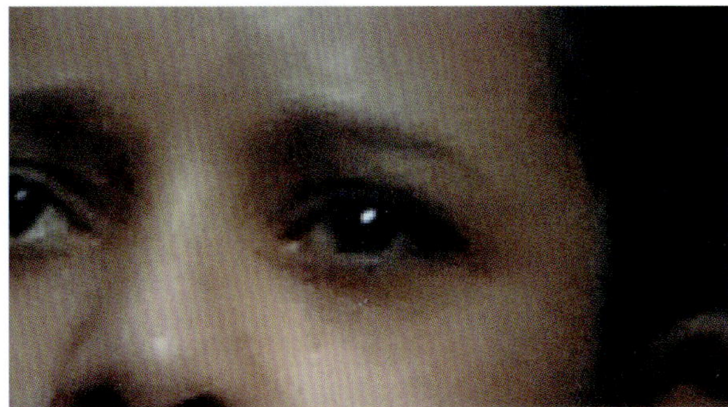

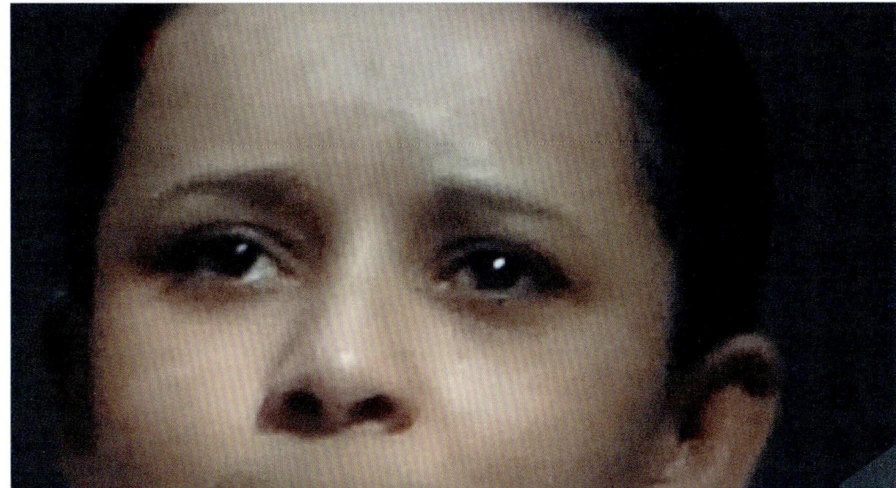

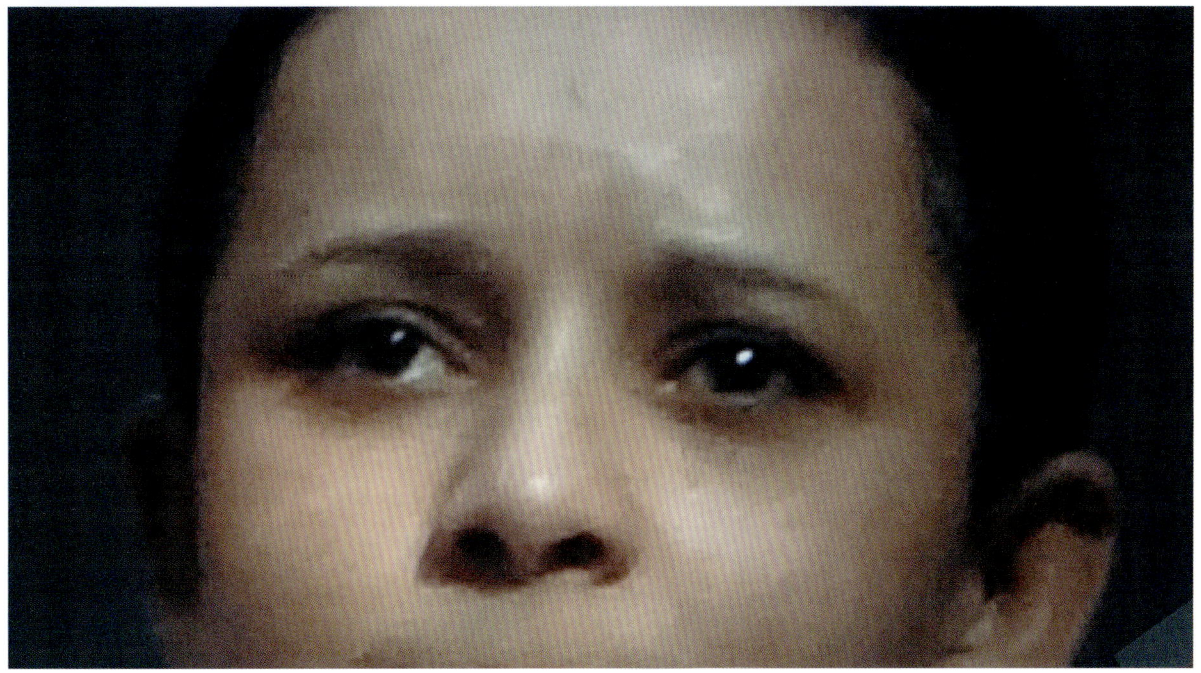

MALL
OF
EUROPE

26:50:00

MALL
OF
EUROPE

SOON (2018) video loop 1'50" without sound

EN

The video loop *SOON* can be seen as an epilogue to the work *WTC.* Both videos are shot at the same location, the 'Quartier Nord/ Noordwijk' neighbourhood in Brussels, but are separated by a three-year difference in time. After the tensions around the World Trade Centre towers became somewhat neutralised by forcefully evacuating people from the park, new building plans were communicated throughout the area again. The announcement 'SOON, office to let' is forecasting yet another future, seemingly promising a clean slate to cover the past.

FR

La boucle vidéo *SOON* peut s'envisager comme un épilogue à l'œuvre *WTC,* réalisée trois ans auparavant sur le même site, le « Quartier Nord » bruxellois. Emma Van der Put y promène à nouveau son objectif : le climat de tension qui régnait autour des tours World Trade Center a été plus ou moins neutralisé par l'évacuation forcée des réfugiés occupant le square local, et de nouveaux chantiers ont été projetés. Une communication *ad hoc* s'affiche dans tout le quartier : *« SOON, offices to let »* (« BIENTÔT, des bureaux à louer ») — comme une énième projection sur l'avenir, comme une promesse d'absolution générale censée faire table rase du passé.

NL

De videoloop *SOON* kan gezien worden als een epiloog van het werk *WTC.* Beide video's zijn opgenomen in de 'Noordwijk' in Brussel, maar met een tijdsverschil van drie jaar.
Na meerdere hardnekkige pogingen om alle mensen uit het park te verdrijven, lijken de spanningen rondom de WTC-torens enigszins te zijn geneutraliseerd. Er verschijnen opnieuw bouwplannen voor de wijk; de aankondiging 'SOON, office to let' voorspelt wederom een nieuwe toekomst, een schone lei die het verleden lijkt uit te kunnen wissen.

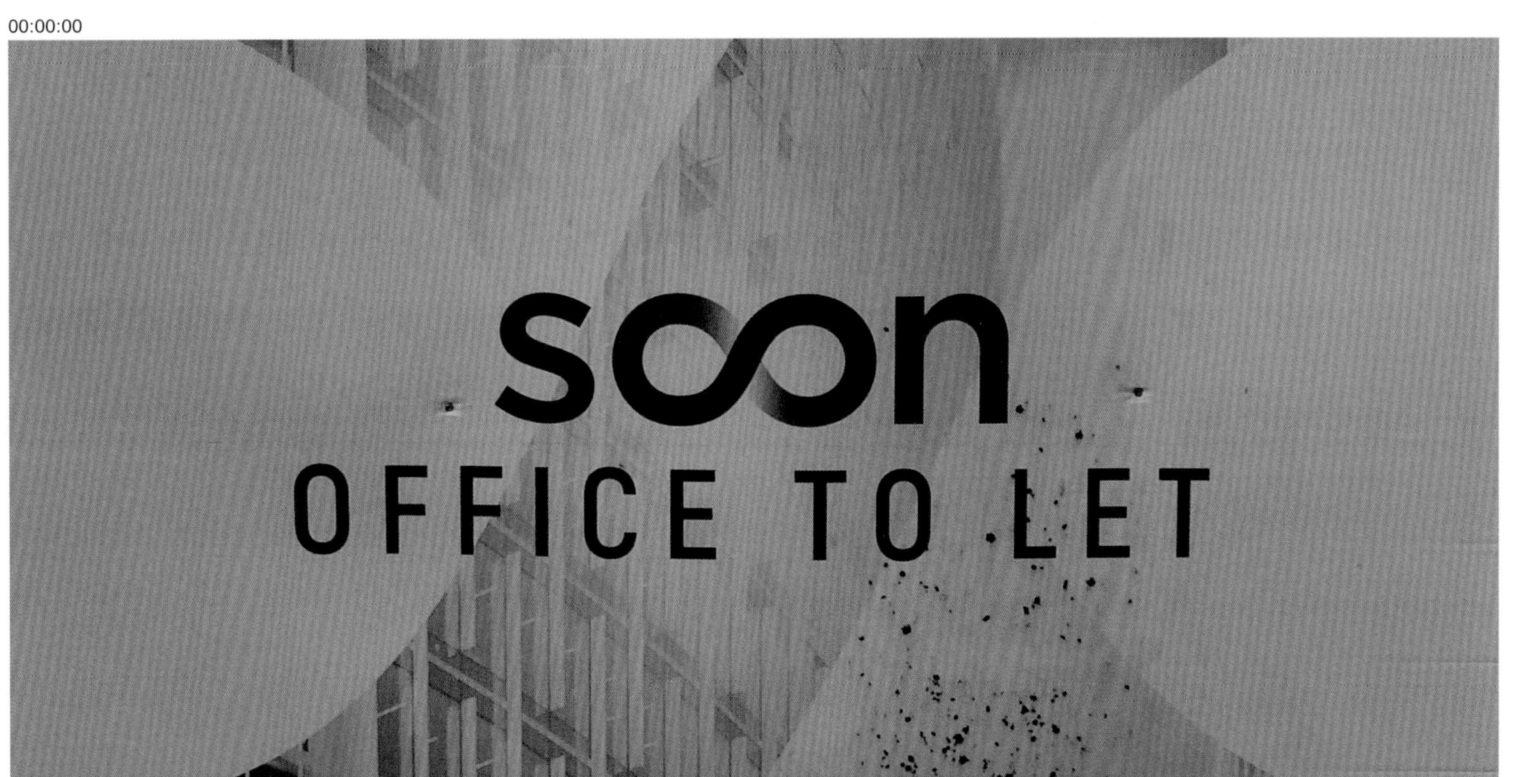

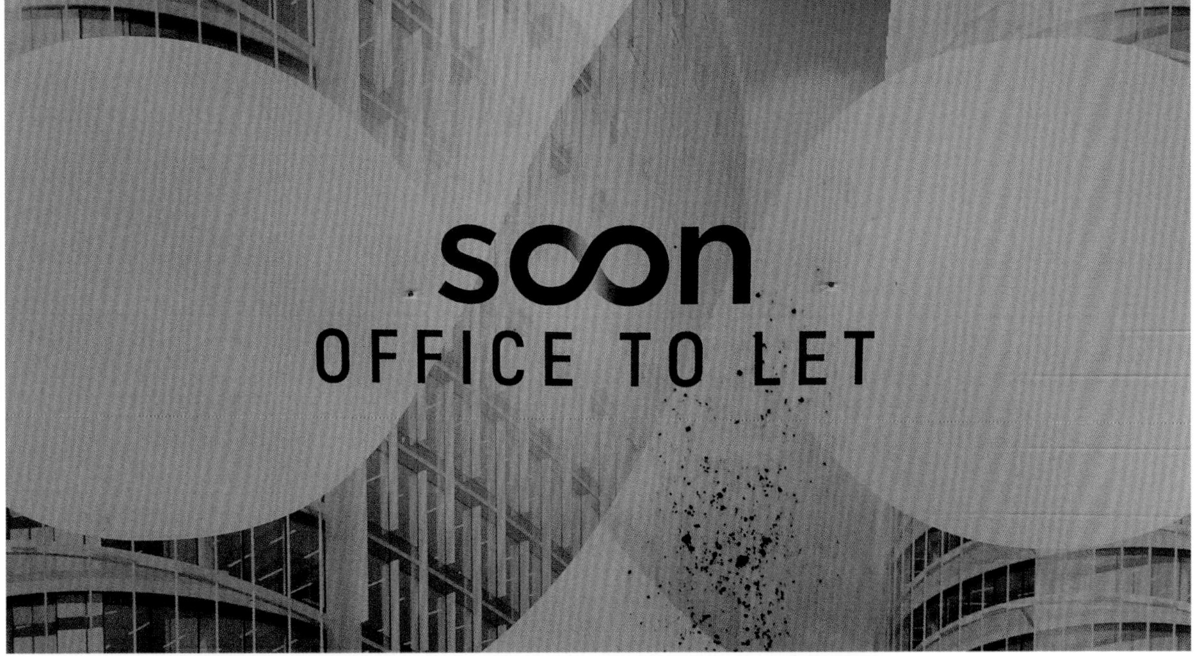

SOON

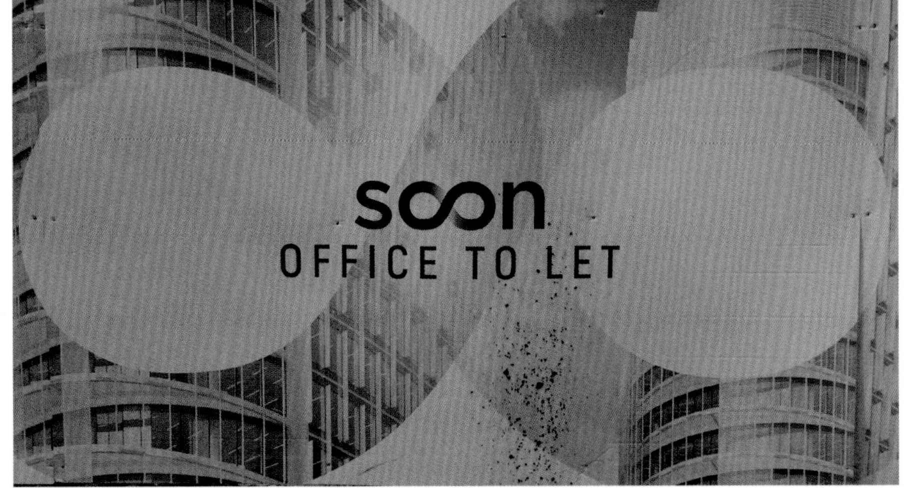

00:20:16

SOON

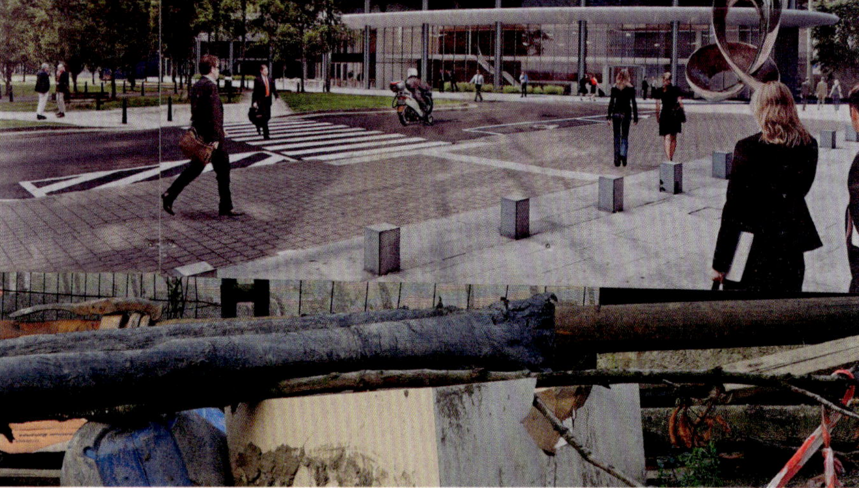

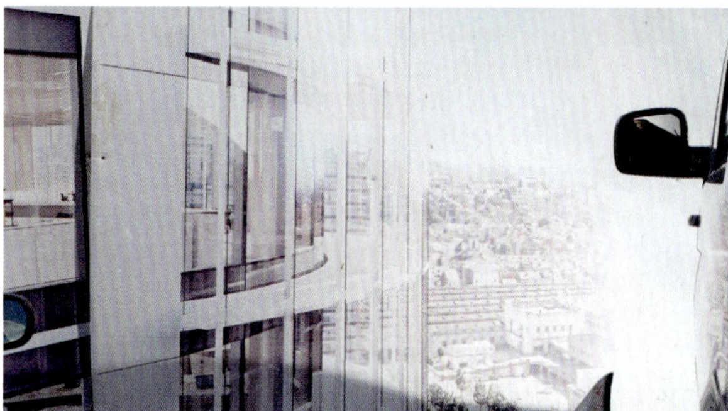

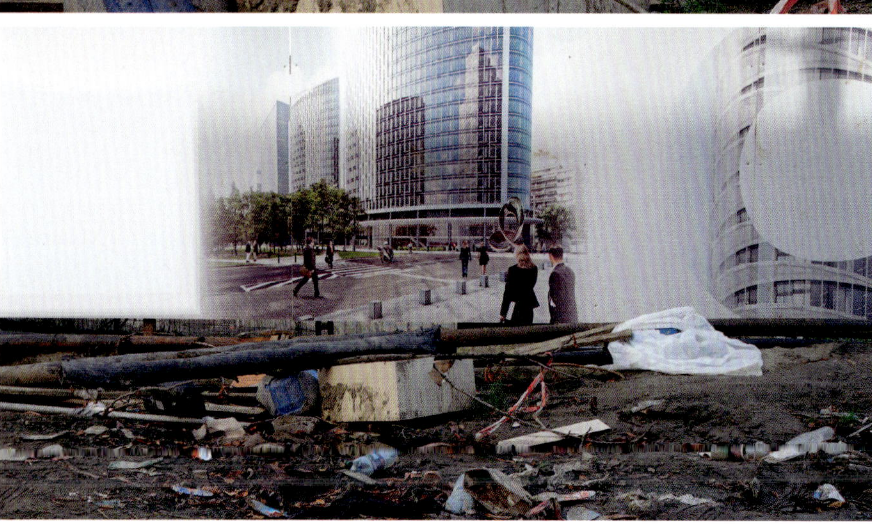

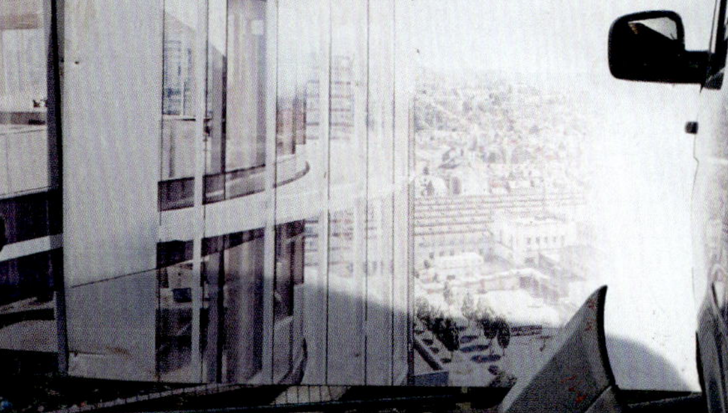

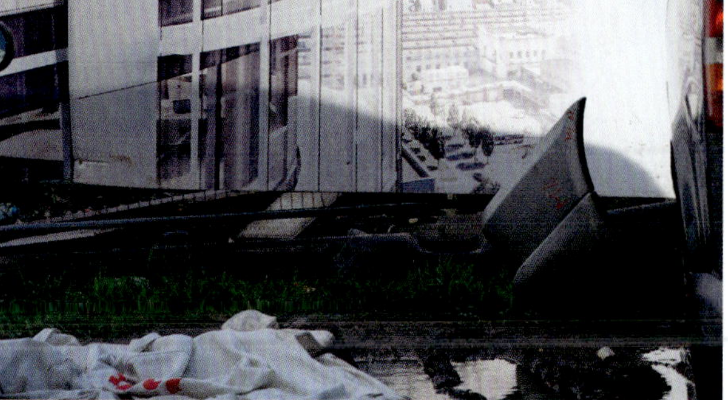

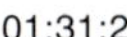

01:31:23

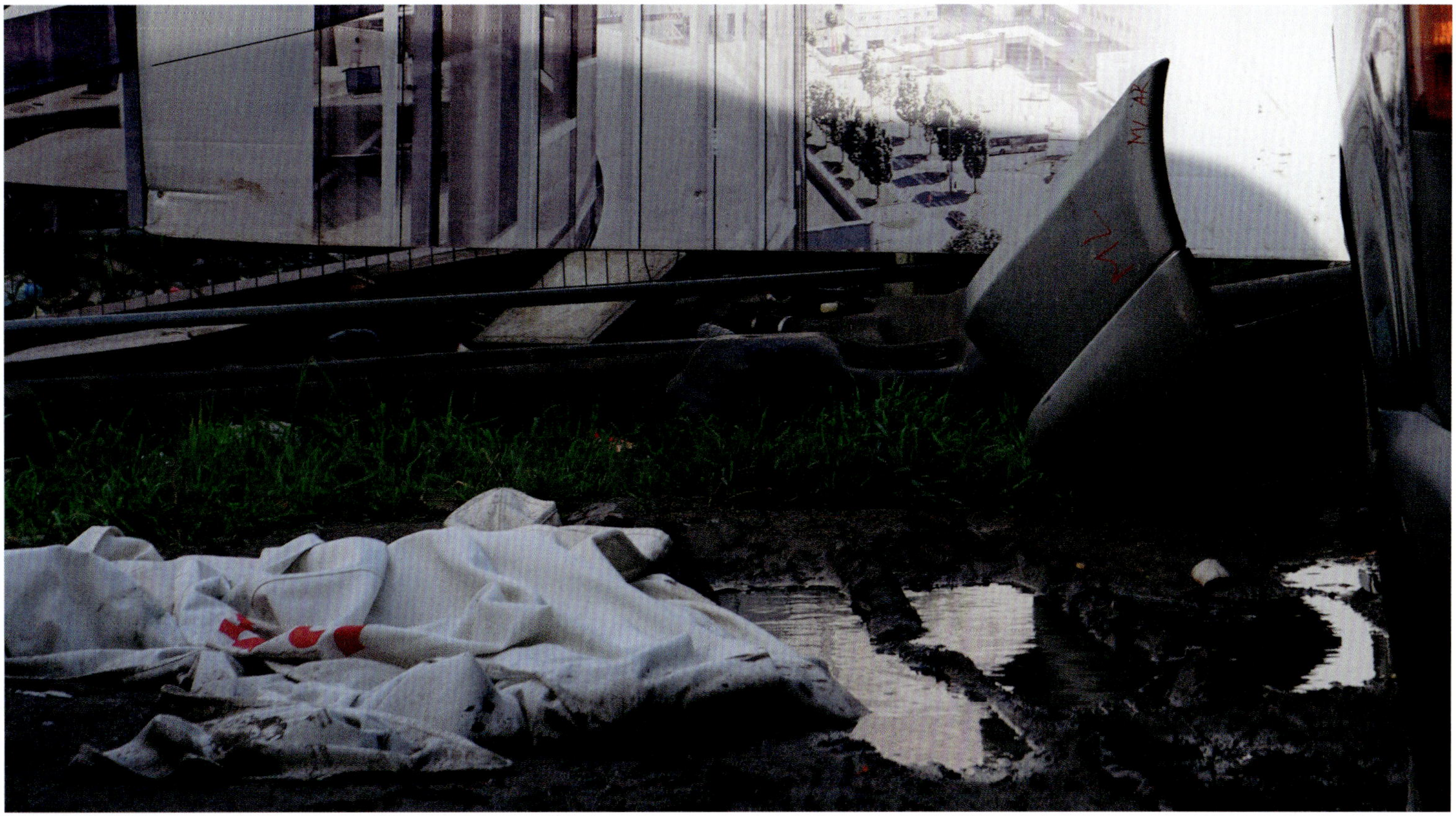

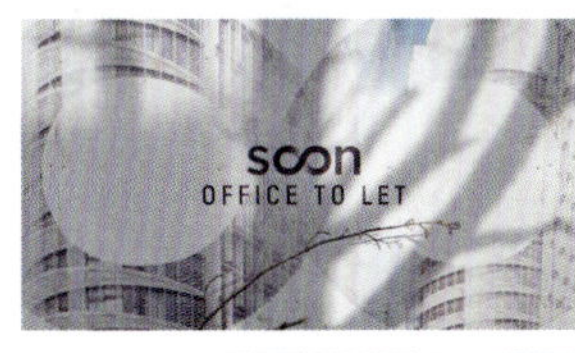

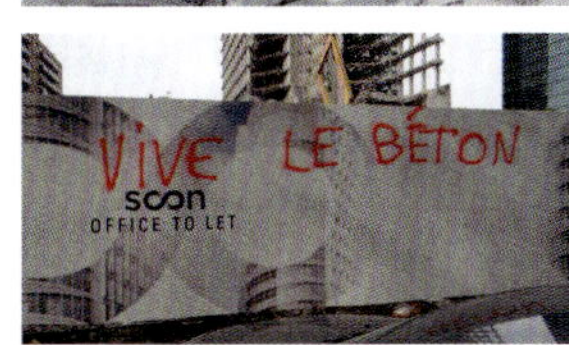

SOON

01:48:24

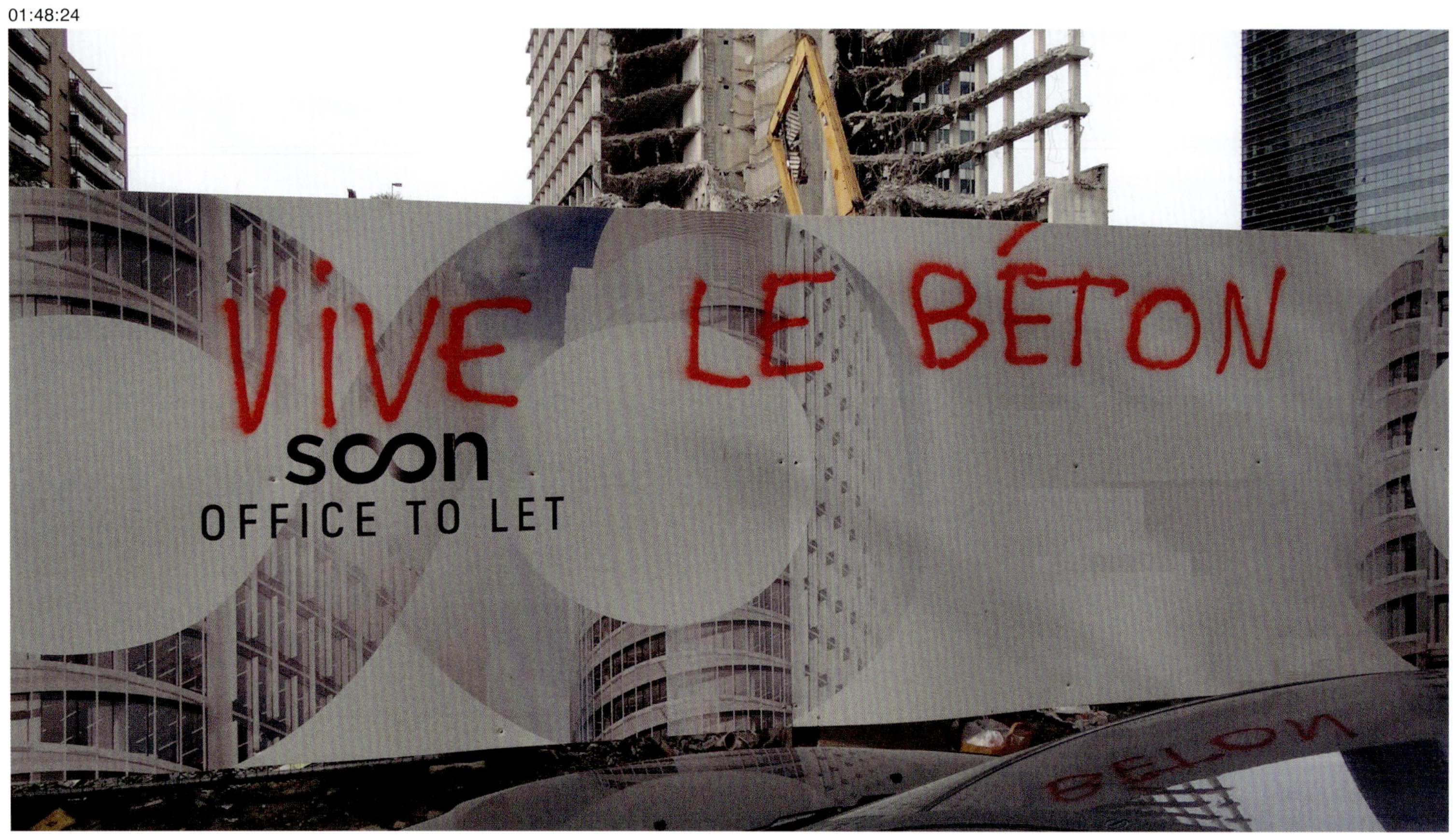

SOON

Projections:
Mall of Europe

Text by:
Steyn Bergs

Projections: *Mall of Europe*

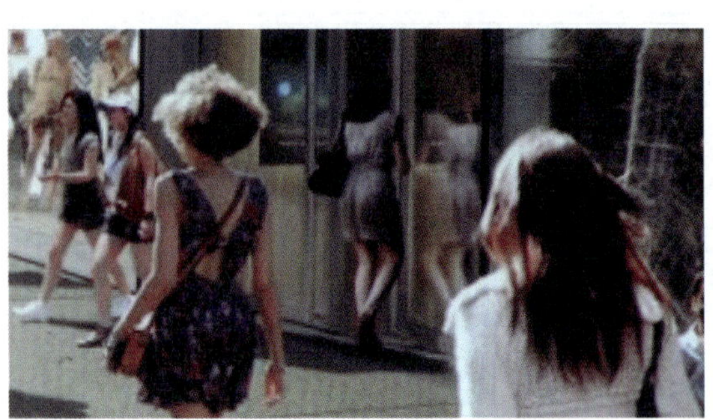

In what follows, I engage with *Mall of Europe,* a 26-minute, single-channel video by Emma van der Put that looks into the traces of historical and contemporary ideas on urban development, (technological) progress, and globalization that can be found within the 'Heysel/Heizel' neighborhood of Brussels, which is the site where its world fairs were held. *Mall of Europe* is essentially a slideshow of photographic images, devoid of any 'diegetic,' on-screen sounds—though it is accompanied by an inconspicuous, low-key soundscape, composed by Maxime Rouquart. My textual contribution presents an effort not just to think *about* the video (as its 'subject matter') but also, to the extent that this is possible, to think *with* it. In this sense, the text is very much an essay in the true sense of the word, which is to say, an attempt. And as an attempt, it is partially structured not only by the possibility of failure (which is always with us anyhow), but also by an impossibility built into its very premise. This essay, then, is marked by the certainty of another, more determinate and hopefully generative, kind of failure. I will come back to this at the end of the text.

Briefly put, the premise of this essay is to articulate conceptually some of the things that *Mall of Europe* conveys visually. The text is organized around three distinct yet related meanings of the term "projection": the presentation of an image on a surface, a forecast of the future informed by the perception of the present, and the conscious or unconscious transferal of desires and affects to an external object or person. In what may well be interpreted as a violation of the principles of analytical clarity, the essay tries to retain, emphasize, and indeed exploit some of the ways in which these senses of "projection" are at once disparate and mutually interdependent. Many others before me have pointed to the cinematic and psychoanalytic resonances that projection, both as a technical and a commonsense term, is ripe with. For my part, I am less interested here in tracing such connections than I am in offering a careful, concentrated reading of *Mall of Europe* that is anchored and afforded by a consideration of projection's various connotations in relation to the video. This is to say that, though in what follows some more generalizing (and therefore more properly 'theoretical') arguments and statements are developed about the world we live in, these arguments and statements are mostly secondary to and supportive of the attempt to look better at the video by writing about it.

Projection: the presentation of an image on a surface

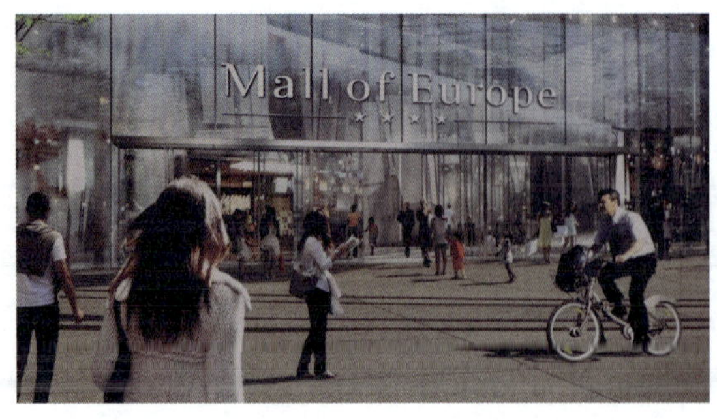

Like much of Emma van der Put's recent work, *Mall of Europe* is suffused with images of images. Pictures photographed from advertising signs, from billboards, and from computer screens are scattered throughout its cinematic slideshow. *Mall of Europe* lends its title from one of the first images it shows: an eerie architectural rendering of a shopping mall, aptly called *Mall of Europe,* registered on camera by Van der Put on the site where the mall in question is to be built. In *Mall of Europe,* Van der Put locks certain images in their frames, keeping them still and immobile, while scanning steadily over the surfaces of others. Different images are invariably separated from one another by the cut—a technique that Van der Put's otherwise uncomplicated and restrained cinematography exploits to maximum effect, often to underline the contrasting and sometimes contradictory claims that different images make on us. Very broadly put, what images of images do, or what they can do, is direct our attention to the organization of visuality. They place us at a remove from the visual environments that we are habitually enveloped by and immersed in, allowing us to reflect upon the logics that structure and underlie those environments but tend to elude conscious perception.

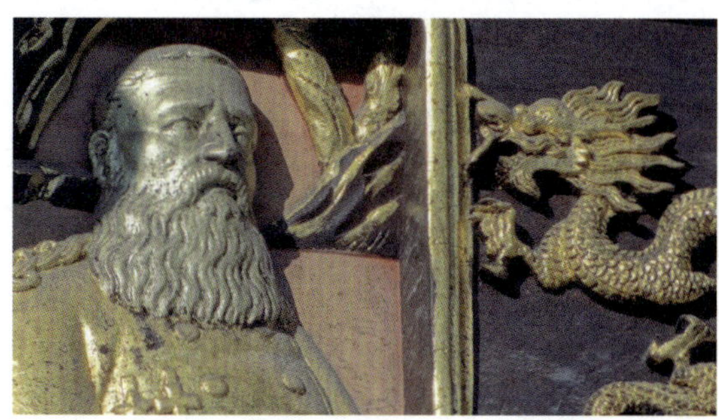

Not coincidentally, much of Van der Put's recent work is shot on sites designed and built to attract and accommodate the spectatorial gaze. For instance, the short piece *Chinese Pavilion,* also from 2018, shows an orientalist construction, erected in the royal gardens of the Brussels municipality of Laken as an 'exotic' attraction for the Belgian royal family. The video ends with an arresting image of a gilded bust of Leopold II in the building's wooden frieze. Leopold II, king of Belgium, had passed away six months prior to the finalization of the pavilion in 1910. He is notorious for his horrific and gruesome exploitation of Congo, which he held as a privately owned colony from 1885 until 1908, when he 'gifted' it to the Belgian state. *Chinese Pavilion* is relevant to mention here because it functions as a coda and a counterpoint to *Mall of Europe*—where, as will be shown, issues of coloniality are ever-present, but only ever latently so, hidden *in* (rather than hidden *underneath)* surfaces of all sorts.[1]

[1] In a 2018 exhibition at A Tale of a Tub in Rotterdam, this counterpunctual relationship of *Chinese Pavilion* vis-à-vis the much longer piece *Mall of Europe* was highlighted by the spatial set-up of the works, which encouraged seeing *Chinese Pavilion* as a complementary afterthought or footnote to *Mall of Europe.*

Mall of Europe itself is a more extended meditation on the Brussels Expo area, where several world fairs were held—including, most notably, the 1935 world fair and the much-glorified Expo '58. Much of the video focuses on the architecture of the modernist 'model neighbourhood' built for the 1958 exhibition, but the world fair is brought into a constellation with other sites of intensified scopic traffic as well. The 'Mini-Europe' tourist attraction, trade fairs for travel agencies and interior decorators, and indeed the shopping mall itself: *Mall of Europe* conjoins these places and these phenomena not just because they all happen to be in close geographical proximity to the 'model neighbourhood', but also because they are all underpinned by a logic of looking highly similar to that of the world fair.

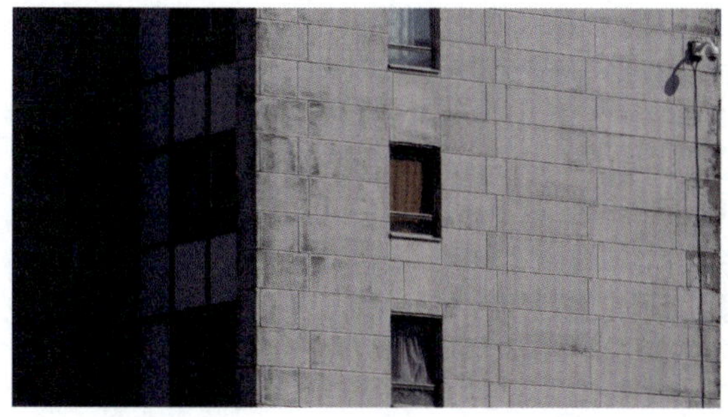

The 'Chinese pavilion', the world fair, and all the other phenomena brought into a constellation in *Mall of Europe* are paradigmatic instances of what sociologist Tony Bennett has influentially called the exhibitionary complex—which is the term he uses to discuss the organization of visuality specific to Western modernity. From the nineteenth century on, Bennett argues, several institutions arose that built on—but ultimately also superseded—the early modern institutions whose disciplinary effects and whose particular concatenations of power and knowledge were famously assessed by Michel Foucault. Bennett wants to demonstrate that, with the exhibitionary complex, discipline and surveillance do not so much disappear as become one aspect of a more intricate—indeed, a more complex—entanglement of power relations.

Fundamental here is the fact that, at least in principle, the new nineteenth-century institutions were public in character. Unlike the carceral or clinical systems that Foucault was interested in, all of Bennett's examples—he mentions museums, art galleries, fairs, expositions and department stores—are concerned with "simultaneously ordering objects for public inspection and ordering the public that inspected."[2] In the exhibitionary complex, spectators are expected first and foremost to sympathize and identify with a certain totalizing gaze; power is not only imposed on subjects from without, but is also operative from within them. According to Bennett, the exhibitionary complex ultimately amounts to "a self-monitoring system of looks in which the subject and object positions can be exchanged,

[2] Tony Bennett, "The Exhibitionary Complex," *New Formations,* No. 4 (1988): 74.

in which the crowd comes to commune with and regulate itself through interiorizing the ideal and ordered view of itself as seen from the controlling vision of power—a site of sight accessible to all."[3] For Bennett, this dynamic is most evident in the case of world fairs, where predominantly Western viewers were quite literally placed in a position of "specular dominance over a totality." World fairs, he writes, "sought to make the whole world, past and present, metonymically available in the assemblages of objects and peoples they brought together" and subjected to a "controlling vision."[4]

[3] Bennett, "The Exhibitionary Complex," 82.

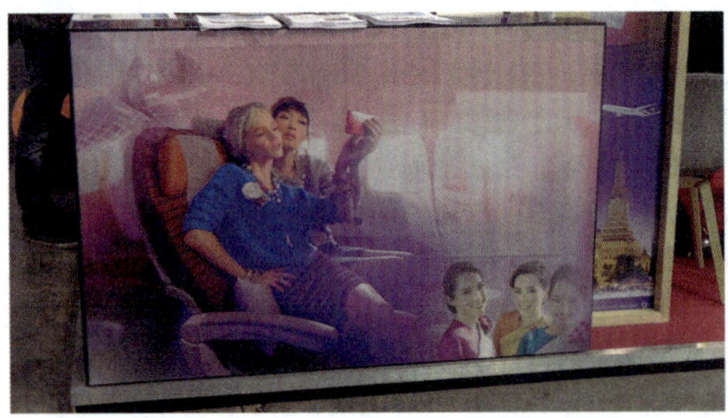

Van der Put's slideshow videos are riddled with viewers who are simultaneously the subject and object of visual contemplation and scrutiny. Indeed, the photographs that make up Van der Put's pieces often exude a sense of distanced observation; they are themselves charged with overtones of surveillance and voyeurism, and establish their own relations—and asymmetries—of power vis-à-vis the people that appear in them. Van der Put's work, in other words, is itself immanent to the exhibitionary complex, fully partaking in it not only because the work is typically shown in museums and assorted exhibition spaces, but also because of the media Van der Put employs.[5] It is significant that the history of the photographic image—whether still or moving—is inextricable from the historical constitution (and continuation) of the exhibitionary complex and the concomitant ways of seeing that are explored in Van der Put's videos.

[4] Bennett, "The Exhibitionary Complex," 79.

[5] The many historical ties between world fairs and the contemporary (globalized) art works are unraveled in Caroline A. Jones, *The Global Work of Art: World's Fairs, Biennials, and the Aesthetics of Experience* (Chicago: Chicago University Press, 2017).

Intellectual historian Martin Jay has noted the more or less simultaneous emergence, around 1850, of photographic technology, widespread tourism, and the world fair, all of which extend the latter's logic of "gazing curiously at the other" and encourage and facilitate seeing the world as exhibition.[6] Like Bennett, Jay stresses the colonial and imperialist dimensions and implications of this projected visual dominion over the world. The forms of exoticism and orientalism that gain currency in the West from the mid-nineteenth century onward are by no means to be seen as innocent, then. What Jay describes as the "visual appropriation of exotic locales and the no less photogenic natives (or fauna) inhabiting them" is a corollary of the *actual* appropriation of such locales through colonization, exploitation, and plunder, as well as of the violent subjection and dehumanization of their "photogenic natives."[7] Witness the inclusion, as late as 1958, of a *village Congolais* ("Congolese village") in the Brussels world exhibition—which was therefore effectively a human zoo.

[6] Martin Jay, *Downcast Eyes: The Denigration of Vision in Twentieth-Century French Thought* (Berkeley: University of California Press, 1993), 140.

[7] Jay, *Downcast Eyes,* 140.

None of this is ever made quite so explicit in Van der Put's work, which is nonetheless replete with references to the colonial past. Importantly, this past is treated not just as something that has passed, but rather as something that problematically continues to shape, inform, and undergird the historical present in myriad ways. Where *Chinese Pavilion* points in a straightforward way toward the persistence of colonial heritage in the materiality of the urban fabric, *Mall of Europe* is more concerned with demonstrating the present-day actuality of the othering gaze. In showrooms and commercial fairs for interior decoration, 'primitive' artefacts and sculptures are removed from their cultural contexts and used as aestheticized, decorative props. Travel agencies' promotional images flaunt the 'authentic' alterity of the destinations they have on offer. Exoticism and orientalism reveal themselves to be in full force—not merely as residual or anachronistic remainders from a bygone era, but as elements fully integral to the historical present.

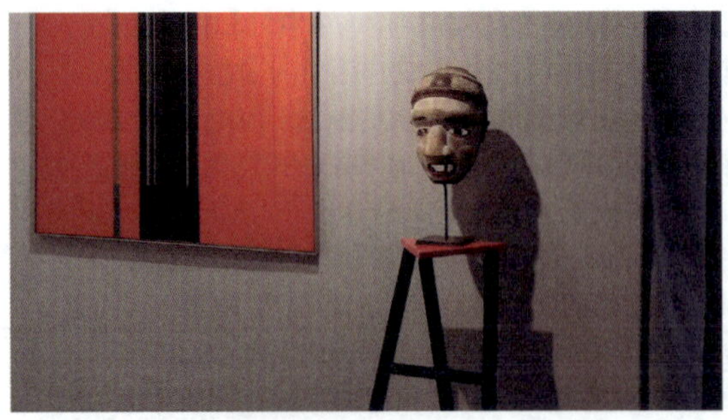

Coloniality, it has been argued, is inseparable from a modernity that we still have not exited.[8] This is what constitutes

[8] This is a fundamental point for the decolonial school of thought, where the two terms are often written together (as "modernity/coloniality") to emphasize the inseparability of the two. See, for instance, Walter Mignolo, *The Darker Side of Western Modernity: Global Futures, Decolonial Options* (Durham,: Duke University Press, 2011).

its relation—which may at first seem rather tangential—to another important aspect of *Mall of Europe:* the centrality, in the work, of modernist architecture. Modernist architecture appears mostly in its post-World War II guise, as Van der Put's focus is on the 1950s housing blocks in the Expo area, and particularly the still-inhabited 'Model Neighbourhood' built especially for the '58 world fair. In a notably salient passage in *Mall of Europe*—where, again, it is an image of an image that is crucial—an old archival photograph of two under-construction housing towers is juxtaposed with Van der Put's registrations of these towers in their present state. Today, worn down by time and use and marked by graffiti, these housing blocks no longer look quite so modern.

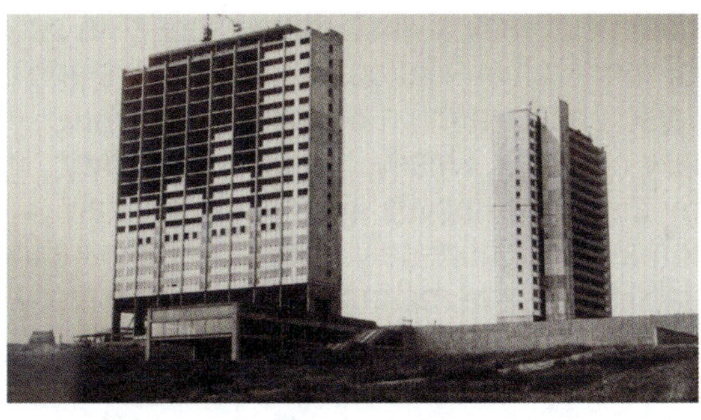

This failure of the buildings to live up to their own image is testimony to a future that never was. As such, it is also telling of the fate of modernism in architecture more generally. In his critique of modernist architecture, Manfredo Tafuri writes that "architecture as ideology of the plan is swept away by the *reality of the plan* when, the level of utopia having been superseded, the plan becomes an operative mechanism."[9] In a similar vein, Masao Miyoshi has commented on the "inescapably utopian" character of modernist architectural discourse and architecture, which "is only fully itself while it is a blueprint under construction and thus still addressing a future condition."[10] In other words, modernist architecture was, and was always going to remain, a *project.*

[9] Manfredo Tafuri, *Architecture and Utopia: Design and Capitalist Development* (Cambridge: MIT Press, 1976), 135.

[10] Masao Miyoshi, "Outside Architecture," in *Trespasses* (Durham: Duke University Press, 2009), 152.

But even though the blueprint or the *plan*—that cipher of rationalized coordination and planning, imbued with promise and potentiality—rather than any actual building is emblematic of modernist architecture, plans are nowhere to be seen in *Mall of Europe.* Instead, Van der Put shows a similar but perhaps more contemporary type of image: the architectural rendering. Like the plan, the architectural rendering appeals to and heralds a future state. Unlike the plan, however, the rendering is of little to no immediate *technical* importance to the realization of the particular future state it expresses; these digital simulations are designed for their aesthetic—and, by extension, ideological—effects only.

Despite the fact that the rendering is not directly instrumental in the way the plan is, what both nonetheless have in common is that they are images that figure the future, that somehow play an active role in the realization of what they depict, coaxing it into existence. In the case of the rendering, this can result in some rather simulacra-like effects: nowadays, "whole cities pretend to be YouTube CAD tutorials," as Hito Steyerl has observed.[11] In other words, the priorities of the real and the representational, the reference and the referent, get all mixed up and muddled. A sense of this is conveyed in the specific manner in which Van der Put shows these renderings in her slideshows. Often, she photographs them in such a way as to highlight their unsettling and uncanny qualities—having the frame of the renderings coincide with the frame of her own pictures, allowing for the rendering to be momentarily confused for a an image indexing something that is really out there already. The same technique is further explored and exploited in *SOON* (2018), another shorter video piece by Van der Put that can be read as a supplement to *Mall of Europe.*

[11] Hito Steyerl, "Too Much World: Is the Internet Dead?," in *Too Much World: The Films of Hito Steyerl,* ed. Nick Aikens (Berlin: Sternberg Press, 2015), 31.

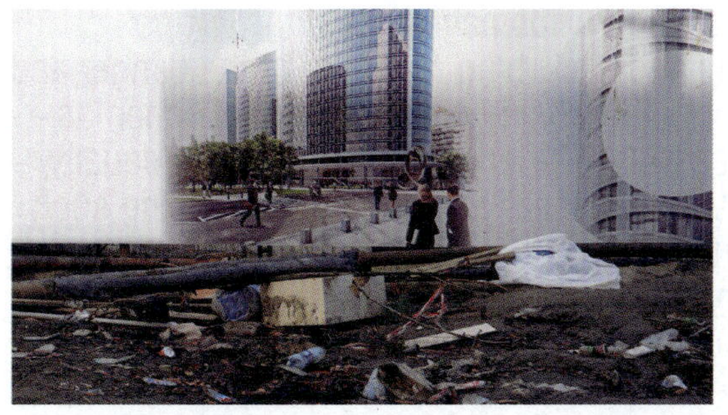

The plan and the rendering are important here because they are illuminating examples of projection. If we take projection to mean the presentation of an image on a surface, then it is evident that this always involves the reduction of a visual *world* into a visual *field.* It involves a certain fixing and flattening of sight—the scanning restlessness of which must be arrested, its spatial wanderings

[12] In this regard, Mary Ann Doane has written on the relation between the (cinematic) projected image and the map. "Projection also names quite specifically the representation on a flat surface of a sphere or a section of a sphere (preeminently, the globe, hence its strong connection with mapping." Mary Ann Doane, "The Location of the Image: Cinematic Projection and Scale in Modernity," in *The Art of Projection,* ed. Stan Douglas and Christopher Eamon (Ostfildern: Hatje Cantz, 2009), 157.

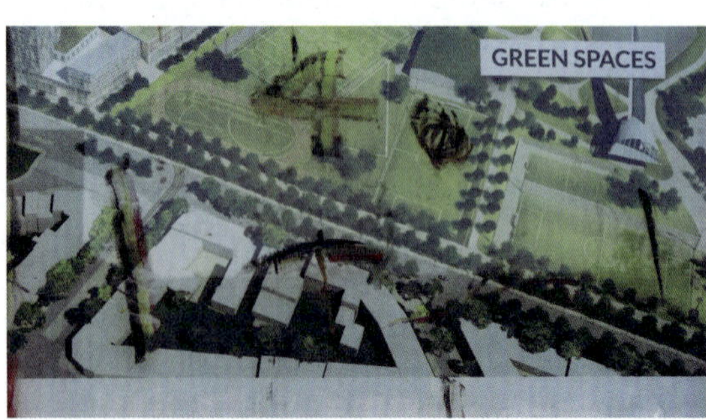

[13] Tafuri, *Architecture and Utopia,* 52.

[14] It is important to emphasize that this characterization does not only suit capitalist manifestations modernity, but applies as well to modernity on the side of the (radical) left. The promethean nature of state socialism in the Soviet Union–with its fixation on planning–is only the most obvious example in this regard. Also instructive in this respect is Cornelius Castoriadis' work on the "revolutionary project". Castoriadis wants to retain confidence in the perfectibility of history while also acknowledging the limitations to human knowledge of and power over the world. That is why revolution, for him, is not a matter of technique or planning, but of a form *praxis*—essentially, a reflexive form of political agency that complicates the distinction between ends and means. See Cornelius Castoriadis, *The Imaginary Institution of Society* (London: Polity Press, 1987), 71–100.

restrained, its holistic integration in and collaboration with the other senses suspended. Projection in this sense is therefore a simplification and a schematization, one that is operative in and on the world. As such, it has often been the product of fantasies of mastery and control—fantasies that, at the same time, it has also often solicited and facilitated. [12] Notions of mastery and control, of course, are precisely what underlie and connect what may at first glance appear to be rather disparate phenomena of modernity—like colonial enterprise and modernist architecture. They also underpin the modern organization of visuality into the exhibitionary complex. Finally, projective mastery and control—as epitomized by the *plan*—inevitably and immediately engender a temporal dimension as well, intimately related as they are to a certain belief in the manipulability and the manufacturability of history.

Projection: a forecast of the future informed by the perception of the present

For Tafuri, modernist architecture—in its initial 'heroic' as well as in its more pragmatic post-war manifestations—is a material exemplification of modern and instrumental thought, the "dominant theme" of which "is that of a future into which the entire present is projected, of a 'rational' dominion of the future, of the elimination of the *risk* it brings with it." [13] In architecture as elsewhere, the plan offers a means of coping with the contingencies of the future by containing them. It is a tool for dealing with the open and the unknown, for managing uncertainty as well as the anguish that it causes. The plan is identical to the project in that it installs and pushes forward a certain vision or imaginary of the future. It is in this sense that both the plan and the project are inextricably bound up with the hubristic confidence, so typical of modernity, in the malleability and perfectibility of history—which is to say, of the future—and in 'Man' as the self-determining historical subject and agent par excellence. [14]

Modernity, in other words, is tantamount to the ideology of progress. The most basic—and literally the most *straightforward*—representation of its temporal structure is the timeline. Hence, world fairs like the Expo '58 purported to represent the 'state of the art' in a world understood to be firmly in the grip of a singular, linear, and universal process of modernization. However, it is important here to stress once more that this conception of the world as a single homogenized time-space would be quite unthinkable without colonialism, which is in turn legitimized by notions of 'backwardness' that such a conception allows for. Hence, at the '58 Brussels exhibition, the simultaneous presence of both the hyper-futuristic Philips sound pavilion (designed by Le Corbusier and Iannis Xenakis, and removed after the fair) and the *village Congolais,* both subsumed under a narrative of the progressive development of human history—with the former exhibit exemplifying the 'vanguard' position, while the latter was supposed to illustrate what it would mean to lag behind on the world-historical stage.

The co-presence of the Philips pavilion and the *village Congolais* serves as a painful and disturbing reminder of the danger and the violence intrinsic to the act of imposing neat conceptual schemas—like the lofty notion of progress—on the course of history. But equally, it shows how history has a way of partially resisting and refusing such impositions, of demonstrating how the ideology of progress produces all sorts of complications and contradictions for itself. For one thing, the very idea of progress necessitates a historical awareness that continually threatens to undermine it. In what is only an apparent paradox, modernism—the perpetual negation of the past in the present by the new—creates, as its by-product as it were, a heightened sensibility to historicity, which only truly becomes perceptible with the waning of tradition as something self-evident.[15] The modernist obsession with museums and public monuments (which also feature prominently in *Mall of Europe)* is no coincidence; in modernism, the projective gaze forwards is mirrored by the historicist contemplation and study of a past seen as having shaped, conditioned, and determined the present. The constant surpassing, eclipsing, or demolishing of the old occasions "a perception, not only of the pastness of the past, but of its presence."[16]

Van der Put's videos attest to and engender precisely such a sense of the historical: one that insists on—that holds onto—the concurrent pastness and presence of the past (as well as of possible futures). There is one particular photograph in *Mall of Europe* that epitomizes this more than others. A slow scan upwards over the surface of the image reveals first—and closest to the camera—an excavator, or a part thereof, placed in front of a rendering offering a panoramic view of what the area is supposed to look like after having undergone the planned transformations. Also in the rendered image is a man in his late twenties or early thirties; he is white, ostensibly middle-class, and otherwise rather nondescript. He is scaled so that his relative size dwarfs that of the landscape behind him. The panning movement of the image soon reveals that he has his arms crossed and is looking upward, smiling fatuously at something beyond the frame of the rendering—at some horizon or heavenly body that we, the viewers, do not get to see. To his top left, there is an icon derivative of the Google maps location indicator; it has a yellow-greenish hue and bears the inscription 'NEO 2021'. Moving further upward still, it becomes clear that the screen that bears the rendered image conceals a building—the decorative top frieze of which towers up from behind the screen. The frieze supports two large classicist sculptures, in bronze, of winged female figures. It also bears the inscription of the year of the building's completion, 1935—the year of the fourth Brussels world fair. From what can be glimpsed from Van der Put's photograph, the largely concealed building is typical of the interbellum art déco style, itself an eclectic blend of historicist and modern, 'forward-looking' elements and idioms.

Part of a larger sequence that combines photographed renderings with shots of construction work in the Expo area, this image captures the strange entwinement of past, present, and future like no other moment in the video. Van der Put's work is concerned with showing how the Expo area (and, by extension, the entire city of Brussels, which is the décor to all her recent pieces) is, in ways both literal and metaphorical, built upon and around the vestiges of the past—more specifically, the vestiges of a modernity which is, therefore, still very much with us. The work does more than expose the tangible actuality of historical traces, however. Scratching away at different layers of historicity at once, the image under discussion here conducts a mini-archaeology of the historical present—a present that is clearly shown to be overdetermined not just by history and its presence, but also, and at the same time, by hopes, expectations, and anticipations of the future.[17] In this particular instance, which can stand metonymically for *Mall of Europe* as a whole, the historical present is understood and presented as a kind of push-and-pull, as *conjuncture.* Importantly, though, 'conjuncture' in this context does not merely mean the wreathing of divergent historical forces as they shape and animate the moment of the present; it includes as well an orientation toward the future, a prospective reckoning with the as-yet-unknown that folds back

[15] Peter Osborne has stated that what we call modernism is essentially "a form of historical consciousness, an abstract temporal structure". Because it is a structure that comprises many different 'contents,' "modernity is *not,* as such, a project, but merely its form." Peter Osborne, *The Politics of Time: Modernity and Avant-Garde* (London: Verso, 1995), 23.

[16] T.S. Eliot, quoted in Edward Saïd, *Culture and Imperialism* (London: Chatto & Windus, 1993) 2. Saïd continues to say that "even as we must fully comprehend the pastness of the past, there is no just way in which the past can be quarantined from the present. Past and present inform each other, each implies the other and, in the totally ideal sense intended by Eliot, each co-exist with the other."

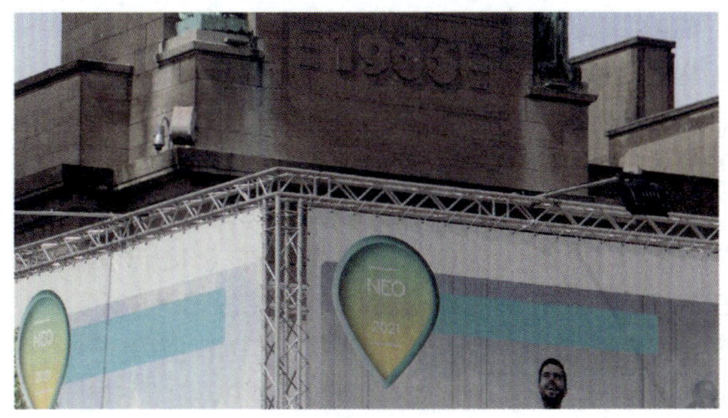

[17] Louis Althusser calls "overdetermination" the complex process whereby various, often mutually contradictory, historical forces bundle to 'cause' a certain event to take place. According to him, recognition of the overdetermined nature of historical events is necessary to move beyond a schematic and reductive (Hegelian) interpretation of history. Louis Althusser, "Contradiction and Overdetermination," *New Left Review,* No. 41 (1967).

onto the present to affect decisions, actions, and behaviours in a very concrete manner. The present moment is constituted not only by the past and the perception thereof, but also by the projections it fosters of the future.

As such, *Mall of Europe* shows that projection exerts, on the future as well as on the immediate present, a force that is as restrictive as it is creative. In installing and pushing forward one particular vision or imaginary of the future, it forecloses the articulation and actualization of others. In producing something new out of the matrix of the present, it prevents the emergence of the *novum*—of the new as something radically different from and discontinuous with the now. Projection, in this sense, cannot be reduced to forecasting alone—to probabilistic conjecture about the future on the basis of present tendencies and developments. With projection, the ideational image that is conjured up of the future is flung forward much more effectively; it is pressed and foisted upon future time. It plays an active, constitutive role in its own actualization—and hence in the elimination of other possible futures. Moreover, what is cast forward with projection also boomerangs back, as the anticipation of its actualization already influences what happens here and now.

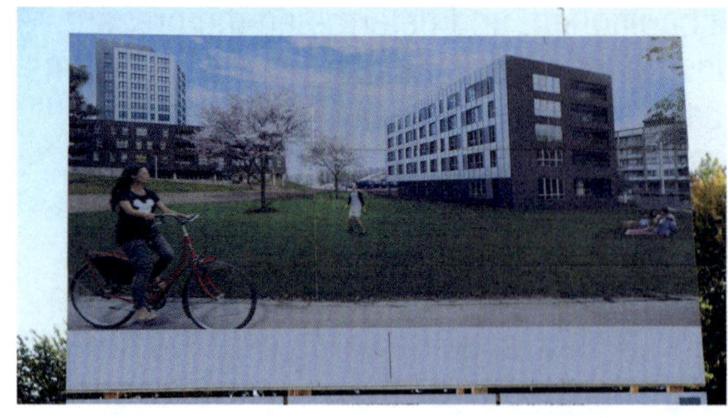

In its second sense, too, projection is a form of schematization. It is an attempt to geometricize historical time, an effort at construing it as mappable, controllable, transparent. This, again, is why it is so closely bound up with modernist fantasies of control and dreams of absolute human sovereignty and self-determination—fantasies and dreams which, needless to say, have had very real and very catastrophic consequences. *Mall of Europe,* however, challenges and disturbs such orderly visions. In the work, the historical present manifests itself as a thick entanglement of historical determinations (which are not properly or exclusively 'historical' in that they are still in force, still tangibly present) and orientations toward the future (which are already effective now). It is not—as the unrealized but lingering visions of modernity attest—the only possible and 'logical' outcome of developments in the past, nor does it hold within itself the ingredients for a mechanistic prediction or production of the future. The present, quite simply, is the mess that we find ourselves in. As such, it contains a vast plurality of possible outcomes—some of which may be well beyond the reach of the projective imagining of the future from the vantage point of the present.

Here, finally, some thoughts on projection's relation to the utopian are in order. Clearly, when authors like Miyoshi and Tafuri characterize modernist architecture (and, by extension, the whole notion of the plan more generally) as utopian through and through, they use utopia in its more pejorative, and limited, sense. Utopia, as they employ it, is essentially a misadventure of idealism, an extreme (and therefore dangerous) figure of the modernist over-confidence in human comprehension and competency. As Kathi Weeks has written, though, a more true and more truly desirable version of utopianism—a utopianism worthy of the name—would be one that emerges not exclusively out of cognitive praxis, but also from the affective thrust of *hope.* For Weeks, the function of hope "is to think these two elements of concrete utopia together: the commitment both to the real-possible and to the novum." [18] According to her, "the hopeful subject affirms not only a possible as opposed to an impossible future, but also a radically different future, one that is both grounded in the real-possible and ventures far beyond it." [19] Utopian thought and practice, as theorized by Weeks, have in common with projection that they grapple with the

[18] Kathi Weeks, *The Problem With Work: Feminism, Marxism, Antiwork Politics* (Durham: Duke University Press, 2011), 197.

[19] Weeks, *The Problem With Work,* 196.

future from the concrete vantage point of the present—the coordinates, developments, and tendencies of which are felt to inform what will happen next. It diverges from it, however, in that utopianism actively fosters an imagination of and an openness toward the unpredictable, toward radical break and rupture—all things that projection ultimately works to preclude. What Weeks would term a politics of concrete utopianism requires not a projective perspective on the relation between the present and the future, but rather an insistence on the opaque and contingent nature of that relation. Though the work is not utopian—at least not in any readily recognizable way—*Mall of Europe* does harbour such an insistence.

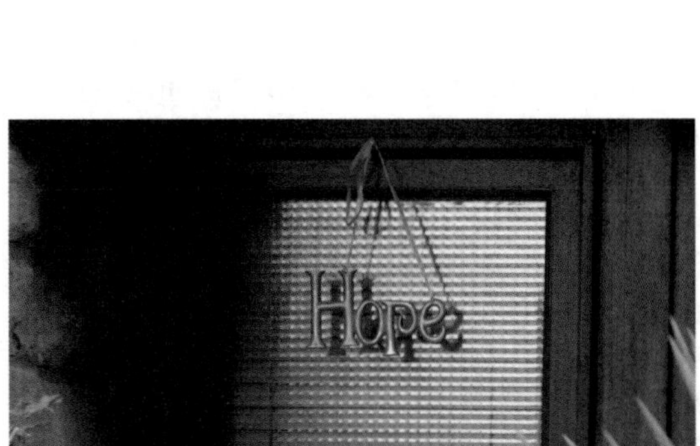

Projection: the conscious or unconscious transferal of desires and affects to an external object or person

Hope as a (potentially) political affect makes an appearance in *Mall of Europe* in the guise of a kitschy doorpiece. The appearance is brief and would hardly be significant if not for its resonance with what is perhaps the main theme of the video: consumerism. If "kitsch" signals an emotional (over)investment in objects that are supposed to be in poor taste, then it is important to note that this entire category marks only a difference in degree with the commodity fetishism that is rampant everywhere. Commodity fetishism, whatever else it may also be, involves a cathexis with objects that is crucial to the projective promises of (Western) modernity. The ideology of progress was and is inextricably bound up the presupposition that a generalized consumerism would and will ultimately make good on the hope for the good life—read: liberal democracy—for all. As attested by the popularity of the world fairs (those immense accumulations and concentrations of commodities), the amassing of material wealth was modernity's—secular and worldly, yet profoundly theological—*telos.* [20] Susan Buck-Morss has argued that, in the twentieth century, images in advertising and cinema (but also, we might add, the world fair) contributed to the fostering of virtual worlds in the collective imaginary, the realization of which subsequently "becomes the social project." However, "the fact that this project is the doubling of a dream image lends to its material construction a phantasmagoric quality." [21] Anyone who has ever set foot in a shopping mall is likely to be familiar with the dream-like and phantasmagoric quality that Buck-Morss writes of.

As pointed out earlier, Van der Put's images of images—including, especially, the architectural renderings and publicity images that appear throughout *Mall of Europe*—emanate a sense of the unnervingly oneiric, and as such resonate with Buck-Morss' discussion of modernity as dreamworld. This is especially the case for the opening sequence, where architectural renderings of the grand entrance of the underconstruction 'Mall of Europe' are used interchangeably with photographs taken outside an actual shopping complex near the Expo area, occasioning moments of confusion between what is image and what is material construction. This is a productive confusion in that it makes tangible and concrete what Buck-Morss expresses in writing, while also rendering it apparent that the program of the material construction of the world on the basis of (dream) images is something that cannot be relegated to a now-historicized and distant modernity alone: it is ongoing. Likewise, the pleasures and comforts on offer in advertising (advertising for tourism, for food, for housing, for the very act of consumption

[20] Sylvia Wynter writes that the ethic of Western modernity is essentially based upon the pursuance of the "supraordinate goal of higher and higher 'standards of living'". It thus projects a form of material redemption, "whereas in the feudal order the behavior-orienting goal was that of *Spiritual Redemption.*' Sylvia Wynter, "No Humans Involved: An Open Letter to my Colleagues," *Forum N.H.I.* 1, No. 1(1994), 61.

[21] Susan Buck-Morss, *Dreamworld and Catastrophe: The Passing of Mass Utopia in East and West* (Cambridge: MIT Press, 2000), 149. For Buck-Morss, this observation applies as much to the history of Soviet Russia as it does to that of the West (always epitomized by the United States). "'Doubling' duplicated virtual realities as material phantasmagorias that could really be experienced. This gave a special dream character to industrial production in the case of the USSR, and to commodity consumption in the case of the United States." Buck-Morss, *Dreamworld and Catastrophe,* 150.

itself) would suggest that "material redemption" is still very much a "behaviour-orienting goal"—is still very much a projection that most of us live by most of the time.

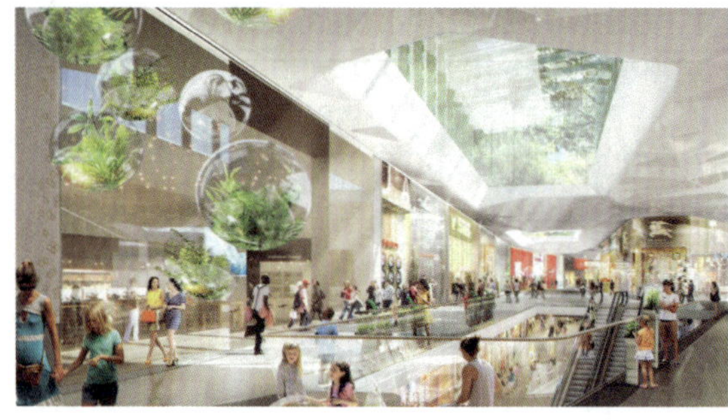

Such is the nature of commodity fetishism that consumption of and investment in the object turn out to (also) be consumption of and investment in the object's image—that the use and enjoyment of the seemingly most concrete, material, sensuous, and tangible of things prove to be bound up with mirage-like illusions of all sorts. This is highlighted in analyses of the society of the spectacle or of the aesthetic populism of postmodernity, but is present in germinal form already in the famously dense section on 'The Fetishism of the Commodity and its Secret' in *Capital.* In this text, Marx is at pains to explain that the commodity's exchange-value is the product of a set of social relations between people rather than a quality that would be in any way innate or even related to the physical properties of the commodity in question. This is not how the commodity appears, however: the relations which determine the commodity's exchange-value remain phenomenologically unavailable, just as the labour that has been invested in making the commodity is invisible in the final product. Marx resorts to a comparison with optical processes to drive home his point that commodities are "sensuous things which are at the same time supra-sensible or social."

The comparison goes as follows: "In the same way, the impression made by a thing on the optic nerve is perceived not as a subjective excitation of that nerve but as the objective form of a thing outside the eye. It is a physical relation between physical things. As against this, the commodity-form, and the value-relation of the products of labour within which it appears, have absolutely no connection with the physical nature of the commodity and the material *[dinglich]* relations arising out of this. It is nothing but the definite social relation between men themselves that assumes here, for them, the fantastic form of a relation between things."[22] The point is that, even with 'ordinary' commodities like the simple wooden table that Marx refers to elsewhere in this chapter, all kinds of qualities and properties are projected onto the commodity that do not properly belong to it. Those qualities and properties subsequently become the object of and motivation for consumption just as much—or more—as do the commodity's *actual* qualities and properties, its use-value.

[22] Karl Marx, *Capital Volume I* (London: Penguin Publishers, 1990) 165. It has often been noted that Marx had a penchant for such optical analogies or metaphors. Compare, for instance, how the inverse projection of the outside world in a camera obscura is called upon to explain the concept of ideology (and its relation to material, historical processes) in *The German Ideology:* "If in all ideology men and their circumstances appear upside-down as in a *camera obscura,* this phenomenon arises just as much from their historical life-process as the inversion of objects on the retina does from their physical life-process." Karl Marx, "The German Ideology," accessed October 29, 2019, https://www.marxists.org/archive/marx/works/1845/german-ideology/ch01a.htm.

Mall of Europe, especially in the moments when it focuses on advertising images or trade fairs, depicts the process whereby the consumption of such use-values seems to become increasingly subordinate to the expenditure of things that are much more elusive—like images, or feelings, or images of feelings. One advertisement in the video appears simply to publicize "The Experience," and consists of nothing but those two words, in a Disney-esque font, against a white background. Another shows a scene by the side of a pool and heralds "Privileged life." The commodity fetishism that is on view in *Mall of Europe* involves processes that are not only analogous to projection in the technical or optical sense of the word, but that also dovetail with the Freudian denotation of "projection" as the attribution or the transfer of emotions to an external object or person. The middle-class lifestyle propagated in the architectural renderings makes it blatantly clear: contemporary consumerism involves a strong affective investment (not in the least of hopes and aspirations for the future) in commodities, which is to say in images of commodities. Beauty as *promesse du bonheur* is alive and well here.

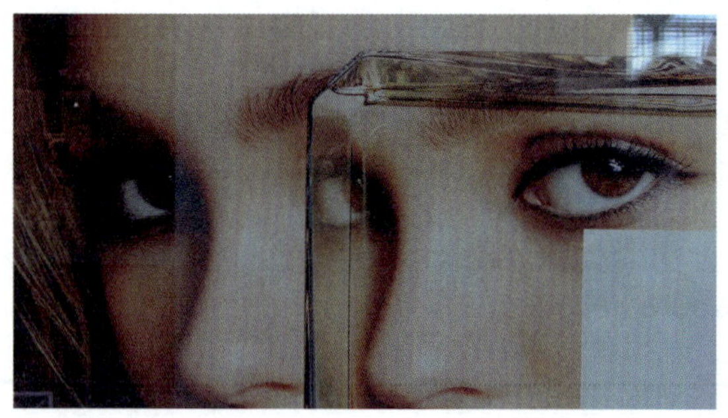

Moreover, the work places these manifestations of "late

capitalism" (if that kind of periodization still holds up) in a constellation with phenomena that belong to modernity proper, with aspects of the exhibitionary complex that can be seen as prototypical of the current, advertising-driven visual regime. World fairs in particular have been a crucial and paradigmatic moment for the relative autonomization of the (mystificatory, enchanting) appearance of the commodity from the commodity itself as a material object.[23] This process of autonomization, whereby the commodity's image is severed from the materiality of the commodity and increasingly starts to live its own life, eventually becoming a commodity in itself, is continued and intensified in advertising. Taken as a whole, then, *Mall of Europe* sketches the outlines of a long-term view (or at least a long*ish*-term view) of the development, out of the exhibitionary complex, of current forms of the organization of visuality.

At this point it becomes tempting to stress how we have come full circle, how we are back at projection as an image presented on a surface, and how it has therefore turned out that the different aspects and senses of "projection" are indeed entangled and interdependent—which was anyhow the presupposition of this essay. Pleasing though this would be, to close the circle here would also be to square it—to overly impose the formal and compositional principles of this essay on *Mall of Europe.* Probably the best way to go about this would be to fall back on the established jargon and the habitual operations of critique, to conclude by claiming that *Mall of Europe* "reveals" and "lays bare," in a more or less determinate and forceful way, the things that have been highlighted here in the reading of the work. Such a claim would not be wrong. Van der Put's video indeed possesses a distinctly critical dimension, engaging as it does with the work of unconcealment, especially where it attempts to establish (historical) connections between apparently disparate and unrelated phenomena. The thing is, though, that that is not all.

It is not without some sense of embarrassment that I want to note that there still is much in *Mall of Europe* that exceeds my reading of it here. In attempting to articulate conceptually what the work conveys visually or aesthetically, this essay inevitably enacts and dramatizes a specific kind of failure: the failure of theory to fully account for either the experience of looking or its significance. One reason why this essay is committed to such failure is because it has the advantage of indexing—albeit negatively—that which ceaselessly resists translation into abstraction, of setting off the kind of understanding that conceptualization just does not really know what to do with. In *Mall of Europe,* this resides in an engagement with and of vision that is much more complex, mysterious, and raw than can properly be accounted for here—and which highlights the historical irony of the etymological provenance of "theory" from spectatorship. The work's treatment of advertising images is exemplary in this regard. It seems to me that *Mall of Europe* is not only about the demystificatory gesture of dispelling the enchantment of commodities—even though that gesture is certainly there as well, insofar as this enchantment is oftentimes shown to be banal, shallow, and cheap. At the same time, however, there is a desire to hold on to the fetish character of the commodity, to inhabit its image, to indulge in the cheapness of its spell. There is, in other words, a visual pleasure at work here that cannot merely be reduced to a symptom of a kind of complicity that it does, however, betray as well. *Mall of Europe* is animated by an interplay and an oscillation between demystification and visual enthrallment that does much more than unambiguously reinforce

[23] Concerning the 1851 world exhibition, held in the Crystal Palace in London, Giorgio Agamben has written: "The transfiguration of the commodity into *enchanted object* is the sign that the exchange value is already beginning to eclipse the use-value of the commodity. In the galleries and the pavilions of its mystical Crystal Palace, in which from the outset a place was also reserved for works of art, the commodity is displayed to be enjoyed only through the glance at the *enchanted scene.*" Giorgio Agamben, *Stanzas: Word and Phantasm in Western Culture* (Minneapolis: University of Minnesota Press, 1992), 38.

the priority or the power of the former. Still, this is not *not* critique; it is just taking more seriously than usual the notion of revelation that critique's rhetoric has always relied on in crucial ways. The kind of revelation that I think the work is getting at is both the stuff of magic and of the everyday. *Mall of Europe* stages such revelation by making an appeal to the wonderful, worrisome thickness of seeing—which troubles projection's cruel geometry and cleanliness more than any critical exposition in and of itself ever could.

Bibliography

Agamben, Giorgio. *Stanzas: Word and Phantasm in Western Culture.* Minneapolis: University of Minnesota Press, 1992.

Althusser, Louis. "Contradiction and Overdetermination." *New Left Review,* no. 41 (1967): 15-35.

Bennett, Tony. "The Exhibitionary Complex." *New Formations,* no. 4 (1988): 73-102.

Buck-Morss, Susan. *Dreamworld and Catastrophe: The Passing of Mass Utopia in East and West.* Cambridge: MIT Press, 2000.

Castoriadis, Cornelius. *The Inaginary Institution of Society.* London: Polity Press, 1987.

Doane, Mary Ann. "The Location of the Image: Cinematic Projection and Scale in Modernity." In *The Art of Projection,* edited by Stan Douglas and Christopher Eamon, 151-166. Ostfildern: Hatje Cantz, 2009.

Jay, Martin. *Downcast Eyes: The Denigration of Vision in Twentieth-Century French Thought.* Berkely: University of California Press, 1993.

Jones, Caroline A. *The Global Work of Art: World's Fairs, Biennials, and the Aesthetics of Experience.* Chicago: Chicago University Press, 2017.

Marx, Karl. *Capital Volume I.* London: Penguin Publishers, 1990.

Marx, Karl. "The German Ideology." Accessed October 29, 2019. https://www.marxists.org/archive/marx/works/1845/german-ideology/.

Mignolo, Walter. *The Darker Side of Wester Modernity: Global Futures, Decolonial Options.* Durham: Duke University Press, 2011.

Miyoshi, Masao. "Outside Architecture." In *Trespasses.* Durham: Duke University Press, 2009.

Osborne, Peter. *The Politics of Time: Modernity and Avant-Garde.* London: Verso, 1995.

Saïd, Edward. *Culture and Imperialism.* London: Chatto & Windus, 1993.

Steyerl, Hito. "Too Much World: Is the Internet Dead?." In *Too Much World: The Films of Hito Steyerl,* edited by Nick Aikens, 30-40. Berlin: Sternberg Press, 2015.

Tafuri, Manfredo. *Architecture and Utopia: Design and Capitalist Development.* Cambridge: MIT Press, 1976.

Weeks, Kathi. *The Problem With Work: Feminism, Marxism, Antiwork Politics.* Durham: Duke University Press, 2011.

Wynter, Sylvia. "No Humans Involved: An Open Letter to My Colleagues." *Forum N.H.I.,* no. 1 (1994): 42-73.

Projections : *Mall of Europe*

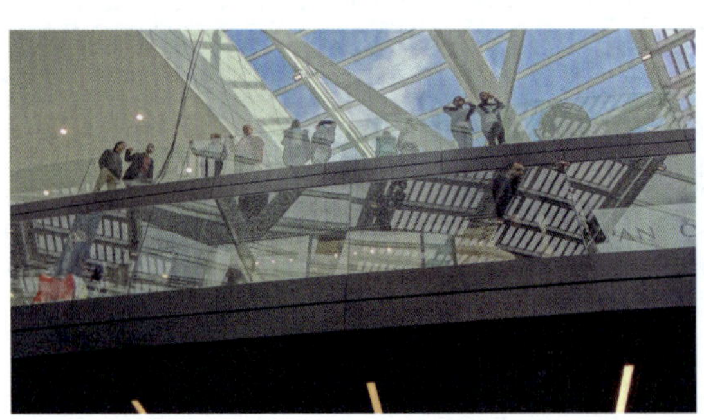

Je me confronte dans ce qui suit à l'œuvre d'Emma van der Put, *Mall of Europe,* vidéo monocanal de 26 minutes. L'artiste y examine les traces laissées par différentes approches — passées et présentes — du développement urbain, du progrès (technologique) et de la mondialisation, que l'on peut trouver dans le quartier du « Heysel », où se tenaient les expositions universelles. *Mall of Europe* est en fait un diaporama d'images photographiques, dépourvu de tout son « diégétique » pris sur place, mais ponctué d'une discrète bande-son minimaliste composée par Maxime Rouquart. Ma contribution tient non seulement à une réflexion écrite *au sujet de* cette vidéo, mais s'efforce aussi de penser *avec* elle, *grâce à* elle, autant que possible. En ce sens, ce texte est bien un essai au sens plein du terme, c'est-à-dire une tentative. En tant que tentative, sa structure dépend en partie de son échec potentiel (possibilité qui, de toute façon, nous accompagne toujours), et au surplus d'une impossibilité inhérente à son principe même. Ainsi cet essai relève-t-il d'un type d'échec bien particulier qui sera, espérons-le, plus fertile. J'y reviendrai à la fin de ce texte.

En deux mots, cet essai a pour principe de développer sur le plan conceptuel certaines choses que *Mall of Europe* exprime visuellement. Il s'articule autour de trois significations distinctes mais corrélées du terme « projection » : la présentation d'une image sur un support, une prédiction du futur influencée par la perception du présent, et le transfert conscient ou inconscient de désirs et affects sur un objet ou une personne extérieurs. Dans ce qu'on pourrait bien interpréter comme une entorse au principe de clarté de la critique ou de l'analyse, cet essai entend mettre au jour, mettre en lumière et même mettre à profit quelques-unes des façons dont ces trois sens de « projection » sont à la fois disparates et interdépendants. Bien d'autres avant moi ont souligné les nombreux échos filmiques et psychanalytiques que recèle la projection, en tant que terme technique aussi bien que dans son usage courant. Ici, il s'agit moins de retracer de telles connections que d'offrir une lecture rigoureuse et attentive de *Mall of Europe,* inscrite dans (et permise par) l'examen des connotations variées de la projection que cette vidéo fait résonner. Autrement dit, si des arguments et assertions plus générales — et donc plus « théoriques » à proprement parler — surgissent au fil de texte à propos du monde dans lequel nous vivons, ce sera peu ou prou au service de la présente tentative : *mieux regarder* cette vidéo en écrivant à son sujet.

La projection comme présentation d'une image sur un support

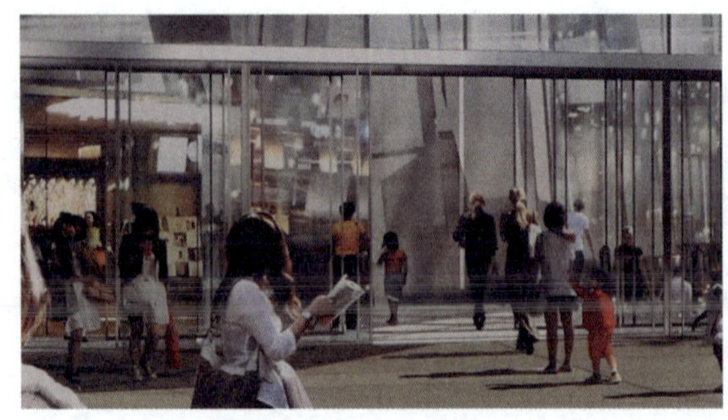

De même qu'une large part du travail récent d'Emma van der Put, *Mall of Europe* regorge *d'images d'images :* le diaporama photographique fait apparaître à plusieurs reprises des photos d'images figurant sur des affiches, des panneaux publicitaires, des écrans informatiques. D'ailleurs, le titre *Mall of Europe* est emprunté à ce qui apparaît sur l'une des images qui ouvrent le film : l'étrange et inquiétante modélisation architecturale (ce qu'on appelle souvent aussi : « vue d'artiste ») du centre commercial « Mall of Europe », capturée par l'appareil photo de Van der Put aux abords du site en chantier. Le montage de *Mall of Europe* alterne plans fixes et travellings sur les photographies à l'image, les figeant dans leur cadrage originel ou bien les animant par des sortes de « scans » lents et réguliers. Sa grammaire cinématographique simple et retenue exploite cependant l'effet de *coupe,* qui rythme systématiquement le passage d'une image à une autre. L'artiste l'utilise à son degré d'efficacité maximum, souvent afin de souligner combien l'impact que peuvent avoir ces images sur nous est plein de contrastes voire de contradictions. Les images d'images sont globalement capables d'attirer notre attention sur la « visualité », sur le régime du visuel et sa structure. Ainsi, les images d'images créent une distance entre nous et les environnements visuels qui nous enveloppent voire submergent habituellement. Ce faisant, elles nous permettent de réfléchir aux logiques qui structurent et sous-tendent ces milieux, mais qui ont tendance à échapper à notre perception courante.

Ce n'est pas une coïncidence si nombre des travaux récents d'Emma van der Put ont été tournés dans des lieux destinés à attirer des visiteurs et conçus pour leur « regard spectatorial ». Par exemple, la courte vidéo *Chinese Pavilion,* datant également de 2018, se concentre sur une construction orientaliste dans le domaine royal de Laeken, au nord de Bruxelles, sorte d'« attraction exotique » construite à l'intention de la famille royale belge, et se termine justement par un plan sur l'étonnant buste doré du roi de Belgique Léopold II, en bas-relief dans la frise en bois au fronton du pavillon. Léopold II, mort six mois avant que soit finalisé le pavillon courant 1910, est bien connu pour l'exploitation cruelle et sans pitié qu'il a fait subir au Congo, colonie dont il garda la propriété exclusive de 1885 à 1908, jusqu'à ce qu'il en fasse « cadeau » à l'État belge. Mentionner ici l'œuvre *Chinese Pavilion* est d'autant plus pertinent qu'elle fonctionne à la fois en contrepoint et en post-scriptum à *Mall of Europe,* où les questions de colonialité sont omniprésentes, mais de façon latente, cachées *dans* (plutôt que cachées *sous)* des surfaces de toutes sortes. [1]

[1] Dans le cadre d'une exposition en 2018 au centre d'art de Rotterdam A Tale of a Tub, la scénographie soulignait la nature contrapuntique de *Chinese Pavilion* par rapport à *Mall of Europe,* d'une durée bien plus longue, exposant la première vidéo comme s'il fallait la considérer comme une arrière-pensée ou une note de bas de page relative à la seconde.

Pour sa part, *Mall of Europe* entreprend une plus longue spéculation au sujet du quartier des expositions à Bruxelles, où ont eu lieu plusieurs expositions universelles, notamment celle de 1935, et la fameuse Expo '58. La vidéo se concentre sur l'architecture moderniste de la « Cité modèle » construite pour l'Exposition de 1958, mais l'intègre aussi à une constellation d'autres sites où se déploie la même sorte de « trafic scopique », comme l'attraction touristique Mini-Europe, des foires commerciales pour des agences de voyages ou des décorateurs d'intérieur, et bien sûr le centre commercial « Mall of Europe ». L'œuvre de Van der Put rassemble ces lieux — et les échanges de regard qui s'y jouent — non seulement parce qu'ils se trouvent être à proximité géographique de la « Cité modèle », mais aussi parce qu'ils sont tous déterminés par une logique scopique très semblable à celle d'une exposition universelle.

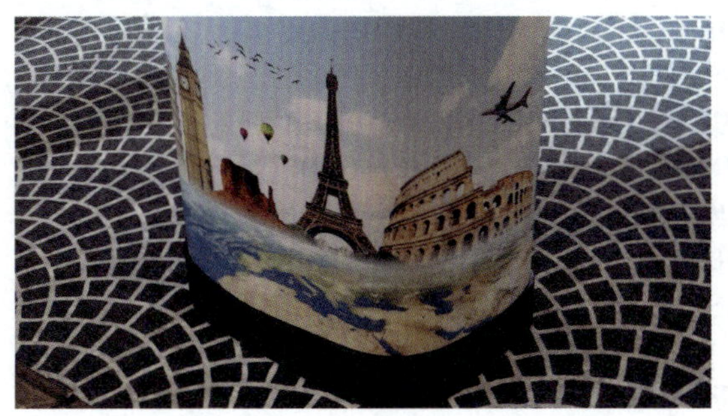

Le « pavillon chinois », les expositions universelles et tous les processus qu'agrège en constellation l'œuvre *Mall of Europe* sont des exemples paradigmatiques du « système expositionnel » (« *exhibitionary complex* »), expression du sociologue Tony Bennett qui a fait florès, qu'il utilise pour analyser le régime de visualité propre à la modernité occidentale. T. Bennet postule qu'à partir du XIXe siècle, plusieurs institutions émergent à partir de celles, pré-modernes, dont Michel Foucault a décrit dans ses fameux ouvrages le système disciplinaire et l'imbrication qui s'y joue entre savoir et pouvoir. Ces institutions finissent par totalement remplacer les anciennes, et T. Bennet entend montrer que discipline et surveillance ne disparaissent pas au sein du système expositionnel, mais deviennent des aspects parmi d'autres d'un enchevêtrement de relations de pouvoir plus emmêlé, et en effet plus « complexe ».

De manière cruciale ici, il faut se rappeler que ces institutions créées au XIXe siècle étaient, au moins en théorie, publiques. Au contraire des systèmes carcéraux et médicaux auxquels s'intéressait Foucault, tous les exemples de Bennett — musées, galeries d'art, foires, expositions, grands magasins... — touchent au fait de « policer l'ordonnancement des objets en vue de leur inspection publique mais aussi, simultanément, la régulation du public chargé de cette inspection ».[2] Au sein du système expositionnel, on attend d'abord et surtout de la part des spectateurs qu'ils adoptent avec empathie un certain regard totalisant — le pouvoir ne s'impose pas seulement de l'extérieur au sujet, mais opère aussi de l'intérieur, depuis le sujet lui-même. Selon Bennett, cela aboutit en fin de compte à « un système scopique auto-régulateur où l'on peut permuter les positions d'objet et de sujet, et où la foule en vient à communier et s'organiser grâce à une conception idéale et ordonnée d'elle-même, considérée du point de vue d'un pouvoir dominateur — un lieu d'observation accessible à tous ».[3] Bennett remarque que cette dynamique est particulièrement évidente dans le cas des expositions universelles, où les visiteurs-spectateurs, principalement occidentaux, sont effectivement placés dans une position de « domination spéculaire envers une totalité ». Ces foires « ont pour but la mise à disposition, par métonymie, du monde entier, passé aussi bien que présent, via les assemblages d'objets et de peuples qu'elles rassemblent et présentent [...] pour le soumettre à une forme de surveillance ou contrôle visuel ».[4]

[2] Tony Bennett, « The Exhibitionary Complex », *New Formations,* n° 4, 1988, p. 74 [trad. Lucas Faugère pour toutes les citations].

[3] *Ibid.*, p. 82.

[4] *Ibid.*, p. 79.

Les diaporamas d'Emma van der Put sont peuplés de nombreux spectateurs à la fois sujets et objets d'une contemplation qui s'avère aussi surveillance. En effet, les photos qui fournissent la matière des œuvres de l'artiste produisent souvent une impression d'observation distanciée, et portent en elles-mêmes des connotations de surveillance et de voyeurisme. Elles tissent leurs propres relations de pouvoir — parfois asymétriques — vis-à-vis des personnes qu'elles représentent. Autrement dit, le travail de Van der Put est lui-même immanent au système expositionnel, non seulement parce qu'il est typiquement présenté dans des musées ou dans divers espaces d'exposition, mais aussi parce qu'il utilise comme matériau le médium photographique.[5] D'ailleurs, l'histoire de celui-ci — dans sa version fixe comme sa version animée, le cinéma — est inséparable de celle de l'émergence et de l'affirmation du système expositionnel, et de fait aux manières de voir concomitantes que les vidéos de Van der Put explorent.

[5] Voir l'examen des liens historiques entre expositions universelles et les œuvres d'art contemporain (à l'heure de la mondialisation) dans : Caroline A. Jones, *The Global Work of Art: World's Fairs, Biennials, and the Aesthetics of Experience,* Chicago (IL), Chicago University Press, 2017.

L'historien des idées Martin Jay a noté l'émergence quasi-simultanée, autour de l'année 1850, de la photographie, du tourisme de masse et des expositions universelles, qui prolongent tous le principe de la foire, « contempler l'autre avec curiosité »,[6] et encouragent à voir le monde comme une exposition. Comme T. Bennett, M. Jay souligne les aspects et implications colonialistes et impérialistes d'un tel arraisonnement visuel du monde. Ces projections rendent d'autant moins innocentes les formes d'exotisme et d'orientalisme qui montent en puissance en Occident à partir du milieu du XIXe siècle. Ce que M. Jay décrit comme « l'appropriation visuelle de sites exotiques remarquables et des populations indigènes (ou de la faune) non moins photogéniques qui y habitent »[7] constitue un corollaire de l'appropriation *effective* de ces lieux par leur colonisation, exploitation, ou pillage, ainsi que du violent assujettissement ou déshumanisation de ces « indigènes photogéniques ». En témoigne l'inclusion d'un « village congolais » dans l'Exposition universelle de Bruxelles de 1958, avatar très récent et très concret des « zoos humains » d'autrefois.

[6] Martin Jay, *Downcast Eyes: The Denigration of Vision in Twentieth-Century French Thought,* Berkeley, University of California Press, 1993), p. 140.

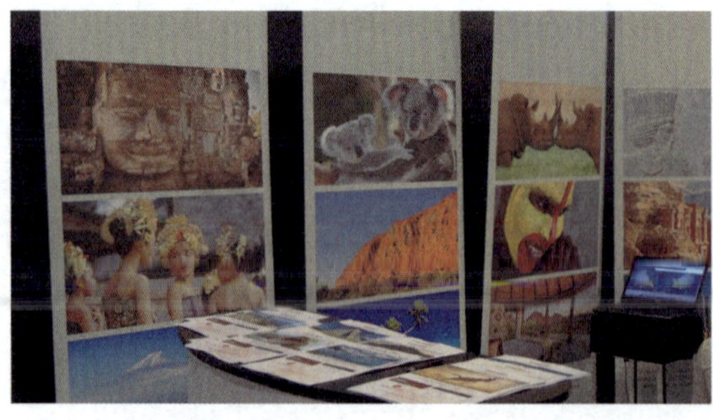

[7] *Ibid.*, p. 140.

Rien de tout cela n'est vraiment à ce point explicite dans le travail d'Emma van der Put, mais les références au passé colonial y abondent néanmoins. Crucialement, le passé n'y est pas traité comme quelque chose de révolu, mais plutôt comme ce qui continue, de manière problématique, à modeler, influencer et sous-tendre le temps présent de mille et une façons. Si *Chinese Pavilion* fait directement signe vers la persistance de l'héritage colonial dans la réalité du tissu urbain, *Mall of Europe* s'attache plus à démontrer combien un regard « altérisant » est à l'œuvre encore aujourd'hui. Ainsi, dans les *showrooms* ou les foires commerciales de décoration d'intérieur, les artefacts et sculptures « primitives » se trouvent déconnectés de leurs contextes culturels respectifs, et sont utilisés comme accessoires esthétisés, à but décoratif. De même, les images promotionnelles des agences de voyages mettent en avant l'altérité « authentique » des destinations qu'elles proposent. Exotisme et orientalisme se révèlent fonctionner à plein, non pas en tant que maigres vestiges anachroniques d'une époque révolue, mais bien comme éléments constitutifs de notre présent.

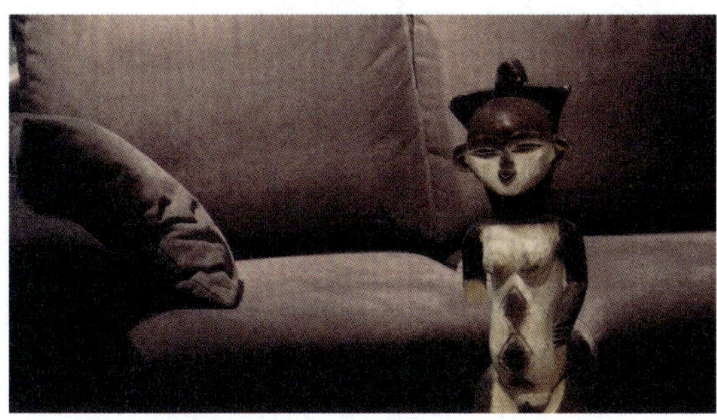

Certains postulent que la notion de colonialité ne peut être dissociée de la modernité, idéologie avec laquelle nous n'avons pas tout à fait rompu.[8] Dans *Mall of Europe,* cette relation (qui pourrait de prime abord sembler plutôt anecdotique) se noue autour d'un autre aspect central de la vidéo : l'importance de l'architecture moderniste. Celle-ci s'y manifeste principalement dans sa version post-Seconde guerre mondiale, puisque Van der Put se focalise sur les immeubles résidentiels du quartier des expositions, construits dans les années 1950, et en particulier la « Cité modèle » construite spécialement pour l'Expo '58, actuellement toujours dépourvue d'habitants. Dans un passage tout à fait remarquable de la vidéo qui mobilise crucialement, une fois de plus, l'image d'une image, Emma van der Put juxtapose à ses propres relevés photographiques contemporains une vieille photo d'archive documentant la construction de deux tours résidentielles. L'état actuel des immeubles de logements, marqués par le temps et recouverts de graffitis, montre bien que leur aspect « moderne » n'est plus vraiment visible aujourd'hui.

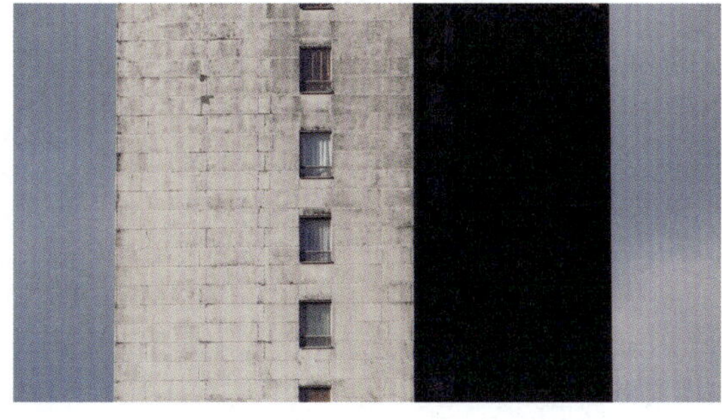

Jamais ces bâtiments ne seront-ils donc à la hauteur des projections qu'ils suscitaient, témoignant en creux d'un futur rêvé mais non réalisé. Un tel constat peut plus largement s'appliquer à la postérité du modernisme en architecture. Critiquant ce courant, Manfredo Tafuri affirme qu'« une architecture qui a pour idéologie le plan se voit balayée par la *réalité effective du plan* dès que l'on dépasse le stade de l'utopie et que le plan doit devenir mécanisme opératoire ».[9] De la même manière, Masao Miyoshi a commenté le caractère « inévitablement utopique » du discours architectural moderniste, et combien cette architecture « n'est toute entière elle-même que lorsqu'elle se trouve encore au stade du plan préparatoire, donc face à une situation future encore en développement ».[10] Autrement dit, l'architecture moderniste s'apparente toujours à un *projet,* et ne pourra jamais vraiment prétendre à être autre chose.

Mais bien que l'architecture moderniste soit mieux représentée par ce genre de *plans* préparatoires que par n'importe quel bâtiment, on n'en voit nulle part dans *Mall of Europe.* Plutôt que le plan, cet emblème de coordination et planification rationnelles, empreint de promesses et potentialités, Van der Put choisit de nous montrer une catégorie d'images similaires et peut-être plus contemporaines : celle des vues d'artiste ou des modélisations en trois dimensions. À l'instar du plan, une modélisation 3D porte en elle la promesse d'un état à venir, mais à son inverse, elle n'a presque aucune importance *technique*

[8] C'est un point fondamental du courant de pensée décolonial, où l'on écrit d'ailleurs souvent les deux termes en un seul syntagme, « modernité/colonialité », soulignant ainsi leur indissociabilité. Voir, par exemple, Walter Mignolo, *The Darker Side of Western Modernity: Global Futures, Decolonial Options* Durham, Duke University Press, 2011.

[9] Manfredo Tafuri, *Architecture and Utopia: Design and Capitalist Development* Cambridge, MIT Press, 1976, p. 135.

[10] Masao Miyoshi, « Outside Architecture » (1996), *Trespasses. Selected Writings* Durham, Duke University Press, 2010, p. 151–157, ici p 152.

immédiate par rapport à la concrétisation de la potentialité qu'elle exprime en particulier. Ces simulations informatiques sont produites en raison de leurs effets esthétiques et, par extension, idéologiques.

Malgré le fait que ces modélisations 3D ne soient pas directement utiles comme peuvent l'être les plans, ces deux outils ont néanmoins en commun leur dimension prospective : ils représentent le futur et, d'une manière ou d'une autre, jouent un rôle actif dans la concrétisation de ce qu'ils préfigurent, facilitant leur venue au monde en quelque sorte. Dans le cas des modélisations, cela peut aller jusqu'à produire des effets proches du simulacre, comme ces « villes entières qui semblent évoquer des tutoriels YouTube pour [le logiciel de modélisation architecturale] CAD », [11] relevées par Hito Steyerl. En d'autres termes, les hiérarchies entre réel et représentation ainsi qu'entre référent et référence sont brouillées, inversées, mélangées. On le sent d'ailleurs dans le mode par lequel Van der Put inclut ces modélisations dans ses diaporamas. De manière singulière, elle les photographie souvent de façon à souligner leur caractère étrange voire inquiétant, par exemple en alignant les bords de sa photo sur ceux de la modélisation, ou en ménageant un moment d'hésitation sur la réalité ou non de ce que celle-ci représente. Ces techniques sont explorées et exploitées plus avant dans *SOON* (2018), une autre vidéo plus courte de Van der Put qui peut s'interpréter comme un supplément à *Mall of Europe.*

Plan et modélisation constituent des exemples parlants d'une « projection », et sont à ce titre d'autant plus importants pour notre argument. Si l'on considère la projection dans son premier sens, la présentation d'une image sur un support, il faut toujours se rappeler que ce processus implique toujours la réduction d'un *univers* visuel à un *champ* visuel, voire à une « simple » *surface.* La vue, la vision s'y trouvent figées, aplaties, et il faut suspendre leur déchiffrement constant du monde, leur vagabondage à travers l'espace, et leur relation holistique aux autres sens ou leur collaboration avec eux. En ce sens, la projection est donc synonyme de simplification, de schématisation agissant sur le monde, dans le monde. En tant que telle, elle a souvent été la conséquence de rêves de maîtrise ou contrôle — fantasmes qu'elle a aussi souvent requis, et facilités. [12] Bien sûr, ces notions de maîtrise et de contrôle sont précisément celles qui sous-tendent et relient ensemble des phénomènes de la modernité qui pourraient à première vue sembler disparates, comme le projet colonial et l'architecture moderniste. Ces notions fondent également l'organisation moderne de la visualité au sein du système expositionnel. Enfin, notons que la maîtrise et le contrôle que l'on peut atteindre dans une projection — comme l'exemplifie bien le *plan* — sont inévitablement et immédiatement créateurs d'une certaine dimension « temporelle », tant ils sont étroitement liés à une forme de croyance en la possibilité de manipuler ou fabriquer l'histoire.

La projection comme prédiction du futur influencée par la perception du présent

Pour Manfredo Tafuri, l'architecture moderniste — dans ses manifestations initiales de type « héroïque », comme dans sa version plus pragmatique d'après-guerre — est une illustration concrète de la pensée moderne et de la « rationalité instrumentale » (Max Weber), dont le « thème dominant est celui d'un futur dans lequel on peut projeter le présent tout entier, d'un futur soumis à une domination "rationnelle", d'un futur débarrassé de tout le *risque* qu'il porte en lui ». [13]
En architecture comme ailleurs, un plan constitue un moyen de gérer

[11] Hito Steyerl, « Too Much World: Is the Internet Dead?, in Nick Aikens (éd.), *Too Much World: The Films of Hito Steyerl* Berlin, Sternberg Press, 2015, p. 29–40, ici p. 31.

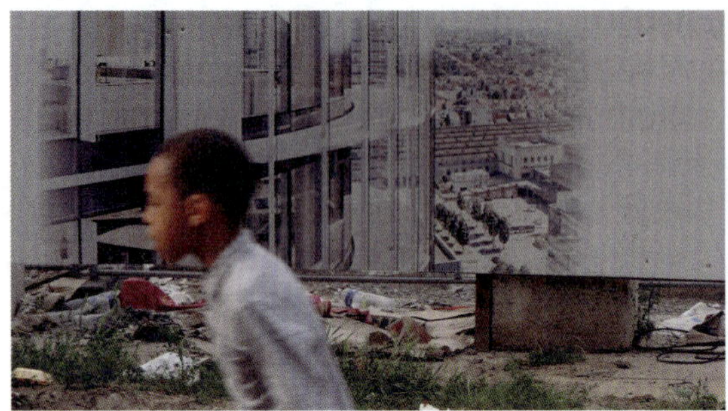

[12] « Voir ce qu'a écrit Mary Ann Doane sur la relation entre carte et image (cinématographique) projetée : « "Projection" désigne aussi très spécifiquement la représentation, sur une surface plane, d'une sphère ou d'une section de sphère (en premier lieu, le globe terrestre), d'où son rapport étroit aux questions de cartographie. » : Mary Ann Doane, « The Location of the Image: Cinematic Projection and Scale in Modernity », in Stan Douglas et Christopher Eamon (éd.), *The Art of Projection,* Ostfildern, Hatje Cantz, 2009, p. 151–166, ici p. 157.

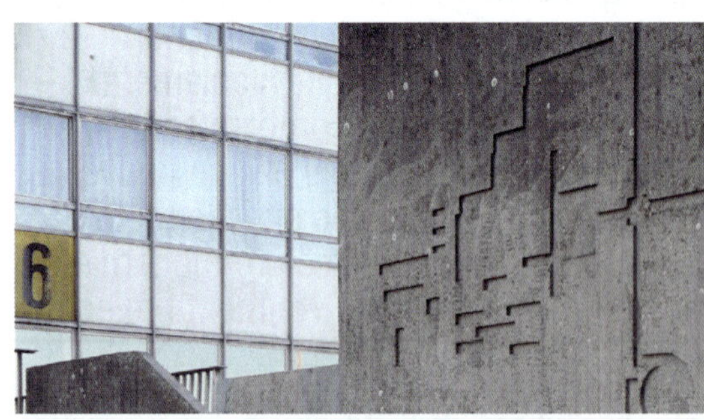

[13] « [...] the dominant theme is that of a future into which the entire present is projected, of a "rational" dominion of the future, of the elimination of the risk it brings with it. » : M. Tafuri, *Architecture and Utopia op. cit.*, p. 52.

les éventualités possibles en les circonscrivant, un outil pour aborder ce qui reste ouvert, inconnu, incertain, un antidote à l'angoisse que le futur peut susciter. Le plan est proche du « projet » au sens où tous deux établissent et encouragent une certaine vision ou un certain imaginaire de l'avenir. À ce titre, ils sont inextricablement liés à une forme de confiance — un *hybris* ! —, symptomatique de la modernité, envers la malléabilité et la perfectibilité de l'histoire (c'est-à-dire du futur) et envers le fait que « l'Homme » soit le sujet et acteur historique autodéterminé par excellence.[14]

La modernité est donc pour ainsi dire équivalente à l'idéologie du progrès. Sa chronologie fournit la représentation la plus basique — littéralement *linéaire,* et directe — de sa structure temporelle. De ce fait, les expositions universelles — telle l'Expo '58 — visaient à représenter « l'état de l'art » dans un monde considéré comme résolument engagé dans un processus de modernisation unique, linéaire et universel. Il faut ici absolument rappeler, une fois de plus, combien cette conception du monde comme espace-temps homogène unifié resterait impensable sans l'appui du colonialisme — colonialisme justement légitimé en retour par l'opposition entre pays « avancés » et pays « arriérés » qu'encourage cette conception. En découle la présence simultanée à l'Exposition universelle de 1958 à Bruxelles du pavillon « sonique » de la marque Philips, futuriste au dernier degré (conçu par Le Corbusier et Iannis Xenakis, et démantelé après la fin de la foire), et d'un « village congolais ». Ces deux *exhibitions* participaient d'un récit de l'histoire humaine tendant au développement et au progrès, la première témoignant d'une position d'« avant-garde », et la seconde illustrant celle de « retardataires » sur la scène de l'histoire globale.

Cette coexistence choquante du pavillon Philips et du « village congolais » nous rappelle avec force les risques et la violence intrinsèques au fait d'imposer sur le cours de l'histoire des grilles conceptuelles strictes — comme celle qu'exige le si noble idéal du progrès. Elle montre également combien l'histoire, cependant, tend à résister et refuser de telles surimpositions, au moins en partie, et à révéler la façon dont l'idéologie du progrès produit toutes sortes de complications et contradictions internes. En premier lieu, l'idée même de progrès requiert une certaine conscience historique, qui justement menace constamment sa pertinence. Ce n'est paradoxal qu'en apparence, mais un effet secondaire, si l'on peut dire, du modernisme — défini comme négation perpétuelle du passé dans le présent grâce au nouveau — est d'amplifier notre prise en compte de l'historicité, notion qui ne devient véritablement sensible qu'après un certain affaiblissement du caractère évident de la tradition.[15] L'obsession moderniste pour les musées et les monuments publics (qui apparaissent beaucoup également dans *Mall of Europe)* n'est pas une coïncidence : dans le modernisme, le « regard projectif » tourné vers l'avenir a pour pendant la contemplation et l'examen historicistes du passé, où celui-ci est compris comme ayant modelé, conditionné, déterminé le présent. Le constant dépassement de « l'ancien », son escamotage, sa démolition, suscitent « non seulement une perception de la passéité du passé, mais aussi de sa présence ».[16]

Justement, les vidéos d'Emma van der Put attestent d'une telle conception de l'histoire, et y contribuent. Cette conception du passé (mais aussi des futurs possibles) souligne et tient pour cruciale la concomitance de sa passéité et de sa présence. Une photo utilisée dans *Mall of Europe* illustre ceci entre toutes : l'image à l'écran procède d'un lent glissement vers le haut et fait d'abord apparaître une (partie de) pelleteuse, au premier plan de la prise de vue, puis l'on distingue

[14] Il faut absolument souligner que cette caractérisation s'applique non seulement aux manifestations capitalistes de la modernité, mais aussi à ce qu'en fait la gauche (radicale). Parmi de nombreux exemples, l'un des plus frappants fut la nature prométhéenne du socialisme d'État en Union soviétique, et son obsession pour la planification.
Le travail de Cornelius Castoriadis sur le « projet révolutionnaire » est également instructif à cet égard, puisque le philosophe s'essaye à préserver une certaine foi dans l'idée de la perfectibilité de l'histoire, tout en reconnaissant les limites du savoir humain, et celles de sa mainmise sur le monde. C'est pourquoi la révolution n'est pas, selon lui, une question de technique ou de planification, mais de *praxis* – c'est-à-dire une forme réflexive d'action politique qui complexifie la distinction entre moyens et fins. Voir Cornelius Castoriadis, *The Imaginary Institution of Society* Londres, Polity Press, 1987, p. 71–100.

[15] Peter Osborne affirme que ce que nous appelons modernisme est essentiellement « une forme de conscience historique, une structure temporelle abstraite ». Et parce que cette structure englobe une grande variété de « contenus », « la modernité *n'est pas,* en tant que telle, un projet, mais tout au plus sa forme » : Peter Osborne, *The Politics of Time: Modernity and Avant-Garde* Londres, Verso, 1995, p. 23.

[16] T. S. Eliot, cité par Edward Saïd, *Culture and Imperialism* Londres, Chatto & Windus, 1993, p. 2. E. Saïd poursuit en écrivant que « même si nous devons tout à fait prendre en compte la passéité du passé, il n'y a pas de façon satisfaisante d'absolument séparer le passé du présent. Le passé et le présent agissent l'un sur l'autre, se déterminent l'un l'autre et, au sens tout à fait idéal où l'entend Eliot, coexistent dans l'un comme dans l'autre »

derrière l'engin une affiche où figure une vue panoramique en modélisation 3D de ce à quoi ressemblera la zone en travaux une fois sa transformation achevée. On peut aussi voir sur l'affiche la photo d'un homme autour de la trentaine, blanc, appartenant clairement à la classe moyenne mais sinon tout à fait lambda, et représenté de manière disproportionnée par rapport au paysage qu'il écrase de sa présence. Le mouvement de caméra révèle rapidement ses bras croisés, son regard levé au ciel et son sourire béat adressé à quelque chose d'extérieur au cadre de l'affiche, vers un horizon ou une créature céleste que nous, simples spectateurs, ne pouvons voir. Dans le coin supérieur gauche de l'affiche se trouve un logo qui rappelle le repère indiquant une position dans Google Maps, portant les mots « NEO 2021 » inscrits dans un dégradé du bleu au jaune. L'image de la vidéo continuant son mouvement ascendant, on comprend que le support de la vue d'artiste cache un immeuble, d'autant plus qu'apparaît la partie supérieure du bâtiment au surplomb de l'affiche. Ce fronton est flanqué de deux grandes sculptures classicistes de femmes ailées, et porte l'inscription de son année d'inauguration, 1935 — date de la quatrième Exposition universelle de Bruxelles. De ce qu'on peut voir sur cette photo de Van der Put, ce bâtiment en grande partie caché par l'affiche est typique du style Art Déco de l'entre-deux-guerres, c'est-à-dire que ses traits éclectiques mêlent des éléments traditionnels ou historiques à d'autres plus modernes voire avant-gardistes.

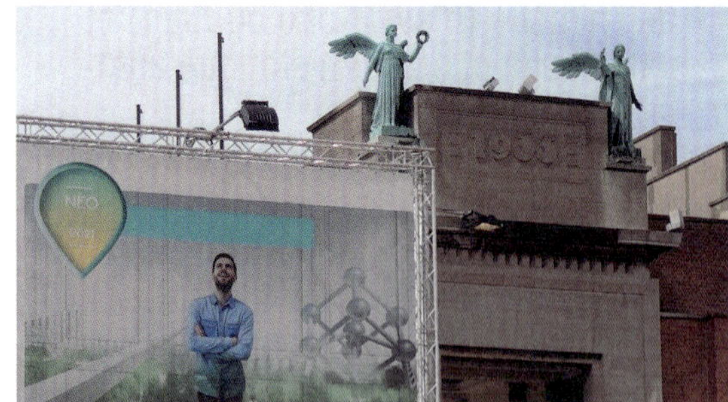

Si d'autres images de la vidéo combinent également des vues de chantier et des photos de modélisations 3D récoltées dans le quartier des expositions de Bruxelles, c'est bien ce moment précis de *Mall of Europe* qui capture le plus singulièrement cet étrange enchevêtrement du passé, du présent et du futur. Le travail d'Emma van der Put s'attache à montrer combien la zone du quartier des expositions (et par extension, toute la capitale belge, toile de fond de toutes ses œuvres récentes) est au sens propre comme au sens figuré construite sur les vestiges du passé — et plus particulièrement sur les vestiges de la modernité, laquelle reste donc encore et toujours présente. Dans la photo en question ci-dessus, l'artiste met en lumière la tangible contemporanéité des traces historiques, mais mène aussi, en mettant au jour simultanément différentes couches d'historicité, une sorte d'archéologie du temps présent — présent dont elle montre ici clairement à quel point le surdéterminent non seulement l'histoire et sa rémanence, mais aussi l'avenir et tous les espoirs, attentes et anticipations que nous y plaçons.[17] Dans ce cas-ci (qui vaut cependant pour toute la vidéo, par métonymie), le temps présent est conçu et donné comme une sorte de va-et-vient entre deux pôles — comme une *conjoncture.* Soulignons ici que, dans ce contexte, « conjoncture » ne désigne pas simplement l'entrelacement de forces historiques divergentes donnant forme et vigueur à un moment du présent, mais exprime aussi une tension vers le futur, une orientation prospective prenant en compte « ce-qui-n'est-pas-encore-connu » et son influence bien concrète sur le présent, sur les décisions, actions ou comportements qui s'y jouent. Ainsi le temps présent est-il fondé sur le passé et la perception que nous en avons, et de plus sur les projections du futur qu'il abrite.

Mall of Europe démontre donc que la projection exerce une force restrictive autant que créative sur le futur comme sur le présent immédiat. En mettant en place une vision unique, en mettant en avant un seul imaginaire de l'avenir, la projection empêche d'énoncer — et a fortiori concrétiser — toute autre perspective. En produisant quelque chose de nouveau à partir de la matrice du présent, elle empêche

[17] Louis Althusser désigne par « surdétermination » le processus complexe dans lequel des forces historiques, entrant souvent en contradiction les unes avec les autres, se regroupent et « provoquent » tel ou tel événement. Selon lui, il est nécessaire de reconnaître la nature surdéterminée des événements historiques afin de dépasser une interprétation (hégélienne) schématique et réductrice de l'histoire. Cf. Louis Althusser, « Contradiction et surdétermination (Notes pour une recherche) », *La Pensée* no 106, décembre 1962, p. 3–22.

l'émergence de tout *novum,* c'est-à-dire d'un nouveau qui serait radicalement différent, et en rupture avec le contemporain. En ce sens, la projection ne peut être simplement réduite à une prédiction ou prévision, à une conjecture probabiliste au sujet du futur, basée sur les tendances actuelles et leur évolution. L'image idéelle du futur que l'on convoque dans la projection est bien plus efficacement *lancée* — elle se superpose et s'impose au temps futur. Cette image projetée joue un rôle actif voire incontournable dans sa propre concrétisation, et donc dans l'élimination d'autres futurs possibles. Et de plus, ce que la projection lance finit par aussi revenir, à l'instar d'un boomerang, puisque le fait d'anticiper sa concrétisation influence toujours déjà ce qui arrive ici et maintenant.

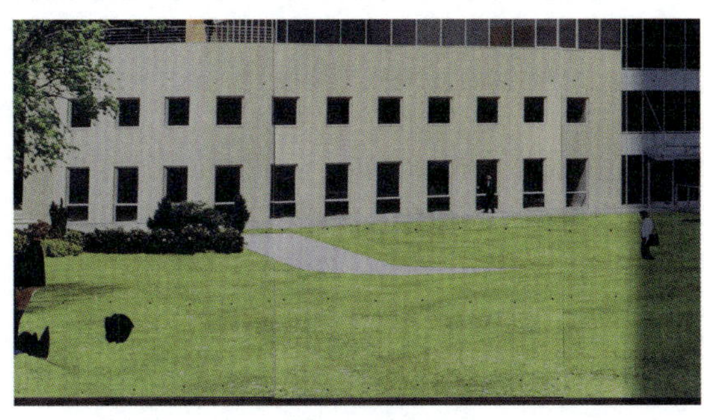

Si l'on revient au second sens de projection, on y trouve également une forme de schématisation : c'est une tentative de rendre géométrique le temps historique, c'est-à-dire cartographiable, maîtrisable, transparent. Voilà pourquoi la projection est une fois de plus si étroitement liée au fantasme moderniste du contrôle total, et à ses rêves de souveraineté et autodétermination absolue des humains — fantasmes et rêves qui, est-il besoin de le rappeler, ont eu des conséquences bien réelles et tout à fait catastrophiques. *Mall of Europe* s'attaque justement à ces visions, et perturbe la belle harmonie dont elles s'autorisent. Dans l'œuvre de Van der Put, le temps présent procède d'un entremêlement inextricable de déterminations historiques (qui ne sont pas à proprement parler ou exclusivement « historiques », puisqu'elles sont encore en action, encore palpables aujourd'hui), et de disposition en vue du futur (qui sont déjà effectives actuellement). Comme en témoigne la persistance, même ténue, de visions de la modernité restées à l'état de projet, le présent ne peut se concevoir comme la seule conséquence possible ou l'aboutissement « logique » des événements passés. Et il ne peut non plus fournir à lui seul tous les « ingrédients » nécessaires pour prédire — et encore moins produire — le futur de manière mécanique. En fait, le temps présent c'est simplement l'imbroglio où nous nous trouvons jour après jour. C'est pourquoi il renferme une vaste pluralité de développements et aboutissements possibles, dont une bonne partie se trouve peut-être tout à fait hors de portée de toute projection imaginant le futur depuis un point de vue ancré dans le présent.

Penchons-nous à présent sur la relation entre projection et utopie : lorsque des auteurs tels que M. Miyoshi ou M. Tafuri définissent comme totalement utopique l'architecture moderniste (et par extension la notion de « plan » toute entière), ils utilisent le terme dans son sens le plus péjoratif et le plus restreint. Sous leur plume, l'utopie se résume à un fourvoiement idéaliste, à une figure extrême (et donc dangereuse) de la trop grande confiance du modernisme dans l'intelligence et les capacités des humains. Comme le défend au contraire Kathi Weeks, une version plus exacte de l'utopie, et à vrai dire plus souhaitable — un utopisme digne de ce nom — ne découlerait pas seulement d'une « praxis cognitive », mais aussi du ressort affectif que peut constituer l'*espoir.* Pour K. Weeks, l'espoir a pour rôle de permettre « une réflexion qui tient ensemble les deux faces d'un utopisme pratique : s'attacher à la fois au réel potentiel et au *novum* ».[18] Selon elle, « le sujet qui espère affirme non seulement un possible opposé à un futur impossible, mais aussi un futur radicalement différent, qui serait à la fois ancré dans le réel potentiel et capable de s'aventurer bien au-delà ».[19] La pensée et la pratique utopiques, telles que les formule K. Weeks, partagent avec la projection le fait d'envisager le futur depuis le point de vue concret du temps présent, et de considérer que la situation, l'évolution et les

[18] Kathi Weeks, *The Problem With Work: Feminism, Marxism, Antiwork Politics*, Durham, Duke University Press, 2011, p. 197.

[19] *Ibid.*, p. 196.

perspectives du présent auront une influence sur ce qui s'ensuivra. Elles diffèrent en revanche dans leur attitude envers l'imprévisible, envers une scission ou rupture radicale : l'utopisme encourage activement un imaginaire et une forme d'ouverture à leur encontre, tandis que la projection travaille en fin de compte à les prévenir. Ce que K. Weeks qualifierait de « politique utopiste pratique » ne requiert pas une perspective projective quant à la relation entre présent et avenir, mais plutôt une attention à la nature opaque et contingente de cette relation. Bien que l'œuvre ne soit pas utopique — du moins d'une façon immédiatement identifiable —, *Mall of Europe* déploie en effet une telle attention.

La projection comme transfert conscient ou inconscient de désirs et affects sur un objet ou une personne extérieurs

L'espoir en tant qu'affect (potentiellement) politique fait une apparition dans *Mall of Europe,* par le truchement d'un ornement de porte assez kitsch. Cette brève apparition n'aurait qu'une signification anecdotique si elle n'entrait pas en résonance avec ce qui constitue peut-être le thème principal de la vidéo : le consumérisme. Si l'on considère que « kitsch » désigne un (sur)investissement émotionnel à l'égard d'objets censément de mauvais goût, alors il est important de noter que cette étiquette et tout ce qu'elle recouvre ne diffèrent qu'en intensité du « fétichisme de la marchandise » (Karl Marx) dont on retrouve partout l'influence. Ce fétichisme de la marchandise, dans toutes ses incarnations possibles, implique une cathexis envers des objets qui est cruciale aux promesses projectives de la modernité (occidentale). L'idéologie du progrès était et est encore étroitement liée à la présupposition suivante : au bout du compte, la généralisation du consumérisme satisferait pleinement l'espoir d'une vie heureuse pour tous — il faudrait ici traduire « vie heureuse » par « vivre dans une démocratie libérale ». Comme en témoigne la popularité des expositions universelles, immenses concentrations de biens et marchandises, le *telos* (séculaire et temporel quoique profondément théologique) de la modernité équivaut à l'accumulation de richesses matérielles.[20] Au XXe siècle, selon l'analyse de Susan Buck-Morss, les images issues de la publicité et du cinéma (mais aussi celles des expositions universelles, pourrions-nous ajouter) contribuent à l'émergence de mondes virtuels dans l'imaginaire collectif, dont la concrétisation « devient le projet de société » par la suite. Cependant, « le fait que ce projet dédouble une image rêvée confère une dimension fantasmagorique à sa mise en œuvre matérielle ».[21] Toute personne ayant déjà franchi les portes d'un centre commercial devrait pouvoir comprendre cette qualité fantasmagorique ou onirique évoquée par S. Buck-Morss.

Comme nous le remarquions plus haut, les images d'images d'Emma van der Put — et notamment les modélisations 3D, vues architecturales et autres images promotionnelles ou publicitaires rencontrées dans *Mall of Europe* — ont une qualité onirique tout à fait déconcertante, et font ainsi écho aux réflexions de S. Buck-Morss sur la modernité comme « monde de rêve » (« *dreamworld* »). La séquence d'ouverture de la vidéo en témoigne tout spécialement : les vues d'artiste de l'entrée principale du « Mall of Europe » en chantier alternent avec des photos prises devant un centre commercial bien réel, proche du quartier des expositions — une interchangeabilité qui suscite à plusieurs reprises une confusion momentanée entre images virtuelles et constructions matérielles. Cette confusion est ici productive, au

[20] Sylvia Wynter décrit à quel point l'éthique de la modernité occidentale est basée sur la poursuite d'un « objectif suprême : des "conditions de vie" de plus en plus élevées ». Ce faisant, cette éthique projette une forme de rédemption « matérielle », « alors que le régime féodal orientait les comportements vers l'objectif d'une *rédemption spirituelle* » : Sylvia Wynter, « No Humans Involved: An Open Letter to my Colleagues », *Forum N.H.I.: Knowledge for the 21st Century,* vol. 1, no 1, « Knowledge on Trial », automne 1994, p. 42–73, ici p. 61.

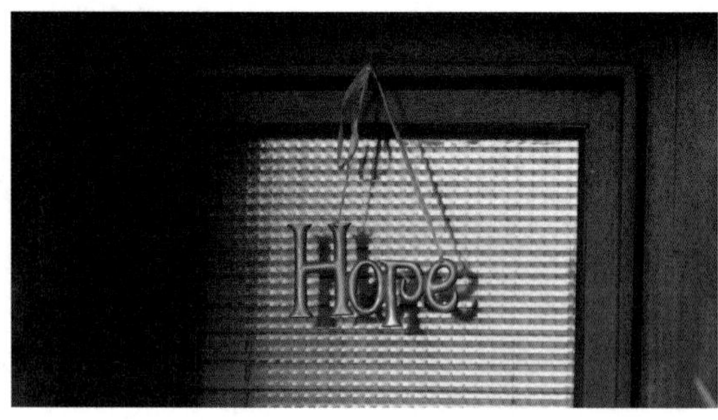

[21] Susan Buck-Morss, *Dreamworld and Catastrophe: The Passing of Mass Utopia in East and West,* Cambridge (MA), MIT Press, 2000, p. 149. Pour la chercheuse, cette observation s'applique autant à l'histoire de la Russie soviétique qu'à celle de l'Occident (toujours incarné par les seuls États-Unis) : « [Ce processus de] "dédoublement" dupliquait des réalités virtuelles en fantasmagories matérielles dont on pouvait vraiment faire l'expérience. Cela conférait une dimension onirique particulière à la production industrielle dans le cas de l'URSS, et à l'achat de biens de consommation aux États-Unis » : *Ibid.*, p. 150.

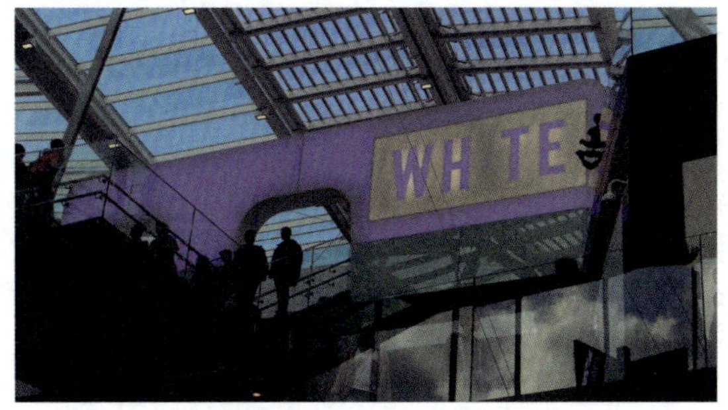

[22] « Aber beim Sehen wird wirklich Licht von einem Ding, dem äußeren Gegenstand, auf ein andres Ding, das Auge, geworfen. Es ist ein physisches Verhältnis zwischen physischen Dingen. Dagegen hat die Warenform und das Wertverhältnis der Arbeitsprodukte, worin sie sich darstellt, mit ihrer physischen Natur und den daraus entspringenden dinglichen Beziehungen absolut nichts zu schaffen. Es ist nur das bestimmte gesellschaftliche Verhältnis der Menschen selbst, welches hier für sie die phantasmagorische Form eines Verhältnisses von Dingen annimmt. » : Karl Marx et Friedrich Engels, *Das Kapital. Kritik der politischen Oekonomie* (1867), Berlin, Dietz Verlag, 1968, p. 86.

Le penchant de Marx pour de telles analogies ou métaphores relatives à l'optique a souvent été relevé. Notons par exemple son utilisation du phénomène d'inversion d'une projection du monde extérieur dans une *camera obscura* pour expliquer le concept d'idéologie (et sa relation à des processus matériels et historiques) : « Si, dans toute idéologie, les humains et leurs relations apparaissent inversés comme dans une camera obscura, cela découle de leur processus vital historique, exactement de la même manière que l'inversion des objets sur la rétine est causé par leur processus vital physique. » [« Wenn in der ganzen Ideologie die Menschen und ihre Verhältnisse wie in einer Camera obscura auf den Kopf gestellt erscheinen, so geht dies Phänomen ebensosehr aus ihrem historischen Lebensprozeß hervor, wie die Umdrehung der Gegenstände auf der Netzhaut aus ihrem unmittelbar physischen. »] : Karl Marx et Friedrich Engels, *Die deutsche Ideologie* (1845–1846), Berlin, Dietz Verlag, 1969, p. 26.

sens où elle rend tangible ce qu'expriment les écrits de S. Buck-Morss, tout en faisant clairement apparaître l'actualité du projet global de construction « matérielle » du monde à partir d'images (oniriques). Ainsi, on ne peut le cantonner à une modernité aujourd'hui mise à distance, historicisée : ce projet est en cours. De même, les plaisirs et commodités promis par la publicité (pour des destinations touristiques, de la nourriture, des logements... et pour l'acte même de consommer) indiquent sans doute combien la « rédemption matérielle » joue encore largement son rôle d'« orientation des comportements » — et combien elle constitue toujours une projection orientant la vie d'une grande partie d'entre nous.

La fétichisation des marchandises est de telle nature qu'elle révèle comment le fait de consommer un objet — et de (s')y investir — revient aussi à consommer son image. C'est-à-dire que l'utilisation voire l'usufruit d'une chose en apparence absolument concrète, matérielle, sensible, tangible, implique en fait irrémédiablement des illusions et mirages de toutes sortes. Les analyses renvoyant à la « société du spectacle » (Guy Debord) ou au populisme esthétique de la postmodernité (Fredric Jameson) soulignent bien ces effets, mais on en trouvait déjà la trace dans le chapitre du *Capital,* célèbre pour sa difficulté, intitulé « Le caractère fétiche de la marchandise et son secret ». Marx y explique laborieusement la façon dont la valeur d'échange d'une marchandise est déterminée par un ensemble de relations sociales entre des individus, et non pas inhérente ou même corrélée d'une façon ou d'une autre aux propriétés matérielles du bien en question. Cependant les marchandises ne se présentent pas ainsi : les relations dictant la valeur d'échange de la marchandise restent phénoménologiquement inaccessibles, de même que le travail investi dans sa fabrication reste invisible dans le produit fini. Marx a recours à une comparaison avec une notion d'optique pour étayer sa caractérisation des marchandises comme étant « des choses sensibles mais en même temps des choses suprasensibles ou sociales ».

Voici cette comparaison : « De la même manière, l'impression lumineuse d'un objet sur le nerf optique n'est pas perçue comme une excitation subjective de ce nerf, mais comme la forme objective d'une chose extérieure à l'œil. C'est un rapport physique entre des choses physiques. Cependant la forme-marchandise et le rapport de valeur des produits du travail n'ont absolument rien à voir avec leur nature physique ou avec les relations matérielles qui en découlent. C'est en fait seulement un rapport social déterminé entre des hommes qui prend ici, à leurs yeux, la forme fantasmatique d'un rapport des choses entre elles. »[22]

Il faut comprendre ici que, même dans le cas de marchandises « ordinaires », comme la simple table en bois à laquelle Marx se réfère ailleurs dans le même chapitre, une infinie variété de qualités ou propriétés sont projetées sur une marchandise, sans qu'elle ne les possède à proprement parler. Ces qualités ou propriétés deviennent en conséquence l'objet — et la raison — de la consommation, tout autant sinon plus que les *véritables* qualités ou propriétés de la marchandise qui constituent sa valeur d'usage.

Mall of Europe décrit le remplacement — de plus en plus prégnant, semble-t-il — d'une consommation basée sur la valeur d'usage par une dépense tournée vers des choses bien plus insaisissables, comme une image, un sentiment, ou même l'image d'un sentiment, et ce d'autant plus lorsque l'œuvre se focalise sur les images publicitaires ou sur les foires commerciales. Ainsi, l'une des publicités apparaissant dans la vidéo semble tout bonnement vanter « une expérience » singulière, en affichant simplement ces deux mots, *« The*

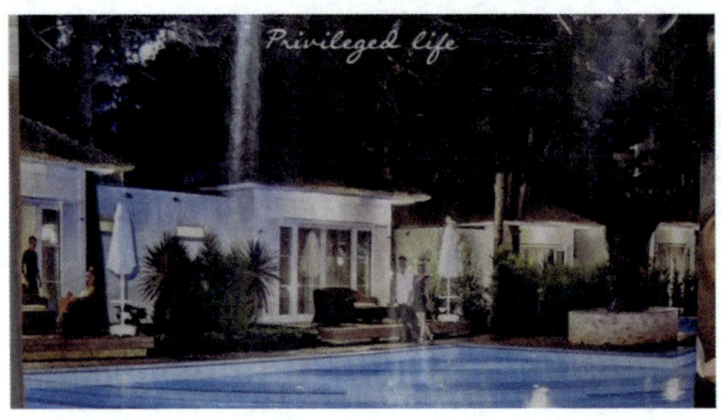

[23] Voir Giorgio Agamben au sujet de l'Exposition universelle de 1851 à Londres dans la halle du Crystal Palace : « La transformation des marchandises en *objets féeriques* signale que la valeur d'usage de la marchandise a déjà commencé à s'éclipser derrière sa valeur d'échange. Dans le cadre mystique des galeries et pavillons du Crystal Palace – prévu, dès sa conception, pour accueillir aussi des œuvres d'art –, les marchandises sont exposées pour être appréciées du regard, dans un *coup d'œil féerique* » [« La trasfigurazione della merce in *objet féerique* è il segno che il valore di scambio sta ormai cominciando a eclissare nella merce il valore d'uso . Nelle gallerie e nei padiglioni del suo mistico palazzo di cristallo, in cui fin dall'inizio si fece posto anche alle opere d'arte, la merce è esposta per essere goduta solo attraverso lo sguardo nel *coup d'œil féerique.* »] : Giorgio Agamben, *Stanze. La parola e il fantasma nella cultura occidentale* Turin, Giulio Einaudi, 1977, p. 46.

Experience », dans une police évoquant l'univers Disney, sur un fond blanc. Une autre annonce « une existence privilégiée » (« *Privileged Life* ») au-dessus d'une piscine. Le fétichisme de la marchandise que *Mall of Europe* donne à voir implique des processus qui ne sont pas seulement comparables à la projection au sens technique ou optique, mais rejoignent aussi une définition plus freudienne du terme, où elle équivaut au transfert, à l'attribution d'émotions à une personne ou un objet extérieur au sujet. La promotion d'un mode de vie « de classe moyenne », omniprésente dans les vues d'artiste en 3D, fait clairement ressortir la forte composante affective du consumérisme contemporain, marqué par notre investissement émotionnel envers les biens de consommation, et donc en fait envers leur image. La beauté fonctionne bien ici comme une « promesse de bonheur ».

De plus, l'œuvre dessine une constellation où figurent ces manifestations du « capitalisme tardif » (si une telle périodisation est encore opérante) aux côtés de phénomènes relevant bien de la modernité, interprétant certains aspects du système expositionnel comme prototypiques du régime actuel, orienté par le visuel et même le publicitaire. Les expositions universelles en particulier incarnent un moment crucial et paradigmatique de l'autonomisation relative de l'apparence (mystificatrice voire « féerique », ensorcelante) de la marchandise par rapport à la marchandise en tant qu'objet matériel.[23] La publicité prolonge et intensifie ce processus d'autonomisation, dans lequel la matérialité et l'image de la marchandise se trouvent déconnectées, la seconde s'émancipant progressivement jusqu'à devenir une marchandise elle-même. Au total, *Mall of Europe* esquisse les contours d'une vision à long terme (ou, du moins, à moyen terme) de l'évolution et affirmation des formes actuelles qui structurent la visualité, à partir du système expositionnel.

À ce stade, j'éprouve la tentation de pointer que nous voilà revenus à notre point de départ, puisque de nouveau la projection s'assimile à une image présentée sur un support, et que voilà prouvé le présupposé de cet essai, puisqu'en effet les différents sens et dimensions de « projection » se sont révélés être résolument enchevêtrés et interdépendants. Mais quelque séduisante soit cette tentation, s'y abandonner reviendrait à imposer abusivement les principes, la structure, la forme de cet essai à l'œuvre qu'est *Mall of Europe.* Nous pourrions idéalement nous retrancher derrière le jargon habituel et recourir aux opérations critiques les plus classiques, en concluant à la « révélation » et la « mise à nu » de ce qu'établissent ou soulignent ici nos interprétations, de manière plus ou moins précise, et plus ou moins véhémente. Nous ne serions pas dans l'erreur : la vidéo d'Emma van der Put possède en effet une dimension critique évidente, et s'attache à mettre au jour ce qui est dissimulé, surtout lorsqu'elle s'efforce d'établir des connexions (historiques) entre des phénomènes apparemment disparates et sans rapport. Tout ceci est vrai — mais l'œuvre est loin de s'y réduire.

C'est avec une certaine gêne qu'il me faut avouer ici combien ce que recèle *Mall of Europe* échappe encore à la présente analyse, ou la dépasse. En souhaitant dégager sur le plan conceptuel ce que l'œuvre exprime sur le plan visuel ou esthétique, cet essai performe et dramatise inévitablement une forme d'échec bien particulier : l'échec de la théorie à tout à fait rendre compte de l'expérience du visuel, et a fortiori de sa signification. Si ce texte ne recule pas devant la perspective de cet échec, c'est parce qu'il réussit à consigner — quoiqu'en négatif — ce qui résiste sans cesse à l'abstraction conceptuelle, et parce qu'il donne accès à un mode de compréhension que la conceptualisation ne sait pas vraiment gérer. Dans le cas de *Mall of Europe,* cela demande une réflexion sur le visuel bien plus complexe, mystérieuse, entière que ce dont nous pouvons en toute honnêteté rendre compte ici, une réflexion engagée qui n'esquive pas l'ironie historique qui rapproche la « théorie » de l'attitude du spectateur, via l'étymologie *(theorein* en grec : « contempler, observer, examiner »). Le travail sur les images publicitaires dans *Mall of Europe* illustre bien cette exigence. Justement, il nous semble que l'œuvre ne se résume pas à son effort de démystification du charme féerique de la marchandise, sa mise en lumière à plusieurs reprises du caractère banal, superficiel, *cheap* d'un tel envoûtement. Car elle exprime aussi le désir de sauvegarder le côté fétichiste de la marchandise, de s'investir dans son image, de s'abandonner à son charme facile. En d'autres termes, un certain plaisir visuel y est en jeu, un plaisir qui révèle une certaine complicité mais qu'on ne peut réduire seulement à un symptôme de celle-ci. *Mall of Europ*e oscille entre démystification et jouissance visuelle, les fait jouer ensemble, et accomplit bien plus qu'un renforcement univoque du pouvoir ou de la primauté de l'une sur l'autre. Cependant ce n'est pas *pas* de la critique ; simplement, la notion de révélation — sur laquelle repose crucialement toute rhétorique critique — y est prise en compte plus sérieusement. Le genre de révélation qui est ici en ligne de mire relève à la fois du quotidien et du magique. *Mall of Europe* met en scène un tel type de révélation en convoquant toute l'ampleur — merveilleuse autant qu'inquiétante — de ce que *regarder* veut dire, jetant ainsi le trouble au cœur de la stricte et cruelle géométrie de la projection, plus que toute exposition critique n'eût jamais pu le faire.

Projecties: *Mall of Europe*

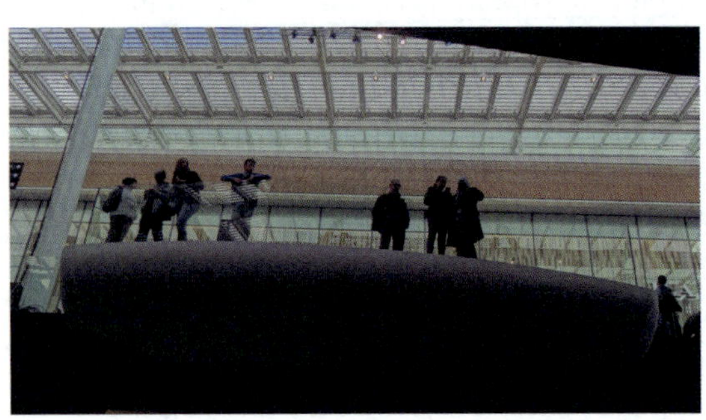

In dit essay verdiep ik me in *Mall of Europe,* een 26 minuten durende single-channel video van Emma van der Put. Het werk onderzoekt historische en hedendaagse ideeën over stedelijke ontwikkeling, (technologische) vooruitgang en globalisering die te vinden zijn binnen de 'Heizel', het wereldtentoonstellingsgebied van Brussel. De video *Mall of Europe* is opgebouwd uit een opeenvolging van fotografische beelden, vergezeld door een subtiele, sobere geluidsband, gecomponeerd door Maxime Rouquart. Mijn tekstuele bijdrage is een poging om zowel na te denken over de video (als 'onderwerp'), maar ook, voor zover mogelijk, mee te denken *met* de video. In die zin is deze tekst een essay in de ware zin van het woord: een poging. Een essay wordt ten dele gestructureerd zowel door de mogelijkheid van mislukking (die ons hoe dan ook steeds volgt), als door de onmogelijkheid daarvan — in zoverre het doel een poging is, kan het immers niet falen. Deze tekst wordt aldus gekenmerkt door de zekerheid van een ander soort mislukking, doelmatiger en hopelijk productiever. Ik kom hier aan het eind van het essay op terug.

Het uitgangspunt van dit essay is, kort gesteld, om een aantal zaken die *Mall of Europe* visueel aandraagt, conceptueel te specificeren. De tekst is georganiseerd rond drie verschillende maar verwante betekenissen van de term 'projectie': het tonen van een beeld op een oppervlak, een prognose van de toekomst op basis van de gewaarwording van het heden, en een bewuste of onbewuste overdracht van eigen verlangens en affecten op een extern object of persoon. Dit essay tracht, in wat als een schending van de principes van analytische helderheid kan worden gezien, een aantal manieren waarop deze betekenissen van 'projectie' tegelijkertijd verschillen en onderling afhankelijk zijn, te consolideren, te benadrukken en zelfs uit te buiten. Velen vóór mij hebben gewezen op de cinematografische en psychoanalytische resonanties van 'projectie' als een zowel technische als alledaagse term. Ik ben hier minder geïnteresseerd in het opsporen van dergelijke verwijzingen dan in het geven van een zorgvuldige, gerichte lezing van *Mall of Europe,* verankerd en gemedieerd door een beschouwing van de verschillende connotaties van 'projectie' in relatie tot het werk. Hoewel er dus meer generaliserende (en daarom meer specifiek 'theoretische') argumenten worden ontwikkeld en uitspraken worden gedaan over de wereld waarin we leven, zijn deze meestal ondergeschikt en ondersteunend aan mijn poging om beter naar de video te kijken door er over te schrijven.

Projectie: het tonen van een afbeelding op een oppervlak

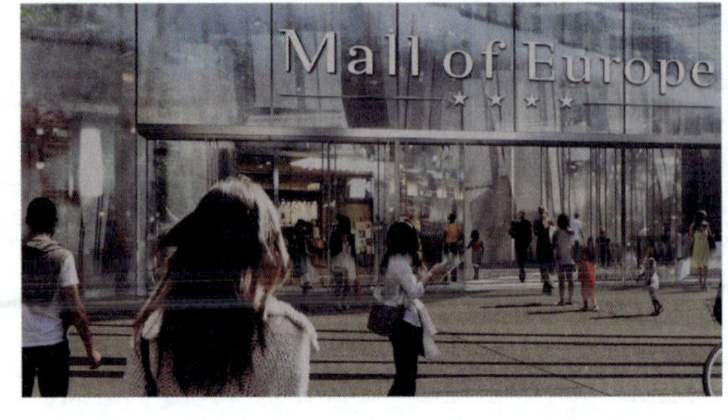

Zoals veel van Emma van der Put's recente werk is *Mall of Europe* doordrenkt met afbeeldingen van afbeeldingen. Foto's van reclameborden, billboards en computerschermen zijn in deze cinematografische diavoorstelling veelvuldig aanwezig. *Mall of Europe* ontleent zijn titel aan één van de eerste beelden die het toont: een spookachtige architectonische *rendering* van een winkelcentrum met de treffende naam *Mall of Europe,* door Van der Put's camera vastgelegd op de plek waar het winkelcentrum in kwestie zal worden gebouwd. In *Mall of Europe* sluit Van der Put bepaalde afbeeldingen op in hun kaders, houdt ze stil en onbeweeglijk, terwijl ze gestaag over het oppervlak van andere beelden glijdt. De afbeeldingen worden steeds van elkaar gescheiden door cuts, een techniek die Van der Put's verder ongecompliceerde en ingetogen cinematografie maximaal tot haar recht laat komen, vaak om de contrasterende en soms tegenstrijdige aanspraken te onderstrepen die verschillende afbeeldingen op ons maken. Wat afbeeldingen van afbeeldingen doen of kunnen doen, is onze aandacht richten op de organisatie van het visuele. Ze geven ons een kritische afstand van de zichtbare omgevingen die ons gewoonlijk omringen en opnemen, waardoor we kunnen reflecteren op de logica die deze omgevingen structureert en onderbouwt, maar de neiging heeft om aan bewuste waarneming te ontsnappen.

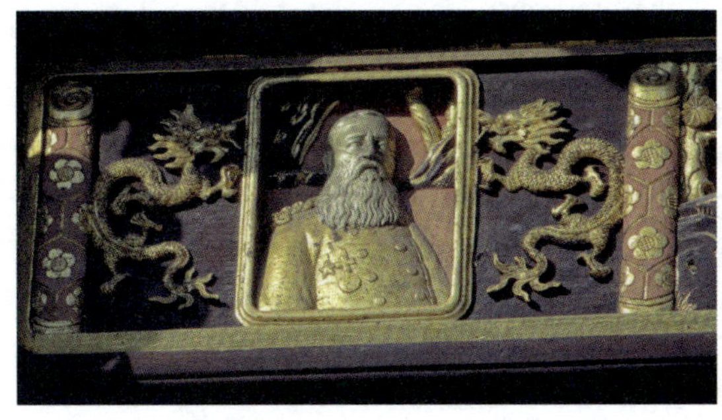

Niet toevallig is veel van Van der Put's recente werk opgenomen op plekken die zijn ontworpen en gebouwd om de blik van het publiek te trekken en vast te houden. Zo toont het korte werk *Chinese Pavilion,* eveneens uit 2018, een oriëntalistische constructie, opgetrokken in de koninklijke tuinen van de Brusselse gemeente Laken als 'exotische' attractie voor de Belgische koninklijke familie. De video eindigt met het opzienbarende beeld van een vergulde buste van Leopold II in de houten fries van het gebouw. Leopold II, koning van België, overleed zes maanden voor de voltooing van het paviljoen in 1910. Hij is berucht om zijn weerzinwekkende uitbuiting van Congo, die hij van 1885 tot 1908 als privé-kolonie in zijn bezit had, tot hij deze aan de Belgische staat 'schonk'. *Chinese Pavilion* is hier relevant omdat het functioneert als coda en contrapunt van *Mall of Europe* — waarin kolonialiteit, zoals ik zal laten zien, altijd aanwezig is, maar steeds latent, verborgen in (en niet zozeer onder) allerlei soorten oppervlakken. [1]

[1] In een tentoonstelling in A Tale of a Tub (Rotterdam, 2018) werd deze relatie tussen *Chinese Pavilion* en *Mall of Europe* benadrukt door de opstelling van de werken, waardoor *Chinese Pavilion* werd gezien als een aanvullende gedachte, of voetnoot, bij *Mall of Europe.*

Mall of Europe zelf is een meer uitgebreide meditatie op het gebied waar verschillende wereldtentoonstellingen werden gehouden, waaronder de wereldtentoonstelling van 1935 en de veelgeprezen Expo '58. Een groot deel van de video focust op de architectuur van de modernistische 'Modelwijk' die voor de tentoonstelling van 1958 werd gebouwd, maar de wereldtentoonstelling wordt ook gerelateerd aan andere locaties binnen het Expo-gebied met een intensief scopisch verkeer. Zoals de toeristische trekpleister 'Mini-Europa', beurzen voor reisbureaus en binnenhuisarchitecten die in de Expo beurshallen worden gehouden, en ook het winkelcentrum zelf: *Mall of Europe* brengt deze plaatsen en fenomenen samen, niet alleen omdat ze zich rondom de Modelwijk bevinden, maar ook omdat ze allemaal gebaseerd zijn op een visuele logica die sterk lijkt op die van de wereldtentoonstelling.

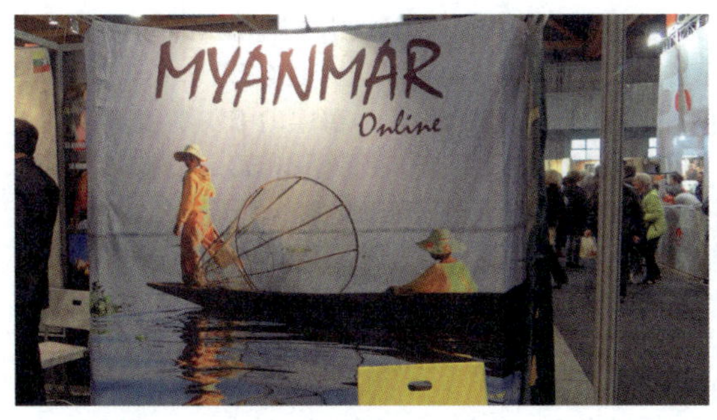

Het 'Chinees Paviljoen', de wereldtentoonstelling en alle andere fenomenen die in *Mall of Europe* zijn samengebracht, zijn paradigmatische voorbeelden van wat socioloog Tony Bennett het *exhibitionary complex* heeft genoemd — de invloedrijke term die hij gebruikt voor de organisatie van het zichtbare, welke specifiek is aan de Westerse moderniteit. Vanaf de negentiende eeuw ontstonden er volgens Bennett verschillende instituten die voortbouwden op, en uiteindelijk ook de plaats innamen van, vroegmoderne instituten waarvan de tuchteffecten en de vervlechting van kennis en macht op befaamde wijze door Michel Foucault zijn beschreven. Bennett wil laten zien dat het *exhibitionary complex* tucht en controle niet doet verdwijnen maar eerder onderdeel maakt van een meer ingewikkelde — inderdaad, 'complexere' — verstrengeling van machtsverhoudingen.

In dit verband is het essentieel dat de nieuwe negentiende-eeuwse instellingen, althans in principe, een publiek karakter hadden. In tegenstelling tot de gevangenissen en ziekenhuizen waarin Foucault geïnteresseerd was, zijn alle voorbeelden van Bennett — hij noemt musea, kunstgalerijen, kunstbeurzen, tentoonstellingen en warenhuizen — gericht op het "tegelijkertijd ordenen van objecten voor beschouwing door het publiek, en het ordenen van het publiek dat ze beschouwt." [2]

[2] Tony Bennett, "The Exhibitionary Complex," *New Formations,* No. 4 (1988): 74.

In het *exhibitionary complex* wordt van de toeschouwers in de eerste plaats verwacht dat ze sympathiseren en zich identificeren met een zekere totaliserende blik: de macht wordt niet alleen van buitenaf aan het subject opgelegd, maar werkt ook van binnenuit. Volgens Bennett komt het *exhibitionary complex* uiteindelijk neer op "een zelfcontrolerend beschouwingssysteem waarin de posities van subject en object uitwisselbaar zijn, waarin het publiek zich verenigt en reguleert door het geïdealiseerde en geordende zelfbeeld, dat de controlerende machtsvisie voor hen ziet, te verinnerlijken — een zichtveld dat voor iedereen toegankelijk is." [3] Voor Bennett is deze dynamiek het duidelijkst zichtbaar bij wereldtentoonstellingen, waar voornamelijk westerse bezoekers letterlijk in een positie van "speculair gezag over een totaliteit" werden geplaatst. Wereldtentoonstellingen, schrijft hij, "probeerden de hele wereld, van vroeger en nu, metonymisch beschikbaar te maken in de assemblages van voorwerpen en volken die ze samenbrachten", en onderwierpen de wereld aan een "controlerende blik". [4]

Een terugkerende figuur in Van der Put's video's is de beschouwer die tegelijkertijd subject en object is van visuele bespiegeling en controle. De foto's waaruit Van der Put's werk is opgebouwd, stralen vaak een afstandelijk soort observatie uit: ze zijn geladen met connotaties van surveillance en voyeurisme, en tonen hun eigen machtsverhoudingen — en -asymmetrieën — ten opzichte van de mensen die erin voorkomen. Van der Put's werk neemt, met andere woorden, volledig deel aan het *exhibitionary complex,* niet alleen omdat het werk gebruikelijk in musea en andere tentoonstellingsruimten wordt getoond, maar ook vanwege het medium dat Van der Put gebruikt. [5] Het is veelzeggend dat de geschiedenis van het fotografische beeld — zowel stilstaand als bewegend — onlosmakelijk verbonden is met de historische vorming (en voortzetting) van het *exhibitionary complex* en de manieren van kijken die daarmee gepaard gaan die Van der Put in haar video's verkent.

Intellectueel historicus Martin Jay heeft opgemerkt dat de fotografie, het wijdverbreide toerisme en de wereldtentoonstellingen rond 1850 gelijktijdig opkomen en allen beheerst worden door een "nieuwsgierig naar de ander kijken", en hiermee een aanschouwing van de wereld als tentoonstelling bevorderen en faciliteren. [6] Net als Bennett benadrukt Jay de koloniale en imperialistische dimensies en implicaties van deze geprojecteerde visuele dominantie over de wereld. De vormen van exotisme en oriëntalisme die vanaf het midden van de negentiende eeuw in het Westen aan belang winnen, kunnen dan ook geenszins als onschuldig worden beschouwd. Wat Jay omschrijft als "de visuele toe-eigening van exotische plaatsen en de al even fotogenieke inboorlingen (of fauna) die hen bewonen" is een uitvloeisel van de feitelijke toe-eigening van deze plaatsen door kolonisatie, uitbuiting en plundering, en evenzeer van de gewelddadige onderwerping en ontmenselijking van hun "fotogenieke inboorlingen". [7] Zie het 'Congolese dorp' op de wereldtentoonstelling in Brussel van 1958, in feite een menselijke dierentuin.

Dit alles wordt in het werk van Van der Put, dat toch vol staat met verwijzingen naar het koloniale verleden, nooit zo expliciet gemaakt. Belangrijk is dat het werk dit verleden niet behandelt als iets uit het verleden, maar eerder als iets dat het historische heden op talloze problematische manieren vorm, inhoud en onderbouwing blijft geven. Waar *Chinese Pavilion* wijst op de hardnekkigheid van koloniaal erfgoed in de materialiteit van het stedelijk weefsel, is *Mall of Europe* meer gericht op het tonen van hedendaagse vormen van 'othering', vormen van beschouwing die een ander tot 'de ander'

[3] Bennett, "The Exhibitionary Complex," 82.

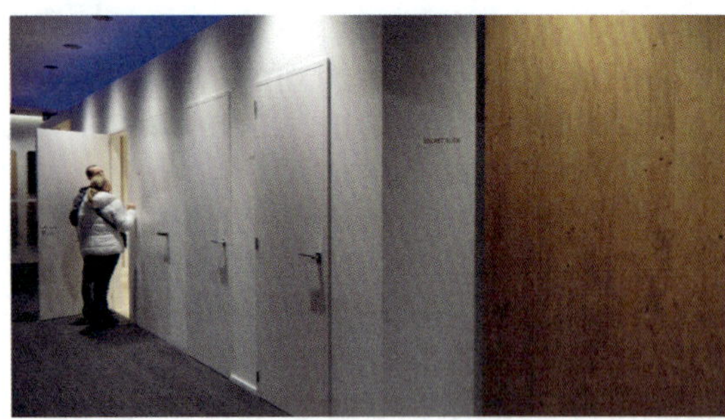

[4] Bennett, "The Exhibitionary Complex," 79.

[5] De vele historische banden tussen de wereldtentoonstellingen en de hedendaagse (geglobaliseerde) kunstwerken worden uiteengezet in Caroline A. Jones, *The Global Work of Art: World's Fairs, Biennials, and the Aesthetics of Experience* (Chicago: Chicago University Press, 2017).

[6] Martin Jay, *Downcast Eyes: The Denigration of Vision in Twentieth-Century French Thought* (Berkeley: University of California Press, 1993), 140.

[7] Jay, *Downcast Eyes,* 140.

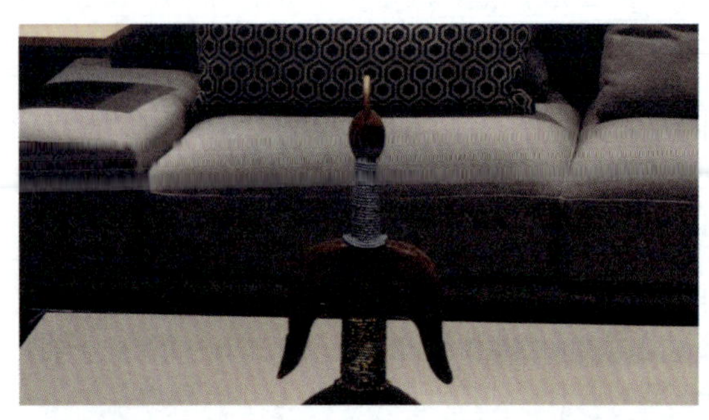

maken. Binnen interieurbeurzen en -winkels worden 'primitieve' artefacten en sculpturen uit hun culturele context gehaald en gebruikt als geësthetiseerde, decoratieve attributen. Vakantiebeurzen pronken met promotiebeelden van het 'authentiek' anders-zijn van de bestemmingen die ze aanbieden. Exotisme en oriëntalisme betuigen zich ten volle van kracht — niet alleen als restanten of anachronistische resten uit een vervlogen tijdperk, maar als elementen die volledig deel uitmaken van het historische heden.

Kolonialiteit, zo wordt betoogd, is onlosmakelijk verbonden met een moderniteit die we nog niet achter ons hebben gelaten.[8] Hierin ligt ook de relatie tussen kolonialiteit en een ander belangrijk aspect van *Mall of Europe,* dat op het eerste gezicht echter onverwant kan lijken: de centrale rol van modernistische architectuur. Die architectuur verschijnt vooral in haar naoorlogse gedaante, want Van der Put richt zich op de woonblokken uit de jaren vijftig in het Expo-gebied, en met name op de nog steeds bewoonde Modelwijk die speciaal voor de wereldtentoonstelling van '58 is gebouwd. In een bijzonder saillante passage in *Mall of Europe* — ook hier betreft het een afbeelding van een afbeelding — wordt een oude archieffoto van de bouw van twee woontorens geplaatst naast Van der Put's opnamen van deze torens in hun huidige staat. Vandaag de dag, versleten door de tijd en gebrandmerkt door graffiti, zien ze er niet meer zo modern uit.

[8] Dit is een fundamenteel punt van het dekoloniale denken, waar de twee termen vaak samen worden geschreven (als 'moderniteit / kolonialiteit') om de onafscheidelijkheid van de twee te benadrukken. Zie bijvoorbeeld Walter Mignolo, *The Darker Side of Western Modernity: Global Futures, Decolonial Options* (Durham: Duke University Press, 2011).

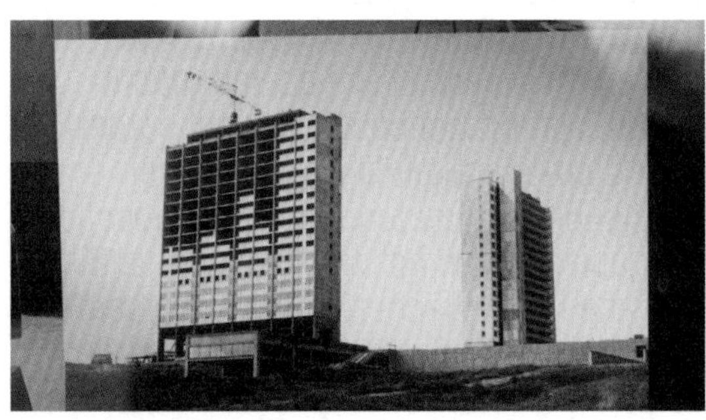

Dat de gebouwen er niet in slagen om hun eigen imago waar te maken, getuigt van een toekomst die nooit heeft mogen zijn. Dit zegt ook veel over het lot van het modernisme in de architectuur in het algemeen. In zijn kritiek op de modernistische architectuur schrijft Manfredo Tafuri dat "architectuur als 'de ideologie van het plan' ter zijde wordt geschoven door de *realiteit van het plan* wanneer het utopische gehalte achterhaald is en het plan een werktuigelijk mechanisme wordt."[9] En Masao Miyoshi beschreef de "onontkoombaar utopische" aard van het modernistische architectuurdiscours en van modernistische architectuur zelf, die "slechts zichzelf is op de tekentafel of in aanbouw, dus zolang ze zich nog tot een toekomstige toestand richt."[10] Met andere woorden, de modernistische architectuur was, en blijft, een *project.*

[9] Manfredo Tafuri, *Architecture and Utopia: Design and Capitalist Development* (Cambridge: MIT Press, 1976), 135.

[10] Masao Miyoshi, "Outside Architecture," in *Trespasses* (Durham: Duke University Press, 2009), 152.

De tekentafel of het bouwplan — symbool van gerationaliseerde coördinatie en planning, met een aura van belofte en potentieel — is meer dan enig feitelijk gebouw emblematisch voor modernistische architectuur. Toch zien we geen bouwtekeningen in *Mall of Europe.* In plaats daarvan toont Van der Put een soortgelijk, maar misschien meer eigentijds type beeld: de architectonische *rendering.* Net als het bouwplan spreekt en kondigt de rendering een toekomstige toestand aan. In tegenstelling tot het bouwplan is de rendering echter van weinig tot geen direct technisch belang voor de realisatie van de specifieke toekomstige staat waarvan het een uitdrukking is: de digitale simulaties zijn slechts ontworpen omwille van hun esthetische, en in het verlengde daarvan, ideologische effecten.

Renderings zijn niet zo direct functioneel als bouwplannen, maar beide stellen de toekomst voor, beide spelen een actieve rol in de realisatie van wat ze afbeelden, en beide wekken dat tot leven. In het geval van de rendering kan dit resulteren in simulacra-achtige effecten, zoals Hito Steyerl opmerkt: "hele steden doen zich tegenwoordig voor als CAD-instructiefilmpjes op YouTube".[11] Met andere woorden, de verhoudingen tussen het echte en het representatieve, de betekenaar en het betekende, worden door elkaar gehaald en vertroebeld. Dit komt tot uiting in de specifieke manier waarop Van der Put deze renderings in haar video's laat zien. Vaak fotografeert ze de renderings zo dat

[11] Hito Steyerl, "Too Much World: Is the Internet Dead?," in *Too Much World: The Films of Hito Steyerl,* red. Nick Aikens (Berlijn: Sternberg Press, 2015), 31.

hun ongemakkelijke en unheimliche aspecten benadrukt worden: het kader van de rendering valt samen met het kader van haar foto's van de huidige locatie, waardoor de rendering kortstondig verward kan worden met een beeld dat verwijst naar iets wat al bestaat. Dezelfde techniek wordt verder onderzocht en gebruikt in *SOON* (2018), een kort videowerk van Van der Put dat, net als *Chinese Pavilion,* gelezen kan worden als voetnoot bij de langere film *Mall of Europe.*

Bouwplannen en renderings zijn hier van belang als verhelderende voorbeelden van projectie. Projectie in de betekenis van de weergave van een afbeelding op een oppervlak, draait duidelijk steeds om de reductie van een visuele *wereld* tot een visueel *vlak.* Het behelst een gefixeerd en vervlakt soort kijken, een kijken waarvan het rusteloze zwerven moet worden opgevangen, de ruimtelijke omzwervingen ingeperkt, de holistische integratie in en de samenwerking met de andere zintuigen opgeschort. Projectie is in die zin dus een vereenvoudiging en een schematisering, die in en op de wereld werkzaam is. Als zodanig is projectie vaak het resultaat geweest van fantasieën van macht en controle — fantasieën die het fenomeen zelf tegelijkertijd ook vaak uitlokt en faciliteert.[12] Noties van macht en controle liggen aan de basis van wat op het eerste gezicht eerder uiteenlopende verschijnselen van de moderniteit lijken te zijn: het koloniale project en de modernistische architectuur. Ze liggen bovendien aan de basis van de moderne organisatie van het zichtbare, zoals die in het *exhibitionary complex* gestalte krijgt. Aangezien geprojecteerde macht en controle (beide belichaamd door het *plan)* nauw verbonden zijn met een geloof in de maakbaarheid en kneedbaarheid van de geschiedenis, omvatten ze ten slotte onvermijdelijk en onmiddellijk ook een temporele dimensie.

[12] Mary Ann Doane schreef over de relatie tussen het (filmische) geprojecteerde beeld en de plattegrond: "Projectie is ook heel specifiek de naam van de afbeelding op een vlak oppervlak van een bol of een deel van een bol (bij uitstek de wereldbol, vandaar het sterke verband tussen projectie en het in kaart brengen)." Mary Ann Doane, "The Location of the Image: Cinematic Projection and Scale in Modernity," in *The Art of Projection,* red. Stan Douglas and Christopher Eamon (Ostfildern: Hatje Cantz, 2009), 157.

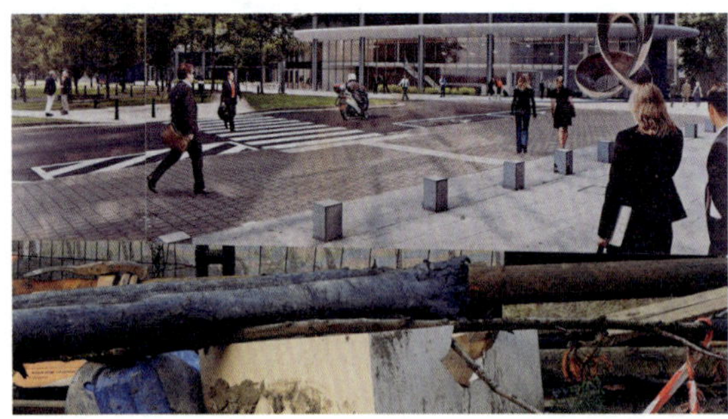

Projectie: een prognose van de toekomst op basis van de gewaarwording van het heden

Voor Tafuri is modernistische architectuur — zowel in haar aanvankelijke 'heroïsche' als in haar naoorlogse, meer pragmatische vormen — een materieel voorbeeld van modern, werktuigelijk denken, met als "overkoepelend thema een toekomst waarin het heden als geheel wordt geprojecteerd, een 'rationele' heerschappij van de toekomst, ontdaan van het *risico* dat de toekomst met zich meebrengt."[13] Een *plan* is, in de architectuur en in andere domeinen, een middel om het onvoorziene van de toekomst te beheersen, juist door het te voorzien. Het is een middel om zich te wapenen tegen alles wat open en onbekend is, om de onzekerheid en de angst die dat veroorzaakt te beheersen. Het (bouw)plan is identiek aan het project in die zin dat het een bepaalde visie of verbeelding van de toekomst voorstelt en naar voren schuift. Wat dat betreft zijn beide onlosmakelijk verbonden met het zo kenmerkende vertrouwen van de moderniteit in de kneedbaarheid en de volmaakbaarheid van de geschiedenis — dat wil zeggen, van de toekomst — en in de Mens als zelfbeschikkend historisch subject en actor bij uitstek.[14]

Moderniteit staat met andere woorden gelijk aan de ideologie van vooruitgang. De meest elementaire — en letterlijk de meest rechtlijnige — weergave van haar tijdsstructuur is de tijdslijn. Zodoende waren wereldtentoonstellingen zoals Expo '58 bedoeld om de 'state of the art' te vertegenwoordigen van een wereld die geacht werd in de greep te zijn van een enkelvoudig, lineair en universeel moderniseringsproces. Het is echter belangrijk om hier nogmaals te

[13] Tafuri, *Architecture and Utopia,* 52.

[14] Het is van belang om te benadrukken dat deze karakterisering niet alleen van toepassing is op kapitalistische uitingen van moderniteit, maar ook op (radicaal) linkse opvattingen van moderniteit. Het prometheïsche karakter van het staatssocialisme in de Sovjet-Unie, met zijn fixatie op planning, is hierin slechts het meest voor de hand liggende voorbeeld. Ook inzichtelijk in dit opzicht is Cornelius Castoriadis' "revolutionaire project". Castoriadis wil het vertrouwen in de volmaakbaarheid van de geschiedenis behouden maar tegelijkertijd de beperkingen van de menselijke kennis en macht over de wereld erkennen. Daarom is revolutie voor hem geen kwestie van techniek of planning, maar van een praktijk – in essentie een reflexieve vorm van politiek handelen zonder eenduidig onderscheid tussen doel en middel. Zie Cornelius Castoriadis, *The Imaginary Institution of Society* (Londen: Polity Press, 1987), 71–100.

benadrukken dat deze opvatting van de wereld als één enkele gehomogeniseerde tijd-ruimte ondenkbaar zou zijn zonder kolonialisme, dat op zijn beurt gelegitimeerd werd door noties van achterhaaldheid en achterstand die een dergelijke moderniteitsopvatting mogelijk maakt. Vandaar dat de wereldtentoonstelling van '58 in Brussel zowel het hyperfuturistische geluidspaviljoen van Philips (ontworpen door Le Corbusier en Iannis Xenakis) presenteerde als het 'Congolese dorp', beide gehuld in een narratief over de voortschrijdende ontwikkeling van de menselijke geschiedenis — waarbij eerstgenoemd paviljoen symbool staat voor de 'voorhoede' en het laatstgenoemde moest illustreren wat het zou betekenen om achter te blijven op het wereldhistorische toneel.

De gezamenlijke aanwezigheid van het Philipspaviljoen en het 'Congolese dorp' kan dienen als pijnlijke en verontrustende herinnering aan het gevaar en het geweld dat inherent is aan het opleggen van strakke conceptuele structuren op de loop van de geschiedenis — zoals de verheven notie van vooruitgang. Maar het laat ook zien hoe de geschiedenis dergelijke structuren gedeeltelijk weerlegt en weigert; het toont aan hoe de ideologie van de vooruitgang allerlei complicaties en tegenstrijdigheden ten opzichte van zichzelf impliceert. Ten eerste vereist het idee van vooruitgang een historisch besef dat het vooruitgangsideaal voortdurend dreigt te ondermijnen. In een schijnbare paradox schept het modernisme — de permanente ontkenning van het verleden in het heden door het nieuwe — als een soort bijproduct een sterke gevoeligheid voor historiciteit, die pas echt waarneembaar wordt wanneer traditie als iets vanzelfsprekends naar de achtergrond verdwijnt.[15] De modernistische obsessie voor musea en openbare monumenten (ook in *Mall of Europe* prominent aanwezig) is geen toeval: in het modernisme wordt de naar voren geprojecteerde blik gespiegeld door de historistische beschouwing en studie van een verleden, waarvan wordt aangenomen dat het het heden gevormd, geconditioneerd en bepaald heeft. Het voortdurend overtreffen, overschaduwen of afbreken van het oude schept "een perceptie van een verleden dat niet alleen voorbij is, maar ook aanwezig."[16]

Van der Put's video's getuigen van en scheppen precies zo'n begrip van het historische: een begrip dat een verleden benadrukt — en vasthoudt — dat tegelijkertijd verstreken en present is (en dus ook verschillende mogelijke toekomsten impliceert). Er is één beeld in *Mall of Europe* dat dit meer belichaamt dan enig ander. Een langzame beweging naar boven over het oppervlak van de afbeelding onthult op de voorgrond eerst een graafmachine, of een deel daarvan. De machine is voor een rendering geplaatst die een panoramisch uitzicht biedt op hoe het gebied eruit moet gaan zien na de geplande transformaties. De rendering toont ook een man van eind twintig of begin dertig, wit, schijnbaar middenklasse, en verder vrij onopvallend. Hij is zo geschaald dat zijn relatieve grootte die van het landschap achter hem in het niet doet vallen. De opwaartse beweging toont al snel hoe hij met zijn armen over elkaar geslagen naar boven kijkt, onwerkelijk glimlachend naar iets buiten het kader van de rendering — naar een horizon of hemellichaam dat wij, de kijkers, niet te zien krijgen. Links boven hem is een geelgroen icoon geplaatst dat lijkt op een 'locatiespeld' van Google Maps met het opschrift 'NEO 2021'. Verder naar boven glijdend wordt het duidelijk dat het scherm waarop de rendering is geprint een gebouw verbergt, waarvan het decoratieve fries boven de rendering uit torent. Het fries draagt twee grote bronzen classicistische beelden van gevleugelde vrouwenfiguren en toont ons de inscriptie van het jaar waarin het gebouw voltooid werd, 1935 — het jaar van de vierde Brusselse wereldtentoonstelling. Van der Put's beeld laat zien dat het

[15] Peter Osborne heeft gezegd dat wat wij het modernisme noemen in wezen "een vorm van historisch bewustzijn, een abstracte tijdsstructuur" is. Omdat het een structuur is met veelsoortige inhoud, is de "moderniteit niet als dusdanig een project, maar slechts gevormd als een project." Peter Osborne, *The Politics of Time: Modernity and Avant-Garde* (Londen: Verso, 1995), 23.

[16] T.S. Eliot geciteerd in Edward Saïd, *Culture and Imperialism* (Londen: Chatto & Windus, 1993) 2. Saïd stelt vervolgens dat "er geen terechte manier is waarop het verleden uit het heden geïsoleerd kan worden, zelfs als we de voorbije aard van het verleden volledig moeten doorgronden. Het verleden en het heden vormen elkaar, geven elkaar betekenis en, in het door Eliot bedoelde geïdealiseerde begrip, bestaan beide naast elkaar."

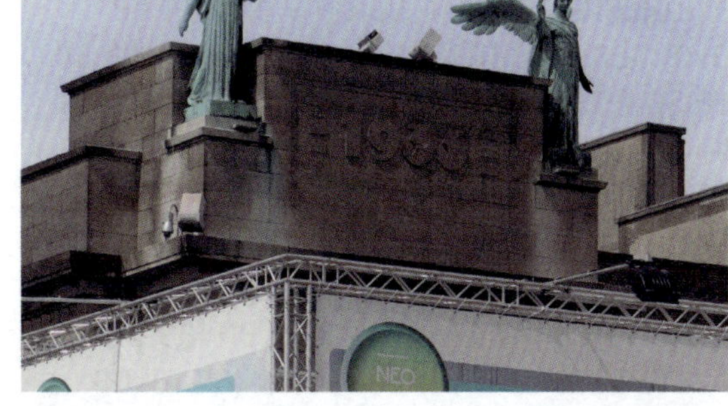

grotendeels verborgen gebouw typerend is voor de art-decostijl uit het interbellum, zelf een eclectische mix van historiserende en moderne, 'vooruitstrevende' elementen en vormentalen.

Dit beeld is deel van een langere scène waarin gefotografeerde renderings gecombineerd worden met opnamen van de huidige bouwwerkzaamheden in het Expo-gebied, en belicht meer dan enig ander moment in de video de vreemde verstrengeling van verleden, heden en toekomst. *Mall of Europe* is erop gericht om te laten zien hoe het Expo-gebied (en in het verlengde daarvan de stad Brussel in het algemeen) zowel letterlijk als figuurlijk is gebouwd op en rond de overblijfselen van het verleden — meer bepaald de overblijfselen van een moderniteit die daarom nog erg dicht bij ons is. Maar het werk legt meer dan slechts de tastbare tegenwoordigheid van historische sporen bloot. De hierboven besproken afbeelding brengt verschillende lagen van historiciteit aan de oppervlakte, als een mini-archeologie van het historische heden — een heden dat 'overbepaald' is door de steeds aanwezige geschiedenis en gelijktijdig, door verwachtingen van, en hoopvolle anticipatie op, de toekomst.[17] In dit specifieke geval, dat als metonymie kan gelden voor *Mall of Europe* als geheel, wordt het historische heden begrepen en voorgesteld als een getouwtrek, als conjunctuur. Belangrijk is echter dat 'conjunctuur' in deze context niet alleen de ineenvlechting is van uiteenlopende historische krachten die het moment van het heden vormgeven en voortbewegen. 'Conjunctuur' omvat hier ook een oriëntatie op de toekomst, een vooruitblikkende berekening van het nog onbekende dat zich terugplooit op het heden om beslissingen, handelingen en houdingen concreet te beïnvloeden. Het huidige moment wordt niet alleen gevormd door het verleden en onze waarneming ervan, maar ook door de projecties op de toekomst die het aanwakkert.

[17] Louis Althusser gebruikt de term 'overbepaling' (Frans: surdétermination, Engels: overdetermination) voor het complexe proces waarbij een bepaalde gebeurtenis wordt 'veroorzaakt' door verschillende, vaak tegenstrijdige, historische krachten. Volgens hem is de erkenning van het 'overbepaalde' karakter van historische gebeurtenissen noodzakelijk om verder te gaan dan een schematische en reducerende (Hegeliaanse) interpretatie van de geschiedenis. Louis Althusser, "Contradiction and Overdetermination", *New Left Review,* nr. 41 (1967).

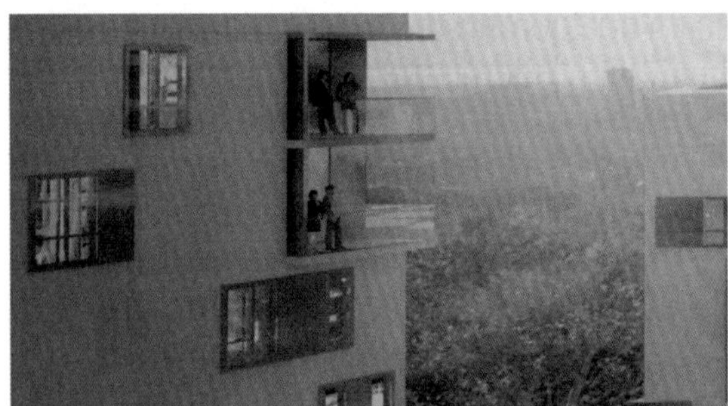

Zo laat *Mall of Europe* zien dat projectie op de toekomst en het directe heden een kracht uitoefent die zowel scheppend als beperkend van aard is. Door één bepaalde verbeelding van de toekomst voor te stellen en naar voren te schuiven, verhindert een dergelijke projectie dat andere toekomstvisies geuit en verwezenlijkt worden. Iets nieuws produceren met het heden als model, verhindert de verschijning van een *novum* — het nieuwe als iets dat radicaal verschilt en ontkoppeld is van het nu. Projectie kan in deze zin niet gereduceerd worden tot een prognose — een probabilistisch vermoeden over de toekomst op basis van tendensen en ontwikkelingen in het heden. Projectie kan zeer effectief een ideevormend beeld van de toekomst katapulteren en op de toekomende tijd opdringen. Projectie speelt een actieve, vormende rol in de eigen verwezenlijking — en daarmee in het uitschakelen van andere mogelijke toekomsten. Wat met projectie naar voren wordt gebracht, kaatst bovendien ook weer terug, omdat de verwachte verwezenlijking ervan invloed heeft op wat er gebeurt in het hier en nu.

Ook in deze tweede betekenis heeft projectie iets schematisch. Het is een poging om de historische tijd geometrisch te maken, tot iets dat in kaart gebracht kan worden, controleerbaar en transparant is. Ook daarom is projectie zo nauw verbonden met de controlewaan en de dromen over absolute menselijke soevereiniteit en zelfbeschikking die het modernisme tekenen — wanen en dromen die zeer reële en catastrofale gevolgen hebben gehad. *Mall of Europe* zet dergelijke al te overzichtelijke zienswijzen echter op losse schroeven. In het werk manifesteert het historische heden zich als een kleverige verstrengeling van historische bepalingen (die niet werkelijk of uitsluitend 'historisch' zijn, aangezien ze blijvend van kracht en tastbaar aanwezig zijn) en uitingen die zich op de toekomst richten (en reeds

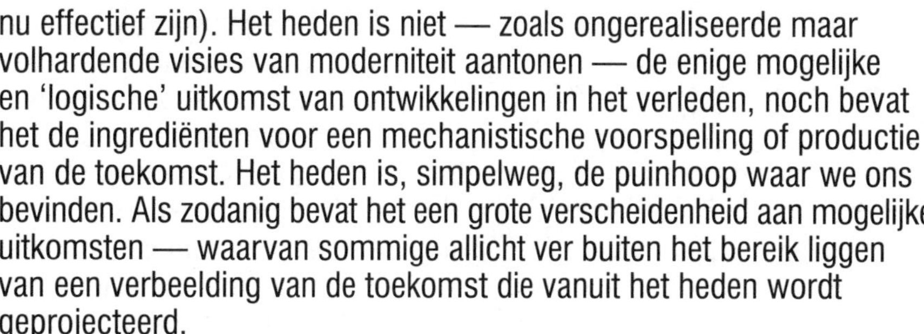

nu effectief zijn). Het heden is niet — zoals ongerealiseerde maar volhardende visies van moderniteit aantonen — de enige mogelijke en 'logische' uitkomst van ontwikkelingen in het verleden, noch bevat het de ingrediënten voor een mechanistische voorspelling of productie van de toekomst. Het heden is, simpelweg, de puinhoop waar we ons bevinden. Als zodanig bevat het een grote verscheidenheid aan mogelijke uitkomsten — waarvan sommige allicht ver buiten het bereik liggen van een verbeelding van de toekomst die vanuit het heden wordt geprojecteerd.

Ten slotte zijn hier enkele gedachten over de relatie van projectie tot het utopische gepast. Wanneer auteurs als Miyoshi en Tafuri modernistische architectuur (en, in het verlengde daarvan, de notie van het plan meer in het algemeen) als door en door utopisch bestempelen, gebruiken ze 'utopie' in een pejoratieve, beperkte, betekenis. Utopie is in hun begrip in wezen een misvatting van het idealisme, een extreem (en dus gevaarlijk) geval van het excessieve vertrouwen in het bevattingsvermogen en de kundigheid van de mens dat met het modernisme wordt geassocieerd. Een meer waarachtige en wenselijke versie van het utopisme — een utopisme dat de naam recht doet — zou er volgens Kathi Weeks echter een zijn die niet alleen voortkomt uit een cognitieve praktijk, maar ook uit *hoop* als affectieve drijfveer.Weeks beschrijft de functie van hoop als "het samenbrengen van de twee bestandsdelen van de utopie als iets concreets: het omarmen van zowel het reëel mogelijke als het novum." [18] "Het hoopvolle subject bekrachtigt een toekomst die niet alleen mogelijk is (in plaats van onmogelijk), maar ook een radicaal andere toekomst, een toekomst die geaard is in het echt mogelijke maar ook ver daarbuiten durft te gaan." [19] Utopisch denken en handelen hebben, zoals Weeks het theoretiseert, met projectie gemeen dat ze vanuit het concrete perspectief van het heden kampen met een toekomst waarvan de coördinaten, ontwikkelingen en tendensen worden aangevoeld om inhoud te geven aan wat er vervolgens zal gebeuren. Toch verschillen ze van elkaar, in die zin dat het utopisme actief een verbeelding en een openheid voedt ten opzichte van het onvoorspelbare, van een radicaal breken — terwijl projectie dat juist tracht te ondervangen. Wat Weeks een 'politiek van concreet utopisme' zou noemen, vereist geen projecterend perspectief op de relatie tussen het heden en de toekomst, maar een vasthoudendheid aan het ondoorzichtige en voorwaardelijke karakter van die relatie. Hoewel *Mall of Europe* niet utopisch is — althans niet overduidelijk — bevat het werk een dergelijke vasthoudendheid.

[18] Kathi Weeks, *The Problem With Work: Feminism, Marxism, Antiwork Politics* (Durham: Duke University Press, 2011), 197.

[19] Weeks, *The Problem With Work,* 196.

Projectie: de bewuste of onbewuste overdracht van eigen verlangens en affecten aan een ander object of persoon

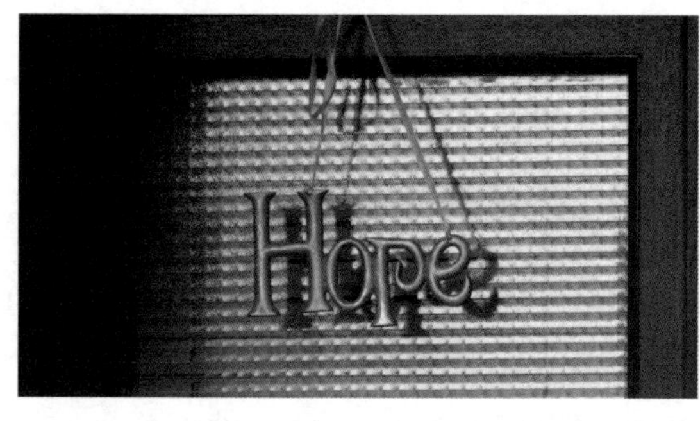

Hoop als (potentieel) politiek affect komt in *Mall of Europe* voor in de gedaante van een kitscherige deurdecoratie. De verschijning is kortstondig en zou nauwelijks betekenisvol zijn, ware het niet dat ze resoneert met wat beschouwd zou kunnen worden als het hoofdthema van het werk: consumentisme. Kitsch kan worden begrepen als een (te grote) emotionele investering in objecten die vaak worden geassocieerd met slechte smaak. Het is dan relevant dat de categorie 'kitsch' en het goederenfetisjisme slechts een gradatieverschil belichamen. Goederenfetisjisme gaat, onder andere, gepaard met een emotionele overinvestering die cruciaal is voor de projecterende beloftes van de (Westerse) moderniteit. De ideologie van de vooruitgang was en is onlosmakelijk verbonden met de vooronderstelling dat een

[20] Sylvia Wynter schrijft dat de ethiek van de westerse moderniteit in wezen gebaseerd is op het nastreven van het "bovennatuurlijke doel van steeds hogere 'levensstandaarden'." Het projecteert dus een soort materiële verlossing, "terwijl de feodale orde *Spirituele Verlossing* voorstaat als doel om gedrag te sturen." Sylvia Wynter, "No Humans Involved: An Open Letter to my Colleagues," *Forum N.H.I.* 1, No. 1 (1994), 61.

[21] Susan Buck-Morss, *Dreamworld and Catastrophe: The Passing of Mass Utopia in East and West* (Cambridge: MIT Press, 2000), 149. Voor Buck-Morss geldt deze constatering evenzeer voor de geschiedenis van Sovjet-Rusland als voor die van het Westen (steeds belichaamd door de Verenigde Staten). "Dit 'kopiëren' dupliceerde virtuele werkelijkheden als materiële fantasmagorieën die men werkelijk zou kunnen ervaren. Het gaf een soort droomkarakter aan de industriële productie in de Sovjetunie, en aan goederenconsumptie in de Verenigde Staten." Buck-Morss, *Dreamworld and Catastrophe,* 150.

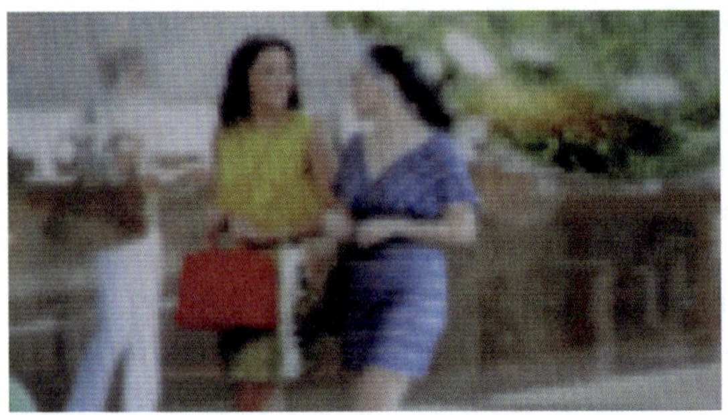

alomtegenwoordig consumentisme uiteindelijk voor iedereen de hoop op het goede leven — lees: de liberale democratie — zou en zal waarmaken. De populariteit van wereldtentoonstellingen — immense ophopingen en concentraties van handelswaar — laat zien dat het vergaren van materiële rijkdom de seculiere en wereldlijke, maar ook diep theologische *telos* van de moderniteit was.[20] Susan Buck-Morss heeft betoogd dat twintigste-eeuwse beelden in reclame en film (evenals wereldtentoonstellingen, zou men kunnen stellen) hebben bijgedragen aan virtuele werelden van de collectieve verbeelding. De verwezenlijking daarvan wordt vervolgens "het sociale project". Echter, "het feit dat dit project een droombeeld kopieert, maakt de materiële constructie ervan iets fantasmagorisch."[21] Wie ooit in een winkelcentrum is geweest is waarschijnlijk wel bekend met de droomachtige en fantasmagorische kwaliteit waarover Buck-Morss schrijft.

Zoals gezegd stralen Van der Put's beelden van beelden — met name van de architectonische renderings en reclamebeelden die doorheen *Mall of Europe* verschijnen — een verontrustende droomsfeer uit, en resoneren als zodanig met Buck-Morss' beschouwing van moderniteit als droomwereld. Dit geldt vooral voor de openingsscène, waarin de architectonische renderings van de grote entree van de eigenlijke 'Mall of Europe', die op dat moment in aanbouw is, worden afgewisseld met foto's die bij een echt winkelcomplex in de buurt van het Expo-gebied zijn genomen. Het schept momenten van verwarring tussen afbeelding en gebouwde constructie. Dit is een productieve verwarring omdat ze tastbaar en concreet maakt wat Buck-Morss omschrijft, waarbij ook zichtbaar wordt dat het bebouwen van de wereld op basis van (droom)beelden, als modernistisch programma, niet slechts kan worden afgedaan als een nu gehistoriseerde, lang vervlogen moderniteit: het duurt voort. Ook het plezier en comfort dat in reclame (voor toerisme, voedsel, huisvesting, het consumeren op zich) wordt aangeboden suggereert dat "materiële verlossing" nog steeds een "doel om gedrag te sturen" is — een projectie waar de meesten van ons het grootste deel van de tijd mee leven.

De aard van het warenfetisjisme blijkt ertoe te leiden dat de consumptie van en de binding met materiële voorwerpen (eveneens) de consumptie van en binding met de afbeelding van die voorwerpen betekent — het gebruik en genoegen van de meest concrete, materiële, zinnelijke en tastbare dingen blijkt gebonden te zijn aan illusies die op luchtspiegelingen lijken. Dit komt naar voren in analyses van de spektakelmaatschappij en van het esthetische populisme van de postmoderniteit, maar de kiem ervan is al aanwezig in de befaamde compacte sectie van *Het Kapitaal* over 'Het fetisjkarakter van de waar en zijn geheim'. Daarin tracht Marx uit te leggen dat de ruilwaarde van waren het product is van een reeks sociale relaties tussen mensen en niet zozeer van een kwaliteit die op enige wijze inherent is aan, of zelfs verband houdt met, de fysieke eigenschappen van de waren in kwestie. Die sociale relaties worden echter niet zichtbaar in de verschijning van consumptiegoederen: de relaties die de ruilwaarde van het product bepalen, zijn niet zintuiglijk voorhanden, net zoals de geïnvesteerde arbeid onzichtbaar is in het eindproduct. Marx neemt zijn toevlucht tot een vergelijking met optische processen om zijn argument kracht bij te zetten dat koopwaren "zintuiglijke dingen zijn die tegelijkertijd bovengemiddeld redelijk of sociaal zijn."

De vergelijking is als volgt: "Zo doet de lichtreflectie van een object op onze gezichtszenuw zich niet voor als een subjectieve prikkeling van die zenuw, maar als een concrete vorm van het object, dat zich buiten het oog bevindt. Maar bij het zien wordt werkelijk licht geworpen van het ene ding, het externe object, op het andere, het oog. Het is een fysische verhouding tussen fysische zaken. In tegenstelling hiermee hebben de warenvorm en de waardeverhouding van de arbeidsproducten, waarin deze vorm tot uitdrukking komt, absoluut niets te maken met de fysische eigenschappen van de waren en met de daaruit voortvloeiende materiële [dingliche] betrekkingen. Het is slechts de bepaalde maatschappelijke verhouding van de mensen zelf, die voor hen de fantasmagorische vorm van een verhouding tussen dingen aanneemt."[22] Het punt is dat, zelfs bij 'gewone' handelswaar zoals de eenvoudige houten tafel waar Marx elders in hetzelfde hoofdstuk naar verwijst, allerlei kwaliteiten en eigenschappen op de waren worden geprojecteerd die er eigenlijk niet bij horen. Die geprojecteerde kwaliteiten en eigenschappen worden vervolgens net zo zeer onderwerp en reden voor consumptie als de werkelijke kwaliteiten en eigenschappen, de gebruikswaarde van het product.

Vooral wanneer het zich richt op reclamebeelden of handelsbeurzen, verbeeldt *Mall of Europe* het proces waarbij de consumptie van de gebruikswaarde ondergeschikt lijkt te worden aan zaken die veel minder tastbaar zijn — zoals afbeeldingen, gevoelens, of afbeeldingen van gevoelens. Eén advertentie in de video lijkt alleen maar reclame te maken voor "The Experience" en bestaat uit niets anders dan die twee woorden, in een Disney-achtig lettertype, tegen een witte achtergrond. Een andere toont een zwembadtafereel met het predicaat "Privileged life" ("Bevoorrecht leven"). Het warenfetisjisme dat in *Mall of Europe* te zien is, omvat processen die niet alleen gelijkaardig zijn aan projectie in de technische of optische zin van het woord, maar ook aan processen die aansluiten bij de Freudiaanse notie van "projectie": de toeschrijving of overdracht van emoties aan een object of ander persoon. De levensstijl van de middenklasse die in de architectonische renderings wordt gepropageerd, maakt het onverholen duidelijk: het hedendaagse consumentisme gaat gepaard met een grote investering (niet in het minst van hoop en aspiraties voor de toekomst) in handelswaar, of preciezer: in afbeeldingen van handelswaar. Schoonheid als *promesse du bonheur* is hier springlevend.

Bovendien plaatst het werk deze uitingen van het 'laatkapitalisme' (als dit soort periodisering nog standhoudt) in verhouding tot fenomenen die horen bij de moderniteit zelf, met aspecten van het *exhibitionary complex* die gezien kunnen worden als prototypen voor het huidige, reclame-gedreven beeldregime. Vooral wereldtentoonstellingen zijn cruciaal en paradigmatisch geweest voor de relatieve autonomie van de (mystificerende en betoverende) verschijning van consumptiegoederen ten opzichte van de materiële goederen zelf.[23] Dit proces van autonomie, waarbij de afbeelding van het consumptiegoed los komt te staan van diens materialiteit, steeds meer een eigen leven gaat leiden, en uiteindelijk een handelswaar op zich wordt, wordt intensiever voortgezet in de reclamewereld. In zijn geheel genomen schetst *Mall of Europe* dus de contouren van een langetermijnvisie (of toch een visie van redelijk lange termijn) op de ontwikkeling van hedendaagse manieren waarop het visuele is georganiseerd vanuit het *exhibitionary complex.*

Hier is het verleidelijk om te benadrukken dat de cirkel rond is, dat we terug zijn bij projectie in de betekenis van een afbeelding die op een oppervlak wordt gepresenteerd, en hoe is gebleken dat de verschillende aspecten en betekenissen van "projectie" inderdaad verstrengeld en onderling afhankelijk zijn — hetgeen in ieder geval de vooronderstelling van dit essay was. Hoe fijn dat ook zou zijn, betekent het sluiten van de

[22] Karl Marx, *Het kapitaal, Kritiek van de politieke economie* (Amsterdam: Boom, 2010) 69–70. Het is vaak opgemerkt dat Marx een voorliefde had voor dergelijke optische analogieën en metaforen. In *The German Ideology* bijvoorbeeld, wordt de omgekeerde projectie van de buitenwereld in een camera obscura beschreven om het begrip ideologie (en de relatie tot materiële, historische processen) in te verklaren: "Wanneer in heel de ideologie de mensen en hun verhoudingen op hun kop lijken te staan als in een camera obscura, dan vloeit dit fenomeen uit hun historisch levensproces voort, net als de omkering van de objecten op het netvlies uit hun direct fysieke levensproces." Karl Marx, "De Duitse ideologie," geraadpleegd 30 december 2019, https://www.marxists.org/nederlands/marx-engels/1845/duitse_ideologie/index.htm.

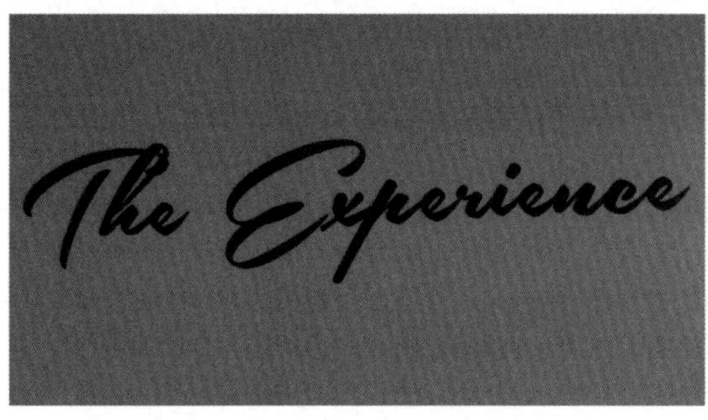

[23] Giogio Agamben schreef over de wereldtentoonstelling van 1851 in het Crystal Palace in Londen: "De transformatie van het goed in een betoverd object is het teken dat de gebruikswaarde van het goed reeds overschaduwd wordt door de ruilwaarde. In de galerijen en de paviljoens van het mystieke Crystal Palace, waar vanaf het begin ook plaats was voor kunstwerken, wordt de waar alleen getoond om van te genieten middels het bekijken van het betoverde tafereel." Giorgio Agamben, *Stanzas: Word and Phantasm in Western Culture* (Minneapolis: University of Minnesota Press, 1992), 38.

cirkel hier ook dat de vormelijke en compositorische principes van dit essay al te zeer zouden worden opgelegd aan *Mall of Europe.* Dat zou waarschijnlijk het beste gedaan kunnen worden door terug te vallen op het gangbare jargon van (kunst)kritiek, en af te sluiten met de bewering dat *Mall of Europe* op een min of meer dwingende wijze de zaken die in deze lezing van het werk naar voren zijn gekomen "toont" en "blootlegt". Een dergelijke bewering zou niet verkeerd zijn. Van der Put's video heeft inderdaad een uitgesproken kritische dimensie, die zich bezighoudt met onthulling, vooral waar deze probeert (historische) verbanden te leggen tussen schijnbaar verschillende, niet-verwante verschijnselen. Maar het geval wil dat dit nog niet alles is.

Niet zonder enige schaamte wil ik opmerken dat er nog steeds veel in *Mall of Europe* is dat mijn lezing ervan hier overtreft. In een poging om conceptueel te verwoorden wat het werk visueel of esthetisch overbrengt, wordt in dit essay onvermijdelijk een specifiek soort falen voltrokken en gedramatiseerd: het falen van theorie om de ervaring van het kijken, of de betekenis ervan, uitputtend te verklaren. Een van de redenen waarom dit essay zich wijdt aan een dergelijke mislukking is het voordeel dat zo'n mislukking — zij het negatief — iets in kaart brengt wat zich onophoudelijk verzet tegen een abstracte vertaling, iets wat het soort begrip op gang brengt waartoe een conceptualisering nooit werkelijk in staat is. In *Mall of Europe* is dit een engagement met en middels het zichtbare, dat veel complexer, mysterieuzer en rauwer is dan hier talig weergegeven kan worden — het belicht de historische ironie dat "theorie" etymologisch verwant is met toeschouwerschap. Het gebruik van reclamebeelden in het werk is een goed voorbeeld in dit opzicht. *Mall of Europe* lijkt niet alleen de demystificerende handeling te tonen waarin de betovering van consumptiegoederen wordt opgeheven — ook al is dat gebaar er zeker ook, en blijkt die betovering vaak banaal, oppervlakkig en goedkoop. Tegelijkertijd is er echter het verlangen om vast te houden aan het fetisjkarakter van de koopwaar, om op te gaan in de afbeelding ervan, om zich over te geven aan de goedkope aard van de betovering. Met andere woorden, er speelt een visueel genot dat niet kan worden gereduceerd tot een symptoom van medeplichtigheid, hoezeer het die medeplichtigheid tegelijkertijd ook aan het licht brengt. *Mall of Europe* wordt gedreven door wisselwerking en oscillatie tussen demystificatie en visuele bekoring. Deze wisselwerking doet veel méér dan slechts het ondubbelzinnig versterken van de kracht van de demystificatie. Toch is dit niet *geen* kritiek. De notie van openbaring, waar de retoriek van de kritiek altijd al op cruciale wijze op heeft gesteund, wordt hier simpelweg serieuzer genomen dan gebruikelijk. Het soort openbaring waar het werk volgens mij op uit is, is zowel magisch als alledaags. *Mall of Europe* ensceneert die openbaring door een beroep te doen op de even wonderlijke als verontrustende ondoorgrondelijkheid van het kijken — dat projectie, met haar harde geometrie en hang naar zuiverheid, meer in de weg staat dan enige kritische uiteenzetting ooit zou kunnen.

COLOPHON

APE#159
SOON
Emma van der Put

ISBN 9789493146372
www.artpapereditions.org
www.emmavanderput.com

First edition of 600 copies
January 2020

Editing and design: 6'56"
French translation: Lucas Faugère
Dutch translation: Jesse van Winden
Printing: UNICUM Tilburg

This book is released in context of the solo exhibition
Mall of Europe by Emma van der Put at Mu.ZEE, Ostend.

Thanks to: Steyn Bergs, Ilse Roosens, Lien Van Leemput, Jurgen Maelfeyt, Har & Michelle van der Put, Timmy van Zoelen, Aline Hernández, Pietje Tegenbosch, Martin van Vreden, Maxime Rouquart, Noor Mertens, C.o.C.A. Foundation, A Tale of A Tub Rotterdam, Needcompany, Kuiperskaai, Cinemaximiliaan.

Emma van der Put is represented by
tegenboschvanvreden, Amsterdam.

With the generous support of:
Mu.ZEE, Mondriaan Fund, Jaap Harten Fonds, The Dutch Embassy in Belgium

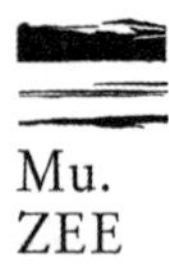

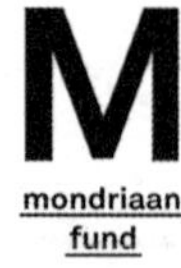

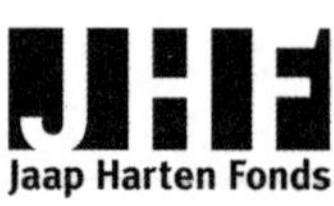